Ethnic Nationalisr
of Empires

MW00574641

Ethnic Nationalism and the Fall of Empires is a wide-ranging, comparative study of the origins of today's ethnic politics in East Central Europe, the former Russian empire, and the Middle East. Centered on the First World War era, *Ethnic Nationalism and the Fall of Empires* highlights the roles of historical contingency and the ordeal of total war in shaping the states and institutions that supplanted the great multinational empires after 1918. It explores how the fixing of new political boundaries and the complex interplay of nationalist elites and popular forces set in motion bitter ethnic conflicts and political disputes, many of which are still with us today. Topics discussed include:

- The disintegration of the Austro-Hungarian empire
- The ethnic dimension of the Russian Revolution and Soviet state building
- Nationality issues in the late Ottoman empire
- The origins of Arab nationalism
- Ethnic politics in zones of military occupation
- The construction of Czechoslovak and Yugoslav identities

Ethnic Nationalism and the Fall of Empires is an invaluable survey of the origins of twentieth-century ethnic politics and provides an important reassessment of the First World War era in relation to the current turmoil in East Central Europe, Russia, and the Middle East. It is essential reading for those interested in the politics of ethnicity and nationalism in modern European and Middle Eastern history.

Aviel Roshwald is Associate Professor of History at Georgetown University in Washington, DC. He is the author of *Estranged Bedfellows: Britain and France in the Middle East during the Second World War* (Oxford University Press, 1990) and co-editor with Richard Stites of *European Culture in the Great War: The Arts, Entertainment and Propaganda, 1914–1918* (Cambridge University Press, 1999).

Ethnic Nationalism and the Fall of Empires

Central Europe, Russia and the
Middle East, 1914–1923

Aviel Roshwald

London and New York

First published 2001
by Routledge
2 Park Square, Milton Park, Abingdon, Oxon, OX14 4RN
Simultaneously published in the USA and Canada
by Routledge
270 Madison Ave, New York NY 10016

Routledge is an imprint of the Taylor & Francis Group

Transferred to Digital Printing 2005

Typeset in Baskerville by Taylor & Francis Books Ltd

British Library Cataloguing in Publication Data
A catalogue record for this book is available from the British Library

Library of Congress Cataloging in Publication Data
Roshwald, Aviel.
Ethnic nationalism and the fall of empires: Central Europe, Russia,
and the Middle East, 1914–1923 / Aviel Roshwald.
    p. cm.
Includes bibliographical references and index.
1. Europe, Eastern – Politics and government – 20th century.
2. Nationalism – Europe, Eastern. 3. Europe, Eastern –
Ethnic relations – Political aspects. 4. Middle East – Politics
and government – 1914–1923. 5. Nationalism –
Middle East – Ethnic relations – Political aspects. I. Title.
DJK48.5 .R67 2001
320.54'09'041–dc21
                                                        00–042475

ISBN 0–415–17893–2 (hbk)
ISBN 0–415–24229–0 (pbk)

To the memory of my mother, Miriam Roshwald

"Identity is not something separate from responsibility, but on the contrary, is its very expression."

(Vaclav Havel, as quoted in *The New York Review of Books*, 5 March 1998, p. 46)

Contents

Maps

Acknowledgements

This book could not have been written without the encouragement, support, and advice of many friends and colleagues. I am very grateful to the following people for reading and commenting on portions or all of my various draft manuscripts: Gábor Agoston, Tommaso Astarita, Steven Beller, David Goldfrank, MacGregor Knox, John McNeill, Steven G. Marks, Jerry Z. Muller, Richard Stites, and the anonymous readers commissioned by Routledge. I also appreciate the feedback and comments of the Catholic University, Department of History faculty seminar on material from an early draft of this manuscript. My thanks also go to the history editors at Routledge, Heather McCallum and Victoria Peters, who patiently supported and encouraged this endeavor. Needless to say, whatever flaws the book contains arise from my own shortcomings.

It is also a pleasure to thank Georgetown University, which provided me with generous assistance in undertaking this enterprise, in the form of sabbaticals, Graduate School summer grants, and the warm support of many colleagues.

My dear wife, Alene Moyer, and my two delightful stepsons, Joseph and Martin Hood, brought great joy, love, and an invigorating spirit of irreverence into my life amidst the trials and tribulations of completing the final version of this book. I am deeply thankful to them for that.

I am indebted to my parents, Mordecai and Miriam Roshwald, for maintaining a keen interest in this project throughout its prolonged gestation, and for helping keep alive my own faith in its value. My mother would have been most delighted to see the finished product, and it is to her memory that this book is dedicated.

Washington, DC
April 2000

1 Introduction

Nationalism and the idea of the nation-state are among the most pervasive political phenomena of our age and among the least well understood. So interwoven are they with contemporary social, cultural, economic, political, and diplomatic institutions, so deeply embedded in political psychology, so broadly influential in the shaping of human identity and socio-political behavior, that it is almost impossible to tease nationalism apart from the sundry elements with which it interacts or of which it forms part and to study it as a thing unto itself. Is it an ideology or an anthropological phenomenon? Is it an outgrowth of liberal democracy or is it inherently intolerant and conducive to authoritarianism? Is it an aspect of modernity or a reaction against it?[1] These are stimulating and productive questions to ask, but ones to which there is no definitive response because each of them can be answered both in the affirmative and in the negative, depending on what historical context and which manifestation or form of nationalism one has in mind.

This book does not approach nationalism with the assumption that it can be made to fit any single framework of analysis or typological category. Rather, it is concerned with exploring how nationalism evolves over time and how its ideological orientations and institutional manifestations are redefined and transformed by historical forces. More specifically, it focusses on a critical watershed in the evolution of a significant number of contemporary nationalisms: the breakup of multinational empires into independent states deriving their domestic and international legitimacy from the principle of national self-determination.

The monographic literature on discrete nationalist movements highlights the role of historical contingencies, individual personalities, cultural peculiarities, and geopolitical idiosyncrasies in shaping national identities and nation-states. It tends to focus on certain key events that are seen as having a critical, long-term impact on the subsequent development of national consciousness, political culture, and institutional structures among ethnic majorities and minorities alike.

Much of the theoretical literature on nationalism is, by contrast, absorbed by the analysis of the formative impact on nationalism of impersonal, macrohistorical forces such as industrialization, the growth of the state, and the spread of literacy and mass communication. Such approaches have produced remarkable

monographic vs theoretical

insights at a very high level of generalization, yet they are also inherently limited insofar as they tend to treat the development of nationalism as though it proceeded at a relatively even, incremental pace, and as though its full manifestation (itself an idealized and problematic concept) were dependent upon the completion of certain material changes that transform the inner workings of society and produce nationalist forms of political identity. Miroslav Hroch's much-cited study of nationalism among the small nations of Europe, for instance, posits an ideal developmental typology in which the emergence of full-fledged national consciousness is the culmination of a three-stage process of intellectual fermentation, patriotic agitation, and mass mobilization, all linked to a carefully timed sequence of capitalist growth and industrialization. Cases that depart from this paradigm may result in stunted nationalisms or the absence of any well-defined national identity, and, once missed, the opportunity can apparently never be regained.[2]

I do not dispute the role of deep historical forces in shaping nationalist consciousness and the modern nation-state, nor do I reject the utility of certain developmental paradigms, provided they are taken with a grain of salt. Yet approaches that focus disproportionately on such factors run the risk of lapsing into a historical determinism that is in some ways analogous to the teleological mentality that pervades many nationalist ideologies. In the mythology of nationalism, national identity attains its fullest expression when a movement that may have begun as a small band of activists has succeeded in mobilizing the masses around one common conception of nationhood. The attainment of independent statehood is conceived of either as the culmination of this process, or as a step in its progressive realization. In practice, however (as recent events in Eastern Europe and the Soviet Union illustrate), the trappings of political sovereignty often come within the reach of nationalists suddenly and unexpectedly, under extraordinary and short-lived circumstances arising from a regional or global crisis rather than from strictly internal developments. If not grasped immediately, the opportunity to establish a separate polity may not recur for generations. But the attainment of political independence under such circumstances cannot be regarded as part of the ineluctable course of history, nor can the specific institutional and territorial forms that independence takes be seen as the inevitable outgrowth of an incremental process of social and political evolution.

In other words, the sudden onset of independence is often the result of short-term, exogenous factors. Once established under such circumstances, a sovereign nation-state is likely immediately to confront profound internal divisions over how to distribute wealth and power and what political values should animate government and society. In the aftermath of "liberation," a liberal-nationalist intelligentsia may suddenly find itself marginalized in a polity whose broader public is not receptive to its ideas. The overnight transition in the roles of nationalist leaders from resisting the authority of imperial states to wielding power over nation-states may produce deep contradictions between ideological rhetoric and political practice. Old socio-political elites may try to co-opt nationalist themes and symbols in order to legitimize their own continued hold on power. The flow of resources, goods, and services may be drastically disrupted by the drawing of new frontiers across regions that once formed integrated markets; the resultant economic problems are likely to exacerbate political tensions within the new states. Ethnic groups that find themselves unexpectedly reduced to the status of minority communities may react by forming separatist movements of their own. In brief, the particular circumstances of a nation-state's creation can have a dramatic impact on its subsequent evolution, closing off various potential paths of development for nationalist movements and creating a radical new field for the crystallization of national identities – a point that most historical monographs take for granted and that most theoretical works ignore.[3]

This book seeks to help bridge the analytical gap between the monographic and theoretical literatures by adopting a broadly comparative approach to the transformative events that shaped nationalist movements and identities in East Central Europe, Russian-dominated Eurasia, and the Middle East during the brief span of years from the outbreak of the First World War in 1914 to the ratification of the Treaty of Lausanne and of the ethnofederal constitution of the USSR in 1923.[4] The collapse of the three (Habsburg, Romanov, and Ottoman) multinational empires toward the end of the war and the circumstances surrounding the emergence of their successor states set in motion patterns of development that continue to shape national identities in these regions at the turn of the millennium.[5]

Having criticized some of the developmental paradigms that have come to inform the theory of nationalism, I must also acknowledge that I have not been able to do without them. This book's organizational scheme clearly reflects the notion that most nationalist movements begin as intellectual trends, develop into political organizations that seek to expand their popular base through propaganda and agitation, and in some cases succeed in going on to establish independent nation-states. But the idiosyncrasy of the cases addressed here is that the First World War telescoped some stages of their development into a very brief period of time. The war created unusual opportunities and tremendous pressures that served to catapult the idea of national self-determination toward sudden realization across a wide range of societies. To be sure, the cultural, economic, and political conditions in these various lands were extremely diverse; what these cases all have in common is that their transition to political systems based on the idea of national self-determination was very sudden, rather than the result of a steady, evenly paced process, and that it took place within the framework of a common, external contingency – a war that transformed the shape of global politics. Each chapter accordingly focusses on an evolutionary phase or framework of development that these diverse cases shared in common, while at the same time stressing the differences in their material and cultural environments as well as the variation in social and political responses of nationalist movements to some of the sudden pressures and common dilemmas these peoples faced.

In undertaking this project, it has not been my intention to be encyclopedic in coverage. The geographical range encompassed by this topic is enormous, and it would be impossible to be comprehensive in this account or even to give honorable mention to every one of the hundreds of ethnic groups that occupied the length and breadth of the three empires. Moreover, any attempt to give equal attention to every region and each people would limit my ability to explore and compare individual cases with any degree of analytical depth. The typical chapter section will accordingly include a brief narrative overview of developments throughout a given imperial sphere, and then narrow its focus to selected cases that can serve to illuminate the book's broad themes. In East Central Europe, for example, this book pays particular attention to the Polish, Czechoslovak, and Yugoslav states and to their pre-1918 political antecedents, for these cases illustrate with particular clarity the strains between supraethnic and ethnonational conceptions of nationhood that all of the movements and polities in the region – and, indeed, in all three imperial or post-imperial spheres – had to contend with.

In general, the emphasis here lies on the empires' subject nationalities – those populations whose languages, and/or religions, and/or historical and cultural identities, marked them apart from the hegemonic cultures (German and Magyar, Russian, and Turkish, respectively) of the Habsburg, Romanov, and Ottoman empires, and among whom a desire to seek some form of autonomy or independence within newly drawn territorial boundaries was most likely to take root. By the same token, we cannot altogether disregard political movements among dominant nationalities – e.g. pan-Turkism or Russian pan-Slavism – that had a profound impact on subject peoples, or, indeed, that served to define other groups as subject peoples.

Finally, while I have tried to pay equal attention to the three empires, in places, some empires will appear more equal than others. This is partly because not every theme, issue, or developmental aspect manifested itself as dramatically or clearly in one region as in another. It also reflects the fact that the monographic literature for any given period – especially for the war years themselves – is not nearly as extensive for some areas (notably the Arab world and the Russian empire, 1914–1917) as for others.

This leads me to another disclaimer: I make no pretense here of bringing to light original material on any given ethnic group or nationalist movement. This book is a historical synthesis, and its contribution will, I hope, consist in its bringing a comparative perspective to bear on the events in question. Drawing on secondary literature rather than archival sources, I have tried to bring together this wide variety of cases under a common analytical rubric by focussing on a number of interrelated, overarching issues that most nationalist movements have had to face.

One such problem is how to integrate the masses into movements that are usually initiated and led by intellectual or socio-political elites. This raises the broader question of how ideologies propagated by elites interact with mass consciousness in the crystallization (or, indeed, fragmentation) of national identities.

Another pervasive issue involves the tension between the origin of the modern nation-state as a specifically Western European or Euro-Atlantic ideological and institutional creation, and the role it is supposed to play as an authentic embodiment and guardian of each nation's particular culture. On the one hand, nationalist movements around the world have modeled themselves on Western political prototypes and aspired to lead their countries on the road to modernization; on the other hand, they are determined to use the nation-state as an instrument for cultivating their own peoples' heritages and guarding against the erosion of their historical identities. How to reconcile these apparently contradictory roles was an ongoing problem for many of the movements discussed here.

This brings us to the distinction between civic and ethnic forms of nationalism. These are useful typological categories employed by much of the contemporary literature.[6] The term civic nationalism refers to the assertion of a population's collective identity and of its right to political-territorial sovereignty based on its adherence to a common set of political values and on its common allegiance to an existing or prospective, territorially defined state. In its historical origins, it is closely associated with the development of West European countries such as Britain or France, where relatively strong, centralized monarchies emerged in pre-modern times, constituting sturdy political-cultural molds within which state-wide national identities eventually gelled, under the impact of homogenizing forces such as economic development and commercial integration, the bureaucratization of the state, the growth of public education, and the development of print media, electoral politics, and mass communication.[7] Because, in principle, civic nationalism is inclusive of all who choose to participate in the common political culture, regardless of their parentage or mother tongue, most authors associate it with liberal, tolerant values and respect for the rights of the individual.[8]

Ethnic nationalism is a phrase used to denote the assertion of a collective identity centered around a myth of common biological descent – an extension of the kinship principle to a large population – and, as its corollary, a claim to territorial sovereignty. The term can also refer to any movement that focusses on common, objective cultural characteristics (linguistic, religious, folkloric, or any combination thereof) as the foundation of political nationhood. Modern ethnic nationalism originated among intellectual elites in nineteenth-century Central and Eastern Europe, who were alienated from imperial states (or from sub-national principalities, as in Germany and Italy) that lagged behind the West European pace of political and economic modernization, and that could not or would not accommodate new elites' aspirations to political empowerment. In the multiethnic empires, populations were culturally and linguistically so diverse that any assertion of the modern notion of popular (as opposed to dynastic) sovereignty was likely to unleash centrifugal rather than integrative forces (with fragmented Germany and Italy representing the inverse of this pattern). Because of its fascination with the idea of the nation's organic unity, rooted in common ancestry and/or expressed in specific cultural forms, ethnic nationalism is seen as conducive to intolerant, chauvinistic, and authoritarian forms of government.

In this book, I have taken the liberty of using these terms in reference to a variety of political movements and ideas. It should be understood that this application of recent social science terminology to early twentieth-century movements is anachronistic. I hope it may be excused insofar as it provides a common frame of reference for the comparison of diverse political cultures. At one and the same time, I must stress that I wish to avoid simplistically categorizing entire peoples as belonging to either the ethnic or civic nationalist camps. It is my sense that more interesting questions can be posed about the nature and evolution of nationalist ideologies if one thinks of ethnic and civic elements as cohabiting uneasily, and competing, with one another within any given construction of national identity.[9] It is indeed one of political liberalism's greatest challenges to find ways of reconciling the principle of civic equality with the ethno-cultural dimension of collective identity.[10] As will become readily apparent, my interest in this problem, and my frustration with the difficulty of resolving it, lends much of the discussion that follows a distinctly normative edge. For this I make no apologies. The human cost of ethnic nationalism taken to its logical conclusion is all too apparent in our day, as is the futility of pretending that civic identity can be defined in culturally neutral terms. To take a dispassionate interest in the history of this problem is to take no interest in it at all.

A further note on terminology: in this book I will use the terms "ethnic group" and "nationality" interchangeably to denote a population sharing common cultural characteristics and/or seeing itself as being of common descent or sharing a common historical experience. "Nation" will refer to any group that thinks of its common identity (however defined) as a basis for claiming some form of collective, political-territorial self-determination, or any population in its aspect as a group on behalf of which such claims are made. "Nationalism" refers to any ideology based on the articulation of such claims and that serves as the framework for political action designed to further them. "Nation-state" will signify a polity that bases its legitimacy on its claim to embody or represent the identity of a sovereign nation (however controversial such a claim may be). Clearly, there is considerable room for overlap among these various notions.[11]

2 Ethnicity and Empire
An Historical Introduction

This book focusses on the development of nationalist movements within the three multiethnic empires that were destroyed by the First World War: the Austro-Hungarian empire, the Russian empire, and the Ottoman empire. Each of these enormous and unwieldy political entities had taken shape through a process of gradual territorial accretion and incremental military conquest over the course of hundreds of years. As of 1914, each of them had been ruled continuously for several centuries by a single dynasty. By the same token, all three regimes had recently permitted (or been forced to accept) the creation of elected parliaments, institutions whose very existence could be seen as fundamentally incompatible with the principle of monarchic authority.

The emergence of electoral politics was one of the most visible manifestations of the process of economic and socio-political change that was engulfing these societies. The imperial regimes faced the prospect of modernization with profound ambivalence. On the one hand, they sought to promote industrial and commercial development, educational advancement, technological innovation, and administrative reform as a means of catching up with the spectacular accumulation of material wealth and military power by the world's major industrial states (Britain, Germany, France, the United States). On the other hand, such changes threatened the authority of existing institutions and undermined the stability of social hierarchies. The exposure of hitherto isolated rural economies to the vagaries of global commodities markets, the social and geographical displacement of economically marginalized populations, the emergence of spirited new social elites eager for a share of power, the growth of cities, the crystallization of an urban working class, the birth of mass movements, broad exposure to Western ideas and values – these characteristic features and side-effects of modernization were manifest to varying degrees in the three empires. Even in their most embryonic form, such changes were deeply unsettling to established traditions and modes of thought. All three regimes were hard put to find a way of reaping the benefits of modernization without calling into question their own legitimacy.

One of the most universal features of political modernity has been the idea that the state is an expression of popular identity. Such notions were essentially incompatible with the authoritarian monarchism of the three empires. Yet these regimes recognized that the ability fully to mobilize the energies of society was the ultimate test of a modern state's power. Their dilemma was how to meet this challenge without undermining the dynastic, patrimonial principles that formed the basis of their political legitimacy. The multiethnic composition of the Habsburg, Russian, and Ottoman empires made this problem particularly daunting: any attempt to stimulate patriotic emotions among the masses almost necessarily involved an appeal to their ethno-cultural identity; yet unleashing such sentiments among any given segment of a highly diverse population could only serve to alienate all the other segments.[1]

If exploiting the politics of ethnicity carried enormous dangers, ignoring them was impossible. Some of the most basic, technical aspects of the modernization process, such as standardizing the languages of education and administration, became explosive political issues as ethnic minorities feared that their tongues or dialects would be marginalized and that their opportunities for advancement in the system might become limited.[2] Economic development and fuller integration into global markets tended to have a highly differential impact on these multiethnic societies: members of some nationalities (such as Greeks and Armenians in the Ottoman empire) were well positioned to take advantage of it while other ethnic groups were economically marginalized; the result, of course, was an aggravation of ethnic tensions. Nationalist ideas seemed to attach themselves to every imaginable social and political movement. Even socialism often achieved its greatest potency as a mobilizing force when it incorporated nationalist themes. The haphazard, inconsistent policies pursued by the imperial regimes only aggravated interethnic tensions and stimulated separatist sentiments among their subject peoples. Moreover, the geographical propinquity of the three empires, combined with the often hostile relations among them, provided their governments with tempting opportunities for the incitement of ethnic troubles across each other's borders.

In the multiethnic composition of their populations, and in the consequent dilemmas and challenges that their regimes faced, the three empires bore some striking resemblances to one another. But of course, there were also significant differences in the dynamics of ethnic relations within each state and in the policies pursued by each government. A brief overview of the evolution of ethnic politics in each empire is therefore in order.

The Austro–Hungarian Empire

Of the three empires, Austria–Hungary was the most exclusively dependent on the dynastic principle for its legitimacy. No single ethnic group formed an outright majority of its population, and the ethnic Germans, who were one of its two dominant nationalities, constituted a minority of Europe's overall German population, most of which had been incorporated in Bismarck's unified German nation-state in 1871. It was therefore impossible to think of the Habsburg monarchy as the political expression of any particular ethnic identity or national tradition. It seemed to many observers of the Austro-Hungarian political scene

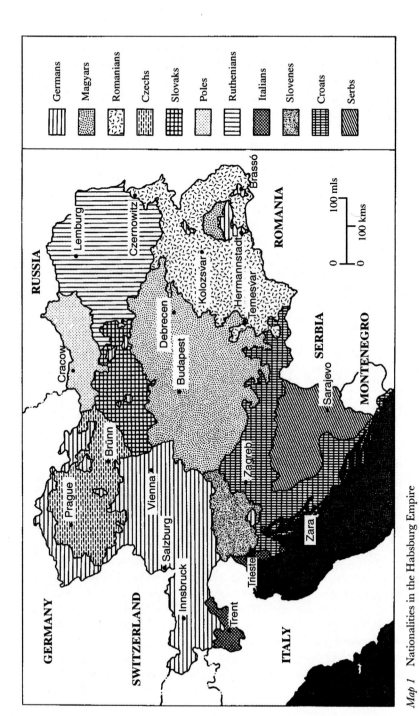

Map 1 Nationalities in the Habsburg Empire
Source: Alan Sked, *The Decline and Fall of the Habsburg Empire*
© Longman Group UK Limited 1989, Reprinted by permission of Pearson Education Limited

that if the empire were to make a successful transition to political modernity it would have to do so as a model of interethnic tolerance and transcendent civic harmony, guiding the rest of Europe beyond the quicksand of militant nationalism. In light of the catastrophic fate that befell its constituent peoples after its collapse, the Habsburg empire came to be viewed with nostalgia by many, as a noble internationalist experiment that somehow failed. In fact, however, no such experiment was ever undertaken. Instead, a series of awkward improvisations and unsatisfying compromises on the part of an ever more desperate ruling house served to aggravate the frustration of, and hostility among, the subject nationalities.[3]

The empire originated as a patchwork of principalities and kingdoms bound together in a personal union under the Habsburgs, whose power base was the group of southeastern German hereditary lands referred to as Austria,[4] and who, with only one brief interruption, consistently held the title of Holy Roman Emperor. The kingdoms of Bohemia (the Czech heartland) and Hungary – to which Croatia had been attached since the twelfth century – entered into dynastic union with the Habsburg lands in 1526–1527. Over the following centuries, the Habsburgs confronted the Ottoman Turks, whose imperial expansion encompassed the entire Balkan peninsula and most of Hungary's territory. Indeed, the Turkish threat had helped precipitate the union of kingdoms under the Habsburg crown. Following the unsuccessful Ottoman siege of Vienna in 1683, the Ottomans began to fall back, with the Habsburg domains growing at Ottoman expense. To the north, the late-eighteenth-century partitions of Poland among Prussia, Russia, and the Habsburg monarchy left the latter in control of Galicia, Poland's southern province.[5]

Drawing their dominions together into a consolidated state with relatively uniform laws and institutions ultimately proved to be a Sisyphean task for the Habsburgs: the more progress they achieved in this direction, the more resentment they incurred among their subjects. The Habsburgs' efforts to centralize state power flew in the face of the historic status of Bohemia and Hungary as distinct states. In the Battle of the White Mountain (1620), Bohemia's aristocratic elite was defeated in its attempt to use Protestantism as a vehicle for challenging Habsburg authority. But the Hungarian gentry, which had also revolted, negotiated an early peace settlement that secured it an amnesty and left its corporate institutions intact.

By the late eighteenth century, the Habsburgs' right to uniform succession within their various territories had gained international recognition. In 1804, the reigning Habsburg monarch declared that his possessions taken together constituted a hereditary empire – a whole that was greater than the historic states that constituted its parts.[6] But during the nineteenth century, the traditional assertion of historic state rights merged with the new doctrine of liberal nationalism in a challenge to autocratic institutions generally, and to the legitimacy of Habsburg rule specifically. The 1848–1849 revolutions took the form of nationalist uprisings in many of the monarchy's provinces, including Bohemia and Hungary.

Although the separatist movements were brutally crushed, the regime's attempt to follow up on its victory by pursuing an energetic program of central-ization ended in failure. Its defeat in its war against Piedmont–Sardinia and France in 1859 (paving the way for Italian national unification), and its humilia-tion in the Austro-Prussian war of 1866 (which led to German national unification), left the Habsburg state shaken. The Hungarian elite took advantage of the situation to negotiate a historic compromise (*Ausgleich*) in 1867. The Hungarians extracted a high price for their continued loyalty to the Habsburgs: full self-rule for the Hungarian kingdom in all spheres other than military and foreign affairs. Personal union under the Habsburgs was not to be called into question, but Austria (a term thenceforth used to refer only to those lands that remained under Vienna's direct jurisdiction) and Hungary were to be recognized as separate and equal political entities under the joint aegis of the Emperor-King. The Habsburg ruler's title was thus modified to reflect the distinction between his status as Emperor of Austria and King of Hungary.[7] The political and administrative division of the state was reinforced by the establishment of separate Austrian and Hungarian parliaments[8] in what had become a constitu-tional Dual Monarchy. In some respects, it could be said that the imperial whole was no longer greater than its parts. The army remained as one of the last major unitary institutions of a very disunited polity.[9]

The *Ausgleich* was a great victory for Magyar (ethnic Hungarian) nationalism. But it did not represent the general triumph of the principle of national self-determination in the Habsburg empire. The landed gentry – and urban professionals of gentry background – who formed the Magyar ruling class justi-fied their demand for self-government by referring to the historical rights of their kingdom. The socio-political foundations of Hungarian government remained very conservative. The vote was restricted to a propertied elite, and this had a disproportionately negative impact on the electoral power of the ethnic minori-ties that made up almost half of Hungary's population. In general, Hungary's leaders approached the nationalities question with a double standard: they regarded the Magyars' right to self-determination within Hungary's historic borders as sacrosanct; the other ethnic groups (such as Romanians, Serbs, Slovaks) were considered culturally inferior peasant peoples who could aspire to nothing higher than assimilation into the Magyar nation. There was to be no question of political autonomy for them, and even promises of cultural autonomy soon gave way to repressive policies aimed at Magyarizing the educa-tional system right down to the elementary school level in linguistically distinct regions such as Slovakia.

The only exception to this trend was the region of Croatia–Slavonia, whose historic status as a kingdom in its own right, if permanently attached to the Hungarian crown, was grudgingly reaffirmed by the Magyars in an 1868 agree-ment (the *Nagodba*). Even in this case, the self-rule granted was very limited, and did not correspond at all to the broad autonomy Hungary had won from Vienna the year before.[10]

In the *Ausgleich*, then, the Magyar ruling class had not only obtained extensive freedom from Vienna's authority, but had won the power to *deny* political and cultural freedoms to Hungary's own ethnic minorities. The Magyars also vigorously opposed any plans for the devolution of power to ethnic groups in Austria, for fear that a dangerous precedent might be set for Hungary. The Habsburgs' historic compromise with Budapest therefore constituted a permanent obstacle in the way of any more systematic reform of the imperial administration. In any case, disputes among the nationalities in the Austrian half of the empire seemed to grow ever more intractable as time went on, while for their part the Habsburg authorities continuously gave mixed signals to the various groups without ever taking a decisive stand on any issue.

In Austria, German-speakers constituted the dominant element in the administration and army. Many members of the political elite were of non-German ethnic background, but had adopted the German language and culture as the price of admission to the ruling circles. However, members of other ethnic groups outnumbered Germans by a margin of two-to-one in the western half of the empire. In Galicia, which enjoyed a measure of administrative autonomy, Poles constituted the local political and bureaucratic elite. However, in eastern Galicia, the Ukrainian[11] peasantry was the largest ethnic group, while the region's major towns and cities were populated largely by Poles and Jews. Bukovina, to the southeast of Galicia, had the most diverse population in the empire, including Ukrainians, Jews, Romanians, Germans, and others, none of whom had a clear majority. In the northwest sector of the empire lay the provinces of Bohemia and Moravia – the homeland of the Czechs. There was also a sizable minority of Germans concentrated along the mountainous fringes of Bohemia (the region later referred to as Sudetenland). Southeast of German-speaking Austria lay the South Slavic zone – provinces inhabited by Slovenes, Croats, Serbs, and Serbo-Croat-speaking Muslims, alongside an admixture of other nationalities (including Germans in partly Slovene Styria and Italians along the Dalmatian coastline).[12] Finally, South Tyrol had a mixed German and Italian population.

The difficulties of ruling over this ethnographic showcase were exacerbated by the conflicting demands and expectations of the various ethnic groups and the high degree of territorial overlap among them. Members of the Polish land-owning gentry (*szlachta*) of Galicia considered themselves the rightful rulers of the province by virtue of their historical role as the governing elite of the Polish–Lithuanian Commonwealth. Their hegemony was disputed by Ukrainians. The Czech social and political elite insisted that their historic homeland – the kingdom of Bohemia – should be accorded autonomy on the Hungarian model. But any concession on Vienna's part to the Czechs instantly raised a chorus of protests from the large ethnic German minority in Bohemia. In general, Austria's German-speaking elite, which included many assimilated members of other nationalities, was convinced that its language was the preeminent medium of high culture and civilization in Central Europe. Indeed, Austro-German liberals were in the forefront of those who decried the assertion of non-German language rights in provincial administrations as an impediment to progress. Right-wing pan-Germanism, on the rise from the 1880s on, contributed to the further polarization of ethnic relations.[13]

The most complex – and ultimately fatal – ethnic problem faced by the Habsburgs was one that straddled the administrative division between Austria and Hungary, and that extended beyond the empire's borders as well. This was the problem of the South Slavs – the speakers of Serbo-Croatian.[14] There were five distinct provinces in the Habsburg empire that were inhabited by Serbs, Croats, or both. The southwestern Hungarian province of Vojvodina was largely Serb in population; Croat-populated Dalmatia and Istria fell under Austrian jurisdiction. As we have seen, Hungary controlled the nominally autonomous province of Croatia–Slavonia (which contained a sizable Serb minority). Finally, Bosnia–Herzegovina, whose population was an ethnic mix of Serbo-Croatian-speaking Muslims, Serbs, and Croats, was jointly administered by Vienna and Budapest.

Nowhere in Europe was the project of constructing national identity plagued by more ambiguity than among the South Slavs. Serbs and Croats were divided by their identification with distinct historical state traditions, different churches (Serbian Orthodox and Catholic, respectively), and different alphabets (Cyrillic and Latin). Yet the Serbs and Croats spoke the same language, as did Bosnia's Muslims.[15]

The result was a variety of nationalist projects – some conflicting, others complementary. There were those who contended that there was a South Slav (Yugo-Slav) nation greater than the sum of its ethnic parts, which potentially included not just speakers of Serbo–Croatian, but also the linguistically and geographically proximate Macedonians to the south and Slovenes to the north. This notion first found expression in the work of the early-to-mid-nineteenth-century Croatian scholars and intellectuals who called themselves Illyrianists and dedicated themselves to forging cultural ties between Serbs and Croats on the basis of their presumed common history and origin. In the mid-to-late nineteenth century, the attempt to build cultural bridges among the South Slavs was carried on by a Croat bishop from Slavonia, Joseph Strossmayer (1815–1905), who founded the Yugoslav Academy of Arts and Sciences in Zagreb in 1867, and who also sought to foster political cooperation between Serbs and Croats within the Habsburg monarchy.

This cooperative vision of Serb-Croat relations was challenged by Ante Starčević (1823–1896), founder of the Party of (Croat State) Right. Starčević responded to contemporaneous Greater Serbian political schemes by articulating an exclusivist Croatian nationalism. He insisted that Croatian political rights were rooted in the historic legacy of the Croatian kingdom, and had been collectively inherited by the Croatian people from the nobility that had founded the state in early medieval times. The Party of Right claimed that all the South Slav lands comprised part of this historic kingdom and, in fact, that people claiming to be Serbs or Muslims were simply Croats who had lost touch with their true identity under the impact of foreign conquest and alien influence. A number of

Serb nationalists duly responded by suggesting that Croats and Muslims were actually nothing more than Serbs suffering from false consciousness.

The ethnic Serbs of Croatia–Slavonia looked beyond the borders of the Habsburg empire to the independent kingdom of Serbia as a frame of reference for their own political identity. The potential for conflict between Austria–Hungary and Serbia was increased by the Habsburgs' official annexation of the formerly Ottoman province of Bosnia-Herzegovina in 1908, after thirty years of *de facto* occupation. This action provoked a wave of vitriolic denunciations on the part of the Serbian government, which itself laid claim to the province. In the following years, the Serbian authorities mounted a propaganda and agitation campaign among ethnic Serb youth in Bosnia, while nationalist officers in Serbian military intelligence recruited young Bosnians to undertake terrorist actions against the Habsburgs. This enterprise culminated in the fateful assassination of Archduke Franz Ferdinand and his wife in Sarajevo by a Bosnian Serb in 1914.

While many of the nationalist programs outlined above were shaped by ethnic elites' interpretations of legal and historical precedents, there was also a strong populist/democratic element to the politics of ethnicity in turn-of-the-century Austria–Hungary. The concept of historic state rights had long been associated with the notion that the land-owning gentry constituted the nation. The elites had not considered the lower classes capable of developing a political consciousness, and certainly had not thought of themselves as sharing a common identity with the peasantry. But the example of the French Revolution had lent growing force to the idea that peoples rather than states were the ultimate repositories of political rights. The intelligentsia – intellectuals and educated professionals with an active interest in cultural and ideological issues – was particularly receptive to such notions, which could be used to challenge authoritarian institutions and legal structures standing in the way of political change and economic reform, and which could also provide a framework of collective identity for members of rising middle classes who did not fit into any of the traditional corporate divisions of society. As early as the late eighteenth and early nineteenth centuries, intellectuals among many nationalities had embarked upon programs of historical scholarship, ethnographic research, literary revival, and myth-making, in a self-conscious effort to build bridges between high and popular cultures and to construct the framework for a unified national consciousness transcending corporate boundaries and class differences. The experience of the 1848 revolutions – where class divisions had frequently undermined the success of gentry- or bourgeois-led nationalist struggles[16] – had demonstrated the importance of mass mobilization for the success of any challenge to the established order. The writings and actions of the Russian *narodniki* (populists) of the second half of the nineteenth century, with their cult of the peasantry as repository of authentic national values, also influenced many of the Habsburg empire's nationalist movements. The result was an increasing tendency on the part of nationalist intellectuals such as Ante Starčević, and even among established socio-political elites such as the Magyar and Polish gentries, to fuse the traditional discourse of historic state rights with the modern rhetoric of popular sovereignty and national self-determination.[17]

While the synthesis of historic claims with populist agendas could serve as a powerful propaganda tool, it contained some obvious contradictions. If popular identity was a critical factor in determining national rights, then discrete ethnic groups falling within a single province's historic frontiers (such as the Germans of Bohemia or Ukrainians of eastern Galicia) must have collective political rights of their own. Yet most nationalists were unwilling to abandon the historic state right framework, precisely because it tended to justify territorial claims that would seem extravagant if popular will and ethnic identity were the sole admissible criteria. Czech leaders demanding autonomy for Bohemia and Moravia were reluctant to abandon all claim to the German-inhabited districts that formed part of the historic kingdom of Bohemia. Poles regarded all of Galicia as part of their heritage and resisted any effort by Ukrainians to challenge their political supremacy throughout the province. The Austro-Germans faced a particularly vexing quandary, for their state tradition was intrinsically imperial rather than national in character. National self-determination for the Austro-Germans would entail separation from the Habsburg empire and merger with the united Germany to the north, as radical pan-Germans in fact called for.[18] Most Austro-Germans, however, voted for parties that unequivocally supported the territorial integrity of the empire while advocating policies that would further institution-alize the hegemonic status of the German language and culture throughout the western half of the Dual Monarchy.[19]

The attempt of the "historic" nations[20] to have their cake and eat it too only served to provoke members of other ethnic groups into cultural "revivals" and nationalist programs of their own. In the absence of indigenous aristocracies and with their populations often composed overwhelmingly of illiterate peasants who spoke a variety of dialects, many of these ethnic groups entered the nine-teenth century without so much as a uniform literary language. A handful of university-educated scholars often played critical roles in selecting one dialect over another as the basis for a standardized tongue. Thus, in the mid-nineteenth century, Ludowít Štúr succeeded in establishing the dialect of central Slovakia as the basis for a standardized Slovak language; this enhanced the distinctiveness of the Slovak tongue, whose western dialect was much more difficult to distinguish from standard Czech.[21] Since they were hard pressed to come up with convincing historical claims to cultural autonomy or self-rule, such movements focussed heavily on populist themes, particularly on the romanticization of peasant culture. This tendency was a distinguishing characteristic of the Slovak, Slovene, and Ukrainian nationalist intelligentsias, among others.[22]

The advance of modernization in the late nineteenth and early twentieth centuries had both centrifugal and centripetal effects on Austro-Hungarian society. It seemed to point the way toward the consolidation of national identi-ties, while concurrently deepening the divisions among the various nationalities. Industrialization and urbanization drew displaced peasants into cities, fostered the growth of middle classes, and eroded differences among people from different regions and speakers of different dialects. Improved communication and transportation systems, the rising rate of literacy, and the growth of the press, all served as catalysts in this process. Yet modernization did not progress evenly throughout the empire; it had a highly differential impact on the Dual Monarchy's various regions, ethnic groups, and social classes, and this bred intense resentments among them.

This pattern was most marked in the many cases where socio-economic status corresponded closely to ethnicity. While the last vestiges of serfdom had been abolished during the 1848 revolutions, economic development and administrative consolidation left subject peoples feeling more vulnerable than ever to the whims of their traditional masters. The steady advance of commercial agriculture was profitable to Polish and Magyar landlords who could afford to develop economies of scale, but left Ukrainian and Slovak smallholders and tenant farmers seriously disadvantaged. The growth of intrusive state bureaucracies staffed by speakers of one language alienated those to whom it was a foreign tongue. New paths of upward social mobility were open to those who were educated in the hegemonic cultures. Correspondingly, literate strata of subject nationalities felt discriminated against by such a system and were particularly strongly motivated to press for their own ethnic group's cultural and administrative autonomy. Schoolteachers and parish priests absorbed the ideas of nationalist intelligentsias and, in turn, helped disseminate them among the masses.[23] Among some of the Slavic peoples of the empire, the Sokol (Falcon) movement – founded in the 1860s by Czech nationalists and soon spawning sister organizations among the Habsburg empire's other Slav peoples – used gymnastic exercise as a means of expressing and instilling a nationalist ethos of disciplined solidarity and youthful vigor.[24]

Ethnic groups that enjoyed economic success did not automatically become satisfied with their status in the empire. On the contrary, the growth of an educated bourgeoisie and politically conscious working class often led to raised expectations of self-rule – expectations that the state could not or would not accommodate. For example, Bohemia became the most highly industrialized region in the empire,[25] and the Czech middle classes and intelligentsia enjoyed a growing sense of prosperity and self-confidence. But the presence of a large ethnic German population in their midst prevented Vienna from devolving power to the region; to do so would have granted administrative dominion to Czechs over Germans – a prospect that the latter militantly opposed. Various efforts to divide the pie or fudge the issue left both sides feeling embittered toward the Habsburg authorities and more hostile than ever toward each other. By the 1890s, urban riots and street clashes between Czechs and Germans had become a favored form of political interaction, and even the Reichsrat was the scene of violent clashes between Czech and German deputies.[26]

The correlation between modernization and the crystallization of diverse national identities was so strongly marked in Austria–Hungary that the Austrian Social Democrats – who constituted the empire's main Marxist party – were obliged to recognize the power of national identity as an independent factor with tremendous potential influence over the behavior of the working masses. At their Brünn (Brno) Congress of 1899, the Social Democrats debated a motion by the South Slav delegation in favor of extraterritorial autonomy as the formula for resolving Austria–Hungary's nationalities problem. Although the Congress was only willing to ratify a modified version of the proposal, the idea of extraterritorial cultural autonomy was further developed and placed in a theoretical framework by two of the party's leading ideologues, Karl Renner and Otto Bauer. These men reached the startling (for Marxists) conclusion that the growth of a modern industrialized proletariat would contribute to the consolidation of national identities, rather than their dissipation. The peasant populations that constituted the demographic reservoirs of the proletariat lived in relatively isolated rural communities with idiosyncratic dialects and customs and parochial mental outlooks. As long as these conditions prevailed, the overarching sense of national consciousness remained confined to the ruling classes, the educated elites. But industrialization and urbanization were breaking down the barriers that stood in the way of cultural integration. Under the impact of mass literacy, the growth of the print media, and the increased mobility of labor, homogeneous national identities based on broad communities of culture were emerging. As long as capitalism survived, class conflict would stand in the way of full national integration, but socialism would bring about complete vertical social integration and, with it, the final crystallization of unified national communities.[27]

To be successful, therefore, socialists would need to find a way of reconciling their Marxist advocacy of economic and political centralization with individual ethnic groups' right to cultural self-expression. The formula of extraterritorial autonomy was designed to do just that. Every citizen of the reformed empire, regardless of his or her place of residence, would be registered as the member of a particular national group. Each nationality would elect, and pay a portion of its taxes to, its own communal council. Each council, in turn, would be responsible for financing and administering its people's cultural and educational institutions throughout the empire. Wherever a group of co-ethnics resided as a minority in a district where the predominant language was alien to them, they could incorporate themselves and draw on their national community's budget to finance their own local schools, orphanages, museums, legal-aid organizations, etc. The standard division of a state into territorial units of administration would thus be complemented by the creation of extraterritorial, national-cultural institutions. This form of expressing national identity would not stand in the way of the inter-national economic and political integration called for by Marxist doctrine – on the contrary, it would facilitate it. Ethnicity would essentially be depoliticized: all citizens would be subject to the same laws and would be free to settle wherever they chose, while enjoying the option of establishing autonomous cultural institutions regardless of whether they constituted a minority or majority of the population in any given province. Labor and capital would flow freely and members of the working class would cooperate fraternally with each other, secure in the knowledge that they could freely express and cultivate their national identities wherever they lived.[28] While orthodox Marxists attacked extraterritorial autonomy as a plan that would fragment the proletariat, the ideas broached at the Brünn Congress and developed by Renner and Bauer soon found very interested audiences among socialist groups in the non-Russian borderlands of the tsarist empire.[29]

Despite their enlightened embrace of multicultural diversity, the Austrian Social Democratic Party's German and Germanized Jewish leaders and ideologues[30] never really abandoned their assumption that German language and culture would eventually prevail as universal media of communication and integration. Interwoven throughout much of their writings is the belief that German is the language of Central European civilization, administrative rationalism, and cultural enlightenment – and that the Slavic peoples operate at a lower cultural plane; in the long run, socialist development and the spread of German culture would go hand in hand with one another.

The Habsburg experiment with constitutionalism failed to defuse ethnic tensions in the empire. In 1907, universal manhood suffrage was established in Austria, but the democratized electoral system only seemed to aggravate the polarization among ethnic groups. All political parties were based on ethnic and regional loyalties, whether they acknowledged it or not. Parties represented in the Reichsrat organized themselves into ethnic blocs, such as the Czech and Polish Clubs. Even in the socialist camp, the largest bloc in the Reichsrat, ethnic tensions could not be surmounted, as the Czech members of the Austrian Social Democratic Party broke away to form their own party in 1911. Close cooperation sometimes occurred between ethnic blocs in the Reichsrat, such as the Czechs and the South Slavs, but these alliances were usually effective only at blocking threatening initiatives proposed by German deputies. It seemed impossible to form a working parliamentary majority that could push through a positive legislative agenda for Austria as a whole. The stalemate of the democratic process left the Habsburg authorities with no option but to rule by decree over the western half of their fractured empire. In Hungary, ironically enough, an attempt by the Magyar government to wrest even more powers away from Vienna was blocked in 1905 by the threat of an imperial decree that would have established universal manhood suffrage in the eastern half of the empire (and would thus have given the vote to the non-Magyars who constituted half of Hungary's population). In the final analysis, the structure of the empire was such that its survival was inseparable from the survival of its dynastic-authoritarian institutions. The Habsburgs employed elements of constitutionalism and democracy very selectively and quite cynically, as instruments with which to play the ethnic groups against each other in a classic game of divide and rule.

By the same token, it would be misleading to characterize the empire in 1914 as poised on the brink of utter disintegration. Few of its nationalist movements advocated full independence for their peoples, many of them had but tenuous connections in any case with the masses they claimed to represent, and the Habsburgs were often tactically astute – if strategically obtuse – in their manipulative approach to ethnic politics. With the outbreak of the First World War, however, the rules of the game began to change too fast for the Habsburgs' adaptive ability.[31]

The Russian Empire

In the tremendous diversity of its ethnic composition, the Russian empire outdid even the Habsburg state. The ethnographic map of Russia was a collage that included dozens of major nationalities and hundreds of small ones. The Caucasus mountains alone were home to scores of different peoples speaking tongues from at least three distinct linguistic families. Islam predominated in Turkestan, the Central Asian (Kazakh) steppe, and much of the Caucasus, Buddhism among groups such as the Buryats in the Far East, and even animism among some small Siberian peoples.

This bewildering diversity was offset by the fact that just under half the empire's population (43 per cent as of 1897) was composed of Russians, the ethnic core group from which the ruling elite was largely drawn. This contrasted sharply with the roughly 23 per cent German share of the Habsburg empire's population.[32] Moreover, the tsarist empire represented the only possible framework for the political expression of Russian nationalism – a situation very different from that of Austria's as an ethnic German-dominated empire lying on the geographical fringe of a dynamic, recently unified, German nation-state. There existed only one Russian-populated state in the world, and this state's tendency to associate itself with Russian nationalism increased over the decades leading up to the First World War. Nonetheless, for much of its history, the tsarist regime retained an ambivalent attitude toward the concept of a Russian nation-state; to its last days, the way in which the empire functioned continued to reflect its multiethnic character.[33]

The Russian empire was the product of a gradual process of territorial acquisition that had taken place over the course of five centuries. Its original geopolitical core was the Muscovite state that had assumed control over most Russian-speaking areas by the sixteenth century, and thereafter expanded steadily into non-Russian regions. Beginning with Ivan the Terrible's conquest of the Tatar khanate of Kazan in 1552, and then again after the rise of the Romanov dynasty in the seventeenth century, Russia pushed its borders outwards in a seemingly endless series of full-scale wars and low-grade conflicts that were motivated by a combination of security considerations, economic interests, and a sense of Russia's religious mission as would-be heir to the Byzantine empire's role as upholder of the Orthodox Christian faith. By the mid-to-late nineteenth century, Russia controlled an expanse of territory stretching from Finland in the north, to Poland in the west, to Transcaucasia and Central Asia in the south, and the Pacific coast in the Far East.

Unlike the Habsburg empire, the Russian empire was largely the product of military conquest rather than dynastic marriage. From the start, therefore, the tsars and ruling elite were able to treat their territories as parts of a single, semi-centralized state, rather than as distinct polities brought together in personal union.[34] Russia was thought of by its rulers as a patrimonial state – that is, its lands, peoples, and resources were, in theory, possessions that were passed on from each tsar or tsarina to his or her heir.[35]

The concept of the patrimonial state was challenged and somewhat eroded by eighteenth-century Enlightenment notions about the rule of law, and nine-teenth-century nationalist ideas about the land as patrimony of the Russian people. However camouflaged or overladen with other constructs, though, the idea of the patrimonial state remained a molding force in tsarist policy to the very end of the regime in 1917. Russian nationalism (closely associated with Russian Orthodoxy) was used to reinforce the tsars' political hegemony and to enhance the cohesion of the state, but it never quite became the state's *raison d'être*. It was certainly the tsars' consistent assumption that the ethnically non-Russian areas of the empire were as integral a part of their domain as was the old Muscovite heartland. Russification was one obvious way in which to try and integrate those territories into the tsarist realm, but the ideas of dynastic right and aristocratic privilege that remained at the core of the ruling elite's political culture could not be fully reconciled with Russian nationalism. In the final anal-ysis, the tsarist regime was neither willing to embrace cultural diversity nor to identify itself unequivocally as an embodiment of Russian popular will.[36]

In practice, of course, the exercise of power over such vast territories and varied populations necessarily involved *de facto* negotiation and tacit compromises with various social groups. In its relations with the ethnic groups that came under its control, the Russian government was often willing to make pragmatic concessions in order to ease the task of integrating newly acquired territories into the state. For example, the Muslims of Central Asia remained exempt from military conscription until 1916. Non-Russian ethnic elites who converted to Russian Orthodoxy (or who were Russian Orthodox to begin with) were inte-grated into the Russian aristocracy. But even when they refused to convert, the social elites of conquered peoples were often allowed to retain some of their traditional privileges and powers, so as to win their allegiance to the tsar. Where pragmatic considerations of this sort came into conflict with the missionary activity of the Church, the former generally took precedence. Thus, Peter the Great's early-eighteenth-century attempt to convert the Tatar nobles from Islam to Christian Orthodoxy on pain of losing their aristocratic status was reversed several decades later by Catherine the Great, who recognized that the policy had only served to antagonize an important social stratum rather than integrating it into the state's official culture. In instances where missionary activity could be pursued without provoking serious resistance (for instance, among the animistic peoples of Siberia), it was undertaken with greater consistency.[37]

It is also noteworthy that Russians as a whole were not the most educated or wealthy ethnic group of the empire. Although Russians did predominate in the officer corps and the bureaucratic elite, most Russians were dirt-poor, illiterate peasants, half of whom were serfs who were not liberated until 1861, and who continued thereafter to be encumbered by laws restricting their freedom of movement. The fact that they spoke Russian did not give them any advantage over peasants who spoke Estonian or Ukrainian or Georgian. Indeed, while many Russian serfs had belonged to non-Russian landlords, Tatars could not become enserfed to members of the Russian nobility. Overall, the conditions for Russian peasants were probably worse than those for most of their non-Russian counterparts.

It was in the northwestern and western sections of the empire that the most educated and economically successful ethnic groups were to be found. In these regions, there was often a significant correlation between ethnicity and class, a phenomenon that was reinforced by the state's inclination to co-opt social elites. Thus, the German elite that had ruled part of the Baltic lands since the region's conquest by the Teutonic Knights in the Middle Ages retained its hegemony over the Latvian and Estonian peasantry, as did the landowning gentry of the former Polish kingdom over the Ukrainians and Belorussians who tilled their fields. Indeed, for many years (until the state's late-nineteenth-century Russification campaign), many of these regional ruling classes were free to pursue their own policies of cultural assimilation (i.e. Germanization, Polonization) toward the generally illiterate ethnic groups under their control. It was also in the Baltic provinces and parts of Poland that late-nineteenth-century industrialization developed most extensively (along with Moscow and St. Petersburg, but in contrast to most of the ethnically Russian provinces).

Although Russians dominated the highest levels of government, educated non-Russians such as Germans and Poles did fulfill important functions in both the regional and central administration of the state, while members of diaspora nationalities such as the Armenians, Jews, and Tatars (as well as many ethnic Germans) played vital roles in building and maintaining the commercial and financial networks that sustained the economy. For much of its history, then, the Russian empire effectively functioned as a multinational state, in which the narrow upper stratum of ethnic Russians controlled political and military power, but in which a number of other nationalities attained higher overall standards of living and education, and filled vital economic and administrative niches.[38] The Russian state was conceived of as a territorial/administrative/dynastic unit encompassing many different nationalities and transcending all of them. In some ways, the Russian-speaking population was but one of those subject peoples. This distinction was even expressed linguistically, in a manner which is lost in the translation: *rossiiskii* (Russian) was the adjective applied to the empire as a whole, while *russkii* (Russian) was used when referring specifically to the Russian language, culture or people.[39]

It was not until the nineteenth century that the tendency to conflate the meanings of *rossiiskii* and *russkii* became part of a concerted policy. The Russification policy that was pursued with varying degrees of zeal during the latter part of the century was part of an attempt to reinforce the legitimacy and consolidate the socio-cultural hegemony of the tsarist autocracy during a period of rapid social and economic change. The Russification campaign was designed to help modernize and consolidate the state bureaucracy by establishing a uniform language of administration throughout the empire's far-flung territories.[40] It was also designed as a repressive and/or preemptive measure directed against certain rebellious ethnic groups (notably the Poles after the crushing of their 1863 uprising). At the same time, pan-Slavism – the idea that all Slavic peoples should unite under the aegis of the mighty Russian state – gained influence among intellectual circles as well as certain segments of the diplomatic and military establishments. Its effect was particularly noticeable in Russia's aggressive Balkan policy of the 1870s and 1880s.[41]

It is important to bear in mind that the regime's linguistic policies were not uniform, nor were they applied consistently in all times and places. In the western provinces – predominantly East Slavic regions that had come to be viewed as a zone of contestation between Polish and Russian cultural influences – Russification was, for a time, pursued with missionary zeal. Attempts by the Ukrainian and Belorussian intelligentsias to revive or develop high cultures based on their own languages were perceived, mistakenly, as part of a Polish plot to draw the local peasantry away from its supposedly Russian roots.[42] Instruction and publication in Ukrainian and Belorussian were accordingly forbidden and the 1839 ban on the Uniate Church of Belorussia and western Ukraine was enforced, all with a view to integrating these regions' Slavic population into the Great Russian mainstream.

In the cases of ethnic groups whose languages were more firmly linked to a well-established high culture, Russification was pursued more sporadically and inconsistently. In Poland, attempts to impose Russian as the language of instruction in the school system were effectively abandoned in the face of widespread resistance, although higher education in Poland remained a Russian-language preserve until the First World War. In the parts of the Baltic provinces roughly corresponding to present-day Latvia and Estonia, the local German landowning aristocracy was regarded as a loyal elite that played a useful role in administering the region and in maintaining social order and the authority of the state (although the spread of German nationalism, especially among the non-aristocratic German urban population in the region, was a source of growing concern). In the last decades of the nineteenth century, the tsarist regime's increasing ambition to exercise direct control in all regions led it to impose Russian as the official administrative, judicial, and educational language in the Baltic provinces and to undercut the ethnic Germans' local dominance by encouraging upward social mobility among the Estonian and Latvian peasantry. But the violent rural unrest that broke out in this region during the 1905 Revolution induced the Russian government to revert to its traditional alliance with the Baltic German barons. In Finland, the loyalty of the Swedish elite to the tsar was suspect, but rather than trying to Russify this semi-autonomous region, the regime fostered the development of Finnish as a literary and official language in order to offset Swedish influence. By the turn of the century, Finnish national consciousness was itself considered too far advanced, and many of the powers of the Finnish Diet were accordingly circumscribed by Nicholas II.[43]

Various nationalities were regarded as intrinsically unassimilable or even undesirable; rather than seeking to integrate them into Russian society, the state institutionalized their marginalization. Little or no effort was made to Russify the Muslim peoples of Central Asia, whose recently conquered lands were coveted as prime areas for colonization by the surplus peasant population of the Slavic heartland. The rebellious Circassians of the western Caucasus were simply driven from their homes and forced to flee to the Ottoman empire. The Jews – who had experienced a short-lived easing of restrictions in the 1860s – were subjected to renewed repression in the 1880s and left unprotected against violent pogroms.[44]

These complex and inconsistent policies reflected the dilemmas faced by a regime hoping to bring the society and government of a multiethnic empire together as part of an organically unified polity under the auspices of a rigidly authoritarian system of government. Some Slavic and/or Eastern Orthodox groups were defined as integral parts of the body politic, vital limbs that needed to be more intimately connected to the Great Russian trunk. Other peoples were designated as alien and unclean elements (in the social-hygiene imagery that was increasingly favored in nineteenth- and early-twentieth-century European political discourse)[45] and were accordingly targeted for persecution, exploitation, and marginalization. The contradictions inherent in these awkward and heavy-handed attempts at political modernization were never fully acknowledged or examined within the ruling circles.

The Russification campaign achieved some degree of success in certain areas (particularly among the population of Belorussia and eastern Ukraine). Overall, though, the regime's ham-fisted methods only alienated non-Russian ethnic groups and stimulated the inception of nationalist movements by their elites. By the same token, the development of a distinctively Russian national consciousness did not necessarily go hand in hand with increased popular support for the tsarist regime; it could just as readily be turned against a government whose inconsistent policies and erratic behavior did not always seem to coincide with any identifiable national interest of the Russian people. During the First World War, the tsarist regime's reluctance to encourage spontaneous contributions by civic organizations and regional bodies to the war effort was perceived as a reflection of its ambivalence toward the potentially democratic-egalitarian idea of Russian nationalism. Nagging suspicions over the tsar's true loyalties were aggravated by the appointment of Boris Stürmer, a reactionary thought to be pro-German, to head the cabinet in the midst of the war and by the undue influence over the tsarina exercised by the Siberian mystic, Grigorii Rasputin – a known advocate of immediate peace talks. Amidst the devastating military setbacks and economic upheaval of the First World War, this growing gulf between Russian nationalist sentiment and the tsarist regime contributed significantly to the revolution of March 1917.[46]

Political agendas, cultural orientations, and social-mobilization patterns among ethnic groups in the Russian empire were extremely varied, but some of the major typologies would have seemed quite familiar to observers of the Habsburg scene. There was, most notably, a contrast between nationalities whose nobilities regarded themselves as guardians of historic state traditions, and ethnic groups that consisted almost exclusively of impoverished peasants with little collective sense of connection to political history. With the passage of time, this contrast became somewhat blurred as the leaders of "historic" nations turned to the masses for support, while the intellectual elites that arose among the "non-historic" peoples compensated for the difficulty of mobilizing illiterate peasants by indulging in intoxicating fantasies about glorious national histories of their own invention.

The Polish nationalism that manifested itself in the futile revolts of 1830 and 1863 was very much a gentry-led affair, although the failure of those uprisings called into question both the wisdom of armed rebellion and the value of gentry leadership. During the latter decades of the nineteenth century, the Polish intelligentsia, gentry, and growing middle class steered clear of romantic adventurism, focussing on economic development and material progress as the most important vehicles for national self-advancement. Cities such as Warsaw and Łódz did in fact become major industrial centers, and the development of urban society led to the creation of mass-based Polish nationalist movements around the turn of the century.

Among predominantly peasant peoples such as the Ukrainians, Lithuanians, and Belorussians, the development of national consciousness was a much slower, more uncertain affair. Ukrainian nationalists saw themselves as reviving the legacy of the Cossack Hetmanate,[47] and Lithuanians identified themselves with the medieval Grand Duchy of Lithuania.[48] These attempts to anchor national consciousness in historic state traditions made up in enthusiasm for what they lacked in conviction: unlike Poland, whose vestigial autonomy had been recognized by the tsarist government as late as 1863 and whose old ruling class remained a prominent social elite, the last substantive manifestations of the Hetmanate and the Grand Duchy had long since disappeared.[49] The tiny handful of intellectuals who committed themselves to the assertion of a distinctive Belorussian cultural and national identity were even more hard pressed to uncover a distinctive political history for their people.[50]

Ironically, it was precisely the tsarist regime's campaign against Polish cultural hegemony in the Ukraine, Belorussia, and Lithuania that spurred efforts by the indigenous intelligentsias in these regions to develop literary languages and educational systems based on the idioms of the common folk. The subsequent ban by the Russian authorities on publishing and teaching in these languages had mixed results, both hampering the diffusion of national consciousness among the masses and radicalizing the attitudes of the activists. In the case of the Ukrainians and Lithuanians, ethnic enclaves across the border (in Austrian Galicia and German East Prussia, respectively) served as bases for the publication of native-language materials that were smuggled into Russia. The Austrian and German authorities were quite willing to encourage dissension among the Russian empire's subject peoples.

Variations on these themes were played out across the length and breadth of the Russian empire. The development of Estonian and Latvian literary languages was actually pioneered by scholars from among the local Baltic-German elite, who took an ethnographic interest in the indigenous languages, as did Swedish intellectuals in the Finnish tongue. These regions' Lutheran culture combined with the growth of a freeholding peasantry to produce relatively high literacy rates in the nineteenth century. This created fertile soil in which to sow the seeds of national cultures.[51] Among the Latvians and Estonians, nationalist emotions were directed first and foremost against the continued socio-political hegemony of the Baltic-German barons.[52]

Among the Jews, disappointment over the rollback of mid-nineteenth-century reforms, and desperation over the unleashing of pogroms against their communities from 1881 on, led to a high degree of political activism, both clandestine and open. Among the wide variety of movements that took root among the Jewish masses around the turn of the century was the Bund (the Yiddish word for "Union") – a Marxist movement popular among the Jewish workers of Poland's industrial towns. The Bund used Yiddish – the language of the masses – as its preferred medium of communication, and claimed the exclusive right to represent the interests of the Jewish working class within the framework of the Russian socialist movement. The Zionists, for their part, upheld Hebrew as the authentic and original language that must be cultivated in preparation for mass migration to the Jewish homeland of Palestine. The Russian authorities were, at times, inclined to tolerate the activities of the Zionists insofar as they promoted the departure of Jews from the Russian empire, although their organizations remained officially illegal. The Bundists were regarded as more dangerous, since they sought to promote an autonomous Jewish working-class culture within Russia while collaborating with other socialists in a common effort to overthrow the regime.[53]

In Transcaucasia, the Armenians were marked by an exceptionally strong sense of collective history and destiny, a distinctive identity that was enshrined in the traditions of their ancient Church[54] and reinforced by a sense of solidarity with the Armenians across the border in the Ottoman empire. Though they did not have their own nobility (aside from the landowning gentry of the district of Nagorno-Karabakh), Armenians were a prominent element among the burgeoning commercial and industrial elites in the major cities of Transcaucasia, from Batum on the Black Sea to Baku on the Caspian. The development of the oil industry in Baku also brought into being a relatively large and politically active Armenian working class. The dynamism of this relatively cosmopolitan ethnic group and its high visibility in the region's urban centers earned it the hostility of other Transcaucasian ethnic groups such as Georgians and Azerbaijanis, whose overwhelmingly rural background left them ill-equipped to compete effectively in the hurly-burly of a rapidly industrializing economy.[55]

The Muslim population of the empire formed a complex cultural and socio-economic mosaic which did not readily arrange itself into cut-and-dried categories of ethnic identity and nationhood. In principle, the Islamic community of the faithful was conceived of as transcending (both spiritually *and* politically) the divisions of class, ethnicity, geography. In practice, a broad variety of historical experiences, cultural orientations, and regional issues shaped the identities of Muslims in the tsarist empire. In Transcaucasia, as we have seen, conflict with the Christian Armenians played a decisive role in the development of the Azerbaijanis' political consciousness. The Muslim peoples of the Caucasus mountains spoke a bewilderingly diverse array of tongues, and their geographic fragmentation was reinforced by the politics of the clan and the blood feud. They did, however, share a common resentment of tsarist political dominance (imposed following the Ottoman empire's forced withdrawal from the region in 1774) and of Russian settlers. In the mid-nineteenth century, the ideal of the Islamic community and the solidarist ethos of the Sufi brotherhood had been successfully transposed to the politics of resistance by the Avar leader Imam Shamil, who was able to bring together a formidable array of Chechen and Daghestani fighters in an anti-Russian rebellion that held out against over-whelming odds for many years.[56]

Most of Muslim Central Asia was formally incorporated into the Russian empire over the course of the nineteenth century, and the khanates of Bukhara and Khiva actually retained their formal sovereignty as Russian protectorates until after the Bolshevik Revolution. Russia's late acquisition of these regions, and its temporal coincidence with the nineteenth-century wave of European overseas imperial expansion, served to accentuate the essentially colonial status of the new territories. To the south, in fertile Turkestan, the cultivation of cotton as a cash crop was virtually imposed on the indigenous peasantry. Both financing of production and purchase of the crop were handled by monopolistic Russian commercial interests on a grossly exploitative basis that created an ever-growing class of landless peasants, while a narrow stratum of indigenous middlemen earned large profits.

The highly stratified structure of these societies and the relatively parochial outlook of their ruling classes rendered them particularly vulnerable to Russian divide-and-rule tactics. The traditional socio-political elites were easily co-opted by the Russian authorities – most notably in the case of Bukhara, a cultural center with enormous regional prestige, whose emir actually relied on Russian assistance to help him reassert control over the rebellious, eastern, Shi'ite regions of his khanate. The clerical/scholarly class (the *ulama'*) was usually willing to promote political docility among the general populace as long as its own social authority and control over educational institutions and religious endowments (*waqfs*) was not intruded upon or challenged. The fact that Arabic was the Muslims' sole liturgical language and Farsi generally the preferred medium of literary expression and official communication among the Central Asian elites, while a variety of Turkic dialects were employed in everyday speech by the masses, made it particularly difficult for would-be political activists to construct sharply delineated cultural and geographical frameworks of national identity or even to agree upon common idioms for the dissemination of their ideas. The Central Asian peasant revolts that broke out sporadically during the last decades of the nineteenth century tended to be fairly spontaneous affairs with little support among the established or educated classes, and were snuffed out with relative ease by the Russian military authorities.

Finally, the Tatars (speakers of a Turkic tongue) of the Volga region had lived in close proximity to Russians for centuries and had been under Russian rule since Ivan the Terrible's conquest of Kazan in 1552. Culturally and economically, they were the Muslim group that had adapted most successfully to life under the tsars; indeed, their commercial and industrial elite played a highly visible role in the empire's modernization efforts. The Tatar intelligentsia's relatively intimate familiarity with the Russian language and culture gave it immediate access to the latest ideological currents shaking up Russian intellectual circles. The influence of Russian populism and pan-Slavism stimulated Tatar intellectuals to think in new ways about their own identity and about their relationship with other Muslim and Turkic peoples, both within the Russian empire and outside it. By the turn of the century, Tatar intellectuals and their publications were playing a prominent role in disseminating novel socio-political ideas among the nascent intelligentsias of Azerbaijan and Central Asia – and even the Ottoman empire (see Chapter 3).

The 1905 Revolution and the short period of liberalization that came in its wake served to intensify ideological fermentation and heighten political consciousness among Russians and non-Russians alike. The brief lifting of censorship led to a flourishing of publications of every imaginable political orientation and in every major language. The creation of a parliament (Duma) provided a forum for public debate and an opportunity for extensive cross-fertilization of ideas among the social and intellectual elites of different ethnic and regional groups. The re-imposition of censorship and the limitations on voting rights that soon followed could not force all these genies back into their bottles. Yet it should also be stressed that most nationalist elites in the Russian empire did not seriously contemplate outright political separatism; talk of cultural autonomy and the possible reconfiguration of the state along federal lines was the norm. Furthermore, while mass movements were clearly emerging among the empire's most urbanized and industrialized peoples, such as the Poles, in most regions political nationalism was still confined to relatively narrow intellectual circles as of 1914.

While the tsarist regime looked askance upon the autonomist or separatist aspirations of ethnic groups within its own borders, it did not hesitate to encourage nationalism in areas impinging on the interests of rival powers. Conservative, pan-Slavic elements among the Galician Ukrainian intelligentsia cultivated close contact with sympathetic officials on the Russian side of the border, as did similar groups among the Habsburg empire's other Slavic nationalities. More significantly, during the last years before the outbreak of war, irredentist politicians and officers in Serbia were convinced they enjoyed Russia's tacit support in their ongoing campaign of propaganda and terrorism directed against the Austro-Hungarian authorities in Bosnia. Of course, the shots that were fired at Sarajevo in June 1914 were ultimately to strike down the tsarist system as well as the Habsburg monarchy.[57]

The Ottoman Empire

Among the three empires examined here, the Ottoman can be said to have been ruled by the most cosmopolitan elite. Whereas the Romanov dynasty flirted with Russian nationalism and pan-Slavism, and the Habsburg emperor was unmistakably Austro-German in culture, the Ottoman ruling family and administrative elite before 1908 could only vaguely and imprecisely be described as Turkish. True, the Ottoman dynasty (named after its founder, Osman I, 1280–1324) traced its origins to a clan of Turkic warrior-nomads whose thirteenth-century military advances against the Byzantine empire placed them in a strong position to replace the declining Seljuk Turks as the major Muslim power in Anatolia. The Ottomans went on to seize the Balkans in the fifteenth century, Constantinople[58] – the last stronghold of the Byzantine empire – in 1453, and the Middle East in the sixteenth century. But by this time, the Ottoman rulers had long since shifted their regime's center of gravity from the saddle to the throne. As Sultans of the Ottoman empire, they drew heavily on Byzantine administrative practices and upheld orthodox Sunni Islam – rather than the mystic sects popular among Turkic horsemen – as the official state religion. Their political culture was molded by the legacy of classical Islamic civilization. Thousands of Arabic and Farsi words were incorporated into Ottoman speech and writing. The Ottoman language that emerged as the medium of imperial high culture was a mixture of vocabularies, grammatical forms, and stylistic devices that was not strictly identifiable as the vernacular of any given ethnic group (although its basic structure remained recognizably Turkic).[59]

Like the other two states we have surveyed, the Ottoman empire contained a highly varied mix of ethnic and religious groups, even after losing control of most of its remaining Balkan territories in 1912–1913.[60] The Sunni Muslims, who constituted a majority of the empire's population, included most of the Turkish speakers of western and central Anatolia and of the empire's remaining Balkan territory around Istanbul and Edirne (Adrianople), many of the Kurds of eastern Anatolia and northern Syria and Mesopotamia, and most of the Arabs to the south. Interspersed among, or adjacent to, these predominantly Sunni Muslim populations were various heterodox and non-Muslim groups such as the Alawites of northwestern Syria, the Shiites of southern Mesopotamia, the Greek Orthodox, Greek Catholics, and Maronite Christians of Syria–Palestine and Mt. Lebanon, the Armenians concentrated in northeastern Anatolia and in cities throughout the region, the ethnic Greeks of the western Anatolian coastline, and the Jewish communities of Anatolia, Mesopotamia, and Palestine.

Even more so than in the case of the Russian empire, the Ottoman state cannot be said to have been of particular material benefit to what was commonly regarded as its dominant ethnic group. The Turkish-speaking regions were actually more heavily taxed than others, and while the empire's administrative and military elite included a disproportionate number of Turks, it traditionally included many members of other nationalities as well. The Ottoman state's central legitimizing principle was its claim to be the expression and protector of the unity of the Sunni Muslims of the world as a community of faith, or *umma*. Being a Sunni Muslim male, cultivating the right social connections, and assimilating into Ottoman culture, rather than belonging to any particular ethnic group, were the necessary conditions for achieving upward mobility in the governing apparatus. At the same time, members of non-Muslim communities, such as Greeks, Armenians, and Jews, played key roles in the development of the state's commercial and financial infrastructure.[61]

Although in principle the Sultan's authority was absolute, by the early nineteenth century he was, in practice, heavily dependent on the support of the semi-feudal landed aristocracy, the Islamic clergy, and the independent-minded "slave" soldiers known as janissaries (who had become more proficient in the art of the palace coup than the battlefield victory). In the absence of a professional imperial bureaucracy, many outlying provinces, such as those in the Arab Middle East, were allowed a considerable measure of autonomy as long as their ruling elites were willing and able to collect revenue and military manpower on the Sultan's behalf.

The empire's Christians and Jews were regarded as infidels but were also recognized as people of the Book (as distinct from pagans). Their longstanding status as *dhimmis* designated them as members of juridically inferior, but protected, communities that were subject to special legal provisions and obligations (such as special tax payments), although full citizenship was formally granted to non-Muslims in 1839. The various non-Muslim religious denominations were organized into *millets* – self-regulating communities defined, not territorially, but in terms of affiliation with a set of religious institutions. The clerical authorities of any given *millet* functioned as its internal leadership, and it was, traditionally, through these authorities that Ottoman power was mediated.[62] This arrangement had originally functioned quite effectively as a system of co-optation and control, with the heads of the various *millets* being held accountable for their respective communities' tax obligations, military-conscription quotas, etc. By the nineteenth century, however, the empire's corporate structuring of power, of which the *millets* were a prominent manifestation, had become a mark of its weakness and inefficiency in comparison to the much more streamlined European polities.

Indeed, the Ottoman empire – once the terror of Europe – had been steadily declining in relative power for centuries. While much of Europe underwent the economic, technological, administrative, and political revolutions commonly referred to as modernization, the once mighty Ottoman empire seemed to stagnate amidst pervasive corruption and half-hearted reforms. Its ultimate collapse was deemed inevitable by most European observers. This was a prospect that was contemplated with varying combinations of eagerness and apprehensiveness by the rapacious Great Powers, each of which was concerned with maximizing its political and economic influence in the Middle East while minimizing that of its rivals. Although this rivalry gave the Ottomans an opportunity to stave off domination by any one power by playing the imperial competitors off against one another, the relationship between the Ottoman empire and the major

European states was a manifestly unequal one. The so-called Capitulations enshrined this inequality in law by providing extraterritorial legal status – amounting to diplomatic immunity – to all Europeans traveling or doing business in the Sultan's territories, with no hint of reciprocity. By the nineteenth century, the growing exploitation and abuse of the Capitulations flagrantly violated contemporaneous European ideas about the sacrosanct quality of state sovereignty.

The inferior status and intermittent persecution of Christian communities in the empire drew the attention of Western public opinion and created opportunities for European intervention in the affairs of the Ottoman state. The Russians, in particular, consistently sought to present themselves as protectors of the empire's Eastern Orthodox communities. The reform plans that European diplomatic conferences regularly sought to impose on the Ottoman empire tended to call for an enhancement of the *millets'* autonomy, and even the granting of territorial self-rule to individual *millets*. During the nineteenth century, this approach had led to the gradual disintegration of Ottoman control over Balkan territories such as Serbia and Bulgaria, where members of Orthodox Christian *millets* constituted a majority of the population. One of the provisions agreed upon at the Congress of Berlin in 1878 was a Great Power guarantee of administrative reform in the six Armenian-populated provinces of northeastern Anatolia (across the border from Russia). Although never enforced, this unfulfilled promise served as a juridical principle in the name of which Armenian nationalist organizations appealed to European governments and public opinion for support. Tensions over the Armenian question spiraled increasingly out of control from the 1890s on, as Armenian activists carried out spectacular paramilitary and terrorist operations against the Ottoman government while the Sultan's regime incited, or turned a blind eye to, the wholesale massacres of Armenian communities in the heart of Istanbul as well as in eastern Anatolia.[63]

As the Ottoman state lost ever more territory in the Balkans, and as the Sultan's nominal authority in North Africa was openly flouted by European imperial powers, the Ottomans struggled to consolidate control over what was left of their once mighty empire. Beginning in 1839, they initiated a series of reforms referred to collectively as the *Tanzimat* (short for *Tanzimat-i Hayriye* – "Beneficent Reorderings"). This modernization effort led to the creation of a large government bureaucracy and a professional officer corps, closer supervision of the provinces by the new bureaucracy, the systematic registration of land ownership throughout the empire with a view to more efficient revenue collection, and an incipient trend away from Islamic law (*shariat*) and toward a more secularized judicial system. Diplomats and top administrators were either sent to Western Europe for their education, or were trained at new institutions of higher and professional education that were established in Istanbul. Most notable among these were the Royal Medical Academy, the Civil Service Academy (the *Mülkiye*), and the War Academy (the *Harbiye*).

In many respects, however, the reforms fell far short of the mark, raising expectations that could not be fulfilled. Indeed, one of the most significant side-effects of the *Tanzimat* was the creation of new, semi-Westernized professional elites who were eager to pursue the reforms to their logical conclusions and were frustrated by the seeming inability or unwillingness of the regime to surmount the many social, cultural, and institutional obstacles that stood in the way of a complete remaking of the Ottoman state. The regime's profound ambivalence about the whole modernization process was encapsulated by Sultan Abdülhamit's response to the Eastern Crisis of 1875–1878. In the face of revolts against Ottoman authority in the Balkans, and in an attempt to ward off the imposition of reforms on the Ottoman empire by the European powers, the Sultan issued a constitution granting equality under the law to all subjects regardless of their faith and creating an elected parliament. But less than a year later (in 1877), he suspended the Constitution and returned to autocratic rule. For the following three decades, the Demand for a restoration of the Constitution of 1876 was to be the common rallying cry of a wide range of political dissidents, many of them graduates of the empire's new educational institutions and members of its new socio-political elites.

The economic development that the reforms were supposed to facilitate was slow to come, and uneven in its social impact. While initiatives by foreign investors led to the undertaking of high-visibility projects such as the construction of the "Berlin–Baghdad" railway, the general infrastructure of the economy remained pre-industrial. The penetration of Middle Eastern markets by Western-manufactured products benefited small groups of middlemen while undermining the livelihood of local craftsmen. The most successful indigenous intermediaries in international commercial and financial transactions tended to be members of Christian minorities, whose Western cultural orientation (commonly reinforced by education in the French-run schools that were established throughout the Middle East during the nineteenth century) and diaspora connections (in the case of Greeks and Armenians) made them natural candidates for such roles. A number of Jewish families also rose to prominence in this fashion. Of course, this pattern reinforced Muslim resentment of the minorities in their midst. Social and economic inequalities within Muslim populations were aggravated by the program of land-ownership registration undertaken in the context of the *Tanzimat*. It was the wealthiest and most influential Muslim landowners and merchants who dominated the local judicial bodies responsible for issuing titles, while the lower strata lacked the education and financial resources needed to make good their claims. The result was a pattern of dispossession of poor peasants, who were forced to become either tenant farmers or landless laborers, while the landed elites consolidated their economic dominance and used their financial power to purchase public office, further strengthening their grip on the regional branches of the expanding state bureaucracy.[64]

For the empire's non-Muslim peoples, the *Tanzimat* were laden with contradictory and paradoxical implications. On the one hand, the regime's efforts to weaken the independent power of the clergy had extended to some of the religious minorities, where it had led to the creation of more secular and representative communal bodies that further institutionalized the *millets*' autonomy. On the other hand, the long-term goal of the *Tanzimat* seemed to be the creation of a more integrated and unified body politic, and the uniform distribution of state power across regions and populations in accordance with modern, European conceptions of political sovereignty. This could be a double-edged sword, bringing a theoretical equality to oppressed ethno-religious groups while in effect subjecting them more directly to the authority of an often brutal and arbitrary government. In general, the half-baked nature of the reform effort created enormous disquiet and uncertainty about the future status of the *millets*, and it clearly contributed to the unrest among the Armenian population in particular.

Finally, it must be noted that during the last decades of the nineteenth century, the Ottoman Sultans laid new emphasis on their claim to be heirs to the classical Islamic Caliphate. As Caliph, the Sultan claimed both spiritual and political authority, not only within the empire, but in principle over all members of the *umma* beyond its borders as well. The Sultan's role as Caliph was highlighted in pan-Islamic propaganda that was disseminated as far afield as Russian Central Asia. By focussing attention on their role as caliphs, the sultans were stressing the intimate connection between the spiritual unity of the *umma* and the political integrity of the empire and trying to create an ideological framework for the state's return to a Great Power role. Yet this pan-Islamic theme ran contrary to the modernizing spirit of the *Tanzimat* and undermined the politically integrative goals of the reform effort as well by drawing attention to the anomalous position of the Ottomans' non-Muslim subjects. In a very loose sense, the Ottomans' pan-Islamic propaganda campaign can be seen as analogous to the tsars' efforts to identify themselves more closely with the idea of Russian nationalism and pan-Slavism. In both cases, imperial regimes were searching for ways of establishing stronger emotional and psychological grips over their subjects, but in appealing to the identity of one community (or group of communities) they ran the risk of alienating everyone else.

Indeed, the nineteenth century witnessed the rise of a particularly strong sense of nationalist or proto-nationalist identity among a number of the empire's Christian peoples. The Orthodox Christian tradition of native liturgies, reinforced perhaps by the institutional precedent of the *millet* system, lent itself readily to the creation of religious frameworks for nation-making, as one branch after another of the Orthodox Church in the Balkans (Serbian Orthodox, Bulgarian Orthodox, etc.) claimed autonomous status within the framework of Eastern Orthodoxy. Indeed, this close association of ethnicity with religion may well have contributed to the fervor and intransigence of Balkan nationalisms; it is interesting to note that forced conversion was a favored method of "integrating" the population of newly acquired territories during the Balkan Wars of 1912–1913.[65]

For its part, as the empire's official religion, Sunni Islam was not structurally linked to any particular regional or ethnic identity, making it difficult for would-be nationalists among the Muslim peoples to reconcile their ideas with religious principles.[66] The sense of humiliation born of the Ottoman empire's relative decline, combined with frustration over the government's failure to follow through effectively on reform initiatives, did stimulate the growth of a militant reform movement – The Committee of Union and Progress, also known as the Young Turks – among the empire's administrative and military elites. As we shall see in the next chapter, the evolution of this movement highlighted the tension between Islamic universalism and the ethnic particularism that was beginning to gain ground among the Muslim intelligentsias during the last years before the First World War.

Epilogue

In discussing the enormous challenges and dizzying complexities with which each of these multinational empires had to contend, it is difficult to avoid creating the impression that they were descending very rapidly toward total collapse and disintegration. It is therefore worth pointing out that all three regimes were still very much going concerns as of 1914; in fact, their resilience in the face of total warfare down to 1917 or 1918 is quite remarkable. Indeed, before the war, most nationalist organizations in the Habsburg, Russian, and Ottoman empires did not explicitly seek outright independence; they focussed instead on advancing various plans for cultural and political autonomy and social reform.

Furthermore, before 1914, it was not clear what political configurations would replace the empires if they ever did reach a point of total collapse. Many of the nationalist movements mentioned here were still in an embryonic phase of development as of 1914; even among those that could already be described as mass movements, there were deep internal divisions over tactics, strategies, and the definition of long-term objectives. The war was to play a decisive role in shaping the evolution of nationalist movements by suddenly and dramatically exposing both the brutality and the fragility of the imperial states, by wreaking havoc upon millions of people who had hitherto remained on the margins of political life and who now found they could not escape politics, and by creating unusual leadership opportunities for certain figures who might not otherwise have risen to prominence. Yet this powerful, across-the-board impact assumed highly differentiated forms among the various intellectual strands and social sectors of each "nation." While the war did create a sudden opportunity for the birth of new states, it did not automatically endow their citizenries with homogeneous collective identities or uniform sets of socio-political expectations. In most instances, it merely created temporary illusions of national unity – and therein lay the peril.

However, before we can explore the impact of the war on nationalist movements, we must take a closer look at the ideological impulses that animated the nationalist intelligentsias that dominated (or even constituted) those movements on the eve of the war.

3 On the Eve of War

The Intelligentsia as Vanguard of Nationalism

At the onset of the First World War, the prospect of national self-determination for the subject peoples of the Habsburg, Ottoman, and Russian empires seemed quite remote. Though facing severe domestic and foreign challenges, these empires were not only still intact, but seemed downright vigorous in many respects. The Habsburg empire had just expanded its territory by formally incorporating the province of Bosnia-Herzegovina in 1908. (It had assumed *de facto* control there in 1878.) For its part, the Ottoman empire was undergoing an ambitious political-reform and administrative-modernization effort under the aegis of the Young Turks, who had consolidated their grip on power following Ottoman military defeats in North Africa and the Balkans that discredited rival elites. Russia's humiliation at the hands of the Japanese in the war of 1904–1905 had only reinforced its ruling elite's zeal for an ever faster pace of industrialization and military modernization, while turning its foreign ambitions away from the Far East and back toward the intricacies of Balkan politics.

Many of the nationalist movements that were to challenge these imperial colossi were little more than fledglings in 1914 in terms of continuous organizational history. Some of them felt ideologically and emotionally linked to a century or more of sporadic uprisings and periodic martyrdoms. There had been Polish revolts against tsarist rule in 1830 and 1863, and the Habsburg empire had been rent by nationalist turmoil during the 1848–1849 revolutions. Yet there was little organic continuity between the leadership of these past rebellions and the nationalist political groupings that emerged onto the political stage around the turn of the century. Some of these movements had begun to garner extensive popular support during the few years since their founding. Others remained almost exclusively elite formations. The overwhelming majority were led by intellectuals and members of the wider intelligentsia – that is, educated professionals who were directly exposed to the ideas of intellectuals and who aspired to implement them. In many cases, these were the people most likely to feel alienated, discriminated against, and limited in their opportunities for upward mobility by the growth of official, state-sponsored nationalism (such as Magyar or Russian nationalism). The intelligentsia was also the social sector most aware of, and obsessed by, the model of the Western nation-state as an instrument of political progress and collective empowerment.[1] To be sure, strong feelings about matters of ethnonational identity readily stirred members of the less educated masses as well. But it was the intelligentsia that took the lead in trying to articulate collective sentiments and that aspired to shape them. It was in the course of the First World War and its aftermath that the pitfalls of this sort of intellectual self-involvement manifested themselves most clearly, as we shall see in subsequent chapters.

A common dilemma for these nationalist vanguards was how to reconcile the cultivation of ethnic particularism with the emulation of foreign models, the quest for cultural authenticity with the embrace of universalistic values. In their effort to find common ground between these conflicting impulses, they tended to embrace very broad definitions of what constituted the nation and who belonged to it. Such expansive conceptions of national identity corresponded most closely to the personal experiences and emotional needs of educated, urban sophisticates and intellectuals whose lives were no longer bound up with the tightly knit socio-cultural fabric of parochial communities, yet who yearned for a sense of morally engaged communal fellowship that would complement rather than contradict their own semi-cosmopolitan lifestyles and outlooks. By defining the nation in the most sweeping terms possible, they also created a potential need for an educated, politically conscious vanguard like themselves to play a leading role in integrating heterogeneous societies into cohesive wholes.

Many members of nationalist elites saw themselves as cultural intermediaries who could draw strength and inspiration from the folk traditions of their peoples, while bringing universal principles of enlightenment to the masses and leading them in the establishment of social and political justice. The achieve-ment of national self-determination – be it in the form of autonomy or independence – was often linked to a vision of harmony and cooperation among nations, whose relations with each other would resemble those of individuals in a democracy.

While liberal-democratic and social-democratic activists played highly visible roles in shaping nationalist ideologies, they did not always go unchallenged. In quite a number of cases, their views were attacked by right-wing rivals who regarded the nation as a quasi-biological organism and contended that ethnic kinship was the only legitimate foundation for political community – and the only valid source of political values. These versions of nationalism were also transformative and expansive – but in far more sinister ways. Rather than focussing on the political integration of diverse communities around a common set of civic values and cultural projects, some right-wing nationalists advocated the purification of the nation by purging it of unassimilable minorities. When looking outward, they rejected democratic universalism, often cultivating aggres-sive visions of territorial expansion instead.

In one form or another, this division cut across many of the nationalist intelli-gentsias in Europe and the Middle East. As long as the multinational empires remained intact, its implications remained largely theoretical – although events such as the Dreyfus Affair in turn-of-the-century France had already shown how pivotal the clash between liberal nationalism and integral nationalism[2] could be in the political development of an established nation-state. The collapse of the empires in 1917–1918, and the consequent triumph-by-default of the principle of national self-determination, was to turn the question of what constituted national identity into a life-and-death matter for millions.

Conflicting Nationalist Agendas in East Central Europe

Poland

Perhaps the most clear-cut example of a nationalist movement riven between inclusive and exclusive visions is the Polish case. By the early years of the twentieth century two very distinct currents had emerged within the broad compass of Polish nationalist politics. Both had arisen in the Russian partition of Poland, the demographic and cultural heartland of the dismantled country, but had established affiliates – or at least close contact with like-minded counterparts – in Austrian-ruled Galicia and in the German partition. Józef Piłsudski led the nationalist wing of the Polish Socialist Party, which embraced an inclusive conception of Polish national identity based on a territorial/political definition of citizenship. Roman Dmowski's National Democratic movement preached a stridently intolerant brand of integral nationalism that identified the welfare of the nation as the supreme ethical and political value, and defined the nation in pseudo-biological terms. Anti-Semitism was a central feature of the National Democrats' ideology and *modus operandi*. While many other political parties and movements (such as the Galician conservatives and new peasant parties) played important roles in Polish politics throughout this period, we will focus in this section upon the figures of Piłsudski and Dmowski, for the rivalry between them – and between the ideas they represented – was to dominate the Polish political scene until Piłsudski's death in 1935.[3]

Józef Piłsudski (1867–1935) was a curious amalgam of aloof aristocrat and radical conspirator, leftist politician and paternalistic autocrat. He was born and raised in the region around Vilnius, whose population was a mixture of Poles, Jews, and Lithuanians. He was himself of Lithuanian aristocratic stock on his father's side and Polish heritage on his mother's. (His brother was to join a Lithuanian national committee in Switzerland during the First World War, at a time when Lithuanians and Poles under German occupation were disputing the future disposition of Vilnius!)[4] Suffering from bouts of severe depression and self-doubt, Piłsudski seems to have taken little interest in his formal studies in Vilnius and Kharkov, and to have found relief and solace in secret reading groups and conspiratorial activities. Positivist and materialist philosophy (Comte, Büchner) was the main form of intellectual nourishment for the young people in his circle, and the terrorist activities of the Russian populist underground organization Narodnaya Volya (the People's Will) the main source of political inspiration.

Piłsudski's involvement in a Vilnius-based secret society linked to Narodnaya Volya led to his trial and sentencing to five years in Siberian exile in the wake of

Narodnaya Volya's unsuccessful 1887 attempt on the life of Tsar Alexander III.[5] Having been exposed to Marxist ideas during his last year in Vilnius,[6] Piłsudski's association with socialism was strengthened by the close bonds he developed with a number of left-wing activists into whose company he was thrown in his village of exile. Following his return to Poland in 1892 at the age of 24, he was quickly drawn to the newly formed Polish Socialist Party (PPS) and rose rapidly to a dominant position within the nascent organization's Central Committee.

The PPS was one of two major Polish socialist parties that came into being during this period. Its rival was the SDKPiL (Social Democracy of the Kingdom of Poland and Lithuania), led from abroad by the exiled Rosa Luxemburg. The SDKPiL adhered strictly to the principle of proletarian internationalism and denounced any form of nationalism as a distraction from the class struggle. For its part, the leadership of the PPS insisted that the interests of Polish workers could best be protected within the framework of Polish national self-determination. As Piłsudski saw it, the peoples of the western borderlands of the Russian empire were more developed economically and culturally and had a politically more conscious working class than the Russian heartland, and were therefore far riper for revolution than the rest of the empire.[7]

This was a Marxist justification for a nationalist program. For Piłsudski, the main attraction of socialism was its potential as an instrument for the mobilization of the Polish working masses on behalf of a separatist movement. Of aristocratic background himself, he felt strong ties to the romantic tradition of militant resistance to foreign occupation. But he also recognized that uprisings such as those of 1830 and 1863 had failed due to insufficient popular support and inauspicious international circumstances. He wished to revive Poland's long-dormant heroic tradition, but to fuse it with modern methods of mass mobilization while leavening it with a measure of *Realpolitik*. With its emphasis on the vital role of an ideological/political vanguard in mobilizing and leading the masses, and its propensity for conspiratorial tactics, revolutionary socialism exerted a powerful attraction on Piłsudski. The prominence he quickly achieved within the PPS (due in part to having joined it at a time when it consisted of no more than one or two dozen members) also satisfied his powerful urge to become a leader of men.

His notion of Polish national identity was closely linked to the historical tradition of the early modern Polish state, which had been dominated by the Polish language and culture but whose ruling class had been a gentry of multiethnic background. He hoped to incorporate most of the territories of the defunct Commonwealth into the future Polish state by structuring it as a Polish-led, multinational federation. He appeared to think of national identity in terms of culture, language, historic tradition, and political values, rather than in narrowly ethnic terms, and was relatively immune to the anti-Semitism which was so pervasive in Polish society. Yet this attitude of tolerance and inclusiveness was not concretized in a clear and consistent political program, and it was hard to say what specific institutional form the PPS's vision of a multinational federation was to take.

Piłsudski's conception of the revolutionary struggle highlighted the cohabitation of romantic and realistic, archaic and modern, elements within his rather enigmatic political persona. While eager to use agitation and propaganda to foster a heightened sense of political and national consciousness among the urban masses of a rapidly industrializing Poland, he retained a strong proclivity for conspiratorial methods even as the PPS grew into a broad-based, mass movement. Much of his energy during the first years of the twentieth century was devoted to the creation of a trained, paramilitary elite organization under his personal command. This strike force – which came to be known as the Combat Organization – was to be held in reserve until the time was propitious for launching an armed uprising against the oppressive Russian state. The Polish Socialist Party and the growing trade union movement affiliated with it were to function as instruments for generating mass support for such an uprising and as recruitment bases for a highly motivated liberation army. The final struggle would take the form of a popularly supported war of independence rather than a social revolution.

The combination of nationalist self-affirmation with the endorsement of working-class interests was a highly attractive package, and by the end of the 1905 Revolution, the PPS had emerged as the largest socialist party in Russian Poland (with 55,000 members, plus 37,000 members of affiliated trade unions). But the growth of the party created internal tensions that it ultimately failed to contain. For many of the younger intellectuals who swelled the ranks of the PPS during these years, Piłsudski's political approach seemed like a throwback to the glorious but futile gentry-led uprisings of 1830 and 1863. The growing left wing of the PPS was convinced that the key to success lay in coordinating the efforts of socialist movements throughout the Russian empire with a view to overthrowing the tsarist system, rather than preparing to confront the Russian army on the battlefield in an old-fashioned military contest.

These ideological and tactical disputes led to a split in the movement in the aftermath of Russia's 1905 Revolution. The party's left wing formed the PPS-Left, which was to join with the SDKPiL after the First World War in forming the Polish Communist Party. Piłsudski's old guard, of which three thousand members of the Combat Organization formed the core, established itself as the PPS-Revolutionary Faction. With its armed struggle reduced to a string of spectacular robberies (including a 1908 mail-train hold-up in which Piłsudski personally participated, bagging a total of 200,000 rubles), the Combat Organization found itself hard pressed by the Russian authorities, who infiltrated its ranks, drew it into traps, and arrested many of its members. Piłsudski himself seemed to retreat into a bitter and self-absorbed cult of resistance for resistance's sake, a quixotic parody of the aristocratic ethos. In a letter composed on the eve of his 1908 train raid, he wrote:

> I fight and die only because I cannot live in the shithouse that is our life. It is an *insult* [underlined in the original] – do you hear me? It insults me as a dignified, unenslaved human being. Let others play at growing flowers, or at socialism, or at Polishness, or at whatever in this shithouse. I cannot! This is not sentimentalism, not procrastination, not a route to social evolution or

anything else. It is ordinary human dignity. I wish to win. And without a fight and a fierce fight at that, I am ... merely a beast of burden beaten with stick or whip. ...[8]

Ultimately forced to retreat from Russian Poland, Piłsudski and a few hundred of his fighters found refuge in Galicia in 1909. Here, Austrian military intelligence looked with favor upon his renewed attempt to create volunteer legions that would be ready to march against the Russians in the event of war among the Great Powers. Yet while Piłsudski looked to the support of the Central Powers against the Russians, his rival Dmowski scoffed at both his organizational tactics and his diplomatic vision as products of romantic self-delusion. The National Democrats, Dmowski insisted, were the only movement capable of uniting the Polish people and leading them to self-government through the pursuit of the hard-nosed politics of realism.

Roman Dmowski (1864–1939) was born near Warsaw to a lower-middle-class family of artisanal background. He attended the Russian University in Warsaw, obtaining an advanced degree in biology in 1892. It was during his university years that he became affiliated with a small, new nationalist organization which he soon gained control of, and which he transformed into the nerve center of a broader political movement known as National Democracy (commonly referred to as the Endecja, after the Polish pronunciation of its acronym, ND).

In developing the Endecja's ideology, Dmowski took elements of Russian populism, scientific positivism, and socialist organizational tactics, and blended them into a novel nationalist synthesis with a decidedly right-wing orientation. He rejected the socialist principle of class struggle as inimical to the national interest. He chided the Polish conservatives for their unwillingness to challenge the political *status quo* and for their single-minded focus on material progress and industrialization to the exclusion of political and cultural development of the nation. Yet he also attacked the tradition of Polish armed resistance to tsarist power, dismissing past uprisings as foolhardy displays of aristocratic bravado which had only brought disaster to the country time and time again.

The most distinctive features of Dmowski's ideology were his explicit and disdainful rejection of many aspects of Poland's historical legacy, his incorporation of virulent anti-Semitism as an integral aspect of his political program, and his advocacy of negotiation and accommodation, rather than direct confrontation, with the Russian government, as the surest means of gaining some form of national self-determination. In Dmowski's view, the supposedly glorious past of the Polish–Lithuanian Commonwealth provided an object lesson in how *not* to organize a state and society. The *szlachta* (gentry) that had dominated early modern Poland had allowed a corrupt and self-serving ethos of individualism to undermine the collective interests of the nation and bring the state to ruin. The lack of a strong, central government had made Poland notoriously vulnerable to the machinations of other powers and had left it virtually defenseless against the neighbors that had partitioned it. The *szlachta*'s reliance on Jews to fulfill the commercial and financial role of a middle class had prevented an indigenous

Polish bourgeoisie from forming until the nineteenth century. The continued presence of a large Jewish minority in Poland, Dmowski insisted, constituted an obstacle to the modernization of Polish society.

As for the international dimension of the Polish problem, Dmowski saw the expansionist and assimilative potential of the strong, industrialized, German state as posing a greater danger to the Poles' long-term prospects than the haphazard and inconsistent abuses of the tsarist regime. In the long run, Dmowski hoped to see a self-governing Congress Poland expand into the Polish-speaking regions of Germany, in the context of an alliance with Russia. As a corollary to this view, Dmowski also contended that it behooved the Poles to forego their claims to the easternmost territories of the defunct Commonwealth, both in order to effect a long-term reconciliation with Russia and because the majority of the population there was non-Polish. Ensuring a relative degree of ethnic homogeneity for the future Polish state was much more important in his eyes than repossessing every inch of ground to which Poland could attach a historical claim.

While the Endecja's leading circles were dominated by members of the intelligentsia, Dmowski aspired to encompass all major Polish social classes in his movement. Separate mass organizations were created for peasants, workers, and university students. The doctrine of class struggle was rejected in favor of a corporatist ethos that stressed the need for cooperation and compromise between workers and industrialists, peasants and landowners, all in the name of national unity. There was also a strong current of anti-clericalism in the movement, whose chief ideologue fancied himself a scientific realist who valued the nation above all competing loyalties. Over the years, the Endecja's mass organizations succeeded in gaining large followings and helped boost electoral support for the party in elections to the Russian Duma, while the movement's leadership continued to function as a semi-conspiratorial elite that shaped the main contours of its affiliated organizations' activities from above.

Dmowski's approach, then, represented an intriguing combination of elitism and populism. In many ways, he was more modern and sophisticated in his political tactics than Piłsudski, who always seemed to prefer working toward his ends through spectacular *coups de main* rather than patient organizational spadework, and who appeared more comfortable conspiring with a small network of loyal confidants than coordinating the activities of a mass movement. Dmowski was willing grudgingly to acknowledge Piłsudski's patriotism, but disdained the romantic elements in his worldview and derided him for choosing the socialist movement as a vehicle for his nationalist agenda.

Like many liberal nationalists, Dmowski thought the intelligentsia must play the role of a vanguard that would raise the cultural and political consciousness of the masses, but his understanding of what constituted political enlightenment was quite distinctive. For Dmowski it was a matter of convincing Poles to cast aside the overly individualistic ethos bequeathed them by the old aristocratic elite and learning to place the collective interest of the nation above the concerns of the individual. Dmowski's justification of this approach represented a crude transposition of biological notions to politics: the nation must be thought of as a living organism with a single, irreducible identity and a natural (if occasionally dormant) survival instinct. Its rules of conduct toward other peoples were to be determined not on the basis of a universalistic code of ethics but by the law of the jungle. Strategic alliances (e.g. with Russia) could be forged on the basis of common interests, but sentiment and conventional notions of morality had no place in determining relations among peoples. Hence his attitude toward the Jews, who constituted some 10 per cent of the population in the territories of the former Commonwealth, and around 30 per cent of the population in many towns and cities. Dmowski regarded the Jews as an alien infestation that had to be dislodged if the Polish national organism was to thrive. A small proportion of them might be assimilated into the body politic through cultural assimilation; the great majority needed to be pushed out of their socio-economic niches and ulti-mately removed physically from Poland. Human rights considerations and the principles of tolerance were luxuries that established great powers like Britain and France might be able to afford. But if Poland was to advance into the ranks of the modernized nations, it must not be distracted by such niceties.

In Dmowski's mind, this approach represented the substitution of scientific method for historical nostalgia (Poland's bane) as the foundation for political action. In its essence, however, his worldview was irrational. The application of biological imagery to politics may add color to theoretical discussions, but to take such metaphors literally and shape one's policies accordingly constitutes an exer-cise in self-delusion rather than the triumph of reason. More specifically, his conception of national integration and his choice of political tactics tended to breed division rather than foster unity. Intent upon transforming his organization into an all-embracing national movement, he set out to destroy potential rivals for mass support. The main National Democratic trade union organization sought to undermine working-class support for the wave of strikes launched by the PPS during 1905–1906. Not only did this result in violent confrontations between rank-and-file members of rival unions, it was accompanied by an orchestrated assassination campaign waged by Dmowski's activists against socialist trade-union leaders in an attempt to decapitate their organizations. Dmowski was ready to engage in a low-level civil war (which cost some 1,000 casualties) in the name of national unity.

When it came to the Jews, he did not feel bound by the slightest pretense of tolerance. Anti-Semitism was an explicit and essential aspect of the Endecja's political program, and, starting in 1912, Dmowski put his beliefs into practice by organizing an economic boycott against Jewish stores and businesses. The idea was that this would function as a sort of ethnic protectionism that could provide an opportunity for the Polish middle classes to supplant their Jewish rivals. Beyond that, common action against the "aliens" in their midst was a way for Poles of every class and region to recognize the commonality of their interests and to express a spirit of national unity.

Although Dmowski drew much of his support from the lower middle classes, his efforts at forging a broader inter-class coalition were not altogether in vain.

Thousands of peasants and workers enrolled in the Endecja's front organiza-tions,[9] and Dmowski was respected as a man of keen intellect and discerning political vision by many members of the intelligentsia. His tactics of mass mobi-lization combined with diplomatic opportunism did not win Congress Poland the autonomy he hoped to gain from Russia; but he did very clearly succeed in marginalizing the old conservatives, many of whom ended up lending support to his movement. He was also successful at securing financial contributions from industrialists and landowners who relied on him to use his influence to contain radical impulses among the working class and the peasantry, and who applauded his zeal in combating the socialists. The split within the ranks of the PPS left the National Democrats as the largest and best-organized mass movement in Russian Poland, with strong organizations in the Austrian and German parti-tions as well. The First World War, however, would give Piłsudski an opportunity to stage a dramatic comeback, and much of the interwar Polish republic's polit-ical history was to be shaped by the rivalry between Piłsudski's and Dmowski's political camps.

Czechs and Slovaks

The advanced stage of industrial development and rich associational life of the Czech lands, combined with the relative tolerance of the Habsburg regime, were conducive to the formation of a less polarized and volatile political culture than that of Russian Poland. A basic core of pluralistic values was shared, to a greater or lesser extent, by all the major movements within the Czech nationalist camp. Czech nationalism was, nonetheless, divided by some important disagreements in emphasis and orientation that loosely paralleled the starker polarities of other East European nationalist movements. This can be seen most clearly in the contrast between the nationalist ideologies of Karel Kramář's Young Czechs and Tomáš Masaryk's Realist Party.

Among the various parties whose central and explicit concern was the asser-tion of Czech national rights, the Young Czechs were one of the most prominent and influential. Their major constituency was the new Czech industrial bour-geoisie that had sprung up in the second half of the nineteenth century. The Young Czechs had split off from the former mainstream nationalist party – thenceforward known as the Old Czechs – in 1874. The Old Czechs' political program was informed by the values of the traditional landowning elite of Bohemia. It strove to reassert the historic powers of the noble- and gentry-dominated Bohemian Diet, and adopted a passive form of resistance (e.g. a boycott of the Austrian Reichsrat) to initiatives associated with the centralization of the Austrian state.[10]

The Young Czechs represented a more modern form of nationalist ideology that incorporated elements of liberal thought, but that stopped short of fully embracing a Western-oriented, democratic universalism. They retained an attachment to the principle of Bohemia's historic state right as a basis for their autonomist demands, while also arguing that the mostly Czech, but historically distinct, province of Moravia should be merged with Bohemia in a self-governing Czech region. Rejecting the Old Czechs' boycott of the Austrian parliament, they jumped at the opportunity to advance their views in the Reichsrat, yet remained rather ambivalent toward the prospect of universal manhood suffrage, from which – as a party of the urban middle classes – they stood to lose electorally.

While the Young Czechs officially disavowed anti-Semitism, they were not above pandering to popular prejudice in their newspapers and public speeches. The fact that Bohemian Jews tended to gravitate toward German language and culture made them suspect in the Young Czechs' eyes, and Jewish commercial enterprises were viewed as yet another source of unwelcome competition for a Czech bourgeoisie that was (rather successfully) striving to challenge the long-standing hegemony of German-speaking elites.

On the other hand, the Young Czechs were rather uncritical in their attitude toward tsarist Russia, with which they strove to cultivate cultural and even political connections on the basis of the romantic notion that the common Slavic heritage of Czechs and Russians somehow transcended the enormous cultural, religious, political, and socio-economic differences between the two societies. The leader of the Young Czechs, Karel Kramář (1860–1937), tried to give concrete expression to the pan-Slavic ideal by organizing the shortlived Neo-Slav movement during the last decade before the First World War. This was an attempt to foster cultural and economic cooperation among all Slavic peoples on the basis of equality. A few international congresses were held under the auspices of this movement, and some prominent East European nationalist figures – including Roman Dmowski of the Polish National Democrats – were drawn into it for a period. But the common ties of blood and soul that were supposed to link all Slavs quickly proved insufficient to withstand the animosities and political tensions between Poles and Russians, liberals and reactionaries, and so on.[11]

One of the prime critics of Neo-Slavism and of the Young Czechs' uneven synthesis of chauvinism and liberalism, romanticism and opportunism, was Tomáš Masaryk (1850–1937). Having initially collaborated closely with Kramář under the rubric of the Young Czech Party, Masaryk broke away and formed his own small party – the Realists – in 1900. Although the Realists never won more than a handful of seats in the Reichsrat, this sufficed to give Masaryk a prominent platform from which to publicize his distinctive brand of liberal nationalism.

Masaryk's political vision for the Czechs reflected his belief that nations could and should serve as mediating bodies between individuals and humanity at large. The Czech nation specifically, he contended, had played a critical historical role in the conception and articulation of universal human values. Masaryk portrayed the early fifteenth-century Czech religious reformer and martyr, Jan Hus, as a central figure in the history of Western civilization who had helped lay the foundations for the modern European Enlightenment. For Masaryk, the Czech national movement was in its essence a spiritual revival that was rooted in the religious legacy of Hus. Czech nationalism should not be construed as being an end unto itself, for it had an integral role to play in humanity's progress through history toward an order based on reason, tolerance, and social responsibility. The Czechs were a small nation, but one that was spiritually elect – a Chosen People in the sense of having an ethical mission to the world. Until 1914, Masaryk also downplayed the theme of historic state rights, emphasizing instead the principle of ethno-cultural self-determination as the most important moral basis for Czech political demands. Common language, culture, historical experience, and values were to serve as the constitutive elements of a self-governing civil society. By the same token, if the Czechs were tempted by chauvinistic or intolerant impulses, it was the duty of their intellectual and political elites not to pander to such sentiments – as the Young Czechs routinely did – but to restrain and educate them. Democratic principles were thus constrained by cultural elitism in Masaryk's political vision, which can best be described as an idiosyncratic blend of Hussite reformism, Platonic philosophy, Old Testament prophetic tradition, and scientific rationalism. The label "Realism" that he applied to this political philosophy was intended to highlight the importance of developing concrete, forward-looking plans for the socio-economic advancement and cultural revitalization of the Czech people.[12]

Masaryk's approach to the Slovak question was closely related to his democratic elitism and to his understanding of the relationship between ethno-cultural identity and civic community. Masaryk became wedded to the notion that Czechs and Slovaks were culturally and linguistically so closely related to one another that they could and should be expected to merge into one Czechoslovak nation. This corresponded to a widespread view among the Czech nationalist intelligentsia to the effect that the more prosperous, industrialized, and culturally vibrant Czechs could serve as a source of inspiration and assistance to the more backward Slovaks as they struggled to preserve their identity in the face of Hungary's oppressively assimilationist policies.

Masaryk and his followers directed their criticism not only against the Hungarian government, but also against the Slovak cultural and intellectual establishment that ran the Slovak National Party. This conservative elite was pan-Slavic and Russophile rather than Western-oriented in its political outlook. The literary figures who dominated this circle made little effort to cultivate grassroots support among the peasant masses, although some novelists paid lip service to the importance of forging a common bond among intelligentsia, gentry, and common people.[13] From the point of view of Masaryk and his followers, the mainstream Slovak cultural elite had, by the turn of the century, become a source of stagnation rather than a force for progress and enlightenment.

Masaryk's own intellectual influence served to promote the crystallization of a small yet vocal alternative Slovak elite. Masaryk's lectures on politics and culture at Charles-Ferdinand University had drawn a devoted following that comprised students from a variety of Slavic nationalities of the Habsburg empire, including Slovenes, Croats, and Serbs as well as Slovaks. For some of the younger members of the Slovak intelligentsia, Prague's cultural and educational institutions offered the most readily available means of escaping Hungarian linguistic assimilation. A number of them embraced Masaryk's Realism as a dynamic model for the rejuvenation of their own Slovak nation. The enthusiastic response of these Hlasists,[14] as they were known, encouraged Masaryk in his own conviction that the Czechs had a special responsibility *vis-à-vis* their Slovak brethren.

Masaryk's conception of the relationship between Czechs and Slovaks may have been a generalization drawn from his own personal experience. A common thread running through his childhood reminiscences was the uncertain nature of his early sense of identity. Growing up as he did in a rural Moravian borderland, and being of mixed Slovak and Germanized Czech parentage, Masaryk's political, intellectual, and national consciousness had evolved from an ill-defined ethno-linguistic identity as a Slovak to a highly articulate and intellectually refined self-definition as a Czech (and, indeed, a provocative reinterpretation of what it meant to be Czech). It is easy to see how, looking back on his own early life, Masaryk might conclude that the Slovaks in general were simply the disadvantaged, poorly educated branch of a Czechoslovak national family, and that the dissemination of Czech culture could serve to raise the Slovaks to a higher level of moral, intellectual, and national consciousness. Moreover, the promotion of a Czech civilizing mission toward the Slovaks may have been a way of concretizing his belief that nationalism should be more than a collective cult of self. Rather than wallowing in an endless celebration of their own ethnicity, the Czechs could focus on fulfilling their responsibility toward their "backward" brethren.

It is apparent from the preceding narrative that Masaryk's brand of nationalism cannot be categorically described as either civic or ethnic. Its essential feature was its attempt to create a synthesis of the two elements. Masaryk insisted that enlightened liberalism was the defining element of Czech national culture. The political and cultural values of the Czechs thus placed them unequivocally in the camp of Western, democratic nations, even if their language and "racial" origins seemed to link them to the autocratic Russians. But this did not mean that Masaryk thought ethnicity was irrelevant to Czech identity. Masaryk saw the German minority in Bohemia as unassimilable into the Czech nation, and he never quite figured out how to reconcile this fact with his civic values. He felt more comfortable with Jews who openly affirmed their distinctive sense of national identity than with those who sought to assimilate into Czech culture. Finally, in the case of Czech relations with the Slovaks, ethno-linguistic affinity was an important consideration for him; it created a medium of direct communication that would enable the Czech intelligentsia to transmit its Western, progressive values to the unenlightened Slovak masses.[15] In a word, Masaryk constantly struggled with the tension between the love of his nation for its own sake and the commitment to a broader, humanistic ideal. It was precisely the fact that he wrestled with this problem that distinguished him from the leaders of the Young Czech Party, who were far more inclined to mystify nationhood and to treat it as a prime value to which all other considerations were subordinate.

The Dream of Yugoslav Unity

Given Masaryk's cultivation of close contact with members of the South Slav political and intellectual elites, it is no coincidence that parallels emerged between the political cultures of the Czechoslovak and Yugoslav nationalist movements. Just as Masaryk hoped that unifying the Czech and Slovak peoples would serve a historically progressive function for them both, so too did some Croat intellectuals embrace cooperation with Croatia's ethnic Serb minority as a way of linking ethnic identities to the development of a broader civic consciousness.[16]

The last decades before the First World War were a period of intense ideological fermentation and bewildering political realignments in the South Slav lands. The repressive, Magyarizing policies of Khuen-Héderváry during his twenty-year tenure as governor of Croatia (1883–1903) led to a split within the Party of Right following the death of its founder, Starčević, in 1896. One faction was led by Josip Frank (1844–1911), a converted Jew who upheld the conservative, Catholic, historic-state-right tradition. Frank's Party of Pure Right (commonly referred to as the Frankists) distinguished itself by adopting a particularly intolerant and antagonistic attitude toward the Serb minority in Croatia, whose support the Hungarian government had periodically tried to cultivate in its effort to isolate the Croatian opposition and whose identification with the neighboring kingdom of Serbia seemed stronger than its loyalty to the Croatian state. Verbal and published attacks against the Serbs, who were portrayed as a fifth column in the midst of the Croatian nation, were used in a demagogic effort to rally popular support for the Party of Pure Right. At the same time, Frank abandoned Starčević's seemingly unrealistic, anti-Habsburg, pro-independence stance, seeking instead to cultivate support in Vienna for the idea of turning the Dual Monarchy into a Trialist system, in which a self-governing Croatia would enjoy equal status alongside Austria and Hungary.

The rival faction, calling itself the Croatian Party of Right, actively sought political cooperation with ethnic Serb parties, in the hope that a united South Slav front would be more effective in obtaining concessions from either Budapest or Vienna. This political reorientation came within the context of a broader ideological shift away from the state-right tradition among a segment of the Croat intelligentsia.

Tomáš Masaryk's teachings and writings played a notable role in shaping some of the alternative ideologies that sprang up among the Croat intelligentsia during these years. The founder of the Croatian People's Peasant Party, Stjepan Radić, was a young intellectual who had been born to a peasant family and had gone on to study under Masaryk in Prague. Radić sought to apply Masaryk's Realist principles to Croatian socio-political conditions. He regarded the state-right principle as an outmoded, elitist notion that failed to address the pressing material needs and spiritual deprivation of the peasant masses. In his view, popular self-determination rather than medieval historical precedents constituted the only legitimate basis for demands for self-rule. But before there could even be any serious talk of formulating a democratic, nationalist agenda, the

most immediate economic and educational needs of the rural populace had to
be addressed. The traditional subservience to landlords and clergy had to give
way to a new sense of political self-reliance and a propensity for collective action,
and it was the duty of intellectuals to commit themselves to the cultivation of
these qualities among Croatia's rural folk. The struggle for economic rights
would generate a political consciousness that would ultimately create an
authentic, grassroots expression of Croatian national identity.[17]

The Masarykian grounding of nationalism in democratic principles rather
than historical claims resonated particularly strongly among the urban intelligentsia of Dalmatia. There was a pragmatic/tactical aspect to such an
orientation: this predominantly Croat-populated coastal province had not been
juridically linked to the historic state of Croatia–Slavonia for centuries, and was
ruled directly by Vienna rather than by Budapest. The principle of national self-
determination was, therefore, more immediately applicable than that of state
right as a basis for changing Dalmatia's status and unifying it with Croatia–
Slavonia. There was also a cultural predisposition here toward liberal nationalism. The urban centers that dotted the Dalmatian coast had a centuries-old
tradition of civic pride; Dubrovnik had been a vibrant commercial entrepôt in
the fifteenth through seventeenth centuries and had maintained its status as an
independent city-state (technically under Ottoman suzerainty) until 1806.
Dubrovnik's legacy as a free republic, as well as the cultural influence of the
local Italian minority, colored the outlook of Dalmatia's Croat urban elites and
enhanced their receptivity to Western liberalism. They saw themselves as an
advanced outpost of enlightenment in the Balkans, a natural aristocracy with a
special role to play in the furthering of economic, cultural, and political progress
in the region.

Urban professionals and intellectuals in Dalmatia looked to Yugoslavism as a
political and cultural ideal that could help the Catholic Croats and Orthodox
Serbs alike to transcend the administrative fragmentation of the region and work
toward a common goal of democratization and modernization. Moreover, given
the intermixture of Serb and Croat communities throughout the Habsburg-
ruled South Slav lands, the demand for popular self-government would gain
credibility and support if it were put forward as a joint Croat–Serb political platform.

Among Croatia's ethnic Serbs, a new generation of leaders – some of them
also influenced by Masaryk's teachings – was impressed by the popular demonstrations in Croatian cities that led to the replacement of Khuen-Héderváry in
1903, and began to question the wisdom of following their community's traditional strategy of boycotting the Croatian Sabor (Diet) and currying favor with
Budapest in return for Hungarian patronage and protection of Serb religious
and cultural identity within Croatia. Grassroots activism and the forging of a
broad popular coalition transcending the Serb–Croat divide might prove a more
effective means of gaining the attention, and possibly cooperation, of Budapest,
and of achieving greater self-rule for a Croatia in which Serb collective rights
won respect from a democratized Croat community. Meanwhile, across the

border in the kingdom of Serbia, a bloody *coup d'état* in 1903 replaced the Obrenović dynasty with the Karadjordjević, and brought to power an aggressively irredentist, anti-Austrian government in Belgrade. The new regime hungrily eyed the Habsburg-administered province of Bosnia-Herzegovina, and eagerly encouraged the development of Croat–Serb cooperation against the monarchy.

It was against this backdrop that, in 1905, at the initiative of two urban intellectuals from Dalmatia, Ante Trumbić (1864–1938) and Frano Supilo (1870–1917), the Croat–Serb Coalition (HSK) was formed as a bloc that initially included all the main ethnic Serb parties and most moderate Croat groupings. The Frankists and Radić's Croatian People's Peasant Party stayed out of the coalition. With its fresh, new, democratic approach, the HSK rapidly moved to the forefront of political life in both Croatia proper and in Dalmatia. In fact, this collaborative effort between Croat and Serb leaders also marked the first exercise in systematic inter-Croat political cooperation across the Dalmatian–Croatian border. The evolution of Croat national consciousness and the forging of Serb–Croat ties seemed to be going hand-in-hand with one another.

On the eve of the First World War, the attitude of the Croat intellectual and political elites toward Serbs remained highly ambivalent. On the one hand, the Croats generally thought of themselves as more sophisticated, educated, economically advanced – in brief, more European – than the Serbs. The Croat leaders in the HSK certainly did not advocate the merging of the Croat and Serb nations, but only their close cooperation within the framework of the Habsburg territories. On the other hand, there was a widespread fascination with, and admiration for, the Serbian tradition of militant independence and the history of Serbian armed resistance against the Turks. Indeed many of the nationalist youth movements (including the Frankist youth movement – Young Croatia) that sprang up throughout the Croat-populated lands during the last years before the First World War tended to idolize the Serbs as true South Slav originals, men of simple virtues and unbending willpower who were unsullied by the effete values and intellectual dilettantism of Central European culture. Austria–Hungary's 1908 annexation of Bosnia-Herzegovina (whose Croat-populated regions were not merged administratively with other Croatian territories), and its maladroit efforts to repress South Slav nationalism, only increased the frustration of Croat elites during the last years before the outbreak of the First World War. Yet the long-term prospects for political cooperation between Croats and Serbs within the Habsburg empire, let alone between Habsburg Croats and the kingdom of Serbia, remained clouded by uncertainty.[18]

Synopsis

By 1914, an ideological bifurcation had, to varying degrees, emerged within the nationalist camps of each of these East Central European societies. On one side of the divide stood those who embraced a progressive, Western-oriented vision of social or liberal democracy as the only valid framework for the expression of national identity. Masaryk's Realists, Slovakia's Hlasists, and the founders of Croatia's HSK fall clearly into this group. All of these parties emphasized the democratic principle of popular self-determination, rather than the older, socially conservative and elitist doctrine of historic state right, as the basis for demands for national autonomy within the framework of a reformed Habsburg monarchy. Piłsudski is somewhat harder to categorize, given his pattern of ideological opportunism and his romanticization of the defunct Polish state and its legacy of gentry nationalism. But this particular state tradition had come to be widely identified (accurately or not) with progress toward a politically liberal and culturally tolerant constitutional system – progress that had been cut off by the country's dismemberment in the late eighteenth century.

In all these cases, there was a strong emphasis on interethnic cooperation, integration, or federation as a key to political success and to the development of a progressive, democratic political culture. Such ideas were clearly marked by the experience of politics in multinational empires, where the central authorities relied heavily on divide-and-rule methods to preserve the *status quo*. Forging cooperative links among nationalities was an obvious way of challenging such tactics. This cooperation was to draw on elements of linguistic similarity and shared historical experience that supposedly made natural partners out of Czechs and Slovaks, Serbs and Croats, Poles and Ukrainians or Belorussians. At the same time, such interethnic nation-building partnerships were viewed as transformative enterprises that would transcend the limitations of self-absorbed folk consciousness and help forge a link between nationalism and socio-political modernization and liberalization.

The right-of-center movements that disputed these views ranged in character and political orientation from the hate-mongering ethno-populism of Poland's National Democrats and Croatia's Frankists, to the Young Czechs' uneven mixture of bourgeois liberalism and Russophile romanticism, to the Slavophile elitism of the Slovak intellectual establishment. Like their more liberal counterparts, many of these movements stressed the importance of developing interethnic cooperation among Slavic peoples, but more on the basis of a sense of primordial kinship and common Slavic spiritual essence than through the joint cultivation of concrete political programs based on explicitly articulated, progressive goals. In their view, ethnic identity and Slavic heritage were somehow to inform political values, rather than vice versa.

Populism, Socialism, and Nationalism in the Russian Empire

The propensity of nationalist ideologues in East Central Europe to project all manner of virtues and flaws, world-historical roles and retrograde characteristics, onto Russia was a function not only of their own conflicting agendas and aspirations, but also of Russia's uncertain self-definition. The Russian empire was a society in flux, and no nationality within it was more riven by disputes over what constituted its national essence than the Russians themselves.

Despite the extreme complexity of Russian political life during the last decade before the First World War, the rough distinction between liberal and integral forms of nationalism that we have drawn in prior instances can be discerned here as well.

At the far right of the political spectrum, parties such as the proto-fascist Union of Russian People presented themselves as defenders of the principles of "Orthodoxy, Autocracy, Nationality," a militantly reactionary slogan that had first been propagated by Tsar Nicholas I's Minister of Education in 1833.[19] They rejected parliamentary constitutionalism as a Western import alien to the spirit of the Russian nation. In the tradition of the nineteenth-century Slavophiles, they adhered to a romantic image of the tsar and the Russian Orthodox Church as the only legitimate sources of political and spiritual authority in Russia. As for ethnic minorities, either they were essentially Russians who had to be brought back into the national-religious fold through the elimination of non-Orthodox churches and by means of linguistic assimilation (this applied to Belorussians and Ukrainians), or they constituted foreign bodies in the Russian organism, to be left alone, marginalized, or repressed, depending on their collective attitude toward the Russian state and the interests of the Russian people.[20]

To the left of center, the Constitutional Democratic Party (Kadets) hoped that the 1905 Revolution was the beginning of a process that would lead to the emergence of a progressive, civil society in Russia based on parliamentary democracy and popular sovereignty. In a multinational state such as Russia, it was also essential that ethnic minorities be actively included in this process of civic development. This meant the revocation of discriminatory and repressive legislation against groups such as the Jews. It would also involve the granting of cultural autonomy and in some cases (notably Poland and Finland) regional self-rule, to non-Russian nationalities. This would defuse ethnic tensions and encourage each group to look upon Russia as a secure political environment within which it could maintain collective dignity through the unhindered cultivation and public expression of its identity, while also participating on an equal basis in the life of society as a whole. Implicit in this program was the assumption that Russian would remain the predominant language of high culture and that a tolerant policy toward minorities would stimulate a natural process of social integration and cultural assimilation analogous to that which had produced modern nation-states in Western Europe.[21]

This optimistic – if not very carefully thought through – approach to the nationality question was shared, *mutatis mutandis*, by Russia's largest left-wing populist movement, the Socialist Revolutionary Party (SRs). While the SRs' vision of radical social reform was based on a romanticized image of an idiosyncratically Russian ethno-cultural phenomenon – the peasant commune – they were convinced that the common quest for social justice would create an unbreakable bond among all the peoples of Russia once the oppressive tsarist regime was overthrown. They went beyond the Kadets by endorsing the principle of political as well as cultural autonomy for all the major ethnic groups, not just the Poles and Finns. Again, the idea here was that granting self-rule to non-Russian peoples would end their sense of humiliation and defuse interethnic tensions, facilitating the strengthening of civic ties that transcended ethnicity.

The Russian Social Democratic Workers' Party (RSDWP; also referred to as the Social Democrats or SDs), which was divided into Menshevik and Bolshevik factions, adhered to a more rigidly Marxist, internationalist understanding of class struggle. From this perspective, nationalism was nothing more than a ploy designed to distract the working classes of all peoples from their common, revolutionary interests. Condemning the tsarist regime's Russification policies, the Social Democrats were confident that in the socialist society of the future, national differences would dissolve into a common proletarian consciousness. Yet precisely because the chauvinistic element in tsarist policy was so alienating to non-Russian nationalities, paying lip-service to the principle of national self-determination did have short-term revolutionary potential. The Bolsheviks would eventually try and exploit this fact for their own purposes, with far-reaching (if unintended) consequences for the evolution of ethnic politics in the region. But that is a story that will be pursued in subsequent chapters.

The non-Russian peoples of the empire were so numerous and heterogeneous that this overview can only touch briefly on a selection of cases designed to illustrate the ideological range of nationalist movements among them. (The case of Poland, which lends itself particularly well to comparison and contrast with the Czechs and South Slavs throughout the period covered by this book, has been included in the previous section of this chapter.)

The dominant modes of political thought and action among nationally conscious minority intellectuals evolved in ways that closely reflected developments among the Russian oppositional intelligentsia. Russian left-wing populism (*narodnichestvo*) was a particularly influential model. The Russian populists (*narodniki*) of the second half of the nineteenth century had undertaken their resistance to the tsarist regime in the name of a peasantry that they romanticized as a repository of cultural authenticity and idealized as heir to a primordial tradition of communal life and social justice. Russian populism was an appealing and highly malleable ideological model for activists of any nationality who were attempting to link ideals of social and political progress to a sense of cultural distinctiveness and rootedness in a tradition of their own, and who were trying to communicate broad conceptions of national identity and political democracy to the parochial and socially conservative world of the rural masses.

While celebrating distinct folk traditions and cultivating separate ethnic identities, left-wing populist brands of nationalism also endorsed the idea of fostering political cooperation among the various peoples of the empire. They shared a common antagonism toward the existing state structure and social hierarchy, which were branded as the main culprits in the oppression and alienation of the masses. If the socio-political order were refashioned so as to reflect the true spirit of the masses, harmony would naturally prevail among the various nationalities. The idea of a federation of peoples replacing the autocratic institutions of empire was particularly appealing to non-Russians who had been educated at Russian universities and exposed to revolutionary ideas.[22] Many of their nationalist projects reflected a life-long search for a way of reconciling and synthesizing their intellectual cosmopolitanism and absorption of Russian culture with their cultivation of ethno-cultural distinctiveness.

Thus, Ukrainian nationalists identified the Russian state, not the Russian people, as the main villain (since the seventeenth century) in their nation's historical saga. Indeed, an early association devoted to the cultural revitalization of the Ukrainian people called itself the Society of Saints Cyril and Methodius, deliberately invoking the legacy of the missionaries who had brought Christianity to all the Orthodox Slavic peoples, rather than choosing the name of a specifically Ukrainian historical figure.[23] In later years, the émigré activist Mykhailo Drahomaniv (1841–1895) drew up a constitutional program that would provide political and cultural autonomy for Ukrainians within the framework of a democratic federation of Slavic peoples.[24]

The most prominent articulator of a liberal-progressive vision of Ukrainian nationalism was Mykhailo Hrushevsky (1866–1934), a scholar and publicist who maintained contact with his compatriots in the Russian empire from his refuge as holder of the first chair in Ukrainian history at the University of Lwów in Galicia (and who was to lead the short-lived Ukrainian Republic of 1917–1918). Hrushevsky embraced the populist-federalist tradition, while cautioning against some of his fellow nationalists' weakness for pan-Slavic programs based on racial chauvinism or naive romanticism rather than democratic principles and enlightened self-interest.[25] Hrushevsky was particularly opposed to Neo-Slavism. He feared that this ostensibly liberal and egalitarian new form of pan-Slavism would play into the hands of reactionary Russian policy and form the basis for Polish–Russian cooperation at the Ukrainians' expense. (Roman Dmowski's initial participation in the movement hardly seemed to augur well for its liberal credentials.) Like Masaryk, Hrushevsky rejected the uncritical cult of ethnic kinship, advocating instead alliances based on shared interests and values. Specifically, he called for Ukrainian cultural exchange and political cooperation with Belorussians and Lithuanians – fellow peasant nations that shared with the Ukrainians a common experience of economic exploitation, political oppression, and forced cultural assimilation at the hands of Polish and Russian elites.[26]

The most influential ideological stream among Armenian political activists also latched onto populism as a framework for the articulation of nationalist aspirations. The Armenian Revolutionary Federation (Dashnaktsutiun – commonly referred to as the Dashnaks) was particularly captivated by the self-sacrificing ethos and the violent and reckless tactics of the second generation of Russian populists – the terrorist intellectuals of the Narodnaya Volya (People's Will) organization. Founded in 1890, the Dashnaktsutiun did not initially direct its paramilitary activities against the tsarist state. The Ottoman empire, where the bulk of Armenians lived, was its first and foremost target. It used Russian Armenia as a base of operations for a campaign of assassination against Ottoman officials, and for spectacular guerrilla and terrorist operations designed to draw the attention of the European powers to the plight of the Armenian people. Administrative reform and autonomy for the six provinces of north-eastern Anatolia (as called for at the 1878 Congress of Berlin) was the Dashnaks' professed objective. Only in 1903, when the Russian authorities threatened the autonomous cultural life of Armenians by seizing control of Armenian Church property and educational institutions (as part of the general effort to Russify and further centralize control over the empire's borderlands), did the Dashnaks turn their wrath against tsarist officials, assassinating several hundred of them over the following two years. The galvanizing impact of Russia's insensitive policy brought thousands of Armenian demonstrators to the streets of Transcaucasian cities, and enabled the Dashnaktsutiun to place itself at the head of a mass movement.[27] The outbreak of violent clashes between Armenians and Turkic Muslims (Azerbaijanis) in Baku during the 1905 Revolution further consolidated popular support for the Dashnaks. At the same time, the party moved toward the formal incorporation (in 1907) of socialist principles into its platform and gained admission into the Second Socialist International, which it hoped to use as an international forum for the airing of its nationalist grievances.[28]

As Russian intellectual movements coalesced into modern political parties around the turn of the century, the Socialist Revolutionaries (SRs) – heirs to the populist and terrorist traditions – emerged as some of the most consistent advo-cates of political autonomy for the empire's nationalities. This, along with the inherent appeal of populist ideology, won the SRs the support of many parties among the ethnic minorities (such as the Dashnaktsutiun). New parties formally affiliated with the SRs also sprang up among groups such as the Jews (Jewish Socialist Labor Party – SERP) and Ukrainians (the Ukrainian Socialist Revol-utionary Party was not founded until 1917, but it rapidly gained a relatively broad mass following as well as the support and leadership of Hrushevsky).[29]

Marxist brands of socialism also gained enormous appeal among sectors of the oppositional intelligentsia and industrial working class in many regions of the Russian empire during the last two decades before the 1917 Revolution. (Indeed, many of the left-wing populist parties discussed above came to incorporate elements of Marxism into their political programs and rhetoric.) In principle, Marxists were not supposed to concern themselves with issues of national iden-tity, and, indeed, many non-Russian Marxists simply joined the Bolshevik or Menshevik factions of the all-Russian Social Democratic Party. Others, however, preferred to maintain some sort of corporate identity within the Marxist move-ment. Marxist organizations sprang up that were organized along ethnic lines and were devoted to the propagation of socialist ideas among the members of their own nationality. Under such circumstances, it was impossible to disentangle issues of class struggle and social justice from demands for cultural autonomy and national self-determination.

As indicated in the previous chapter, most of the empire's heavily industrial-ized cities lay in the non-Russian western borderlands, and it is therefore no surprise that Marxist parties seemed to enjoy greater support among the mostly Polish and Jewish industrial proletariat of these regions than in the less developed

Russian heartland (apart from Moscow and St. Petersburg). The Polish case has been discussed earlier in this chapter. Among left-wing Jewish movements, the Labor Zionists molded Marxist doctrine into a rationalization for their explicitly nationalist program directed at the creation of a Hebrew-speaking, Jewish proletarian-communal society in Palestine.[30] Their position was challenged by the General Jewish Workers' Alliance (the Bund, founded in 1897), which insisted that the destiny of the Jewish masses depended on the outcome of the revolutionary struggle within the Russian empire as a whole. In fact, the Bund played a role in the founding of the RSDWP. But while the Bund rejected nationalism *per se* and insisted that the Jewish proletariat must take up its place alongside its Russian and other non-Jewish comrades in the war of classes, it rapidly came to realize that Yiddish was a far more effective medium of communication with the Jewish masses than was Russian. Its decision to adopt Yiddish as its main language of propaganda and agitation rapidly led the Bund away from the assimilationist impulses of its early years. The demand for Jewish cultural autonomy (meaning the cultivation of Yiddish secular culture, rather than religious or Zionist culture) within a socialist Russia soon became one of the central planks in its political platform. However, the Bund's attempt to gain recognition from the Social Democratic leadership as a fully autonomous organization representing the Jewish proletariat was rebuffed, leading to the Bund's withdrawal from the party in 1903.[31]

Curiously, Marxism struck deep roots in Georgia, whose population consisted overwhelmingly of peasants (some of whom were beginning to seek industrial employment in cities) and an economically rather backward rural nobility. Here, common resentment of the Armenian commercial bourgeoisie's rise to regional prominence may have contributed to Marxism's appeal. The local branch of the Menshevik organization, led by educated Georgians of noble background, rapidly established itself as the dominant mass organization during the first years of the twentieth century. While the Georgian Mensheviks professed their sincere commitment to the ideal of socialist internationalism, their ideological platform and the nature of their popular appeal clearly reflected an ethnopolitical agenda.[32] As Ronald Suny puts it (sardonically?), "in Marxism Georgians had a non-nationalist ideology that was a weapon against both their ethnic enemies: Russian officials and the Armenian bourgeoisie."[33]

Thus, various blends of populist, Marxist, and nationalist themes dominated the political thought of intelligentsias among many of the Russian empire's ethnic minorities. While doctrinal differences pitted opposing parties (such as Zionists and Bundists) against each other in fierce ideological disputes, one can say that one of the central issues all of these groups were contending with was how to reconcile the particular with the universal, how to synthesize ethnocultural identity with internationalist solidarity. Some non-Russian political activists simply joined all-Russian political parties such as the Social Democrats, Socialist Revolutionaries, and Constitutional Democrats. But many others realized that, even if the ultimate goal of their political activity was internationalist in scope, they would fail to mobilize their fellow ethnics unless they appealed to their particularist sentiments. Beyond that, many of the activists were eager to link themselves to an "authentic" folk tradition as part of their rebellion against the hegemony of state-sanctioned high culture and against the culturally leveling aspects of economic and political modernization.

The combination of socialism with nationalism seemed to offer the most coherent resolution of this tension. By bringing about true economic and political equality among human beings, socialist revolution would also bring about equality among ethnic groups. (This was a particularly convincing argument in the many regions where distinctions of class corresponded closely to ethnic differences.) By the same token, asserting one's own (exploited and oppressed) ethnic group's particular rights and interests could only serve to advance the cause of socialist revolution for the empire as a whole. As in the case of the Czech, Slovak, and South Slav liberal-democratic nationalists, the left-wing nationalists of the Russian borderlands thought of nationalism as a transformative project that would draw on selected themes from their ethnic groups' respective cultures and historical experiences in the course of building a fundamentally new social and political order embodying universal themes of modernity and justice.

This created an atmosphere that was highly receptive to the Austro-Marxists' approach to the nationalities question. Their ideas[34] were eagerly seized upon by many left-wing nationalists in the tsarist state as a systematized theoretical and doctrinal framework for their own position, and as a basis for clarifying how relations among ethnic groups were to be structured within the future socialist state. The leaders of the Bund, frustrated by the RSDWP's decision to rebuff their claims, were particularly fascinated by the concept of extraterritorial cultural autonomy, which seemed to offer the perfect solution to the plight of the dispersed Jewish masses. In fact, it was Bundist translations of the Austro-Marxists' works into Russian that facilitated the dissemination of these ideas among the broad array of ethno-socialist movements in the Russian empire. By 1907, a number of parties, ranging from the Armenian Dashnaktsutiun to the Belorussian Socialist Hromada, had declared themselves in favor of combining extraterritorial cultural autonomy with territorial federalism in the future socialist Russia. Geographically concentrated ethnic groups would thus be in a position to enjoy a certain administrative self-determination, while diaspora nationalities as well as transplanted individuals would be free to run state-funded cultural and educational institutions of their own wherever there were enough of them to constitute a community. Acknowledging the legitimacy of ethnic identity would foster mutual tolerance and promote rather than undermine the consolidation of the multinational socialist state. The more channels for ethno-cultural self-expression were created, the more comfortable the various nationalities would feel about cooperating with each other. Such thinking provoked scathing ideological attacks on the part of the Bolsheviks, who paid lip service to the principle of national self-determination but rejected the idea that a socialist movement should actively seek to nurture cultural divisions among the proletariat. Eventually, however, the Bolsheviks would themselves feel obliged to develop a more nuanced (if disingenuous) position on this issue.[35]

The Muslim intelligentsias of the Russian empire stood at the intersection of cultural influences radiating from the Middle East and from Russia. The Islamic modernist movement, which had established itself as a major intellectual force in Egypt under the leadership of scholars and publicists such as the Persian-born Jamal al-Din al-Afghani (1839–1897) and his Egyptian student Muhammad Abduh (1849–1905), was an inspiration to the Tatar intelligentsia. Islamic modernism encouraged the selective adoption of Western ideas and methods as part of a broader effort to revitalize Islamic civilization. The modernists argued that the Islamic world was in apparent decline, not because of flaws that were inherent to its belief system, but precisely because it had lost touch with the essential spirit and values of Islam. The original message of the Prophet, which had formed the basis of a radiant civilization, had over time been covered by layer after layer of false interpretations, arbitrary edicts (issued by religious authorities at the behest of corrupt rulers rather than on the basis of Islamic principle), and superstitious customs. This accounted for the sense of stagnation in the Ottoman empire and for its inability to respond effectively to the Western challenge. The time had come for Muslims to cast off these paralyzing accretions and reconnect themselves with the original spirit of Islam. Islam's great flowering during its classical age had itself been a central source of inspiration to the then relatively backward Europeans, who had acquired their knowledge of science, mathematics, etc., from the Muslim world. In adopting some of the technological and organizational features of modern Western society, the Islamic world would in a sense be rediscovering its own foundations, for the beauty of Islam lay in its perfect marriage of reason with faith.[36]

Islamic modernism manifested itself among Muslim intellectuals of the Russian empire as the Jadid ("new") movement. The Jadids saw themselves as leading the way to a spiritual and material renewal of Russia's Islamic peoples. Their initial focus was on educational reform. The "new method" (*usul i-jadid*: hence the name of the movement) of education that they championed would do away with the narrow-minded scholasticism of the traditional Islamic schools and introduce modern curricula that included the sciences and that would teach students how to think critically. Such ideas clearly threatened to undercut the authority and status of the Muslim clerical and scholarly establishment. Within the Russian empire, Jadidist schools were allowed to develop freely, but in Bukhara – the technically sovereign emirate that was the cultural capital of Turkestan – the emir upheld the authority of the traditional Islamic establishment, forcing the Jadidist schools to operate semi-clandestinely.[37]

The Jadids generally came from wealthy families whose income was derived from commerce, and who constituted a rising bourgeoisie. The Volga and Crimean Tatars, given their longstanding contact and familiarity with Russian culture and education, became the intellectual vanguard of the Jadid movement, infusing it with ideas that reflected the influence of pan-Slavism and populism. The first Muslim newspaper in Russia was established in the 1880s by Ismail-bey

Gasprinsky (1851–1914), a Crimean Tatar who played a pathbreaking role in the development of Jadidism. The overwhelming majority of the periodicals and other publications associated with the Jadids were written in a fusion of modified Crimean Tatar and Ottoman Turkish, a pan-Turkic synthesis that was promoted as a lingua franca among all the Muslim peoples of the empire. This would render the written word more readily accessible to Russia's Muslim masses, most of whom spoke Turkic languages and found it difficult to master the Farsi or Arabic that were the dominant media of traditional high culture.[38] It would also help establish a deeper and more substantive feeling of community among the socially and geographically fragmented Islamic population of tsarist Russia. Pan-Islamic and pan-Turkist elements thus coexisted within a loosely defined intellectual movement that was trying to spearhead cultural renewal and social revitalization, that challenged the authority of the traditional Islamic establishment, but that was vague and uncertain about its long-range political goals.

The 1905 Revolution and its aftermath served to hasten the diffusion of the Jadids' ideas and to politicize the movement's agenda. Muslim delegates in the Duma aligned themselves with the Kadets and issued moderate calls for the institution of regional autonomy throughout the empire. The political crackdown from 1907 on, and the associated restrictions on voting rights, could not roll back the changes wrought by the experience of the previous two years. The overwhelming majority of the Muslim masses may have remained unfamiliar with, and suspicious of, the new political ideas, but the intelligentsias were all the more determined to play the role of a socio-cultural vanguard committed to the enlightenment of the masses and to the transformation of society.

In Turkestan, where the electoral restrictions virtually eliminated the possibility of regional representation in the Duma, local Jadids began to think increasingly in terms of political independence as the only acceptable solution to their predicament. Narrowly ethnic constructions of identity remained completely unappealing, however, for the key to success was considered to lie in unity. Most of Russia's Muslim intelligentsia was in search of an inclusive definition of national identity that could provide a framework for coordinated political action among a wide variety of ethnic groups and social classes. The growing idea that pan-Turkism could constitute just such a framework was reinforced by the events of 1908 in the Ottoman empire. As we shall see, the Young Turks who seized power in Istanbul in that year were themselves strongly influenced by a group of Muslim émigrés from Russia.

Social Elites and Nationalist Intellectuals in the Ottoman Empire

From Ottomanism to Turkish Nationalism

Of all the regions examined in this book, the Middle East was the one where modern political nationalism took root the latest. As in the case of industrial and technological change, however, ideological transformations often take place most rapidly and most violently precisely in those societies whose elites feel they have the most catching up to do. While cultural environment, political institutions, and socio-economic conditions in the Middle East were in many ways fundamentally distinctive, the nationalist movements in this region faced dilemmas that bore some striking resemblances to those confronted by their Central and East European counterparts.

In 1908, a *coup d'état* brought a group of officers, administrators, and intellectuals known as the Young Turks (or the Committee of Union and Progress – CUP) to power in Istanbul. In the following years, the Young Turks gradually consolidated their position, replacing Sultan Abdülhamit II with the more compliant Mehmet V in the wake of an attempted conservative countercoup in 1909, and using military force to unseat an opposition coalition and concentrate arbitrary power in their own hands in 1913.[39] The Young Turk revolution inaugurated the most dramatic and chaotic stage in the checkered history of the Ottoman struggle with reform and modernization that had begun with the *Tanzimat*.[40] Although the Ottoman defeat in the First World War brought an end to the Young Turk movement *per se*, Kemal Atatürk's postwar vision of Turkish nationalism was clearly rooted in the ideas and practices of certain elements within the CUP regime.[41]

Yet it must be stressed that in its original incarnation, the Committee of Union and Progress was not constructed as an explicitly Turkish-nationalist organization. The CUP began its history in 1889 as a group of disaffected intellectuals and highly placed administrators who had been exposed to Western ideas through the reformed Ottoman higher-education system, and who were frustrated by the regime's inability or unwillingness to act on those ideas and to implement modernization on a systematic or thoroughgoing basis. Organizing themselves clandestinely within the Ottoman empire, and operating openly from exile in cities such as Geneva and Paris, the Young Turks regarded themselves as an intellectual elite whose mission it was to gain power (be it through persuasion or by force) within the Ottoman bureaucracy and to use that power to apply the laws of science and the principles of reason to the problems of state and society.

Although some of the CUP's publications played on pan-Islamic themes, most of the Young Turks regarded this as a necessary ploy in the struggle for public support rather than a true reflection of their worldview. In their private writings and conversations, many of them revealed themselves to be militantly secular intellectuals; some professed radically atheistic views. Narrowly conceived forms of positivism and "scientific" materialism (all the rage in mid-to-late-nineteenth-century Europe) were molding forces in their intellectual development.[42] The Young Turks' central demand was for the restoration of the suspended Constitution of 1876, which had briefly created a parliamentary form of government for the empire. The most recent research indicates that this position did not arise from a commitment to democracy as such. Indeed, many of the Young Turks subscribed to Gustave Le Bon's cynical view of the masses as a purposeless, ignorant mob that needed to be guided manipulatively by a forceful elite.[43] The CUP's constitutionalism served as a political platform from which its leaders could pursue their goal of transforming the Ottoman system into a true meritocracy, in which ability to govern and commitment to reform, rather than loyalty to the Sultan, would be the criteria for success – and in which they, accordingly, would assume the reins of power. This is not to say that they were completely insincere in their espousal of parliamentary government; it is just that they saw parliamentary government as an instrument for limiting the Sultan's authority and for transforming society from above, rather than as a medium for the expression of popular opinion.

The CUP's original membership reflected the multiethnic composition of the Ottoman state's administrative elite. Before it came to power, its leading figures included Albanians and Arabs as well as Turks. Graduates of the leading educational institutions of Istanbul, they could all rally around the common struggle for a restoration of the Constitution and the creation of a meritocratic government. This platform was so broad that there was even room on it for the radical Armenian nationalists of the Dashnaktsutiun Party. But what would the practical implications of radical political reform be – the centralization of government or regional self-rule, the creation of a unitary national identity or the cultivation of ethno-cultural diversity? These were questions that began to divide the CUP leadership even before it came to power.

It was the conviction of the CUP's leading figures that the transformation of the empire into a modern, powerful state would entail the crystallization among the masses of an overarching sense of patriotism and identification with the institutions of government. The catchword associated with this notion was Ottomanism – a vague term denoting the cultivation of collective political identity based on civic equality among the peoples of the empire. It remained far from clear how an ethnically and religiously neutral cultural foundation for such an identity could possibly be created. Ottomanism, it soon became apparent, was a very loaded term.

This was reflected in an increasingly acrimonious debate about the future structure of the state, and the scope it would allow for cultural autonomy and regional self-government. For most leaders and supporters of the CUP, the *millet* system was a glaring anachronism that would have to be fundamentally reformed or done away with altogether in a modernized Ottoman state. But what would replace it? If the *millets* were to be integrated into a more unified body politic, would this involve the forcible assimilation of ethno-religious minorities into the Muslim majority? That was an unacceptable prospect for the Dashnaktsutiun and for ethnic Greek supporters of the CUP. If, on the other hand, geographically concentrated (compact) minorities such as the Armenians were to be granted territorial autonomy, would that not play into the hands of interventionist foreign powers and lead to the breakup of the empire?

These issues came to a head in 1902, when an effort was made to create a broad opposition front to the Sultan's regime. The initiative came from Prince Sabahaddin, a disgruntled member of the Sultan's family who had joined the CUP in exile three years earlier. Sabahaddin sought the active cooperation of the Armenian nationalists in the belief that they could help draw the European powers into a military intervention that would assist in unseating the Sultan and placing the CUP in power. It was to this end, and with a view to marginalizing rival leaders within the CUP, that Sabahaddin and his supporters in the organization convened the First Congress of Ottoman Opposition in Paris as a forum for the negotiation of a joint political platform among opposition forces drawn from all the major ethnic groups of the Ottoman empire. As these talks proceeded, a number of Young Turks – led by Ahmed Riza – attacked the idea that foreign intervention was an acceptable means of fostering change in the Ottoman empire. More particularly, they expressed their opposition to the very idea of negotiating with the Dashnaktsutiun as a separate organization. As Ahmed Riza put it:

> According to their own words the Armenians want to reach an agreement with us in order to overthrow the present regime. This type of agreement can be reached between sovereign states. ... But I cannot imagine it between the citizens of the same state who are living in different areas of the Empire.[44]

When, in the end, Sabahaddin's faction accepted language suggestive of a special status for the Armenian provinces, Ahmed Riza and his supporters protested the agreement by splitting away from the CUP. The Young Turk organization fell briefly into abeyance, only to be reconstituted by Ahmed Riza a few years later.[45]

All this seemed to suggest that the restoration of the Constitution would create more problems than it would resolve, unless the various nationalities of the empire could be assimilated into a mainstream, national culture. For Turkish members of the CUP, Turkish identity was the obvious and sole candidate for this role. Rather than trying to construct a modern state purely on the basis of abstract conceptions of civic equality and Western science, the Young Turk movement would draw on what was best and most inspiring about the historical heritage of the Turkish people. Indeed, a growing number of ethnic Turkish leaders in the inner circle of the CUP felt that the old concepts of *umma*[46] and *millet* should not be discarded outright; these notions contained valuable elements that could be adapted and combined in a potent new socio-political formula that synthesized the social solidarism of Islam with the language and culture of the Turkish-speaking masses.[47]

It was one of the ironies of the Ottoman empire that its Christian minorities enjoyed official recognition as autonomous ethno-cultural communities by virtue of the *millet* system, while the masses of Turkish speakers had no such distinct framework for the cultivation of political identity and communal solidarity. According to Ziya Gökalp, who emerged as a leading Young Turk ideologue (and was later to play a similar role under Mustafa Kemal's (Atatürk's) regime), the Turks should be recognized as constituting a *millet* in their own right – not just *a millet*, in fact, but *the millet* whose identity and interests should be embodied by the state. In the vocabulary of Turkish nationalism, *millet* meant nation,[48] and nationalism would constitute the new religion holding nation and state together. Under the old regime, society was fragmented by rigid hierarchies (based on birth rather than merit) and by an unbridgeable gap between a high culture based on alien (Arabic and Persian) foundations, and the culture of the common populace. In a reformed empire, the new intellectual elite would create an official culture based on the language and traditions of the masses (and more specifically, on the popular dialect of Istanbul). This, in turn, would lend that elite the authority to take charge as a leading force in society, a vanguard whose views and decisions would be expressive of the fundamental interests of the nation as a whole.[49]

Many of Gökalp's conceptual frameworks were derived from the work of Durkheim and of a variety of German political thinkers (notably Tönnies). While he insisted on cultural-linguistic, rather than racial, criteria for defining national identity, his brand of nationalism reflected the influence of German, *völkisch* collectivism. His slogan *halka doğru* ("toward the people") was taken from the Russian populist movement of the 1860s, but his was an authoritarian form of populism: the political leadership could have no legitimacy unless it drew its inspiration from the culture of the masses, but it must be ruthless in the exercise of its power and it must use that power to bring civilization (i.e. education, technology, the various material innovations of the West) to the people. Pluralism and individualism were indulgences that would only threaten the organic integrity of the nation. Class conflict was incompatible with the goal of national unity, and updated versions of traditional craft associations combined with state-funded care for the needy would serve to fend off the threat of socialism.

In its synthesis of cultural populism with political elitism and its corporatist economic programs, Gökalp's thought bore some striking resemblances to Roman Dmowski's. Indeed, "scientific" materialism and positivism were molding forces in the intellectual development of the Young Turks and the Polish National Democrats alike. The result in both cases was a pseudo-rationalist political philosophy that was used to justify an autocratic approach to the exercise of power and to legitimize an organicist conception of the nation.[50] It will not be surprising, then, that a growing intolerance toward minorities seemed to go hand in hand with the development of Turkish nationalism. Gökalp toyed for a while with the idea of giving the Muslim Arabs equal status in an Ottoman empire reorganized as a dual monarchy on the Habsburg model and he insisted that any individual who embraced Turkish culture and language must be accepted as a Turk, regardless of his ethnic background. (Gökalp himself was of partly Kurdish ancestry, and had briefly flirted with the idea of fostering Kurdish nationalism before turning to the Turkish ideal instead.) But he insisted that Armenians and Greeks were alien groups whose economic success constituted a hindrance to the development of a Turkish middle class and whose Christian identity made them – unlike the Kurds – unassimilable. They had no intrinsic political rights as communities and dwelt amidst the Turkish nation strictly on sufferance.

Another ideological stream that emerged as a growing force within the CUP in the first years of the twentieth century was pan-Turkism. Pan-Turkist nation-alists defined Turkish identity in explicitly ethnic/racial terms.[51] They pointed to the linguistic affinities between the Turks of the Ottoman empire and the Turkic peoples of Russian- and Chinese-ruled Central Asia, and insisted that they were all descended from the same stock and should therefore be incorporated within one, all-embracing, unitary Turkish state. Political unification on this grand scale was the destiny of the Turks, and only through it could they reconnect them-selves with their early history and achieve their full potential as a nation. If the non-Turkish regions of the Ottoman empire, including the Arab lands, had to be jettisoned in the process, that was a price well worth paying for the realization of the pan-Turkist dream.[52] What the pan-Turkists lacked in political common sense or historical empiricism, they made up for in their taste for romantic imagery; one of the most popular of their poets addressed his co-ethnics as follows: "Oh, race of the Turks! Oh, children of iron and of fire! Oh, the founders of a thousand homelands, oh, the wearers of a thousand crowns!"[53]

This radical, irredentist brand of pan-nationalism, which gained considerable influence within the Young Turk movement from the period just before 1908 to the end of the First World War, was largely the brainchild of Tatar exiles from Russia. As we have seen, the creation and propagation of a Turkic lingua franca was one of the central projects of the Jadid movement, and this cultural enter-prise had obvious political ramifications. For the Tatar and other Turkic intellectuals who fled the censorship and oppression of the tsarist regime, Istanbul was not just a place of refuge (indeed, before the 1908 Revolution, the Sultan's regime regarded them with almost as much wariness as the tsarist government had).[54] The Ottoman empire was also a potential launching pad for a liberation struggle on behalf of Russia's Muslims.

Pan-Turkism, then, was a militant response to the aggressive pan-Slavism of the tsarist regime. A nationalist movement that confined its aspirations to the Turkish inhabitants of the Ottoman empire was of no interest to these men, for they had to define national identity in such a way as to encompass the Turkic peoples of the tsarist empire. This implied an ethno-racial conception of nation-hood that could hardly be inclusive of Arabs or Kurds, let alone Armenians or Greeks. In the pages of their post-1908 publications, and in the cultural and educational societies they established under the aegis of the newly established CUP regime, Russian-born pan-Turkist activists such as Yusuf Akçura, Ağaoğlu Ahmet, and Hüseyinzade Ali struggled to disseminate their views, while hammering as many nails as possible into the coffin of Ottomanism. For them, the state had meaning only as an embodiment of ethnic identity; the idea of a civic culture arising within the framework of a multiethnic state was an anachro-nistic delusion that stood in the way of pan-Turkist destiny. Indeed, the Ottoman empire might eventually collapse altogether, but destiny would still await the Turks.[55]

Following his reconstitution of the CUP under his own leadership, Ahmed Riza focussed the organization's efforts on cultivating support among Turkish officers in the armed forces. It was a military coup launched by officers in

Salonika that brought the Young Turks to power in 1908, and that allowed them to consolidate their political control in the following years.[56] The military officers who soon came to dominate the movement seemed particularly open to cut-and-dried definitions of nationhood that left little scope for nuanced notions of civic identity and interethnic dialogue. The influence of German officers in Ottoman military academies reinforced the tendency to think of the army as the "school of the nation," and to regard the nation as an organic being defined by a unitary culture, rather than a collection of diverse communities held together by common political values.[57]

During their first years in power, certain aspects of the Ottomanist vision did manifest themselves in the Young Turks' legislative initiatives. Laws were passed that secularized the judicial system (although family law was not entirely secularized), enhanced the rights of women in marriage, and in other ways sought to transform the Ottoman empire into a *Rechtsstaat* that could invoke a sense of loyalty and commitment from subjects-turned-citizens.[58]

Yet the means by which the Young Turks sought to foster such a transformation were laden with inconsistencies and contradictions. The restoration of the long-suspended Constitution of 1876 seemed to herald the dawn of a liberal-democratic age, complete with empire-wide parliamentary elections and guarantees of freedom of expression. (The Capitulations were not abolished until October 1914.) But real power was concentrated in the hands of a handful of civilian leaders and military officers who imposed increasingly draconian measures to quell dissenting views and popular manifestations of discontent. Armenian demands for autonomy were followed by a series of massacres that were officially blamed on reactionary elements that the Young Turk authorities seemed – at best – reluctant to curtail.[59] While the CUP continued to present itself publicly as a political vanguard for the peoples of the empire as a whole, rather than for Turks only, recent research by Şükrü Hanioğlu, Erik Zürcher, and others has confirmed what many non-Turkish elites suspected at the time, namely that the CUP's innermost councils were dominated by figures who were wedded to the narrow, Turkish-nationalist agendas that have been outlined above. The outbreak of the Balkan Wars in 1912 greatly strengthened the already powerful ethnonationalist and pan-Turkist elements within the leadership, and this dynamic gathered further momentum during the First World War.[60]

From Ottomanism to Arab Nationalism

The CUP's attempt to modernize the state along the lines of European political and administrative models was initially embraced with enthusiasm by the educated social elites of Damascus, Baghdad, and the other major urban centers of the empire's Arabic-speaking regions. These elites were dominated by landed urban notables – that is, men who derived large incomes from their enormous rural land holdings, but who lived in cities and used their financial independence to pursue an education in Turkish institutions of higher learning, returning to occupy powerful – and lucrative – administrative positions in their native regions. Many of them had been involved in CUP activities and had even held positions of leadership in the organization during the 1890s. By 1908, Arabs were systematically excluded from any positions of power in the CUP, whose leaders secretly derided the Arabs as culturally inferior to the Turkish people.[61] Nonetheless, the Young Turks' reform drive initially seemed to hold forth the promise of creating new avenues of upward mobility for the Arab urban notables. The rigidly stratified Ottoman system seemed to be opening up, and this could only benefit provincial elites.

Or so they thought. It did not take long for disillusionment to set in, for once in power, the Young Turks embarked on a centralizing program that tightened Istanbul's administrative grip on the provinces without providing provincial notables with any commensurate increase in access to central power. Moreover, there were indications of a Turkification campaign in the making, reminiscent of the Russification efforts in the tsarist empire's borderlands. Arab members of the Ottoman parliament who voiced criticisms of these policies found themselves harassed and prevented from running effective re-election campaigns.

Responses in the Arab world were marked by ambivalence and uncertainty. Arab nationalism was still in its infancy in the early twentieth century, and prior to the First World War, most Arab notables and intellectuals did not seek the breakup of the Ottoman empire. While some of them had, since the 1850s, occasionally contemplated the possibility of creating an independent state in Greater Syria, they seemed to have done so more out of a sense that the Ottoman empire might be a sinking ship, easily vulnerable to the depredations of European powers, than out of an intrinsic attraction to the idea of political independence.[62] The policies of the CUP-in-power did clearly provoke a widespread anti-Turkish backlash among Arab social, cultural, and political elites, but this reaction assumed a variety of forms. A number of regional potentates – such as Sayyid Talib in Basra (in southern Mesopotamia) or Sharif Hussein of the Hejaz – seemed ready to flirt with the possibility of foreign alliances or the adoption of oppositional ideologies in their efforts to resist Istanbul's encroachment on their local authority. But such behavior essentially conformed to traditional patterns of center–periphery tensions in the empire, and cannot be said to have reflected a modern nationalist sensibility.[63]

A more recognizably nationalist sentiment can be said to have manifested itself among members of the commercial and intellectual elites of cosmopolitan cities such as Beirut, among younger members of the landowning-bureaucratic notability of the Fertile Crescent, and among Arab officers who found themselves passed up for promotion or reassigned to undesirable posts by their Turkish commanders. Modeling themselves organizationally on the CUP, some of these disaffected elements in Syria and Mesopotamia formed secret societies such as *al-Fatat* (short for *Jam'iyyat al-ummah al-'arabiyyah al-fatat* – The Young Arab Nation Society) and *al-'Ahd* (The Covenant),[64] while openly propagating their views through political parties such as the Cairo-based Ottoman Administrative Decentralization Party. However, even among these activists, who did not number more than 100 before 1914,[65] the majority did not advocate outright Arab political independence prior to 1914. Their activities were principally directed against the Young Turks' centralizing efforts, which threatened to undermine the local and regional power to which Arab elites had been accustomed. Cultivating a sense of pride in the historical significance and originality of Arabic language and civilization, they sought to promote an Arab cultural renascence accompanied by a greater measure of self-rule within the context of a reformed and decentralized Ottoman empire. Equal status and regional self-rule for the Arabs within a democratized Ottoman empire was also the demand of the delegates at the Arab National Congress that convened in defiance of the CUP in Paris in June 1913. Those calling for outright Arab political independence were, during the pre-1914 years, still little more than an isolated minority.[66]

While there was clearly a range of ideological orientations and political agendas represented in these organizations, the main currents within them drew their inspiration from the intellectual movement referred to by latter-day scholars as Arabism.[67] Arabism was several decades old by 1914, and was itself an offshoot of the Islamic modernism discussed earlier in this chapter. Arabism was divided into a number of different streams that differed over such issues as how to define the relationship between Arab identity and Islam, but that shared a common belief that the revitalization of Arab culture and consciousness was essential if the Middle East as a whole was to resist the encroachment of the West. In line with Islamic modernist thought, the Arabists tended to regard political liberty (at least for the educated elite) and constitutionalism as rooted in Islamic and Arabic traditions, which had been abused and perverted over the centuries by the Ottoman sultans.[68]

One of the most influential Arabist thinkers was the Syrian-born Rashid Rida (1865–1935), who propagated his views through his Cairo-based journal, *al-Manar* (The Lighthouse).[69] A student of Muhammad Abduh's, Rida contended that, since Arabic was the language of the Koran and it was the Arabs who had brought the world Islam, an Arab national-cultural revival was a necessary precondition for the revitalization of Islamic civilization as a whole. What was good for the Arabs would be good for all Muslims, regardless of nationality, because Arab identity was directly linked to the universal values of Islam. It thus stood in marked contrast to what Rida regarded as the narrow, exclusive nationalism of the Young Turks.

Indeed, Rida was scathing in his criticism of the ethnonationalist or racial (*jinsi*) element in the Young Turks' ideology, blaming it on their obtuseness and ignorance. He pointed out that the Turks actually stood to lose the most in the game of ethnic politics, since the ethnic principle would reduce their sphere of legitimate authority to Anatolia, and since the European powers would not permit them to compensate themselves by pursuing pan-Turkist fantasies in Central Asia.[70] In his eyes, Turkish nationalism was no more than an updated version of the tribal solidarity – *'asabiyyah* – that had originally given rise to the Ottoman–Turkish state. Disputing Ibn Khaldun's classic paradigm, Rida argued that *'asabiyyah* could not serve as the social cement or foundation of authority in a civilized society. Whereas Ibn Khaldun had contended that *'asabiyyah* was essential to the cohesion and power of the ruling elite in an Islamic state, Rida insisted that *'asabiyyah* was antithetical to Islam. The historic greatness of the Arabs lay precisely in the fact that they had founded a religion that could bring together peoples of many different races under an egalitarian rule of law.[71]

The political implications of this thesis remained vague. Although Rida's central focus was on how to revive Islamic civilization, his insistence on the centrality of the Arabs to any such revival could clearly lend itself to nationalist interpretations. Indeed, in holding up the Arabs as the fount of Islamic civilization and the only hope for its redemption, he was running the risk of falling into precisely the sort of ethnic chauvinism for which he castigated the Young Turks. Yet by the same token, what might be termed Rida's cultural nationalism was constrained by his very real concern with the broader fate of the Islamic world.[72]

The institutional ramifications of his thought were similarly ambiguous. In Rida's vision of an ideal Islamic state, political power over such critical issues as the election of the Caliph would be vested in the hands of a learned and respected elite that represented the interests of the community as a whole. Was this a formula for parliamentary constitutionalism or conservative oligarchy? In later years, when some of his own earlier ideas were being adapted and incorporated into secular nationalist and republican ideologies, Rida retreated in alarm into Islamic fundamentalism. But as late as 1922, he was writing treatises that could be interpreted as attempts to link Arab national consciousness and Islamic values with advocacy of a system of mixed government and rule of law bearing at least some resemblance to a Western-style liberal constitutional order.[73]

It was ideas such as these that – along with the model of the Young Turk movement, the example of separatist nationalism in the Balkans, and the influence of Western values and institutions – formed the intellectual and ideological backdrop to the activities of the Arab political societies that sprouted up during the last half-dozen years before the outbreak of the First World War. One of the premises shared by most Arabist political currents was the notion that Arab identity was rooted in the history of Islam, and vice versa. (In later years, even some Christian Arab nationalists would claim to feel an affinity – in a loose, non-religious sense – with the heritage of Islamic civilization.)[74] In this early form, then, the idea of Arab nationhood evoked the image of an inclusive cultural and historic community which could both accommodate internal minorities and sustain an organic political connection with the Turks, if only the latter would accord it the respect and equality of status it deserved. In principle, Arab identity could be cultivated within the framework of a decentralized Ottoman empire, serving as the catalyst for a reinvigoration of Middle Eastern society as a whole. Should the incompetence of the Young Turks lead to the empire's collapse, the Arabs would draw on their sense of common values and common destiny to fend for themselves.

It remained to be seen whether the high-minded values that informed

Arabism could survive the test of power any better than the liberal aspects of the Young Turks' ideology had.

Conclusion

The most obvious point to emerge from the above discussion is that these nationalist movements cannot be understood in isolation from one another. They took form within multiethnic empires that shared similar problems and common borders, and there were ongoing contacts and mutual influences among the *Czech Nationalism* leaders and ideologues of many of these movements. Masaryk's ideas directly molded the outlooks of some leading Slovak and Croatian intellectuals; socialist and populist parties in Austria–Hungary and Russia were engaged in an ongoing dialogue about the nationalities question; the Neo-Slav movement formed a shortlived framework for contact and contention among a variety of Slavic nationalists; the influences of right-wing pan-Slavism and left-wing Russian populism converged with that of Islamic modernism to produce the Jadid movement among Russia's Muslim intellectuals, who were also stirred by news of the Young Turk revolution of 1908; Tatar intellectuals escaping tsarist oppression brought their pan-Turkist ideas to the Ottoman empire, where they gained considerable influence within the CUP.

Among the diversity of movements surveyed in this chapter, a number of common patterns emerge. The dominant intellectual currents within each of the movements saw themselves as progressive forces that would lead their nations to modernity by building on the most valuable aspects of their historical heritages. Some embraced Western liberalism while others contrasted Western materialism with their own culture's supposed spiritual and communal values, but they were all determined to raise their peoples to Western standards of political cohesiveness and material success by infusing them with an awareness of, and sense of pride in, their own distinctive heritages.[75]

Each of these nationalist projects, then, had to contend with an inner tension between the celebration of the past and the striving for a better future, between the cult of Self and the imitation of the Other, between the idealization of the nation's intrinsic qualities and the commitment to transform it into something better – or to help it realize its full potential, as a nationalist might prefer to put it. This tension manifested itself in a marked tendency to define national identities in broad, sweeping terms that transcended existing boundaries, be they political, cultural, or even linguistic. Masaryk insisted that Czechs and Slovaks were part of a Czechoslovak people, a portion of the Croat and Serb intelligentsias articulated a Yugoslavist program, the Young Turks embraced wildly unrealistic pan-Turkist ideals. Many socialist nationalists synthesized ethnic particularism with proletarian (or peasant) internationalism, and aspired to create broad federations of autonomous nations. The political and ethical implications of these programs ranged the full breadth of the spectrum from racist exclusivism to liberal pluralism, but their one common feature was their incorporation of transformative agendas that were ostensibly rooted in the unique

Czech – collapsed 1993 .

essence of their respective nations. The full realization and expression of national identity was a goal to be achieved; the nation was not simply a pre-existing object of worship, it was a process of becoming. Of course, it was the intelligentsias that were to lead the masses to the realization of their national destinies.

At a personal level, these ambitious constructions of national identity were often expressive of nationalist intellectuals' struggles to reconcile their relatively worldly, or even cosmopolitan, outlooks with their quest for a sense of rooted-ness. It is striking how many of these figures were themselves of mixed ethnic background, or had suffered from a sense of cultural or social marginalization. Masaryk was part Slovak, Piłsudski saw himself as an heir to the Polish–Lithuanian tradition, Ziya Gökalp had some Kurdish background in his family, and the assumed name of another prominent Turkish nationalist publicist – Tekin Alp – was a substitute for his rather unlikely given name – Moïse Cohen.[76] For these people, articulating transformative visions of nationalism was a way of taking an active hand in the creation of communities to which they could unambiguously belong.

While transformative impulses were common to all nationalists, many nation-alist intelligentsias were deeply divided over how to balance and integrate the civic and ethnic dimensions of collective identity. Masaryk's Realists, the Yugoslav activists, the PPS, the liberal wing of the CUP, among others, all emphasized shared political values as cardinal attributes of national community. The leadership of each of these movements regarded its own ethnic group's culture and language (Czech, Croatian, Polish, Turkish) as a medium for the dissemination of progressive, universal values among the population of the ethnic group itself as well as among culturally, linguistically, and/or historically related nationalities (Slovaks, Serbs, Ukrainians, Kurds and Arabs, respectively). The articulators of these programs tended to be blind to the discriminatory potential or cultural-imperialist implications of their own ostensibly tolerant and egalitarian philosophies.

Such political programs were often challenged by alternative constructions of national identity that unapologetically and unambiguously stressed the priority of ethnic bonds over civic values. To varying degrees, Kramář's Young Czechs, the Croatian Party of Pure Right, the Polish Endecja, and the Turkish national-ists and pan-Turkists – among others – envisioned the creation of political communities whose values, structures, and institutions would be a direct expres-sion of their own people's idiosyncratic character, in which civic identity would simply function as the public expression of ethnic kinship. The leaders of these movements were usually quite frank about their ethnocentrism and outspoken about their intolerance toward minorities. At the same time, they were disingen-uous in their self-portrayal as mere mouthpieces for the spirit, traditions, and history of their peoples. These intellectuals' programs were in fact no less trans-formative (perhaps, indeed, more so) than those of their opponents, and the proclivity of some among them for pan-nationalism was an expression of their eagerness for a radical reconfiguration of existing mentalities and communities.

The intelligentsias that nourished these conflicting aspirations all greeted the outbreak of war in 1914 as an opportunity to put words into action and to realize their ideological visions. But the war did more than affect the fate of intellectuals and the evolution of their ideas; it transformed and disfigured the faces of entire societies. The following chapter focusses on the development of national identities under the direct impact of total war.

4 Straining the Imperial Molds, 1914–1918

The First World War was a total war on an unprecedented scale, and no segment of the population in the multinational empires could entirely escape its impact. The military fronts in Eastern Europe cut wide swaths of destruction, massacre, rape, and pillage as they moved to and fro across vast lands like the sickle in the hands of the Grim Reaper. In many of those regions of Eastern Europe and the Middle East that were largely spared the direct wrath of the sword, the scepter of imperial administration took on a hard new edge as military institutions encroached on, or replaced, the authority of civil administrations. Mass conscription, the shock of battle and the *esprit de corps* of combat, the death and maiming of loved ones, the requisitioning of property, shortages and rationing of the most basic commodities, the induction of women into workforces, foreign conquest and military occupation, the outflow and influx of refugees – in these and other ways, the war impinged directly and brutally on most sectors of society. The trauma of the war experience made even people of the least educated classes and remotest regions realize that their daily existence was bound up with politics in ways they might not previously have dreamed possible.[1]

But to say that everyone was affected by the war is not to suggest that the nature of the experience or the types of responses it evoked were fundamentally similar across the board. The war's impact on people's mentalities and identities changed dramatically over time and varied greatly among different regions, cultures, age groups, sexes, and classes – not to speak of the differences between front-line fighters and civilians. Following the initial outbreak of mass euphoria and patriotic solidarity among the urban populations of all the major belligerents during the first days and weeks of the conflict, experiences, perspectives, and reactions began to diverge ever more sharply.

One such pattern of divergence divided subject peoples from dominant nationalities and imperial political elites within the multinational empires. The sense that this endless, draining war was being fought in the interests of the latter groups heightened the collective sense of alienation among the former, as did the ever more widespread belief that the burden of war was being divided unfairly among them. In many instances, these perceptions reinforced myths of national martyrdom and awakened messianic expectations of collective deliverance.

At the same time, it must be stressed that the war's impact on individual ethnic groups was itself far from homogeneous. By 1918, the rhetoric and imagery of national liberation had become a widespread medium for the expression of political resentments and aspirations across a broad spectrum of social sectors within many of these peoples. Yet rather than constituting a common political coinage, nationalism was to assume the form of a multiplicity of denominations whose exchange value was open to question. What were the concrete political and economic implications of national self-determination? Which groups would deserve most credit for achieving it? Who was best positioned to benefit from it? These were unresolved questions, questions that had the potential to be enormously divisive precisely because the language of nationalism raised such high expectations of social solidarity and collective salvation. The answers to such questions, and even the nature of the issues being raised, varied from group to group. Within any given nationality, there were soldiers in imperial armies, volunteers for national legions serving under "enemy" command, middle-class civilians, displaced persons, industrial workers, peasants, domestic political leaders who continued to profess loyalty to the imperial regimes well into the war, and exiled nationalist politicians dedicated to the dismantling of empires, to name but a few categories of action and experience. The range of political and social agendas that had to be reconciled with one another within the framework of "national unity" after 1918 was, therefore, extraordinarily wide.

This chapter will use a selection of cases to explore the range of influences the war had on conceptions of identity among members of subject nationalities[2] within the ever more strained frameworks of the multinational empires. The following chapter will focus on new, wartime arenas of nationalist activity and consciousness that lay outside established imperial frameworks.

War Front, Home Front, and the Politicization of Ethnicity in the Habsburg Empire

In the Habsburg empire, the outbreak of war was the occasion for fervent affirmations of loyalty on the part of mainstream political leaders in Galicia, Croatia, Slovenia, Bohemia, etc. Indeed, it was hoped that a resolute display of wartime loyalty to the crown would earn its reward in the form of greater opportunities for self-rule after the war. Yet the fact that there was a perceived need to proclaim loyalty to the monarch is itself indicative both of the archaic political culture of the Habsburg state, and of its potential incohesiveness.

Massive casualties on the Russian front combined with the enormous economic toll of the war effort did ultimately strain the loyalty of both dominant and subject nationalities. Austria–Hungary presented the incongruous spectacle of a dynastic state fighting a total war; the war's demands were such as could be sustained for the duration only by a state that could inspire its populace with a sense that its national destiny was at stake in the conflict. In the context of the Habsburg empire, this notion might have been vaguely plausible for the

Magyars, but insofar as the conflict intensified their sense of a distinct national destiny, it reinforced their alienation from the imperial edifice whose base remained in Vienna. Indeed, the Hungarian government withheld grain supplies from the Austrian half of the monarchy while accusing the Habsburg military of squandering Magyar lives in disproportionate numbers on the front lines.[3] As for the Austro-Germans, whatever strengthening of nationalist sentiments they experienced not only worsened their conflicts with Czechs and Magyars, but also aggravated the tension between the pan-German ideal and loyalty to the Habsburg state. Berlin, after all, was a far more powerful magnet for German nationalist emotions than was Vienna.

Among many of the other ethnic groups, nationalist feelings were directly associated with sympathy for the Allied cause. To be sure, there were many people of all nationalities who did feel a sense of personal devotion to the elderly patriarch, Kaiser Franz Joseph (reigned 1848–1916), who ruled over the empire. They may have valued the Austro-Hungarian state as a source of stability and the rule of law. The Poles and Jews of Galicia looked to Vienna for protection against what they saw as the barbarous hordes of the Russian army. But a regime that explicitly and necessarily distanced itself from any modern conception of national identity was by definition incapable of igniting that spark of collective zeal that helps a population endure the privations and brutal demands of a total war.

Russia's Brusilov offensive in the summer of 1916 cost the Austro-Hungarian army 750,000 men (over half of them as POWs) before the German army's intervention forced the Russians to retreat in disarray. The Dual Monarchy was left more subservient than ever to Berlin in its prosecution of the war effort, as it submitted to the creation of a joint military command in which the Germans called the tune.[4] In November 1916, the joint Habsburg–German proclamation of a Polish kingdom on territory captured from Russia briefly raised hopes among the Habsburg empire's Slavs for the incorporation of an autonomous Poland in a Habsburg state reconfigured as an ethnic federation. These hopes faded as the new Polish entity turned out to be little more than a façade for German hegemony. Finally, Franz Joseph's death (also in November 1916) after a sixty-eight-year reign removed from the scene a figure that had embodied the images of dynastic legitimacy and dignified paternalism that were so central to Austro-Hungarian patriotism.[5]

The new emperor, Karl I, recognized that the state bequeathed to him was in too brittle a condition to contend with the pressures of the war. He made over-tures to the Slavic nationalities by overtly raising the possibility of a devolution of power to them. The Reichsrat was reconvened in May 1917 after a three-year hiatus. Karl also used private channels to explore the possibility of negotiating a separate peace with the Allies.

When premature public disclosure led to the unraveling of his secret diplo-matic contacts in the spring of 1918, Karl found himself more vulnerable than ever to the demands and pressures of his resentful German ally. For their part, with the prospect eliminated of luring the Habsburg empire away from the war effort, the Allied powers felt they had nothing to lose by promoting its dissolution, and began openly endorsing the idea of full independence for its nationalities.[6] On the domestic front, the reconvened Reichsrat served once again as a forum for Czech–German confrontation rather than reconciliation. An increasingly fragile and polarized Habsburg state found itself unable to derive much benefit from Germany's defeat of Russia in 1917, as widespread mutinies and massive desertions plagued its army. In October 1918, with Allied victory on the Western Front imminent, Karl's last-minute offer of self-rule to the nationalities of the Austrian half of the empire was seen as a sign of weakness rather than magnanimity. The leaders of subject peoples throughout the monarchy responded by proclaiming the independence (or the adherence to neighboring, co-ethnic nation-states) of their respective regions, leaving Austria and Hungary as defeated rump states stranded in the midst of a transformed Central European political map.

To what extent and in what ways was this gradual corrosion and final, sudden collapse of the Austro-Hungarian state connected to mass-based nationalism among its peoples? One can, at a minimum, plausibly assert that the monarchy failed to maintain the allegiance of significant sectors among regional elites and masses, leaving the field open for small but determined groups of separatist leaders. But can one go further and suggest that the war fostered the growth of an active anti-imperial animus among the general public, stimulating the development of nationalist sentiments that were incompatible with the continued existence of the Habsburg monarchy? The answer is elusive, because the relevant source material is relatively sparse. We have at our disposal volumes of collected writings and speeches by political leaders and ideologues; most other people were much less concerned with recording their changing attitudes and mentalities. Nevertheless, by combing through soldiers' letters from the front, military records, contemporaneous newspaper accounts, police reports on public gatherings, and records of court proceedings, and by making plausible inferences from the actions and demands of strikers, mutineers, deserters, demonstrators, resistance bands, and local political leaders, historians have been able to develop working hypotheses about changes in political consciousness across classes and regions during the war years.

In most cases, ethnicity played a powerful role in mediating wartime experiences, while war, in turn, shaped the construction of national identities. These patterns in the development of social and political consciousness were far from uniform, however. By focussing selectively on three distinct yet related arenas of activity – the Habsburg military, the Czech home front, and the South Slav home front – we can develop a sense of the range of responses to the war among members of the empire's subject nationalities.

Loyalties on the (Front) Line

As one of the last all-imperial institutions of the post-1867 Dual Monarchy, the Austro-Hungarian army held a significance beyond that of providing for the security and defense of the state. It was a powerful public symbol of imperial unity as well as an instrument of interethnic integration.[7] Its ability to maintain internal cohesion was therefore doubly essential as the Habsburg empire took on the fateful challenge of total war. By the same token, any centrifugal pressures within its ranks would likely have a powerful ripple effect extending beyond the military realm into the political sphere.[8]

By most accounts, the army performed surprisingly well in the war, given the enormous strains it was under. That is to say, in view of its multiethnic character and its state of relative underequipment, it is remarkable how long the army remained a functioning institution.[9] Although it was not able to achieve decisive victory on any front without direct assistance from Germany, it was able to mount some punishing offensives in the Italian sector and to maintain an effective defense there until September 1918. The army's most cohesive element was its officer corps, which was one of the most ethnicity-blind institutions left in the monarchy; although just over half of those who chose to become career officers were ethnic Germans, promotions appear to have been determined much more on the basis of merit than of nationality.[10] Officers were themselves usually the sons of civil servants, who would likely have moved from one part of the empire to another with their families as they were posted to various provinces over the course of their careers. This typical background of geographic mobility during childhood combined with the ethos of military education prevented most officers from getting caught up in the progressive ethnicization of identity that was gnawing at the monarchy's foundations in the years leading up to and during the war. The overriding loyalty of the typical officer was still directed toward his regiment and toward the Emperor-King, to whom he had taken a personal oath of loyalty.[11]

Among the rank-and-file conscripts, the sense of corporate identity and tradition was much weaker. Habsburg soldiers, most of whom were peasants, could be relied upon to obey orders and to help maintain domestic law and order: they were routinely stationed away from their native provinces as part of a conscious divide-and-rule approach to the nationalities problem. Many of them do seem to have felt a sense of loyalty toward the Emperor-King. But when it came to the rigors of the war, their performance was often shabby and their morale poor. It was only on the Italian front that any degree of enthusiasm for the struggle could be discerned among the uniformed masses, for the entry of Italy (a former ally) into the conflict on the Entente side was seen as a stab in the monarchy's back and Italy's annexationist designs on South Slav territories were successfully exploited by Austrian propaganda among Croats and Slovenes.[12]

The performance and morale of the rank-and-file was hardly helped by the fact that most of the soldiers who entered the war in 1914 were killed, maimed, or captured in its first two years. By 1916, the youths of 1914 had largely been replaced by raw conscripts and reserve formations that had been hastily called up to satisfy the war machine's insatiable appetite. Insufficiently prepared and inadequately clothed and fed, this rag-tag force could hardly take much comfort from the fact that the Russian army was even more run down. The Austro-

Hungarian victory over the Italians at the Battle of Caporetto in September 1917 was the Habsburg army's last hurrah; from that point on, its decline was rapid.

The increasing sense of disdain among common soldiers for the pompous Habsburg autocracy, and their growing impatience with the harsh demands of military discipline, is best captured in the Czech author Jaroslav Hašek's farcical novel, *The Good Soldier Švejk*. The story's Czech anti-hero spends the war threading himself through every available bureaucratic loophole and taking advantage of all possible opportunities for shirking his duties and avoiding combat, all the while maintaining an outward air of innocent simplicity.[13] Indeed, many of those who fought in Austrian uniform did so half-heartedly, and in April 1915, Austrian authorities were shocked by the surrender to the Russians of almost the entire 2,000-man 28th Infantry Regiment from Bohemia, under circumstances that seemed suggestive of desertion to the enemy. This regiment, many of whose soldiers were industrial workers affiliated with the Russophile National Socialist Party, was one of two formations that had flamboyantly protested being sent to fight against fellow Slavs upon their departure from Prague seven months earlier. The regiment's commitment to the war effort had not been strengthened by its experience while stationed in Hungary, where the hostile attitude of the local Magyar population had confirmed the feeling that Austria–Hungary, not Russia, was the true enemy of the Czech people.[14]

Among the South Slavs in Habsburg military service, Serb troops were particularly prone to desert or defect to the enemy (especially on the Serbian and Russian fronts),[15] and the longer the war lasted, the more such incidents multiplied among Slovenes and Croats as well. But it was units posted in the rear – where relative inactivity contributed to low morale and contact with civilian populations sensitized troops to changes in the political atmosphere – that were most prone to challenge authority. Reserve units, composed largely of men exempted from front-line service by virtue of their status as university students, priests, or schoolteachers, were particularly fertile ground for the cultivation of revolutionary and nationalist ideas. Those considered unfit or troublemakers were also consigned to these and other rearguard units, which contributed to the poor discipline and rebellious proclivities of such formations. During early 1918, mutinies dominated by South Slav sailors broke out aboard the Austro-Hungarian fleet that lay idle off the coast of Dalmatia. Although suppressed, they were soon followed by a string of rebellions among South Slav ground units posted in Croatia–Slavonia, Dalmatia, and Bosnia – units that now included tens of thousands of former POWs freshly released from captivity in Russia, where they had witnessed the revolutionary transformation of army and society. Declining food rations helped precipitate such revolts, but they almost invariably took on a heavily political coloration. Rebel agendas usually reflected a mixture of social-revolutionary and nationalist aspirations: pro-Bolshevik slogans were chanted alongside cries such as "Long live Yugoslavia!" or "Long live the Slovenes!"

While individual mutinies in the rear could be forcefully suppressed, by

October 1918 – in the wake of an unsuccessful Habsburg offensive on the Piave river in June – even troops on the Italian front had lost all inclination to fight on in a hopeless cause. Magyar units now deserted the trenches as readily as Slav soldiers did. As the Habsburg monarchy's imminent demise became apparent, that last redoubt of dynastic loyalty – the officer corps – finally disintegrated as well, as a majority of officers placed themselves at the disposal of the national committees that were springing up in their native regions.[16]

What does the above narrative tell us about the role of nationalism in the Austro-Hungarian army? In and of itself, of course, soldiers' reluctance to die in battle or languish in barracks need not be taken as a symptom of separatist nationalism. The French command faced a large-scale mutiny on the Western Front in 1917, and ethnic Russian troops in the tsar's army were not much more eager to fight than those of other nationalities.[17] The cataclysm that was the Great War took its toll on every army's stamina, cohesiveness, and discipline. Conversely, it is accepted wisdom among military historians that the sense of camaraderie within a military unit is much more important than patriotism in sustaining morale and discipline under the extreme pressures of war. When confronting the imminent possibility of a horrific death, the combatants' *esprit de corps* and immediacy of contact become a much more vital dimension of their experience than any broader identification with an "imagined community" possibly could be.[18]

What is misleading about this generalization is that it ignores the possible relationship between the two frames of reference. Patriotism clearly is not a sufficient condition of discipline among troops, but the nature of their political loyalties can play a vital role in defining the common goal toward which they direct their *esprit de corps*. A common resentment of the Austro-Hungarian state and army colored the group spirit of military units such as the Czech 28th Infantry Regiment that readily surrendered to the Russians in April 1915. It can be argued that the internal cohesion of such formations did not break down at all; rather, their collective behavior was reshaped by their national consciousness.[19] The case of the French mutinies of 1917 was qualitatively very different. Here, discipline broke down, but fundamental patriotic assumptions remained intact. The demands of these soldiers centered on immediate concerns such as insufficient leave from the front lines, abusive behavior on the part of officers, inedible rations, etc. Their calls for immediate peace talks took it for granted that the return of Alsace-Lorraine to France would have to be part of a final settlement. The overall righteousness of the French war effort does not seem to have been widely called into question, and there were certainly no mass desertions to the enemy.[20]

It is clear that there was a considerable degree of correlation between ethno-cultural consciousness and differential desertion rates in the Habsburg army. Soldiers of Slavic nationality deserted in higher proportions than did ethnic Germans or Magyars (although by the last months of the war, desertion rates were skyrocketing among these groups as well). Slavic troops were also much likelier to desert on the Russian and Serbian fronts than on the Italian front.

Conversely, ethnically Italian troops (from Austrian-ruled South Tyrol and the Dalmatian coast) deserted in disproportionately high numbers on the Italian front.[21] These patterns suggest that a sense of ethnic affiliation with the enemy undermined some soldiers' loyalty to the empire. It can be conjectured that, for every soldier who took the risky initiative of deserting, there were several others who did not have the opportunity to do so, but nonetheless resented being forced to engage in mortal combat against counterparts whom they did not regard as enemies.[22]

Disaffection with the Austro-Hungarian cause was particularly rife among those soldiers who ended up as prisoners in Russia. In the summer of 1918, a few months after the signing of peace treaties with the Central Powers at Brest-Litovsk, the Bolsheviks began to release hundreds of thousands of German and Habsburg prisoners of war. As soon as these men had returned home, many of them found themselves thrust right back into uniforms and sent off to new fronts. If nothing else had politicized them, this did. Having languished in camps and suffered severe privations for years, these men were hardly eager to be recycled into cannon fodder upon their long-awaited return to their native lands. Moreover, having been in Russia during the revolutionary turmoil of 1917–1918,[23] they had become prone to question authority and keenly aware of the possibilities of employing mass action to challenge the existing order. Former POWs played leading roles in inciting mutinies and rebellions in the Austro-Hungarian army during the summer and fall of 1918, and contributed to the disintegration of law and order in some regions. It was also from the ranks of POWs in Russia that the main contingents of volunteers for Czech and South Slav nationalist legions were recruited (see Chapter 5).[24]

In brief, the army's performance in the war encapsulated both the strengths and the vulnerabilities of the Habsburg empire. For most of the war, the majority of troops took the empire's existence – and their obligation to fight for it – for granted. Yet – except on the Italian front – members of subject nationalities did not generally feel that in doing their duty toward the Emperor-King they were also protecting any vital interest of their own people. Indeed, the military command did not even make a serious effort to instill such feelings in the troops.[25] The Habsburg army's cohesion had always revolved around loyalty to the person of the monarch; ethnic identity and regional attachments were seen as things to be left behind when one entered the ranks. An eleventh-hour effort initiated in March 1918 by military counterintelligence to systematize the patriotic education (*Vaterländischer Unterricht*) of the troops proved hopelessly inept in its heavy reliance on didactic brochures and lectures and woefully traditional in its rigid focus on the value of the Habsburg state and the benevolence and peaceloving nature of its ruler. Pamphlets distributed among the war-weary, embittered soldiers included such pithy gems as: "Only a fair monarch worthy of love and above all party infighting can ensure that everyone receives an equal share of rights and goods."[26]

This sort of propaganda campaign could only serve to reinforce the sense of alienation among the rank-and-file. Indeed, the Hungarian authorities, who did seek to instill a sense of nationalist ardor among Magyar troops, openly opposed this last-ditch effort at reviving their supranational, dynastic loyalties; the unifying principle of the Habsburg army had become an anachronism. Emperor-King Karl's last-minute attempt at the end of October 1918 to strike a new bargain with Hungarian nationalism by releasing Magyar troops from their oath of personal loyalty to him only accelerated the influx of Magyar soldiers into the multinational stream of deserters flowing away from the front lines. In the Habsburg empire's final hour, all its nationalities were as one in their deter-mination to abandon it.[27]

In the final analysis, the multiethnic makeup of the Habsburg army was not the major cause of its military failure: the largely peasant composition of the armed forces, inadequate logistics, the inability of the Habsburg economy to sustain a total war effort, and the final collapse of Austria–Hungary's German ally were the determining factors. But the demoralization associated with this war effort, the disillusionment under these conditions with the notion of personal fealty to the person of the monarch, and the failure of the Habsburg authorities to create an alternative framework of collective motivation, all helped undermine loyalty to the empire among the troops. If only by default, ethnic identity emerged as the most appealing frame of reference for mutinous and deserting soldiers. In other words, ethnic identities did not in themselves cause Habsburg defeat, but the approach of defeat did stimulate the disintegration of the army along ethno-national lines. Without the continued cohesion of the army as both symbol and enforcer of imperial unity, there was nothing left to hold the Austro-Hungarian state together. For the final years of the conflict had also led to dramatic developments on the home front, as the following two cases will illustrate.

The Czech Home Front

Although the Czechs' open defiance of Habsburg authority was to play an important role in the disintegration of the empire as a whole, it was not until 1917–1918 that a determined nationalist spirit manifested itself on a consistent and concerted basis. During the first two-and-a-half years of the war, the activity of the mainstream Czech political parties lacked the focussed intensity of Masaryk's political endeavors in exile (see Chapter 5). It is true that a number of leaders who remained in Prague entertained hopes of liberation by Russia or of an internal collapse of the Austro-Hungarian empire. With this in mind, Karel Kramář and Vaclav Klofáč – the Russophile heads of the Young Czech and National Socialist[28] parties, respectively – were secretly in communication with the Russian government, while the Agrarian Party chief, Antonín Švehla, pursued a dual-track policy of maintaining contact with radical nationalists in exile and at home while concurrently acting within the legitimate framework of Austrian politics. But to risk all in an overt challenge to Habsburg authority seemed like a foolhardy proposition even to these figures. Others, such as the leaders of the Catholic parties, either retained an active sense of loyalty to the monarchy, or had grown used to working within the system and were reluctant to abandon their complacency. In general, hope continued to focus on the possibility of attaining self-rule for the historic Czech lands within the framework of a reformed Habsburg empire. A secret steering committee of radical nationalists known as the Maffie had been set up by Masaryk's associate Edvard Beneš before the latter's departure from the country, but its influence did not manifest itself until 1917.[29]

During the first year of the war, the imprisonment of Kramář, Klofáč, and other nationalists suspected of subversion and contact with the enemy, and the imposition of brutal military rule on parts of the Czech provinces of Bohemia and Moravia that were adjacent to Galicia, cast doubt on the possibility of constructive dialogue with Vienna. On the other hand, the jailing of the most confrontational leaders of the mainstream political parties left more accommodating figures at the forefront of Czech politics. Until 1917, therefore, these parties remained quite cautious, if not timid, in their dealings with the authorities, and reluctant to heed the exiles' calls for confrontation and resistance.

Emperor Karl's November 1916 announcement that the Reichsrat would be reconvened in May of the following year, combined with his amnesty for political prisoners, initially seemed to vindicate the position of those Czech leaders who had insisted on keeping open the lines of communication with the government. New life seemed to have been breathed into Czech "activism" – the term used to describe working actively within the system to bring about meaningful reform. The main threat to Czech interests was seen as coming not from the Habsburg monarchy itself, but from the ethnic-German party bloc. These Austro-German[30] nationalists had been emboldened by the outbreak of the war and the suspension of that circus of ethnic diversity, the Reichsrat, to press for outright political and ethno-linguistic domination of the western half of the monarchy. Now that the Reichsrat was being reconvened, the Czech parties perceived an opportunity to redress the political balance and put an end to the Austro-German bloc's behind-the-scenes intrigues. Such was the faith many Czech leaders continued to vest in the basic integrity of supranational Habsburg institutions.

With a view to creating a cohesive parliamentary opposition to the Austro-German initiatives, the main Czech political parties organized themselves into a Czech Union as well as an extra-parliamentary coordinating council known as the Czech National Committee (to be renamed the Czechoslovak National Committee in July 1918). The two main socialist parties – the Social Democrats and National Socialists – created their own joint council dedicated to the representation of working-class interests, but without questioning the overall authority of the National Committee, in which they were full participants. The Czech Union also established close coordination of parliamentary tactics with the South Slav bloc.

Focussing on cooperating with the imperial government rather than disputing its authority, the Czech Union embarrassed Tomáš Masaryk by publicly repudiating the Allies' January 1917 espousal of Czechoslovak national liberation as a war aim. By the end of May, however, in the wake of the March revolution in Russia and the United States' entry into the war in April, a radicalization had occurred in the Czech Union's position. The statement delivered by the Union at the opening session of the Reichsrat was a much closer approximation of the pro-independence position articulated by the exiled nationalists (see Chapter 5). It claimed the right to self-government for both Czechs and Slovaks within a single political framework, and in so doing it referred not only to Bohemia and Moravia's historic rights, but to the revolutionary principle of national self-determination for the Czech and Slovak peoples. Lip service was still paid to the idea of achieving this objective through a reorganization of the Habsburg state, but the shift toward a separatist mindset was unmistakable. In January 1918, the Czech Union issued an even more brazen statement in favor of the general application of the principle of national self-determination, without referring at all to the continued existence of the Austro-Hungarian state. Such Czech initiatives fanned the flames of South Slav separatism in turn.

As Austria–Hungary drifted into ever greater dependence on Germany and ever worse military and economic straits, the credibility of the old "activist" policy was completely undermined. "Activist" party leaders were stigmatized as little better than collaborators and removed from positions of authority. The influence of the Maffie (and through it, of the exiled Masaryk and Beneš) increased across the Czech political spectrum. Even the Czech Social Democratic Party had forced its leader Bohumir Šmeral out of office as early as September 1917. An ardent internationalist, Šmeral had consistently espoused the view that socialism did not have realistic prospects in the region if the large economic unit of Austria–Hungary were to be broken up into independent nation-states. He was ousted by radical nationalists who rejected the old Austro-Marxist program of cultural autonomy for the nationalities, and who joined forces with the "bourgeois" parties in the campaign for full-fledged national self-determination. For his part, Šmeral went on to become one of the founders of the Czechoslovak Communist Party. By October 1918, as the state's authority collapsed on all sides, the Czechoslovak National Committee peacefully took over administrative responsibilities in Bohemia and Moravia and proclaimed the country's independence.

This, then, is the basic chronology of political events leading up to the creation of Czechoslovakia. The question is, in what ways was this process related to the war's impact on the wider Czech public?

There is no indication that, as of 1914, the Czech public was any more intent on gaining national independence than its political leaders were. Greater autonomy within the framework of a federalized Habsburg monarchy probably represented the closest thing to a consensus objective, support for which cut across Czech social sectors and regional divisions. But to accept the possible utility of a reformed Habsburg monarchy was one thing; to die for an unreformed Austro-Hungarian empire in a war against fellow Slavs from Serbia and Russia was quite another. The reports of the Governor of Bohemia in September 1914 contained accounts of drunken conscripts in Prague tottering off to the front flaunting the Czech national colors and waving a red banner asking why they were being sent to fight the Russians, while sympathetic crowds urged them not to shoot at their Slavic brothers.[31]

Such early outbursts of discontent were soon suppressed, as the Habsburg authorities suspended civil liberties throughout the empire, arrested nationalist leaders, and restored a semblance of order and discipline on the home front. With the passage of years, however, the economic ravages of total war took a steady toll on public morale. Suffering acutely from the British blockade of the Central Powers, the Habsburg monarchy found itself increasingly hard put to provide adequate food and fuel for its civilian population. The army's needs had to come first, and basic supplies such as bread and coal were rationed ever more tightly. Bohemia was the economic powerhouse of the empire, containing over 70 per cent of its heavy industry (including the vast Skoda arms-production complex in Plzen [Pilsen]). Yet by the summer of 1918, the government was able to supply the residents of this vital region with only 45 per cent of their already meager official flour ration of 165 grams a day.

The evolution of wartime public opinion among the Habsburg empire's subject nationalities has been studied by Péter Hanák, whose work is based on thousands of letters collected by the postal censors over the course of the conflict. Hanák has concluded that the war's hardships accentuated the lower classes' dichotomized view of society as divided between rich and poor, and between willful authorities and hapless subjects. The rich could afford to buy scarce goods on the black market, to evade (so it was thought) military service, and to wield influence with the authorities. The poor were objects of conscription, requisitioning, and rationing. In the many instances where class and ethnic distinctions largely coincided with one another, resentment of the rich and powerful meant, by definition, resentment of another ethnic group – thus indirectly reinforcing the oppressed group's own sense of ethnic distinctiveness.

In the case of the Czechs, class and ethnicity were not coextensive, as they largely were in the case of "peasant peoples" like the Ruthenians (Uniate Ukrainians of Galicia) or Slovaks. There were fully developed Czech middle and upper-middle classes, a large and well-organized Czech industrial working class, as well as a relatively well-off and economically sophisticated Czech peasant stratum. In this case, therefore, it cannot be taken for granted that heightened awareness of socio-economic and national identities under the impact of war would be mutually reinforcing; there was the potential for conflict between the two forms of identity. As the hardships of war provoked them into more active political engagement, the Czech masses had to decide whether the primary purpose of that engagement was to confront the propertied classes generally, regardless of ethnicity, or their non-Czech rulers specifically.

That national loyalties generally took precedence over class conflict among the Czechs was due in part to patterns and perceptions of power distribution among the ethnic groups of the empire. For example, the population's bitterness over the acute food shortages described above was aggravated by the continued export of grain from the Czech lands to Germany throughout much of the war, and by persistent rumors that the Hungarian half of the Dual Monarchy was refusing to share its more plentiful agricultural supplies with the western half of the empire.[32] This highlighted the external dependence of the Habsburg crown on Germany and its internal weakness *vis-à-vis* the Magyars. It was indeed increasingly clear that Habsburg survival in this all-or-nothing conflict depended on German victory, and that such a victory would leave Germany as the undisputed hegemon of Europe generally, and East Central Europe particularly. This emboldened the pan-German parties in the Reichsrat in their own bid for domestic political hegemony, while the Hungarian government looked forward to even greater freedom to determine its own affairs – and disregard the interests of Slovaks, Croats, and others – under a weakened Habsburg crown. The political future of the empire's Slavic peoples looked dim indeed, were the Central Powers' arms to prevail. The material difficulties experienced daily by the Czech masses thus assumed a very well-defined political dimension in their minds, as they reinforced the pre-existing perception that the Habsburg empire's Slavs were consistently oppressed and exploited by the Germans and Magyars. Inadequate rations were seen not just as a function of the war in general, but as the more particular consequence of ethnic inequality in Austria–Hungary.

The politicization of Czech economic resentments thus took on a nationalist rather than social revolutionary character from the beginning. The bread riots and looting sprees that broke out periodically in Czech cities did not indiscriminately target all stores or all people who were seen as prosperous; they were directed primarily at German and Jewish merchants and shopkeepers. (The Jews of Prague were usually Germanized, rather than Czechified, in language and culture.) The strikes that engulfed industrial centers in Bohemia tended to be associated with demands for national self-determination at least as much as with calls for social revolution. After all, the authorities who had led society into this catastrophe in the first place were not leaders of the Czech middle or upper classes; they were drawn primarily from the German and Magyar elites. The war made the relative powerlessness of the Czechs within the Habsburg system more tangible than ever before. The nation as a whole was seen as oppressed by outsiders, and resentments over the economic disaster were therefore channeled into a heightened sense of nationalist consciousness.

This trend was reinforced by the Czech cultural establishment, which adopted an ever more defiant anti-Habsburg stance during the last two years of the war, when the liberalization under Emperor Karl made relatively bold gestures possible. In May 1917, 222 writers signed a manifesto drafted by Jaroslav Kvapil, artistic director of the National Theater in Prague, calling for a complete restoration of constitutional liberties in the Habsburg empire. This helped bring pressure on the Czech political leadership (organized in the Czech Union) to revise the cravenly loyalist public stance it had adopted at the beginning of the year (see above). In May of the following year, the fiftieth anniversary of the National Theater's founding was the occasion for a cultural festival attended by numerous delegates from the Slavic regions of the empire, whose rousing speeches called into question the continued legitimacy of Habsburg rule.

The picture that emerges is of a broad convergence of social, cultural, and ideological currents in a common national-democratic stream that rapidly gained force over the final year and a half of the war and that obliged the leaders of political parties to keep pace with it or face marginalization. The contrast between Czech and Austro-German socio-political radicalism during the war is quite revealing. January 1918 witnessed the outbreak of a massive strike movement in Vienna and other Austrian–German cities, which soon spread to Hungary as well. Clearly inspired by the example of the Bolshevik Revolution, the striking workers in some cases set up soviets (popular councils) on the Russian model and articulated their discontent in terms of class conflict and the need for social revolution. Only through an overthrow of the existing socio-economic and political system, they claimed, could the war be ended rapidly on all fronts. The deployment of seven Habsburg combat divisions was required to suppress the strikes.[33]

There was considerable interest in this movement among the Czech working class, and the Czech Social Democratic Party officially expressed its sympathy and support for it. But in concrete terms, the Czechs did not contribute very much. A one-day sympathy strike was organized in Czech factories toward the end of January, by which time the authorities had already clearly gained control over the situation in Austria. Only in the industrial outskirts of the Moravian capital Brno (Brünn) did Czech workers join the strike as soon as it began. The Czech Social Democratic leadership clearly made a deliberate decision to avoid a break with the Czech middle-class parties and to remain a sympathetic bystander rather than become an active participant in the effort to bring about an empire-wide social revolution. The composition of the Social Democratic leadership was itself a reflection of shop-floor sentiments and rank-and-file pressures that had led to the removal of the committed internationalist Šmeral as party boss in September 1917, and the consolidation of power by nationalists within the movement.

Why did national identity become so fundamental a reference point for Czechs of the working as well as middle classes? Among the socio-political dichotomies that Hanák refers to in his analysis of lower-class perceptions are those between rich and poor, lords and peasants, capitalists and proletariat. But the most fundamental dichotomy in the minds of the masses was defined by disparities in power, rather than in material wealth *per se*. That is to say, the material hardships associated with the war did not automatically generate class conflict. Rather, they accentuated the popular distinction between those with power and those without it.

In the case of the lower classes of the socio-economically differentiated Czech population, the predominant perception was that Germans as a group had power, and Czechs as a community did not. It was perfectly clear that it was not the Czech bourgeoisie that had dragged the country into the war (even if individual Czech industrialists might be making a profit from military contracts), or that was shipping grain to Germany. It was the Habsburg state that was arbitrarily imposing these decisions on Czechs of all classes. The feeling that Czechs of all classes were victims of Habsburg and German exploitation reinforced the sense of national community that had already been highly developed before the war. More importantly, it undermined the belief that the nation's rights could be secured within the framework of the Habsburg monarchy. By 1918 it seemed self-evident to most Czechs that any kind of meaningful social reform could only be achieved once the fundamental problem of imperial exploitation had been resolved for good.

The South Slav Lands

It is much harder to provide a coherent or even sequential account of the wartime evolution of national consciousness among the Habsburg empire's South Slavs. The extensive overlap among the respective territorial distributions of Serbs, Croats, and Muslims confounded efforts at clearly delineating national identities in the region, as did the deep divisions within ethnic groups between urban and rural cultures (most notably among the Croats) and between secular-liberal and clerical-religious elements. Wartime pressures complicated matters further, as Habsburg military and civil authorities vied for control of regions in the vicinity of the Serbian front and pursued agendas that were at cross-purposes with each other. In a sense, it is precisely this pattern of chaos and fragmentation that constitutes the organizing principle of this narrative: contem-poraneous historical actors may have been almost as confused as latter-day historians about how to make sense of rapidly shifting political circumstances and wildly fluctuating popular emotions. The war intensified nationalist senti-ments among the South Slav peoples, while further complicating the issue of where to direct those feelings and what would constitute the best cultural and political framework(s) for national self-determination.

The outbreak of the war led to a crackdown on oppositional political activity throughout the South Slav regions of the empire. The civilian authorities retained juridical control of Hungarian-ruled Croatia, but the Habsburg military regarded the region as a war zone and felt free to impose "security measures" with impunity. Hundreds of Serb civilians were put to death and many more deported on the basis of vague or trumped-up charges of espionage. Of course, some Serbs were involved in sabotage networks, and local Serbs in one border zone welcomed the Serbian army with open arms during its brief incursion into the region. But the Habsburg military treated the entire Serb population as suspect, taking advantage of its unusual wartime powers to embark on a campaign of terror designed to eradicate any potential for collective political action on the part of the ethnic Serb minority.[34] The situation was aggravated by an anti-Serb backlash among many Croats, who forgot their pro-Serbian enthusiasm of the previous few years (see Chapter 3) and engaged in violent street protests and riots in Zagreb (as well as in Dubrovnik and Sarajevo) in the wake of the assassination of Habsburg heir apparent Franz Ferdinand and his wife at Sarajevo in July 1914. The Croatian nationalists of the Frankist party enthusiastically endorsed the military's violent crackdown against the Serb minority; their party organ, *Hrvatska* (The Croat), observed that "the Serbs are poisonous snakes from whom you are safe only after you have crushed their heads." The most prominent Yugoslavist activists of the Croat–Serb Coalition (HSK) – which was still the largest grouping in the Croatian Sabor (parliament) – were either already in exile in Allied countries, or now managed to make their way there (see Chapter 5). The HSK was led by Svetozar Pribićević (1875–1936), leader of its Serb wing, who had recently veered back toward an opportunistic defense of Serb collective interest through cooperation with the Hungarian government.[35] Amidst an outpouring of virulently anti-Serbian government propaganda, the cowed HSK hastily declared its loyalty to the Habsburg state and its unwavering commitment to the cause of military victory over Serbia and Russia, while desperately seeking the protection of the civil authorities in Budapest against the depredations of the Habsburg army.[36] In Austrian-ruled Dalmatia, public support for Yugoslavism appeared to hold more steady, but even here this could only be said of the educated, urban middle classes, whose anti-clericalism and commercial orientation alienated the local peasantry.[37]

In Bosnia, whose large Serb population had served as fertile ground for the pro-Serbian Mlada Bosna (Young Bosnia) nationalist youth movement in the years just before 1914, martial law was harshly enforced as soon as the war broke out. Thousands of suspected activists were interned in prison camps and Bosnian Serbs were treated like an enemy population by Habsburg forces under the command of General Sarkotić, a Croat. Summary military justice was the norm; hundreds accused of espionage or sabotage were executed with little or no concern for due process. As part of a deliberate divide-and-rule policy, the Habsburg authorities recruited Bosnian Muslims and Croats into a militia – the *Schutzkorps* (Defense Corps) – charged with suppressing and preempting Serb guerrilla activity. The brutal methods of the *Schutzkorps*, which included the occasional massacre, poured fuel on the flames of the longstanding hostility between Muslims and Serbs in Bosnia, and aggravated Croat–Serb resentments.[38]

The provinces populated by Slovenes were far enough behind the front to be spared extensive administrative interventions by the military, but the Austrian civilian authorities proved harsher in their supervision of Slovene publications than the Hungarian authorities were in their oversight of the Croat press and stage. Indeed, much of Slovene culture was effectively suppressed during the first two years of the war. Newspapers and journals associated with the staunchly conservative, pro-Habsburg, clerical wing of Slovene politics and culture were given free rein to express their views, while the liberal press, which had taken up the cause of Triune Yugoslavism (advocacy of the creation of a self-governing South Slav entity as the third constituent element of a reconfigured Habsburg monarchy) in the pre-war years, was heavily censored and in many cases altogether stifled. Slovene theater life, with its liberal affinities, was also severely constrained, while German-language productions partially filled the resulting vacuum on Ljubljana's (Laibach's) stages. Such policies were hardly conducive to warm relations between the city's German and Slovene communities, nor did they give Slovenes a sense that they stood to benefit from a Habsburg victory in the war.[39]

The repressive measures imposed on the South Slav territories ultimately had a counterproductive impact on popular sentiment from the Habsburg standpoint. By the time censorship and political repression were relaxed under Emperor-King Karl in late 1916/early 1917, the Yugoslav ideal appeared to have bounced back and gained stronger support than ever among the urban population of Croatia and Slovenia. Not only did liberal newspapers renew their call for political and cultural cooperation among the empire's Serbs, Croats, and Slovenes, but leaders – such as the Slovene Anton Korošec – of conservative clericalist parties now added their voices to the Yugoslavist clamor, as did Slovene priests in their Sunday sermons. What was particularly noteworthy about this shift was that whereas, in past years, conservative Croat and Slovene politicians had endorsed the idea of Slovene–Croat autonomy, they now joined liberal Yugoslavists in explicitly including Serbs (despite their Eastern Orthodox religion and suspected sympathies for the Serbian kingdom) in the formula. The initiative of a younger generation of clericalists – more open to change and more attuned to the shifting winds of wartime sentiment – played an important role in fostering this new attitude.

Over the course of 1917–1918, Croat and Slovene literary works and stage productions became increasingly daring in their celebration of Yugoslav themes. An opera entitled *The Witch's Veil* that premièred in Zagreb in 1917 combined modern staging techniques and Wagnerian structure with elements of traditional South Slav melodies in its interpretation of a heroic Serb folk tale. The period also witnessed the founding of literary journals specifically devoted to the promotion of Yugoslav consciousness and cultural synthesis, such as Zagreb's *Književni jug* (*The Literary South* – first published in January 1918), which made a point of inviting contributions in all three South Slav linguistic media (Cyrillic- and Latin-script versions of Serbo-Croatian, and Slovene). In February 1918, a Zagreb-based journal tried to arrange a public celebration of the 100th anniversary of the birth of one of the most famous Illyrianist poets, Petar Preradović. When the formal events were banned, the public thumbed its nose at the authorities through spontaneous displays – closing down stores for the day, displaying the Serb, Croat, and Slovene colors, and laying wreaths at the poet's graveside.

Such cheerfully defiant assertions of liberal-nationalist, Yugoslav solidarity failed to produce strong echoes from the Croatian countryside, where the urban commercial and professional classes were perceived as scoff-laws and shirkers who found ways of avoiding conscription and profiting from black-market trade and inflated prices on commodities, while the peasantry lost manpower to conscription, livestock to military requisitioning, and income to undiminished or increased rates of rent and taxation. This increasingly ugly mood exploded into violent social unrest in the summer and autumn of 1918. Military deserters in the Croatian countryside, their numbers now swelled by an influx of Croat POWs freshly released from Russian captivity and unwilling to be recycled into cannon fodder, joined forces with destitute Croat peasants in a mounting campaign of social banditry. Known as the Green Cadres, these forces numbered in the tens of thousands by the autumn of 1918. They directed their anger against landowners and representatives of state authority, destroyed documentary records used in rent- and tax-collection, and, during the climax of the revolt in October–November 1918, carried out raids on towns throughout Croatia–Slavonia.[40]

This was, first and foremost, class warfare rather than an expression of nationalist sentiment. But in the context of the military and political events of 1918, it could hardly fail to have a serious impact on the development of nationalist politics in the region. Indeed, ethnicity played a direct role in shaping the political frames of reference of rural unrest: Croat peasants favored the declaration of an independent, social-egalitarian Croat republic or even remaining under Habsburg rule rather than merging with Serbia. By contrast, much of Croatia's minority Serb peasantry – which had been subjected to particularly harsh treatment by the Habsburg military over the preceding four years – eagerly anticipated liberation at the hands of the Serbian forces that were, by September 1918, fighting their way north from the expanding Allied bridgehead in Salonika.[41] Ethnic divisions also played a role in shaping patterns of violence. In many of their raids on towns, the Green Cadres vented their rage against any gendarmes and civil servants they could lay their hands on, and plundered a variety of commercial establishments. However, Jewish-owned shops were much more systematically targeted for looting and burning than were non-Jewish stores. In some cases, Serb-owned stores were also singled out for harsh treatment (although in many instances Serb and Croat peasants participated to a similar extent in the general attacks on propertied classes and local bureaucrats). Serb peasants were generally much more enthusiastic about the idea of Yugoslav union (which they interpreted to mean immediate establishment of the Serbian kingdom's authority over the region) than were Croats, and this contributed to inter-communal tension and violence. Fighting between Serbs and Muslims in Bosnia spilled over into Croatian border regions as well. For their part, amidst the collapse of the Habsburg state in October–November 1918, frightened municipal authorities in eastern Croatia (Slavonia) turned to released Serbian POWs (that is, members of Serbia's armed forces who had fallen into Habsburg captivity) for protection against the marauding Croat peasants.[42]

The activities of the Green Cadres were an important link in the tangled chain of events that led to the precipitous unification of Croatia and Slovenia with the kingdom of Serbia in the immediate aftermath of the war. As Habsburg military and political authority melted away in October 1918, enthusiasm for the Yugoslav idea reached a crescendo in the region's urban centers. On 6 October, the major Croat, Serb, and Slovene political parties formed a Zagreb-based representative body called the National Council of the Slovenes, Croats, and Serbs. On 29 October, the Croatian *Sabor* (parliament) declared Croatia's (including Dalmatia) independence and simultaneously declared its merger into a state of the Slovenes, Croats, and Serbs *of the (former) Habsburg lands*, under the authority of the National Council. Such was the enthusiasm over Yugoslav unity at this juncture that the anti-Serb Frankist party declared its own dissolution. (It was soon to reappear.)

While all this was going on, the exiled Yugoslav activists (organized into the Yugoslav National Committee) were trying to negotiate with the Serbian government over the terms for a union of Serbia and the Habsburg South Slav lands – terms that would provide for powersharing and confederal arrangements among the three major nationalities (see Chapter 5).

A variety of factors, among them the need to act swiftly in the face of Italian territorial claims and military moves in Istria and Dalmatia, conspired to pressure the National Council in Zagreb into bypassing the Yugoslav National Committee and accepting an essentially unconditional merger of the Habsburg South Slav lands with Serbia on 1 December. But one of the most critical elements that led to this development was the terror that the Green Cadres inspired in the hearts of the Croat middle class, which feared the spread of violence to the region's towns and cities. With Habsburg forces gone from the scene, and with insufficient ability to maintain order on its own, the Croatian political elite looked to the army of the restored Serbian state as the most ready-to-hand source of salvation from the threat of social revolution and what it saw as peasant Bolshevism. On 5 November, the harried National Council had issued an appeal for Serbian troops to be sent in to restore order. Serbia complied, and by the middle of November, most regions had been forcefully pacified and Serbian troops were in occupation of much of Croatia (among other formerly Habsburg territories). In the hasty political negotiations that ensued, the Serb wing of the HSK dominated the deliberations of the National Council, while Croat leaders felt ill-equipped to resist.[43] Hence the ease with which Belgrade secured an agreement providing for the union of the Habsburg South Slavs with Serbia under the Serbian royal house, with only the vaguest lip service being paid to the protection of non-Serbs' collective rights within the new entity. It is a bitter historical irony that the terms for the establishment of a united Yugoslav state were determined more by the Croats' internal disunity and the Serbian regime's shortsighted opportunism than by the overarching strength of Serb–Croat–Slovene solidarity.

Synopsis

Péter Hanák's study of Habsburg public opinion during the war suggests that the conflict awakened a wide variety of political sentiments among members of subject nationalities. The general political apathy and passive sense of suffering of the first two years of conflict gave way from early 1917 on to more active anticipation of, and widespread engagement in, radical social-political activism. Dramatic external events served to stimulate new fears and expectations during the latter period: key watersheds were marked by the death of Franz Joseph in November 1916, the overthrow of the tsar in March 1917, the American declaration of war in the following month, the Bolshevik Revolution of November

1917, and the Russo-Central Powers Peace of Brest-Litovsk of March 1918. Perceptions of the opportunities and dangers that such events created varied across social classes. Middle-class people began to focus on the possibility of gaining national independence if the Allies – with the Americans now at their side – won the war; they feared the possibility of social revolution inspired by events in Russia. For their part, during late 1917 through early 1918, many peasants, laborers, working women, and other segments of the underclasses took a strong and positive interest in the possibility of a socialist revolution that would bring about an early end to the conflict on all fronts.

Ultimately, actions speak louder than words: lower-class sympathy for revolutionary causes did not automatically erase ethnic boundaries. Hence the failure of the Austro-German and Magyar strike movement of January 1918 to win active support among the majority of the Czech industrial proletariat: public opinion among members of all Czech classes had to a large extent converged around a common sense of being the victims of exploitation by non-Czechs. Social change was still hoped for by the working class, but it could only come, most of them believed, within the framework of national self-determination. The failure of the strike movement, in turn, convinced many lower-class members of ethnic minorities across the length and breadth of the Habsburg monarchy that social revolution had poor prospects, leaving national independence as the likeliest scenario for bringing about some sort of change for the better.[44]

While ethnic boundaries stood in the way of socialist internationalism, they did not necessarily foster unity within individual nationalities. The degree of social consensus prevalent within any ethnic group was dependent on a variety of factors; the contrast between the Czech and Croat cases is quite striking in this respect. The longstanding political conflict, cultural clash, and economic rivalry with the ethnic Germans of Bohemia provided a common foe for Czech workers, bourgeoisie, and peasantry alike. Wartime trends in both the foreign policy and domestic politics of Austria created the impression among Czechs of all classes that the Habsburg state was itself becoming nothing more than the tool of German interests, that the system therefore could not be reformed, and, hence, that national independence might be the only means of safeguarding Czech interests. Moreover, Czech national solidarity extended beyond the urban framework into the countryside – a function of the relatively high degree of integration between urban and rural economies and societies in Bohemia. (This pattern was less strongly developed in Moravia.) Finally, the prospect of a possible merger with Slovakia (see Chapter 5) was not a major source of division among Czechs; there was relatively little demographic overlap – and hence limited pre-existing tension – between the two groups, and Slovaks had no established polity of their own that might threaten to dominate a future union.

Among the Croats, the war seemed only to aggravate pre-existing uncertainties about the nature of national identity and to heighten tensions along multiple ethno-social axes. Should Croats look to Vienna to protect them from Budapest, or to the Hungarian authorities to shield them from the arbitrary wartime power of the Habsburg military? Were the Serbs natural, cultural, and political partners for Croats, or were they enemies of Catholicism who would ride roughshod over Croat rights and sensibilities in the event of Croatia's merger with the Serbian kingdom? Sentiments on such issues swayed back and forth over time and divided Croats along ideological, class, and regional lines. In August 1914, Croatia's cities were the scenes of anti-Serb riots. Over the course of the war years, popular opinion in Croatia's urban centers did converge around a reinvigorated, if vaguely defined, Yugoslav ideal. But the Croat peasantry had little acquaintance with, or sympathy for, this notion. By the final months of the war, hard-pressed Croat peasants were venting their rage against Serb shopkeepers and Croat propertied classes alike. For Croatia's frightened urban elites, a hasty and poorly negotiated merger with Serbia represented not so much the fulfillment of a broadly shared national ideal as a quick escape route from their own hostile, rural underclass.

Ethnic identity, then, played a powerful role in shaping mass behavior throughout the Austro-Hungarian empire during the final stages of the war, and the war in turn contributed to a politicization of ethnicity. But fixing the cultural and territorial boundaries between nationalities, and determining the relationship between ethnicity and nationhood, were contentious issues that undermined the very unity that nationalism was supposed to foster. Similar paradoxes manifested themselves in the other two multinational empires during this period.

The Ethnic Dimension of War and Revolution in Russia

The overthrow of the tsarist regime in March 1917[45] took place against a backdrop of grotesque mismanagement of the war effort by a government neither psychologically nor organizationally capable of effectively mobilizing the country's human and natural resources. The initially successful Brusilov offensive of 1916 had disintegrated into a chaotic retreat as German forces pressed hard against a Russian army whose logistical infrastructure and morale were breaking down completely. The Provisional Government that replaced the tsar remained doggedly committed to the Allied cause, but its attempt to revive the Russian war effort only guaranteed its own undoing at the hands of the Bolsheviks, who seized power in a *coup d'état* in November 1917.

Wartime propaganda efforts in tsarist Russia had failed to create a sustainable framework of patriotic solidarity uniting society and state. The initial wave of optimistic faith in tsar, people, and motherland that spread swiftly through the urban and educated sectors of Russian society in August 1914 soon fragmented into a myriad of broken ripples and dangerous undertows. Dynastic imagery rapidly lost its popular appeal as a patriotic reference point, practically vanishing within months from media of high and popular culture alike and persisting only in the stodgy publications of officially endorsed propaganda organs. By the time it collapsed, the regime had succeeded in completely alienating all classes of society; even the most educated members of the liberal intelligentsia shared in the widespread but unfounded suspicion that the tsar or those close to him were actively colluding with the enemy. But if most Russians came to agree that the *ancien régime* did not embody the nation's identity, there was no consensus about what did.[46]

While the war aggravated the Russians' identity crisis, it accelerated the crystallization of national identities – or at least reinforced a collective sense of alienation from things Russian – among a number of the empire's minorities. Those most affected were groups stigmatized by the Russian military and administrative authorities as having dual loyalties. Ethnic Germans were an obvious target of such accusations. Ukrainians adhering to the Uniate Church were suspected of maintaining questionable ties with their brethren in Austrian-ruled Galicia, where, in turn, the brief Russian occupation of 1914–1915 was associated with the suppression of Ukrainian-language publications and harassment of Uniate clergy, further antagonizing both the local Ukrainian population and ethnic Ukrainian troops among the Russian occupation forces.[47] The Turkic peoples of Central Asia were assumed to sympathize with the Ottoman cause. The Jews were the objects of wild accusations of treachery and collusion with the enemy; the military authorities targeted them for wholesale deportation from western border regions, while the government effectively banned the publication of material in Hebrew characters.[48] Such reductionist images of peoples – disseminated through both official and unofficial propaganda, and acted upon through repressive or discriminatory policies – had a self-fulfilling quality. Forced into confining ethnic pigeonholes and labeled as threats to the welfare of Russia, people naturally became eager for "liberation" at the hands of the enemy and more inclined to think of themselves in unidimensionally ethnic terms.[49]

Ethnicity played an important role in determining the nature of non-Russians' participation in the war effort and in shaping their behavior as soldiers. Many of the nationalities of Siberia, the Caucasus, and Central Asia, as well as the Finns, were exempt from conscription.[50] As we shall see below, the government's violation of the conscription exemption in Central Asia provoked civil unrest in the region. In Finland, the exemption from conscription was honored by the Russian government, but the wartime influx of soldiers and sailors from the Russian army and of laborers from all over the empire assigned to build up Finland's coastal fortifications provoked xenophobic and racist sentiments among the Finnish population and intensified resentment of Russian rule, as did the economic hardships associated with the war.[51]

Among conscripts from those non-Russian nationalities that were subject to military service, desertion from the army's ranks was in most cases even more common than it was among the disaffected Russian peasant troops. Conversely, in cases where the prospect of foreign conquest had particularly ominous implications for a specific ethnic group, its soldiers' commitment to the war effort was unusually high. This was the case with Armenian volunteer units deployed in the Caucasus, whose familiarity with the Ottoman army's habit of slaughtering Armenian communities induced them to maintain a determined military resistance long after the front as a whole had collapsed. Likewise, Latvians formed a special volunteer rifleman force to help defend their territory against the Germans, because a German victory would presumably enable the Baltic Germans to indulge in an even more exploitative local hegemony than they already enjoyed.[52]

The common theme among these otherwise disparate attitudes and experiences is that they all demonstrate how the war reinforced the role of nationality in determining loyalties, defining identities, and creating frameworks for collective action. (Such frameworks could quickly change into arenas for civil strife – but they were no less significant for that.) These patterns became all the more pronounced when the all-encompassing, Russian-imperial frame of reference fell to pieces in 1917.

Nationalism and Separatism under the Provisional Government

The Russian Revolution of March 1917 opened the floodgates to a raging torrent of conflicting social and political demands and agendas that ripped the state from its already fragile moorings and was ultimately to sweep it into the whirlpool of civil war. As the Russian military machine collapsed over the course of 1917, the distinction between army life and civilian sector, military affairs and domestic politics, became ever more blurred. Soldiers in the field formed soviets that pressed for egalitarian reforms within the army while cultivating close ties to left-wing parties active in the workers' soviets of Petrograd[53] and Moscow. Lenin's slogan of "land and peace" struck a particularly resonant chord among the peasant soldiers who made up the overwhelming majority of army conscripts, and the Bolshevized elements in the military played an important role in challenging the authority of the officer corps and the Provisional Government alike.[54] Tens of thousands of soldiers "voted with their feet" (as Lenin put it) by deserting their units and making their way back to their homes, where they added an additional element of violent discontent to the seething cauldron of socio-political conflict. Many of the non-Russian soldiers who deserted the ranks of the military (and they did so in even higher proportions than Russian soldiers) became actively involved in the ethnic conflicts and national-liberation struggles that engulfed the former empire's borderlands, as war against the Germans gave way to civil war.[55]

The formation of the Provisional Government had raised expectations for social and political reform at every level of society and in every region of the country. Resolutions, proclamations, and manifestos issued forth from every corner, and the redress of age-old grievances of every description was impatiently awaited. The various cabinets of March–November 1917 were dominated by coalitions led by either the liberal-democratic Constitutional Democrats (Kadets), the moderate socialist Right Socialist Revolutionaries (Right SRs), or both. The great workers' soviets of Petrograd and Moscow, dominated by a variety of socialist parties including both Right and Left SRs, Mensheviks, and Bolsheviks, were initially cooperative with the Provisional

Government, but soon drifted toward confrontation with it as its insistence on keeping Russia in the war alienated the lower classes and strengthened the hand of the Bolsheviks.

Most parties and movements spoke a common revolutionary idiom of democratic rights and political freedom. But similar words and slogans could take on very different meanings depending on who uttered them and in what context. For radical socialists, the achievement of political democracy was conditioned on the liberation of workers and peasants from economic exploitation; the soviets came to be seen by many as more legitimate repositories of the people's will than the Provisional Government.

The meaning of the popular phrase "national self-determination" was also hotly contested. Democratization and the recognition of popular sovereignty were widely seen as going hand-in-hand with some form of self-rule for individual peoples. Under pressure from the Petrograd Soviet, the Provisional Government justified its continued commitment to the war effort on the grounds that Russia was fighting for a new European order based on the democratic principle of national self-determination.[56] The same concept was frequently mentioned as a guiding principle in the prospective restructuring of the Russian state itself. But did the phrase mean local autonomy for all ethnic groups, or only for those groups that could point to some historical precedent for such a privilege? Did it imply the right to secede altogether from the Russian state?

The Provisional Government was eager to gain widespread legitimacy among the peoples of the empire, yet by the same token, it was afraid of seeing the principle of national self-determination taken to its logical conclusion, which would mean the fragmentation of the entire state. This sort of ambivalence had typified the pre-war attitudes of the two parties that dominated the Provisional Government. The Kadets were on record as favoring cultural autonomy for all nationalities and the restoration of administrative/political autonomy to Finland and Poland; they were opposed to the federalization of the Russian state as a whole on the ground that this would exacerbate ethnic tensions rather than resolve them. The Socialist Revolutionaries' official platform did endorse "the widest possible application of the federal principle to the relations among the individual nationalities," but the party was riven by internal differences over how far the implementation of such a policy could go without causing economic fragmentation and undermining class consciousness.[57]

Upon coming to power, the Provisional Government did away with all legislation discriminating against ethnic and religious minorities and established full civic equality as the basis of the legal system. It also declared its recognition of the Finnish people's right to "internal independence" and issued a proclamation recognizing the right of Poland to self-government.[58] Petrograd's official stance toward other autonomy movements was that the idea of reorganizing Russia as a democratic federation of nationalities – as advocated by a congress of the non-Russian peoples of the Russian empire that met in Kiev in September – was fine in principle, but that the Provisional Government lacked the authority to implement such a policy. Any serious initiative would have to await the election of a

Constituent Assembly. This stance was regarded by nationalist leaders as so much legalistic quibbling that ill-concealed the persistence of Great Russian chauvinism among the country's new leadership. As if to confirm the perception that it could not break with the past, Petrograd proved unwilling or unable to negotiate a compromise even with the leaders of the newly reinstated Finnish parliament (*sejm*), dissolving the assembly instead.

As in its relationship with the soviets and as in its commitment to the war effort, so too in its nationalities policy, the Provisional Government was unable to keep pace with a rising tide of emancipatory expectations. The more it resisted demands for the immediate decentralization and federalization of government, the more it alienated its erstwhile supporters among the intelligentsia and nationalist leaderships of the non-Russian peoples. The lower classes of every ethnic group were embittered by the government's insistence on continuing a draining war effort that seemed ever more futile and purposeless. By November, when the Bolsheviks seized power in a carefully orchestrated coup, the Provisional Government no longer enjoyed mass support in the Russian urban centers, the countryside, or the non-Russian periphery. Moreover, their disappointing relationship with the Petrograd authorities led some nationalists to question whether liberal-democratic, parliamentary values and institutions were really as compatible with nationalist agendas as they had thought (see Chapter 6).

The Socio-Cultural Bases of Ethnic Unrest

The official records of nationalist assemblies and councils that passed resolutions and issued proclamations during 1917 would seem to suggest that every ethnic minority in the country was united in its single-minded determination to achieve self-rule either within a federated union or through outright secession. The truth is that some of these documents were produced by deliberative assemblies that were representative of little more than themselves. Most notably, in the case of Belorussia, where the nationalist Hromada Party organized a National Congress that attempted to establish an independent republic in December 1917, no echo of support for its stance could be discerned among the peasantry that made up the overwhelming majority of the Belorussian population. The group of disgruntled intellectuals who took this dramatic plunge into the nation-building enterprise were members of a tiny Belorussian urban population that was overwhelmingly outnumbered by Poles and Jews even in Minsk, the capital of the new republic. Indeed, in the elections to the Constituent Assembly (conducted over the course of two weeks in November–December 1917), the Bolsheviks had won over 60 per cent of the vote in Belorussia, suggesting that Lenin's slogan of "land and peace" was more appealing to the typical Belorussian peasant than "national self-determination."[59] The only reason the Hromada's proclamation of an independent state had any practical significance at all was that it was followed in February 1918 by a German military advance into Belorussia, whereupon the German high command embraced the idea of a nominally independent state as a convenient fig leaf for the imposition of German rule.[60] German conquest also provided the backdrop for the Latvian declaration of independence.

Yet many of the nationalist movements that were active during this period clearly were able to evoke a positive response among the masses on whose behalf they claimed to speak. Across the length and breadth of the country, economic devastation and the fragmentation of the country's political institutions had cast many communities adrift, forced to fend for themselves in the midst of a Hobbesian nightmare. As any semblance of rule of law vanished into thin air, people turned for help to social networks based on shared cultural identities and common material interests. The attraction of utopian political fantasies based on ethnic separatism and/or social revolution increased correspondingly. Indeed, Ronald Suny has argued that it was in those cases where nationalist agendas could be coupled with socio-economic grievances that political movements were most successful at generating significant support among the masses.[61]

By looking at a few cases out of the hundreds of ethnic groups in the Russian empire, we can gain a sense both of the powerful impetus that the events of this period gave to the spread of nationalist ideas among the popular classes of many nationalities, and of the uncertainties and conflicts that arose as people from different social strata and regions strove to define what, if anything, they had in common as a nation. The Ukrainian example highlights the ambiguity and volatility of the relationship between rapidly evolving class and national identities. An overview of political activism among Russia's Muslims underlines the dilemmas and contradictions involved in defining the geographical boundaries of nationhood.

In the Ukraine,[62] following the tsar's fall, the major nationalist parties convened a national council (Rada) in Kiev. Unanimously electing Mykhailo Hrushevsky as its President, the Rada declared its support for the Provisional Government and put forth demands for Ukrainian self-rule. Petrograd responded ambivalently. It expressed respect for the democratic rights of the Ukrainian people, while insisting on its right to appoint administrators and officials in Ukrainian provinces, rather than ceding that power to the Rada. In June–July, Petrograd beat a tactical retreat, recognizing the Rada as a channel for the transmission of the central government's authority. After a period during which the Rada attempted to cooperate with the Provisional Government on the basis of this ambiguous understanding, it became clear that Petrograd's and Kiev's respective interpretations of the agreement were mutually incompatible. Mounting tensions culminated in November 1917 in the Rada's extension of support to the Bolsheviks in expelling military units loyal to the Provisional Government from some of the Ukraine's major cities. This was immediately followed by the proclamation of a Ukrainian People's Republic.[63]

The evolution of the Petrograd–Kiev relationship was strongly influenced by the pressures of Ukrainian mass politics during this period. The moderate tone of the Rada's initial demands ran against the currents of social and political radicalism that were sweeping across the Ukrainian peasantry in 1917. Popular demands for economic change became closely linked to calls for a tougher stance on the issue of national self-determination. This grassroots movement contributed to a hardening of the Rada's position, as did the increasingly transparent avoidance tactics of the Russian Provisional Government.

The two main catalysts of nationalist radicalization among the Ukrainian peasantry were conscripts' experience of the war and the almost universal resentment of prevalent land-ownership patterns. Compulsory service in the military removed peasants from the narrow radius of their rural existence and brought them into closer-than-comfortable contact with members of unfamiliar ethnic groups as well as with co-ethnics from all over the Ukraine. This must have heightened their awareness of how much more they had in common with fellow conscripts who spoke the same language than they did with those whose customs and tongues were alien and unfamiliar to them. The brutality of the war reinforced the crystallization of ethnic affinities. Hostility came to focus not so much on the officially designated German or Austro-Hungarian enemy as on the Russian-dominated officer corps that was sending conscripts to their deaths. Soon after word of the March Revolution reached the front, Ukrainian soldiers – modeling themselves on the Polish military formations that were taking shape with Petrograd's blessing at this time – began forming organizations that looked to the Rada for leadership and that called for the creation of separate Ukrainian military units. (A parallel process took place among soldiers of many other non-Russian nationalities.) Soldiers based in Kiev organized Ukrainian Military Congresses that convened in May and then again – in defiance of Petrograd's orders to the contrary – in June and October. These volatile assemblies were fora for the articulation of radical demands for full political autonomy regardless of the Provisional Government's legalistic hesitations.

Among the Ukrainian peasantry, the political upheavals of 1917 gave rise to an intense expectation of salvation from economic exploitation and deprivation. This took concrete form in the demand for an immediate redistribution of land, away from the mostly Polish and Russian gentry and to the Ukrainian peasantry.[64] The Rada's attempts to negotiate a political compromise with Petrograd during the summer of 1917 held little interest for villagers who were eager to attain their vision of social justice in the agrarian sphere – a vision that was linked to demands for self-rule. It was widely recognized that a land-reform program implemented on a Russia-wide basis might entail the distribution of some of the Ukraine's productive land to "immigrants" from other parts of the country. Moreover, the communal land-tenure system common among Russian peasants was alien to many Ukrainian villagers, who were more accustomed to private ownership. For Ukrainian peasant organizations, therefore, the attainment of political autonomy seemed like an essential precondition for implementing a successful land-reform program on their own terms. As the months slipped by with no apparent move either toward the redistribution of land or toward the clear-cut attainment of Ukrainian autonomy, peasant support for the Rada declined precipitously. At the All-Ukrainian Peasant Congresses of 1917, this sense of frustration expressed itself in increasingly strident demands for Ukrainian self-rule and for a complete break, if necessary, with the Provisional Government.

It was those Ukrainian parties that were able to link the nationalist agenda to the socio-economic grievances of the rural population that gained the broadest support among the masses. The Rada was originally dominated by a coalition of liberal-democratic intellectuals calling themselves the Society of Ukrainian Progressives (TUP was their Ukrainian acronym), a group that Hrushevsky was closely associated with. Although they advocated Ukrainian autonomy, the TUP's leaders were also committed to working in cooperation with liberal-democratic forces in Russia. As the months went by, the TUP found itself isolated in a Rada whose political complexion was steadily becoming more radical under mounting pressure from peasants and soldiers. The TUP soon gave way to a coalition dominated by Ukrainian Social Democrats (USDs), who formed the dominant element during the period of negotiations with Petrograd. The USDs had once been opposed to Ukrainian nationalism on Marxist doctrinal grounds, and were now trying to soften their position in light of popular enthusiasm for the idea of self-rule. However, their failure to achieve a clear-cut agreement with the Petrograd authorities on Ukrainian autonomy, combined with their reluctance to take unilateral action outside a negotiated framework, strengthened the hand of the Ukrainian Socialist Revolutionaries (USRs). The USRs attacked the USDs for their legalistic preoccupations, insisting that the nationalization and redistribution of land within the context of a fully autonomous Ukraine must commence immediately, regardless of whether or not prior agreement had been reached with the Provisional Government. This platform earned the USRs widespread support in local elections, and the surge of popular enthusiasm for the USRs convinced Hrushevsky to join them as their leader. To his shocked former allies in the TUP, Hrushevsky explained that the USRs' radical stance reflected the will of the people; to ignore it or resist it was to swim against the current of history and to violate the populist principles on which his idea of the Ukrainian national movement had always been based.

In practice, the Rada could not enforce its authority in much of the countryside, where, in the context of a growing power vacuum, rogue Cossack units and local peasant militias ran amok, attacking the gentry and seizing lands. The less control it exercised, the more eager the Rada's leadership became to adopt extreme measures that might gain it a loyal following among the masses. The growing pressure from the peasants' and soldiers' congresses and the initiatives of the Ukrainian Socialist Revolutionaries pushed the Rada toward open confrontation with the Provisional Government. The Rada's support for the Bolshevik forces in Kiev in November was the product of a strictly tactical alliance, designed to end Petrograd's authority in the region once and for all and to facilitate the establishment of Ukrainian political independence. Pro-independence sentiment among the peasantry may have had more to do with its eagerness for a land-reform program whose benefits would not be shared with outsiders than with the nationalist ideology of the intelligentsia; nonetheless, mass support for political separation had played a critical role in the developments leading up to the Rada's proclamation of the Ukrainian People's Republic.[65]

Representatives of Russia's Islamic peoples responded to the March Revolution by organizing All-Russian Muslim Congresses that met in Moscow and Kazan during the summer of 1917, and by forming a twenty-five-member, Moscow-based, Muslim National Council (*milli shura*, commonly referred to simply as the Shura) designed to promote Muslim interests throughout Russia. Unfortunately, it proved very difficult to reach a consensus on what the nature of those interests were. Not only were there tensions between conservative clerics and Jadids, but the sudden opportunity of taking political action revealed deep divisions among the reformist elements themselves. The Volga Tatars who dominated the Congresses represented a population that had lived cheek-by-jowl with Russians for centuries and that had successfully carved out a socio-economic niche for itself in the Russian empire by developing a large and enterprising commercial middle class. Their reformers were the most secular in orientation and most fully versed in parliamentary politics and modern administrative techniques. Many of them embraced Socialist Revolutionary or Menshevik political programs, while most other progressive Muslim elites were affiliated with the Kadets. Given that the Volga Tatars lived in the midst of ethnic Russians, and that their commercial interests extended throughout the empire, their leaders advocated support for the principle of extraterritorial cultural autonomy. The Central Asian and Caucasus representatives hailed from economically underdeveloped provinces where the rapid influx of Russian colonists presented an immediate threat to the livelihoods and lifestyles of the indigenous populations; territorial autonomy seemed much more relevant to their needs. Moreover, the idea of extraterritorial autonomy raised the prospect of a central administrative body in charge of Muslim affairs throughout Russia – just the sort of institution that the Volga Tatars would be well positioned to dominate.

The Muslim Congresses sought to paper over such conflicts by passing resolutions in favor of extraterritorial cultural autonomy for all Muslims in the country as well as territorial autonomy for individual Muslim peoples, but this compromise did little to foster substantive cooperation. Their superior organizational and rhetorical talents allowed the Tatars to dominate the Shura, where they continued to promote their idea of extraterritorial autonomy, while many nationalists in Central Asia and Azerbaijan rejected the Shura's authority and formed their own councils in their home regions. Meanwhile, the Provisional Government's reluctance to commit itself to any form of autonomy disillusioned all the Muslim groups and further undermined the Muslim National Council's authority. The Muslim National Assembly (*majlis*) that was convened in Ufa in November 1917 did not last more than two months. As the Russian state itself fell to pieces, the geographic diffuseness of its Muslim populations put an end to any pretense of concerted action among them.[66]

These circumstances tended to bring regional and ethnic identities to the political foreground in many of Russia's Muslim lands. Although pan-Islamic and pan-Turkist themes continued to play an important role, mass support was most readily mobilized around immediate economic issues that were linked to local ethnic conflicts. A notable example is that of the Kazakhs, who had played a central role in the first major wartime revolt in Russia in 1916. The traditional exemption from conscription enjoyed by Central Asian Muslims was abolished in 1916, when the tsarist regime – hard pressed for manpower resources – announced that able-bodied men were to form labor brigades that would serve behind the front lines. This provoked rebellions in the cities and agricultural regions of Turkestan, but it was the Kazakh pastoralists of the steppe who offered the most stubborn resistance. For decades, the tsarist state had been turning over Kazakh lands to Russian agricultural colonists, limiting the pasture available for Kazakh livestock, and circumscribing the nomads' freedom of movement. The conscription order was seen as the latest in a series of attacks on the Kazakh way of life; only the most ruthless severity enabled the Russian army to suppress the ensuing uprising. In its wake, an even more aggressive encroachment on Kazakh grazing rights was initiated by Russian settlers who now felt free to slaughter those who stood in their way with complete impunity.[67]

Traditional tribal leaders and Muslim clerics played key roles in leading and encouraging the rebels, while the handful of secular (Kadet-affiliated) Kazakh nationalists who ran the newspaper *Qazaq* initially advocated compliance with the conscription order as a means of winning concessions from the Russian government. Their alienation from popular sentiment was short lived, though, for the failure of the rebellion discredited the traditional Kazakh leadership and the subsequent fall of the tsarist government created a new political environment that favored the secular intellectuals who were capable of engaging in the revolutionary discourse of 1917. The group, organized around the editorial board of *Qazaq*, took the lead in articulating disappointment with the All-Muslim Congresses and frustration with the Provisional Government's reticence on the nationalities issue. A series of Kazakh political congresses organized by the *Qazaq* group culminated in November 1917 (just after the fall of the Provisional Government) in the proclamation of an autonomous Kazakh governing council called the *Alash Orda*.[68]

In the eyes of the Kazakh nationalists, economic interests and ethnic identity were inextricably intertwined, for the pastoral existence that constituted the basis of the Kazakh masses' economic livelihood was also a defining element of their ethno-cultural identity. The spread of Russian colonists and the impositions of the Russian state threatened to destroy this people's entire way of life; the cultivation of the Kazakh language and culture was a vital element in building up the population's will to resist. The contributors to *Qazaq* made a point of using the Kazakh language rather than Tatar as their medium of communication. They also sought to link their secularism to a specifically Kazakh ethnic identity by playing up the fact that conversion to Islam had come late for most Kazakhs. Indeed, Islamization of the Kazakhs had been initiated in the eighteenth century by Volga Tatar missionaries with the encouragement of Catherine the Great, who hoped that conversion would lead the unruly steppe nomads to emulate their pacific and civilized Tatar brethren. In a sense, then, Islam could be portrayed as a legacy of Russian cultural imperialism![69]

For the leaders of the *Alash Orda*, then, secularization and modernization could in fact reinvigorate the national culture: a progressive educational system could be used to teach Kazakhs how to read and write their own language as well as how to employ more efficient livestock-raising techniques. This would facilitate an adaptation to modern economic conditions within a framework that drew on elements from the Kazakhs' traditional nomadic lifestyle. The reactionary influence of Islamic law (*shariat*) would give way to a progressive legal system that would draw its legitimacy from tribal custom (*adat*). The emancipation of women from the restrictive practices of Islam would allow them to contribute their full energies to the building of the nation.

In Azerbaijan, the Musavat Party commanded overwhelming support among local Muslims during 1917–1920 by promoting a vague but appealing platform that mixed Marxist social reformism with an ill-defined nationalism directed against Russian imperial domination, but more specifically against the domination of regional economic and political life by the Armenian and Russian commercial and working classes of the oil city of Baku. The leader of the Musavat had been in the forefront of opposition to the Tatar program of extraterritorial autonomy for Russia's Muslims and in favor of outright federalism at the Muslim Congress of May 1917. What actually constituted the framework for the national identity of Azerbaijani Muslims was left unclear. There had for many decades been a debate between advocates of a literary language based on local dialects and supporters of Gasprinsky's pan-Turkic lingua franca (see Chapter 3). Some Musavat leaders had a history of active pan-Turkism with an orientation toward Istanbul, and the party essentially welcomed the advance of Ottoman troops into the region with open arms in 1918. It was the actual experience of occupation by the Ottoman military, which violated its professions of fraternal amity by pursuing politically repressive policies, that led to the definitive alienation of the Musavat from pan-Turkism and its unambiguous turn toward an avowedly Azerbaijani nationalism.[70]

Thus, the impact of the war and the chaos of the revolution had damaged the credibility of traditional leaders and undermined the geopolitical frames of reference of the pan-Turkist and pan-Islamic Jadids. In the case of the Kazakhs, the resultant political void was filled by a tiny group of intellectuals associated with a specifically Kazakh ethnonationalism, while the Musavat turned in a similar direction in Azerbaijan. Ethnic and/or regional loyalties prevailed over broader constructions of national identity elsewhere as well. The Jadids of Turkestan gathered in Kokand to proclaim the formation of a Turkestan Autonomous Government in November–December 1917, but Khiva and Bukhara – the cultural capital of Turkestan – remained under the control of their emirs. Although he was willing to form a tactical alliance against the Bolsheviks with the Kokand government, the Emir of Bukhara resisted the Bukharan Jadids' attempts to gain power in his own realm and found it easy to convince the urban mob that these secular intellectuals were apostates who had more in common with the hated Russians than with their own people.[71]

In general, then, Islamic identity played a central role in setting Turkic and other Muslim peoples apart from Russian administrators and settlers; yet it was not a sufficient basis for concerted action on a Russia-wide scale given the absence of a cohesive organizational infrastructure and the collapse of the Russian state itself as a unified forum of activity. Local issues – and hence narrowly defined ethno-cultural and/or regional identities – formed the most meaningful context for political action in the Muslim areas of the empire as they did in many of the non-Muslim regions.

What general conclusions can one draw from the wide spectrum of responses that the events of 1917 elicited from Russia's nationalities? Ronald Grigor Suny has argued that class and ethnic identities cannot be understood in isolation from one another in the context of the Russian Revolution.[72] Both were fluid and conditional forms of self-definition that were constantly being reshaped by ongoing socio-cultural developments and that had a decisive influence on each other's development. In the case of the Armenians, who faced an imminent prospect of physical annihilation at the hands of the advancing Ottoman army in 1918, all social strata united under the banner of the Dashnaktsutiun – an ostensibly socialist-revolutionary organization that functioned in practice as a national-liberation movement for Armenians of all classes. In the case of the Latvians and Belorussians, groups that were composed overwhelmingly of impoverished peasants, an end to the war and a redistribution of land were over-riding priorities that overshadowed any faint glimmerings of national consciousness. This was reflected in their overwhelming support for the Bolsheviks, rather than for their "own" nationalist parties, in the elections for the Constituent Assembly in November 1917. The formation of an independent Latvian state was a byproduct of the German army's conquest of the region in 1918, rather than of an upsurge of popular enthusiasm for national liberation.

It is between the two ends of the nation–class spectrum, Suny contends, that most forms of group identity lay. Thus, the Ukrainian peasant masses were attracted to the nationalist rhetoric and imagery of the Ukrainian Socialist Revolutionaries because the latter linked material grievances to ethnic identity in a manner that resonated among the populace. The slogan of returning Ukrainian land to the Ukrainian people took on a powerful double-meaning, evoking both the issue of the peasantry's relationship to farmland and the nation's relationship to the national territory. When the advancing German army set up a socially reactionary Ukrainian puppet state in 1918, mass support for the nationalist idea dissipated, and the Bolsheviks were subsequently able to gain a broad popular following in the Ukraine as they in turn held forth the prospect of land redistribution. Nationalism in and of itself had no meaning for the masses; only as a medium for the expression of the Ukrainian peasantry's identity and interests *as peasants* did it enjoy mass appeal.

Suny points to Georgia as a case where common ethnic identity provided a framework for the development of a broad-based socialist consciousness. Georgian peasants and gentry alike resented the influence wielded over the rural economy by the largely Armenian commercial and manufacturing classes of the cities. The Georgian intelligentsia (many of whom had roots in the gentry) were drawn to the Marxist discourse that attacked the role of the bourgeoisie, and hence created a coherent ideological framework for opposition to the ethnically alien urban elites. The result was an unusual fusing of socialist internationalism with national identity under the rubric of the Georgian branch of the Menshevik Party. The Georgian Mensheviks, who retained a virtual monopoly of mass support during the period of the Russian Revolution and Civil War, remained committed throughout 1917 to working for social and political change within the overall framework of a reformed Russian state. It was only with the collapse of the Russian state amidst the ongoing advance of Turkish forces that they were left with no option but to go it alone at the head of an independent nation-state.

Suny's approach emphasizes the subjective, cultural basis of collective consciousness. He rejects static and objective definitions of group identity, arguing that class and nation are mutable frameworks of self-understanding rather than fixed compartments of scientific classification. As such, there need be no conflict between them – class consciousness and ethnic identity often evolved into two parts of a seamless whole under the pressures of war and revolution. By the same token, changing conditions (such as the creation of reactionary puppet states by the German occupation forces) could tear apart such syntheses even more quickly than they had been formed, alienating the lowest strata of society from the nationalist paradigm and sending them into the arms of the Bolsheviks.

While, in general, Suny's paradigm constitutes an excellent tool for the analysis of mass politics during the war, it does contain an inherent contradiction. In his theoretical formulation, which draws on the methodology and vocabulary of post-modernism, he emphasizes the centrality of collective discourse in the constitution of popular identities, yet goes on to contend that the process does not inherently favor either class or nation as the framework for the definition of collective consciousness. Surely, though, his own work strongly suggests that sharing a common culture and common language is a fundamental prerequisite for conducting a meaningful discourse, and therefore an almost indispensable precondition for the crystallization of political identity. Class identity could easily become a dominant reference point *within* an ethnic group, as among the Ukrainian peasantry, and this could then serve to hinder or facilitate the consolidation of a national identity, depending on how effectively the nationalist leadership played to its mass audience. But whereas common ethnic identity was often successfully used to create bonds among different classes, class identity rarely transcended the ethnic divide. The Belorussian peasants' electoral support for the Bolsheviks should probably not be taken as an indication that they had a strong sense of class solidarity with the workers and peasants of all Russia. That would represent a highly unlikely leap from local bonds of kinship and village community to sophisticated internationalist consciousness. A more plausible explanation would be that among rural ethnic groups that did not yet have a strong sense of distinctive national identity, the Bolsheviks' rejection of official state patriotism and their promises of peace and land spoke directly to the immediate, local, and personal concerns of illiterate peasants. Where class did serve as the framework for the formation of an imagined community broader than that of the immediate village, it usually did so *within the bounds* of an ethnic group rather than across cultural and linguistic frontiers. Ultimately, as Suny himself points out, the Belorussians proved to be one of the easiest ethnic groups for the Bolshevik state to absorb precisely because their linguistic and cultural characteristics (dare one say their objective ethnic characteristics?) were already so similar to those of the Russians.[73] Similar factors may have contributed to the inconsistency of Ukrainian peasants' attachment to separatist nationalism.

The case of the Latvians does stand out as an anomaly, for the Latvian Bolsheviks were a highly active and engaged component of Lenin's movement who were able to tap into genuinely widespread popular support among their own ethnic group for their avowedly internationalist position. The Latvian language was very distinctive (it was not even Slavic) and literacy rates among Latvians were among the highest in the Russian empire, suggesting that even poor peasants in this region had broader mental horizons than their Belorussian counterparts. The Latvian volunteer riflemen who had fought the advancing German army during the war did not become a nationalist vanguard, but instead proved particularly sympathetic to the Bolsheviks, voting for them in overwhelming numbers in the elections to the Constituent Assembly.[74] A regiment of Latvian riflemen served as the Bolsheviks' Praetorian Guard in Petrograd in the wake of the November Revolution.[75] Had it not been for the German military occupation of Latvia in 1918, it is doubtful whether the middle-class nationalist parties would have been able to gain power.

Part of the explanation may lie in the fact that Latvia was a region where industrialization and commercialization of agriculture had proceeded faster than in almost any other part of the Russian empire. This had contributed to the rapid emergence of new classes with conflicting interests: in the cities, a relatively large Latvian working class resented the growing economic dominance of the Latvian bourgeoisie, whereas the countryside was divided between large numbers of landless peasants and a highly visible minority of relatively prosperous peasant proprietors. All of these groups resented the continued economic and administrative dominance of the Baltic German barons, but they were deeply divided over who should inherit the instruments of political authority once the German elite had been dealt with. Radical Marxism was thus able to tap into a broader popular base in Latvia than in any other part of the Russian empire. For their part, the middle-class nationalists' behavior in 1917 suggested that they did not plan on sharing power with the landless peasants or workers in a self-governing Latvia.[76]

Finally, the very anomalousness of Bolshevism's success in Latvia lent the Latvian Bolsheviks very high visibility and influence within Lenin's party. The support of the Latvian Social Democrats had played a critical role in Lenin's power struggles with the Mensheviks, and from the summer of 1917 on – at a time when the Russian army was generally disintegrating – the Latvian Bolsheviks were able to gain influence and maintain extraordinary discipline and enthusiasm among the riflemen by leading them to think of themselves as the spearhead of the coming socialist revolution.[77] For members of a tiny, long-oppressed ethnic group to assume a highly visible and distinguished role in the unfolding of events that would shape Russia and the world must have been particularly exhilarating – much more rewarding, in fact, than the prospect of vying for power with the Latvian bourgeoisie within the confines of a minuscule nation-state. The very uniqueness of their stance – and the opportunity it created for them to play a disproportionately prominent historico-political role – may have reinforced the commitment of the Latvian Bolsheviks and their supporters to the internationalist dream.[78] Ethnic identity certainly cannot be dismissed as an important factor contributing to the extraordinary solidarity and high motivation of the riflemen; it is just that the role they chose to play as a group was acted out on the grand stage of Russian revolutionary politics rather than in the sideshow of Latvian separatism.

The Provisional Government's failure to act resolutely on the nationalities issue had added to its many enemies and hastened its downfall. The Bolshevik regime that replaced it was to prove far more resolute – but not in the manner that Russia's nationalist and separatist movements might have hoped. As we shall see in Chapter 6, ethnic conflict overlapped with class and ideological conflict in the ensuing civil war, and led the Bolsheviks to formulate a novel approach to the problem of national identity in a socialist state.

The Burden of War in the Middle East

In considering the Ottoman empire in the Great War, it is worth bearing in mind a couple of broad distinguishing features that set it apart from the Austro-Hungarian and Russian cases. One is that the events of 1914 did not constitute quite as clearcut a watershed for Ottoman history as they did for the other two empires, given that the Ottomans had just been involved in three wars over the preceding three years. What with the major territorial losses (in Libya and the Balkans) associated with two of those wars and the ongoing upheaval of the Young Turk revolution, the Ottoman state was already in the midst of a dramatic political and ideological transformation at the time of its entry into the Great War on the Central Powers' side in November 1914. 1914 marked the beginning of a new phase in this transformative process rather than an unheralded departure from previous experience.

Second, the Young Turks maintained the state's cohesion to the very end of the conflict. Cohesion is a relative term, to be sure; throughout the war, individual provincial governors exercised considerable autonomy in the pursuit of their own political agendas and patronage interests.[79] But there was no sudden collapse of the empire or dramatic breaking away of its provinces (other than the Hejaz – which had been only loosely controlled by Istanbul in the first place; see Chapter 5). During the final years of the conflict, the Ottoman army was steadily beaten back by British forces, but the Ottoman state remained intact to the end within whatever perimeter its military could hold. This was due in part to the earlier territorial and political transformations referred to above: the Ottomans had already lost their most independence-minded provinces in the Balkans in 1912–1913; their remaining territories were overwhelmingly Muslim in population and hence more amenable to continued rule by the Sultan-Caliph (who remained in place as a figurehead throughout the Young Turk period).

By the same token, the war did serve as a powerful catalyst for the intensification of previous transformative trends and the initiation of new ones. The fact that pan-Islamism might serve as an integrating rather than divisive ideology within the post-1913 territories of the empire was not lost upon the Young Turk rulers as they entered the fray in 1914. Yet even as they cynically revived this pre-revolutionary propaganda line, they forged ahead with the cultivation of Turkish nationalism – a nationalism now shorn of its erstwhile liberal accouterments and unabashedly chauvinistic and expansionist in its aims. And among the Arab population of the Levant and Mesopotamia, while the majority remained quiescent, a tiny activist minority was caught up in events that would later form the basis of a pan-Arab nationalist myth.

The Radicalization of Turkish Nationalism

The 1908 Revolution that brought the Young Turks to power was but the first in a series of dramatic events that were to alter radically the territorial and political configuration of the empire. From 1908 to 1913, the CUP's Central Committee ruled indirectly, as a secretive oversight body that dictated policy to the government without any public accountability. The Young Turks responded to mounting criticism in parliament by arranging for its dissolution in 1912 and using crude and violent tactics to ensure the election of a more compliant chamber. Leaders of opposition movements were forced underground or into exile. In 1913, renewed opposition combined with military setbacks and territorial losses in the Balkan Wars finally led the CUP to seize direct control of the reins of government, forming a cabinet dominated by Enver Pasha, Talat Pasha, and Jemal Pasha.[80] It was this triumvirate that engineered the Ottoman empire's entry into the First World War on what it gambled would be the winning German side, in the hopes of compensating for the recent humiliations by reconquering Egyptian and Transcaucasian lands lost to the British and Russians in earlier years.

The Young Turks tried to gain popular support for their policies through multiple propaganda campaigns designed to appeal to different sectors of the population. These campaigns were not necessarily consistent with one another, and some of them were more directly indicative of the governing elite's ideological predilections than were others. Specifically, the Turkish-nationalist elements of wartime propaganda appear to have reflected the political agenda of key leaders of the CUP, who saw the war not only as an opportunity to recoup some of the territorial losses of recent years but to fulfill ambitious pan-Turkist dreams.

The Ottomanist idea, to which the CUP had continued to pay lip service long after abandoning it in practice, was now almost completely discarded: a concept of interest to a handful of liberal intellectuals, it clearly was incapable of arousing the sort of mass passions needed to sustain a major military effort. On the other hand, pan-Islamism, which had been propagated by Sultan Abdülhamit's *ancien régime*, was now opportunistically seized upon by the secularist Young Turks as a means of generating support for the war among the Muslim masses of all nationalities. On the government's instructions, the Muslim religious authorities issued a proclamation, to which the Sultan (in his capacity as Caliph) also affixed his name, that defined Ottoman involvement in the war as a *jihad* (divinely sanctioned struggle) against the infidels. This was not only intended to unite Turks, Kurds, and Arabs in the struggle against the Triple Entente; the document also addressed the Muslim populations of the British, Russian, and French empires, calling upon them to rise up in arms against their oppressors.[81]

The separate theme of Turkish and pan-Turkist nationalism that was taken up by wartime propaganda organs in Anatolia was much more directly linked to the ideological convictions and political-administrative practices of the CUP in power.[82] The war served as both an opportunity and a catalyst for experimentation with extreme forms of ethnic nationalism. The course of Ottoman military campaigns over the war years further reinforced the belief that pan-Turkism held the key to the empire's future, as Arab lands were steadily lost to the British while the disintegration of the Russian empire appeared to open up fantastic opportunities for expansion into Turkic lands to the north.

The CUP's growing interest in Turkish nationalism had been powerfully spurred by the Balkan Wars of 1912–1913. The joint Serbian, Montenegrin, Greek, and Bulgarian attack on the Ottomans' remaining Balkan possessions had come as the Italians were completing their conquest of Tripolitania (Libya), which they had invaded in 1911. Rather than heralding the dawn of a new era of progress, the Young Turk revolution seemed only to have awakened the appetites of European states eager to take advantage of internal turmoil in Istanbul and reluctant to see the CUP consolidate control over the empire's outlying provinces. A shift in Balkan alliances enabled the Ottomans to regain control of the province of Adrianople (Edirne) in the Second Balkan War (1913), but Albania, Macedonia, and Thrace had been lost.

The Balkan Wars seemed to provide an object lesson in the power of nationalism. Most of the regions lost in the conflict were populated by non-Turks whose own nationalist impulses had clearly undermined the Ottoman grip over those territories; even the mostly Muslim Albanians had launched a revolt in 1910 in the face of the Young Turks' centralizing policies. On the other hand, some of the most successful actions of the Ottoman army had been conducted by a tightly knit group of Turkish officers under the leadership of Enver, many of whom had earlier volunteered to lead guerrilla operations against the Italians in North Africa. The success of these *fedaîler*'s (volunteers') operations against the Bulgarians had depended on the active support of the local Turkish-speaking population in Edirne and parts of Thrace.[83]

These experiences reinforced the sense that ethnic identity was a critical element in determining mass loyalties and that the future of the Ottoman empire depended largely on the Young Turks' ability to awaken nationalist passions among the Turkish populace. The succession of external military threats and internal political crises had also magnified the influence and prestige of the radical, Turkish-nationalist *fedaîler*, whose growing role as the strong arm of the CUP seemed indispensable. It is no coincidence, then, that the period of the Balkan Wars marked the beginning of the CUP's open sponsorship and encouragement of pan-Turkist propaganda. Most notably, it was in 1912–1913 that the CUP began to encourage the growth of a recently founded pan-Turkist organization called Türk Ocaği (Turkish Hearth). Led by prominent pan-Turkist intellectuals like Yusuf Akçura and Ağaoğlu Ahmet, Türk Ocaği established branches in many cities, where it organized cultural activities designed to foster the growth of pan-Turkist identity among the educated strata.

The Ottoman empire's entry into the First World War accelerated the growth of Turkish nationalist currents enjoying the government's thinly veiled support. Membership in pan-Turkist organizations expanded (the Istanbul chapter of Türk Ocaği boasted over 2,500 members – including many women – by 1918) and their propagandist efforts (pursued through a variety of media, including lectures, plays, and films) intensified. This trend was particularly apparent from 1916 on, when the failure of pan-Islamism to stir the Muslims of the world had become painfully apparent, while the decisive defeat of British-led forces at Gallipoli (the Allied expeditionary force was withdrawn in December 1915) stimulated a surge in popular patriotism among the Turkish urban population.[84] During the last year of the war, Britain's gains in Mesopotamia and steady advance into Palestine–Syria made the collapse of Russia to the north seem all the more providential: leaders such as Enver, who served as Ottoman war minister from 1914 to 1918, looked to a conquest of Transcaucasia and Turkestan as an imminently realizable objective that would not only compensate the empire for the loss of its Arab provinces, but allow it to reconstitute itself as a pan-Turkist superstate. Enver's *fedaîler* played an active role as agents trying to stir up rebellions among the Turkic peoples of Russia, as well as among Turkic and other Muslim groups as far afield as Iran, Afghanistan, and British-ruled India.[85] Enver went so far as to transfer units away from the collapsing Middle Eastern fronts in 1917–1918 in order to press forward into Transcaucasia, where the Musavat Party of Azerbaijan organized active collaboration with the Ottoman forces. Pan-Turkism, then, was not just a propaganda device; it was a political ideology that came to dominate the CUP's definition of state interest during the Ottoman empire's last years. Enver was to continue chasing his pan-Turkist dream after the war, assuming the leadership of anti-Bolshevik guerrilla forces (Basmachis) in Turkestan, where he met a violent end in 1922.[86]

While the grandiose ideal of pan-Turkism came to dominate the external outlook of the CUP's wartime leadership, these years also witnessed domestic policy initiatives that can best be described as Turkish nation-building efforts. Legislation introduced in 1916 further encroached upon the already limited juridical sphere of Muslim religious courts, consolidating civil authority in the hands of the state – and giving the lie to the pan-Islamic propaganda line that had, by now, virtually been abandoned.[87] In the economic arena, the governments of all major belligerents in the Great War found it necessary to undertake unprecedented interventions designed (with varying degrees of success) to marshal resources, allocate raw materials to key industries, ration supplies, and control inflation. In the Ottoman case, such efforts fell under the rubric of an ambitious nationalist agenda that promoted the consolidation of Turkish control over the Anatolian economy. The long-resented Capitulations (see Chapter 2) were abrogated as soon as war had broken out in Europe. This was followed up in the course of the war by initiatives designed to establish state supervision of the economy along proto-corporatist lines. State control, in turn, was employed in an effort to boost the economic power, entrepreneurial initiative, and technical skills of ethnic Turks. Differential tariff regimes were designed to shelter nascent domestic industries in selected manufacturing sectors; the state invested capital in the formation of new, Turkish-run banks and corporations, while encouraging the growth of ethnic-Turkish manufacturing and trading cooperatives and joint-stock companies; selected factory workers and peasants were sent to Germany to learn modern manufacturing and farming techniques. This was a nationalist *étatisme* designed to foster the development of a strong Turkish-dominated economic system led by a Turkish technocracy and Turkish bourgeoisie that would supplant the Armenian and Greek commercial classes that had long dominated the trade and financial sectors of the economy and were seen as having benefited from the Capitulations regime. Freeing Turkey from foreign encroachments was to go hand-in-hand with ridding it of the internal influence of "alien" ethnic groups.[88]

The actual implementation of these policies was haphazard and inconsistent, and in many respects only impeded the empire's ability to tolerate the strain of a drawn-out conflict. Government intervention in key economic sectors such as the grain trade simply created opportunities for rapacious profiteering by people with connections to the inner circle of the CUP. The incitement of mob violence against Greek and Armenian merchants led to the flight of thousands and the consequent disruption of essential commercial and financial networks; the Turks who were encouraged to seize their abandoned property and occupy their economic niches could hardly transform themselves into an entrepreneurial bourgeoisie overnight. Power struggles between military and civilian authorities, patronage politics, and the flouting of central authority by regional satraps all served to distort the vision of a streamlined, rationalized economy beyond recognition. The army's insatiable demand for manpower and provisions disrupted harvests, drained the rural economy, and combined with speculative grain hoarding to produce horrific deprivation and famine in Anatolia – which lost approximately 20 per cent of its population – as it did elsewhere in the empire, ultimately undermining the material backbone of the war effort itself.

Such profound difficulties only intensified the regime's quest for ideological mechanisms that could help sustain popular commitment to the war. Pan-Turkism was something of a double-edged sword in this respect, for while it provided a stirring rationale for pressing onward against the Russians, it also could be attacked insofar as it suggested that the already sorely pressed Anatolian Turks needed to share their resources with their soon-to-be-liberated Transcaucasian and Central Asian brothers. A separate propaganda line was accordingly developed that extolled the unique virtues and unparalleled patriotic sacrifices of Anatolian Turks. In light of the tremendous strain that conscription and requisitions were imposing on the Turkish peasantry, the CUP founded an organization called Halka Doğru (Toward the People) that romanticized the peasant lifestyle as the ideal manifestation of Turkish national character, in a manner reminiscent of the Russian populist tradition. In practice, however, participation in, and attendance at, the activities sponsored by Halka Doğru was essentially limited to urban, educated people. The organizers of Halka Doğru could talk rhapsodically *about* the peasant masses, but – like the Russian populists before them – found it difficult to communicate *with* them.[89]

Imbuing the masses with a new cultural and political identity based on unfamiliar intellectual constructs was an elusive goal; negative integration through the manipulation of ethnic tensions seemed to promise much more immediate rewards by channeling social tensions and resentments over wartime hardships away from the government. The systematic victimization of minorities became a stock-in-trade of the Young Turk regime during the war, and Enver's *fedaîler* appear to have been responsible for some of the most notorious episodes. Soon after the Balkan Wars, the *fedaîler* had been organized into a secret-operations unit called the Teşkilât-i Mahsusa (Special Organization), which answered to Enver's personal command. Teşkilât-i Mahsusa – whose core units were dominated by ethnic Turks, with regional auxiliary forces recruited from the Kurdish population in eastern Anatolia and Bedouin in Iraq – operated as a dirty-operations unit for Enver Pasha during the First World War. It carried out commando operations and guerrilla warfare against the British in Egypt and Iraq, while engaging in political assassinations and ethnic cleansing on the home front. The organization not only helped instigate the riots against the Greek and Armenian commercial classes in Anatolia's urban centers, but is also thought to have played a central role in organizing the wartime genocide of Anatolia's Armenian population.[90]

The outbreak of war with Russia immediately placed the Armenians in a dangerous position, as they straddled the frontier with the tsarist empire. Armenians on the Russian side of the border formed a special volunteer corps to fight the Ottoman army with a view to achieving the Dashnaktsutiun's goal of Armenian national self-determination. Despite the expressions of loyalty and commitment to the Ottoman war effort on the part of the Ottoman Armenian community's official leadership, the CUP's inner circle clearly regarded the presence of a potentially hostile population on the frontline as a potential menace. In the spring of 1915, an Armenian uprising broke out in the province of Van. Although nationalist activists had been trying to foment a rebellion, it seems that the revolt itself may have come in response to unprovoked anti-Armenian atrocities that had already taken place in the vicinity. In any event, the concerted nature of the CUP's response suggests that a plan of action had been ready well in advance of the Van uprising. Armenians throughout eastern Anatolia (not just the northeast provinces) were deported *en masse* to the Syrian desert under conditions that ensured massive loss of life. Kurdish peasant-soldiers and Teşkilât-i Mahsusa auxiliaries were incited to massacre the deportees along much of their route, and the result was the almost total eradication of Armenians from their traditional homeland. The number who died is conservatively estimated to have been between 600,000 and 800,000, and may well have been in excess of one million.[91]

The atrocities of 1915 should not be viewed simply as excesses associated with the clumsy implementation of improvised, wartime security measures. Strong indirect evidence suggests that leading figures within the governing circle of the CUP were responsible for deliberately turning the deportation into what amounted to genocide. The activities of Armenian radical activists in Anatolia may have served as a pretext for the regime's actions, but the geographic scope of the "deportations" and the scale of the killings suggest that they represented part of a sinister experiment in socio-political engineering designed to transform the demographic composition of Anatolia in line with radical pan-Turkist ideas. For the Young Turk leadership, the presence of a large Armenian population within the empire constituted a perennial opportunity for Great Power intervention in the Ottoman state's internal affairs. More fundamentally, the Armenians were seen as an unassimilable element that stood in the way of national integration and that constituted an unwelcome buffer between the Turks of Anatolia and the Turkic peoples of the Caucasus. The authorities may have convinced themselves that the deportations and massacres were essential for the successful prosecution of the war, but they may also have seen the war effort as a golden opportunity for pursuing a genocidal approach to national homogenization that would have been unthinkable in peacetime.[92]

Many of the nationalist policies pursued by the CUP were monumentally disastrous for the empire's war effort, yet laid the foundation for Mustafa Kemal's (Atatürk's) subsequent reinvention of Turkish nationalism. The Young Turks' economic nationalism destroyed vital Greek and Armenian commercial networks and created opportunities for rampant profiteering by a small number of well-connected Turkish merchants while the rest of the population suffered. Yet these policies formed the basic mold for the *étatisme* and nurturance of an ethnic-Turkish bourgeoisie that became the hallmarks of the postwar Turkish republic's economic policy. Pan-Turkism was an ideological mirage that distracted the empire's elites from the harsh realities of military defeat in the

Middle East and economic disaster on the home front. But Anatolian–Turkish nationalism rested on a firmer foundation of genuine patriotic enthusiasm among the urban population, especially in the wake of Britain's defeat at Gallipoli. Moreover, the wartime proliferation of clubs and organizations devoted to one form or another of Turkish nationalism created an institutional network that served as a framework for the organization of resistance to the Allied occupation forces following the defeat of the empire and the flight of the Young Turk leaders. Although Atatürk distanced himself from the legacy of the CUP in the aftermath of Ottoman defeat and presented himself as the father of a reborn Turkish nation, it is now widely recognized that much of the ideological and institutional infrastructure of Turkish nationhood was created by the wartime policies of the CUP.[93] What we see in retrospect is the curious spectacle of an empire's leadership trying to reinvent its state as a nation, destroying the empire in the process, and thus creating an opportunity for a successor state partially to realize its vision.

One of the fundamental contradictions faced by the Young Turks in their nation-building endeavors was that, until the final stages of the war, half the territory of their empire was populated by Arabs. Although the Arab provinces were lost in battle with the British rather than breaking away in rebellion, there is no question that the conditions of the Young Turks' wartime rule alienated significant sectors of Arab societies. More importantly for the long run, wartime abuses provided the essential ingredients for the creation of a myth of Arab martyrdom and resistance that was to form a legitimizing framework for Arab nationalism in subsequent years.

The Suppression of Dissent in the Arab Lands

The impact of the war on mass consciousness among the Arabs is very difficult to assess; there is a budding literature on mass political culture in Syria, Palestine, Lebanon, and Iraq in the aftermath of the conflict, but little material on the war years themselves. The Ottoman war effort took a heavy toll on the populations of the Arab Middle East, as it did on the empire's other populations. The combination of mass conscription, exorbitant tax rates, ruthless requisitioning, and Allied blockade wreaked economic havoc that was exacerbated by the speculative hoarding of grain by landlords. Famine and disease were widespread in the Levant (present-day Syria and Lebanon) causing hundreds of thousands of deaths. Material conditions were also very difficult in Mesopotamia (Iraq), where Turkish-commanded forces were engaged in a grueling campaign against an invading British–Indian army. The pre-war trend toward centralization and Turkification of the empire's administration accelerated sharply: Jemal Pasha, Ottoman navy minister and a member of the Young Turk triumvirate that ran the empire, assumed personal control of the territories comprising latter-day Syria, Lebanon, Palestine, and Transjordan, and proceeded to appoint his cronies to posts that had long been held by local notables.[94]

The oppressive burden of the Ottoman war effort contributed to the sporadic outbreak of popular revolts, especially among members of the Shiʿite Muslim underclass in places such as the Baʿalbek region in present-day Lebanon and the town of Najaf in Mesopotamia. Although members of the nationalist secret societies helped lead some of these outbreaks, they remained localized, isolated affairs, that were easily suppressed by the Ottoman military. (During General Allenby's military advance into Syria in 1918, armed uprisings did begin to break out on a wider scale behind Turkish lines.) It was only among the disaffected members of urban elites that any kind of geographically broad infrastructure existed for the systematic coordination of anti-Ottoman activities above and beyond the limited arena of local politics. The secret societies, al-Fatat and al-ʿAhd, were the principal fora for such conspiracies.

The wartime intensification of the CUP's abuses of power had deepened the sense of bitterness among those members of Arab notable families, usually the younger sons, who were being denied opportunities for upward mobility that their elders had been able to take for granted just a few years earlier. The responsibilities, perquisites, and status of holding public office were no longer theirs for the taking as the CUP extended its direct bureaucratic control over the region and as Jemal Pasha set up his own patronage system. The members of al-Fatat and al-ʿAhd readily linked their personal feelings of humiliation and frustration to the broader notion that Arab society as a whole – of which they were the natural leaders – was being oppressed. An Ottoman victory in the war could only make matters worse, for it would inevitably strengthen the grip of the Young Turks over the empire and lessen the prospects of political reform. The notion that the Arabs should break away altogether from the Ottoman empire to form an independent state, or confederation of states, thus gained ground among the tiny, but tightly knit, circles of the secret societies, whose wartime membership rose from less than 100 to nearly 200.

Like the founders of the Young Turk movement before them, the leaders of the Arab secret societies sought to broaden their circle of support by drawing military officers into their movement. Contacts were established with Arab officers in the Ottoman army as well as Bedouin chiefs in the hope of stimulating an anti-Ottoman uprising from within the ranks of the military and among the tribal groups. The chances of success for such a revolt would be increased immeasurably if it could be coordinated with British military operations. It was in the context of these plans that Faisal, son of the Sharif of Mecca, was secretly sworn in as a member of al-ʿAhd in 1915, during the first of his two wartime visits to Damascus. This was to set the stage for the revolt of the Hejaz, as we will see in Chapter 5.

In Syria itself, however, Jemal Pasha struck preemptive blows against the nationalist movement by hanging dozens of suspected nationalists in Beirut and Damascus, mostly on charges of collusion with the enemy stemming from their pre-war contacts with French and British diplomats. He also took the precautionary step of transferring a number of suspect Arab army divisions away from Syria. Even had it not been for these measures, it is highly unlikely that an armed rebellion would have had much prospect of success within Syria. The number of army officers in contact with the nationalists represented a minute fraction of the Syrian officer corps, and the very secrecy of organizations such as al-Fatat had limited their ability to agitate or propagandize on a mass scale. Among the dominant Sunni Muslim community, the official Ottoman call for Islamic solidarity against the British resonated at least as strongly as the notion of a distinctly Arab national destiny.

Although Jemal Pasha's repressions intensified anti-Turkish sentiments in the Arab world and provided material for the development of a nationalist marty-rology propagated by Arab nationalist regimes in the aftermath of the Ottoman empire's defeat, most Arab notables remained loyal to the Ottoman empire to the very end. A prominent example is that of Sati' al-Husri, born in Yemen to Syrian parents in 1882. A graduate of the *Mülkiye* (the top Ottoman administrative college) who was more fluent in Ottoman Turkish than in Arabic, al-Husri was to become a leading pan-Arab nationalist ideologue in the interwar years (see Chapter 7). Before the First World War, however, he had made a name for himself as an ardent defender of liberal, multiethnic Ottomanism who had attacked Ziya Gökalp for his narrow, organicist conception of Turkish nationalism. During the First World War, al-Husri held the post of Director of Education in Syria, and though he may have had contact with members of al-Fatat, there is no evidence at all that he supported their activities. Likewise, Yasin al-Hashimi, who was to become a leading figure in Faisal's short-lived Syrian government and subsequently in the Iraqi regime, served loyally as an Ottoman military commander until the final collapse of the empire. The journalist Kurd 'Ali, who had been active in Arab nationalist circles before the war, avoided any hint of disloyalty toward Istanbul during the war and was reduced, in his memoirs, to defensively insisting that he never denounced any of his nationalist colleagues in the course of his many friendly encounters with Jemal Pasha, and that he sought to intercede on behalf of those activists who had been sentenced to death.[95] Among the urban notables of Mesopotamia (Iraq), there was even less support for a complete break with Istanbul than among the Syrian elite.[96]

But although Ottoman power in the Arab lands was defeated by British armed might rather than by indigenous revolution, wartime events did help set the stage for the postwar development of Arab nationalism. Even though the role played by Arab nationalist organizations in the defeat of the Ottoman empire was practically nil, they provided an ideological and organizational kernel around which a more powerful nationalist movement could coalesce in the wake of the postwar partition of the Ottoman empire into League of Nations mandates administered by the British and French. More importantly, perhaps, the war furnished opportunities for creating powerful myths of national resistance. The hangings of political activists by Jemal Pasha were to become one major focal point of nationalist hagiography. But, as we shall see in Chapter 5, center stage in the nationalist drama was held by the political and military leadership of the Arab Revolt, whose springboard lay not in the urban centers of the Fertile Crescent, but on the periphery of the Ottoman empire, in the breakaway province of the Hejaz.

Conclusion

The war left no social class or ethnic group in the Habsburg, Romanov, and Ottoman empires unaffected. Its destruction of lives and property and its disruption of any sense of predictability and order deepened pre-existing grievances and accentuated conflicts across a variety of fault lines. The millions of those whose response was one of complete despair, or who focussed their entire beings on the overwhelming task of day-to-day survival, left little direct imprint on politics – although their very political passivity or alienation could have significant repercussions in the postwar world. But there were many who were drawn into oppositional political activity at a variety of levels and in a multiplicity of forms, ranging from the expression of anti-war or anti-government sentiments in their private correspondence to participation in political movements, public demonstrations, and armed revolts. The common denominator among virtually all the political responses to the war was that they expressed ardent hope for radical change, for a fundamental transformation of the social or political order – a transformation profound enough to lend meaning to the tremendous sacrifices of the conflict and/or to ensure that such a disaster never happened again.

Among many of the subject peoples of multinational empires, the idea of national self-determination gained broader and more intense appeal as a potential framework for the realization of popular aspirations. But the ostensible uniformity of nationalist sentiment could be misleading, for within it were embedded a bewildering diversity of socio-economic agendas, political ideologies, and definitions of identity. Notions of what constituted the nation, who belonged to it, where its demographic and geographic boundaries should lie, and what social tranformations must take place as part of its liberation, varied widely. The broad, federative schemes or pan-nationalist visions of nationalist intelligentsias and urban middle classes often clashed with territorially and ethnically more circumscribed conceptions of political identity among peasant populations. This gap was frequently linked to a disparity between nationalist elites' preoccupation with gaining a dignified role for the nation on the world stage and popular interest in more concrete issues of social justice and the redistribution of resources. Thus, Croatia's urban population turned sharply toward Yugoslavism in the last two years of the war, while the restive peasantry harbored dreams of a Croat socialist republic. Ukrainian nationalist leaders were eager to gain political autonomy as an end unto itself, while for the Ukrainian peasantry self-government was thought of in more instrumental terms as a means of securing a favorable framework for land reform. The liberal reformers of the Jadid movement sought to create national cultural institutions for Russia's Muslims on a pan-Turkist basis, only to encounter anti-Tatar sentiments and ethno-regional particularism among representatives of the Central Asian and Transcaucasian provinces. The members of al-Fatat and al-'Ahd aspired to create a single independent state encompassing most of the Arab provinces of the Ottoman empire, but the sporadic outbreaks of popular violence in Syria and Mesopotamia, as well as the participation of the Bedouin rank-and-file in the Arab Revolt (see

Chapter 5), can most easily be understood as expressions of local and tribal interests and loyalties.

During the final countdown to the collapse and/or military defeat of the multinational empires, rapidly intensifying nationalist sentiments, indecisiveness and loss of confidence among the political authorities, and administrative breakdown all reinforced each other in what became an inescapable vicious circle. Eleventh-hour efforts to appease nationalist feelings – such as Kaiser Karl's October 1918 offer to federalize the Habsburg monarchy or the Russian Provisional Government's promise of varying and ill-defined forms of autonomy to Russia's national minorities – only served to invigorate separatist impulses by creating frameworks within which they could more readily be acted out or by raising expectations that could not really be accommodated within the existing political order. Their inability to control such centrifugal forces added to the demoralization and disorientation of the central authorities, and in many cases left them unwilling to use whatever power remained at their disposal to try and restore order.

As they departed the scene, the multinational empires took with them the longstanding geopolitical frames of reference within which national identities had evolved. For some groups, this meant a removal of limitations under which they had chafed; this was the case for Yugoslavists who could now openly embrace the goal of uniting the South Slav provinces of Austria–Hungary with the kingdom of Serbia. By contrast, ethnic leaderships that had espoused the ideal of ethnic autonomy within a multinational, federal framework now found themselves cast adrift with no apparent alternative to political independence; this was briefly the experience of Georgia's Mensheviks and of the mainstream Arab political elites. And everywhere, the elimination of overarching imperial structures left the field open to violent contestation of the boundaries of national identity.

In this chapter, we have focussed on the dynamics of nationalism within empires at war. Before turning to the aftermath of empire, we must shift our attention to the novel, extra-imperial arenas for nationalist activism that were created by the war.

5 New Arenas of Action

Nationalisms of Occupation and Exile, 1914–1918

The force fields of separatist nationalism were not entirely congruent with, or contained within, the borders of imperial states, nor was the wartime evolution of ethno-national identities shaped exclusively by the internal political dynamics of the multinational monarchies. Successful challenges to political authority in one empire could set powerful precedents for discontented elements in other monarchies; we have already seen how strong an impression the revolutionary turmoil in Russia made on a broad array of ethnic groups and social strata in Austria–Hungary. But the war did not merely intensify the power of example; it brought into being new geopolitical frames of reference and arenas of action within which nationalist experiments could be undertaken and hitherto marginalized programs propagated and developed to an unprecedented degree.

This chapter focusses on three such wartime spheres of nationalist experimentation and improvisation. One is the military occupation zone – of which the most important examples are the German occupation zones in Eastern Europe. The second is the politics of exile – not a new dimension in and of itself, but one that gained new significance and influence in the context of the war and its immediate aftermath. The third frame of action is that of the volunteer legions that were formed either in wartime exile or in occupation zones. Each of these fora lay outside the established frameworks of multinational empires, and for much of the war what transpired there seemed to have little significance for the development of the nationalities problems within the imperial polities. But as the imperial edifices came crashing to the ground in 1917–1918, many elements that had been confined to the wings suddenly appeared poised to occupy center stage.

Zones of Occupation

Poland and Lithuania

The successful German-led Eastern offensive of 1915, which rolled Russian forces back along a broad front stretching from eastern Galicia to the Baltic, created a new sphere of administrative ambiguity and political uncertainty in the large stretch of territory that was wrenched away from the Russian empire. The bulk of Russian Poland was divided between German and Habsburg occupation zones (with headquarters in Warsaw and Lublin, respectively). The German occupation zone was administered by General Beseler, who answered directly to the authority of the Kaiser. To the north, a zone designated as Ober Ost (Upper East) – roughly corresponding to the medieval Grand Duchy of Lithuania and including urban centers such as Kaunas and Vilnius – came under the direct and exclusive jurisdiction of the German Supreme Command in the East.[1]

Large question marks hung over the future disposition and status of these territories. German Chancellor Bethmann-Hollweg entertained the hope of using Germany's gains to negotiate a separate peace with Russia, but was unwilling to retreat to the pre-war border and faced strong pressure from Generals Hindenburg and Ludendorff, who assumed overall command of Germany's armies in August 1916, to extend Germany's sphere of control even further east. The Habsburg authorities toyed with the idea of merging Congress Poland with Galicia in a Polish kingdom that would form an autonomous entity under the Habsburg crown, but Berlin had no intention of allowing its venerable partner to profit on such a grand scale from a successful military campaign that had been spearheaded by German forces. Talks between Vienna and Berlin culminated in a joint November 1916 proclamation of an "independent" Polish kingdom under the interim authority of a Provisional State Council appointed by the German military authorities in Warsaw. To the north, Ober Ost remained under the direct administration of the German Eastern Command.

The German authorities had no carefully designed blueprint for the absorption of these occupied regions into their hegemonic sphere. Their policies bore the marks of hasty improvisation and conflicting calculations. But a common thread running throughout the Germans' wartime activity in Eastern Europe was their confrontation with the reality of the population's multinational composition and their ensuing struggle to find a way of turning various manifestations of ethnic consciousness into conduits for the dissemination of German influence. The diverse attempts to achieve this all backfired in the end, but in the process, the Germans played a greater – if often unwitting – role in shaping the politics of East European nationalism than did Woodrow Wilson.[2]

The longstanding Polish aspirations for a restoration of national sovereignty constituted the most obvious and visible issue to contend with. In the course of their 1915 military campaign, the Germans had presented themselves in their propaganda as liberators who would free Poland from its subjugation to Russia.[3] By creating the framework for a sovereign Polish kingdom in November 1916, the Germans and Habsburgs did briefly succeed in gaining the active political cooperation of a certain segment of the Polish socio-political elite, as well as of Józef Piłsudski and his followers, who had returned to Warsaw from their Galician exile in the wake of the Russians' withdrawal. Piłsudski's anti-Russian orientation seemed to make him a natural partner for the Germans in their attempt to forge an alliance with Polish nationalism, and he agreed to join the Provisional State Council.

However, it soon became clear that Berlin had nothing more in mind than a compliant Polish puppet state that would do the Germans' bidding and devote its efforts to the mobilization of Polish resources and manpower on behalf of the German war effort. As we shall see below, Piłsudski responded by turning from cooperation to resistance, finally resigning from the State Council in July 1917 and being imprisoned by the Germans shortly thereafter. When the remaining members of the Provisional State Council resigned two months later, the Germans tried to salvage their credibility by designating a new Regency Council as the sovereign authority for Poland pending the crowning of a monarch. Dominated by a handful of conservative, aristocratic figures still willing to collaborate with the Germans, this body failed to gain any significant measure of political support. But by creating an institutional precedent for Polish independence on the one hand, while frustrating nationalist aspirations on the other, the Germans had laid the groundwork for Piłsudski's triumphant assumption of power in November 1918 (see below). Moreover, the economic hardships and political failures experienced under the conservative leadership of the Regency Council, offset by the wartime expansion of both public and clandestine activities by Polish mutual aid societies and mass-oriented political parties, helped foster broad-based, popular support for Polish national self-determination under a republican form of government.

Meanwhile, Ober Ost was administered by the German Supreme Command in the East as its own colonial enterprise, a political laboratory where it could experiment with the manipulation and reconfiguration of the local political economy, ethnic identities, and cultural values. The successful establishment of German political and cultural hegemony here might serve as an instructive model elsewhere, as victorious German armies carried the banner of *Kultur* ever further eastwards.[4] No single ethnic group clearly dominated this region, which contained a bewildering mix of Lithuanians, Poles, Jews, Belorussians, and others. Initially uncertain over how to bring order to this ethno-cultural carnival, the Germans soon developed a divide-and-rule strategy that was designed not just to maximize their control, but to facilitate the transformation of the land and its peoples in the German image.

The most distinctive feature of this multifaceted – and often self-contradictory – approach was the attempt to facilitate the crystallization of standardized national cultures among all of the region's ethnic groups. Rather than enshrining one language as Ober Ost's official tongue, the German military administration in Kaunas encouraged the use of all locally spoken languages. In the face of dialect variation within a speech community, the Germans endeavored to promote a uniform standard. The establishment of school systems for each ethnic group would contribute to the remolding of peasant populations that had hitherto had little exposure to any form of written culture. Official decrees were issued in seven different languages by the military administration's press section, whose staff of translators were also responsible for publishing newspapers in local languages as propaganda vehicles for the Ober Ost command. Official identification cards were issued to every individual in the territory, each printed in its bearer's own native tongue.

The cumulative – and intended – effect of these policies was to institution-alize ethnic identity in Ober Ost to an unprecedented degree. But this approach was not the expression of a refined multicultural sensibility among the German officer corps. Rather, it stemmed from the notion that clearly structured cate-gories of identity constituted an essential aspect of a modern society and, furthermore, that the consolidation of ethno-national frames of reference would facilitate the dissemination of German social and cultural values. As V.G. Liulevicius has argued, the Ober Ost authorities saw the transformation of land use patterns (combining scientific principles of agronomy with idiosyncratically German notions about the taming and cultivation of nature) and the reshaping of the land's native peoples as complementary elements in a project of inte-grating the region into the German political-cultural realm. Drawing clear distinctions between overlapping ethnic identities and furthering the develop-ment of a standardized culture (through publications, cultural exhibits, crafts fairs, and theatrical productions in indigenous languages) for each nationality, would all serve to bring the population in line with German ideas about what a modern society should look like. This process of modernization would itself make each ethnic group more receptive to German ideas about disciplined work habits, bureaucratic regimentation, and respect for authority and the rule of law. The use of native tongues to diffuse such ideas would make them seem less alien and more readily comprehensible; at the same time, the study of German would become compulsory in every ethnic group's schools. In brief, the policy repre-sented an attempt to create cultures that were national in form, but Germanic in content.[5] In fact, the similarity to later Soviet efforts to create cultures "national in form, socialist in content" is so striking that one cannot help wondering whether Lenin's and Stalin's nationalities policies (see Chapter 6) were influenced by this precedent – as Bolshevik War Communism was influenced by the model of the German war economy.[6]

This utopian (or dystopian) program for socio-cultural modernization ran afoul of numerous obstacles and pitfalls. Not least among these were the exploitative aspects of Ober Ost's own policies, as dictated by considerations of wartime expediency and as facilitated by the myriad opportunities for abuse of power inherent in the very nature of a military-occupation regime. Tens of thou-sands of men from all ethnic groups were dragged off to perform forced labor, leaving their families with little or no means of support. Massive requisitions of grain and livestock left agricultural communities destitute. Rigid bureaucratic controls on internal travel and commercial activity caused economic fragmenta-tion and aggravated material hardships, as well as contributing to the growth of a black market and smuggling trade whose effective functioning depended on the venality of German soldiers and officers.[7]

Lithuanian nationalism comes of age

The impact of this self-contradictory pattern of governance was indeed to reinforce the centrality of ethnicity as a framework for collective action and mutual
support, but in ways that did not necessarily coincide with the purposes of Ober
Ost's nationalities policy. It was thus that Lithuanian nationalism came of age
under the stimulus of German occupation. The military administration
employed heavyhanded methods in its attempts to cultivate Lithuanian
consciousness while limiting its expression to a narrow range of approved topics
and opinions. For example, it encouraged the establishment of Lithuanian
schools, then imposed a Germanophile curriculum on them; it published its own
Lithuanian-language newspaper, but refused until September 1917 to permit the
establishment of an independent paper – and then sought to muzzle it through
censorship. Such policies only served to stimulate diverse forms of resistance. An
underground educational system spread through the countryside alongside polit-
ical-mobilization and propagandist activities carried out by Lithuanian
nationalists under the cover of the officially sanctioned Lithuanian Refugee Aid
Committee. The severe regimen of requisitions and forced labor created a receptive audience for nationalist agitation among the peasantry. While much of the
wartime rural unrest in Ober Ost took the form of banditry, there was at least
one incident of armed resistance that was clearly linked to clandestine nationalist
activity.[8]

In 1917, a new framework of activity arose for Lithuanian nationalists. It was
early in this year that the Provisional Government came to power in Russia and
that the United States entered the war, both governments espousing the doctrine
of national self-determination as the basis for a non-annexationist peace settlement. In July 1917, the German Reichstag (lower house of parliament) passed a
resolution calling for a peace without forcible annexations. On the other hand,
Russia's military disintegration held forth the prospect of further expansion of
German military might in the East.

It was within this political and military context that Lithuanian political
nationhood was summoned forth by none other than the Ober Ost authorities as
the designated vehicle for the legitimization of their imperial project. This was
designed to counter the impact of Russian revolutionary propaganda by demonstrating that German rule was compatible with national self-determination.
Cultivation of Lithuanian nationalism could also serve to counterbalance and
contain the restive Poles.

The result was the convening of a conference in Vilnius in September 1917
that elected a twenty-member council – the Taryba – considered broadly representative of Lithuanian society. Coming under intense pressure to call for union
with Germany, the Taryba soon showed that it had a mind of its own. It made
tactical concessions to the military authorities while simultaneously insisting on a
greater measure of autonomy for Lithuania than Ober Ost was prepared to
grant. In February 1918, in protest over the exclusion of Lithuanians from
involvement in Germany's peace negotiations with the Bolsheviks, the Taryba
declared Lithuania independent, separately reaffirming a previous commitment

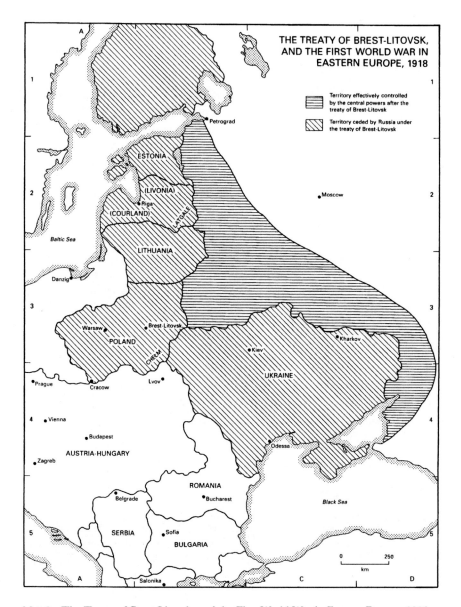

Map 2   The Treaty of Brest-Litovsk, and the First World War in Eastern Europe, 1918

Source: Richard and Ben Crampton, *Atlas of Eastern Europe* (London: Routledge, 1996)

to maintaining military and economic union with Germany. An awkward political dance ensued, with the military authorities cracking down hard on open manifestations of dissent, while the Taryba tried to circumvent the Ober Ost system by employing political ties with sympathetic elements among the Catholic Center Party in the German Reichstag to gain the Kaiser's formal, if conditional, recognition of Lithuanian independence in March 1918. This had few practical implications as long as the German military remained in effective control, but with the collapse of the German war effort in November, this skeletal framework for self-government could begin to take on substance. The point is that, its worst intentions notwithstanding, the German occupation regime had contributed significantly to the consolidation of Lithuanian national identity and the creation of an institutional framework for Lithuanian territorial independence – and all this through policies that had been intended to mold the local population into pliable objects of German cultural and political imperialism.

The Jews under German occupation

The case of the Jews also vividly illustrates not only what a transformative impact the German occupation had on the development of national identities, but also how varied the modes of influence were. While every European country had a Jewish minority, the East European lands that fell to the Germans in 1915 formed part of an extensive swath of territory containing the largest concentration of Jewish population on the continent; Jews constituted approximately 10 per cent of the area's general population, and often 30 to 50 per cent of the population in towns and cities. The ethno-cultural distinctiveness of most East European Jews was manifest in every aspect of their existence – religion, language, dress, occupational patterns, neighborhoods. What the German occupation did was to create opportunities for the development and/or expansion of modern institutional, political, and cultural frameworks for the expression of Jewish identity in its multiplicity of forms and orientations. This was the case both in Ober Ost and in German- and Austrian-occupied Poland.[9]

The most immediate and obvious impact of German occupation on Jewish life in the region was the relief it offered from the systematic wartime persecution of the Russian authorities, who had treated Jews as potential spies, sent tens of thousands of them from border regions into internal exile, banned correspondence and publication in Hebrew letters, and physically destroyed numerous Jewish settlements and neighborhoods during the Russian army's retreat in 1915.[10] Just as German propaganda in 1914–1915 promised the Poles a better lot under the Kaiser's benevolent hand, so too did it play on the theme of Russian abuses to win Jewish sympathy for the Central Powers' cause.[11] The introduction of German military rule was associated with abuses of its own, but these took the form of an equal-opportunity system of exploitation that, at least officially, did not single out the Jews for harsher treatment. Moreover, because of the linguistic affinity between Yiddish and German, a disproportionate number of Jews were employed as interpreters and in other low-level clerical roles in the German occupation regimes.[12]

German occupation not only brought an end to Russia's 1915 ban on Hebrew and Yiddish publication, but created unprecedented opportunities for Jewish cultural innovation and political activism. In Ober Ost, the occupation regime's unusual nationalities policy meant that Yiddish was recognized as the official language of the Jews, and that Jews were encouraged to develop a modern, Yiddish-language school system as well as Jewish vocational schools and a number of Hebrew-language schools.[13] In Poland, the Germans' attempt to curry favor with Polish nationalists led to the designation of the Jewish minority as a religious group rather than a nationality. Yet here too, German rule created unprecedented opportunities for the development of new Jewish educational and cultural institutions.[14]

In the political realm, German reforms in municipal election procedures broadened the franchise and opened up the playing field to fuller participation by Jewish socialist and Zionist parties whose scope of action had been severely circumscribed by the tsarist regime. This, along with such parties' involvement in refugee assistance and relief work, created the opportunity for their rapid expansion into mass movements. The General Zionist Party's success in reaching the masses was marked by its collection of 238,000 signatures on a 1917 petition in support of the Jewish claim to Palestine.[15] The founding of other Jewish political parties – notably the Orthodox Agudat Israel – that were to play significant roles in Poland during the interwar years also took place under the German occupation regime.[16]

This pattern of German administrative initiatives and Jewish responses constituted but one strand in a thick web of social, cultural, and political interactions between occupiers and occupied. Rival German-Jewish organizations, whose ideological orientations ranged from assimilationism, to religious Orthodoxy, to Zionism, sent relief missions, investigatory and advisory groups, and teachers to the Jews of the occupied East, stimulating and reinforcing local initiatives. In efforts that paralleled the political activity of some highly placed Austrian and Prussian Poles and a handful of Prussian Lithuanians on behalf of their respective national causes,[17] German Jews lobbied the German government and occupation authorities on behalf of their own various policy recommendations (that ranged from programs for the Germanization of Yiddish-speaking Jewry to advocacy of national-cultural autonomy for the Jews of the East).[18] Intercession by German-Jewish officers in the Ober Ost administration's Press Section facilitated the establishment of the first major modernist Yiddish theater in Vilnius (the Vilna Troupe)[19] and enabled the company to tour the entire Lithuanian–Polish region, bypassing normal travel restrictions.[20]

Many of the above initiatives were elements in a general tendency toward vertical integration on the part of rival ideological movements, each of which claimed to embody the essence of Jewish identity. By vertical integration, I refer to the creation and consolidation of school systems, youth movements, press organs, and other cultural and social institutions under the aegis of mass-oriented political parties. Many of these initiatives were necessarily fragile and limited in scope under conditions of wartime occupation, but they created modern institutional frameworks for the development of a multifaceted Jewish national-cultural life in interwar Poland.

Synopsis

The German occupation of Russian Poland and Lithuania thus served to lend new impetus to the crystallization of ethno-national identities and/or to the consolidation of modern political and institutional expressions of identity among the diverse peoples of the region. It played this catalyzing role in a variety of ways, both indirect and direct. For one thing, harsh and exploitative though they were, the German occupation regimes in Ober Ost and Poland were in some respects less politically and culturally repressive than the tsarist authorities had been. By introducing a semblance of the rule of law,[21] the Germans facilitated the growth of new frameworks and opportunities for various forms of communal self-organization and cultural experimentation.

In Ober Ost, the German military deliberately imposed an ethno-cultural grid (to paraphrase Liulevicius) on its new subjects, promoting the crystallization of mutually exclusive categories of collective identity. While these policies were intended to promote the transmission of German norms and values and to reinforce German hegemony over the population, they were implemented in a haphazard and inconsistent manner and rarely served the purpose they were designed for. The bureaucratization of cultural policy was a process that lent itself to subtle forms of subversion, as in the case of the *melamdim* (Torah teachers in traditional Jewish schools) summoned to Kaunas from surrounding small towns for a certification course taught by German-Jewish instructors. The *"melamdim"* enrolled in the class turned out to be petty traders who had misrepresented themselves as a means of obtaining travel permits so as to market their wares in the big city.[22] The Lithuanian Taryba's refusal to play the docile role expected of it by the German authorities is a more dramatic example of German ethno-political manipulation being turned on its head. Sympathetic elements within the German military administration and in the Reichstag also aided in the carving out of small but significant niches of cultural autonomy on the part of subject communities in the occupied lands.

Finally, the self-contradictory qualities of German policy in Lithuania and Poland, which fostered ethno-cultural awareness and/or self-government on the one hand while withholding any substantive form of national self-determination on the other, and which purported to be directed at the betterment of local conditions while in practice severely aggravating the already intense material hardships of wartime, served to fan the flames of resistance. This ran the gamut from spontaneous manifestations – such as the hit-and-run attacks on German troops carried out by armed bands of Lithuanian men evading forced labor service[23] – to clandestine activities undertaken by disciplined organizations such as Piłsudski's Polish Military Organization (of which more below).

All of the above factors contributed to an intense preoccupation on the part of Polish, Jewish, and Lithuanian communal leaders, press organs, and literate publics with the possible prospects and forms of national self-determination in the framework of a German-dominated Eastern Europe. With the collapse of German power in 1918, Wilsonian rhetoric became the predominant frame of reference for these debates and disputes as the contending forces brought their cases to the Paris Peace Conference. But it was in the context of the German and Austrian occupation of the region that concern with these matters had engaged the interest of a broader public than ever before and that many of the key institutional and organizational mechanisms for political and military action and mass mobilization within each ethnic community had taken form.

Serbia

The Central Powers' occupation of Serbia followed a different pattern from that of Poland–Lithuania. The cultural policies pursued here were much more unambiguously and straightforwardly repressive, and were variously designed either to impose cultural assimilation on the Serb population or to eliminate any meaningful form whatsoever of cultural expression. The net effect, however, was to reinforce the Serb masses' sense of political identity by feeding directly into their national myths of collective resistance and martyrdom.[24]

The kingdom of Serbia already was an independent nation-state long before 1914, and had, of course, been directly involved in the outbreak of the war. It merits our attention, however, because the wartime development of its government's political agenda and of its society's national consciousness had long-term repercussions for the South Slavs of Austria–Hungary.

Coming close on the heels of the country's impressive military performance in the Balkan Wars of 1912–1913, the onset of the First World War found Serbia's largely peasant population already gripped by powerful nationalist emotions. Indeed, among all the Balkan countries, the rural tradition of the blood feud had been effectively transposed to the level of interethnic and inter-state relations. The brutal massacres that had characterized the advance and retreat of Ottoman, Greek, Romanian, Bulgarian, Montenegrin, and Serbian armies in 1912–1913 had left a warm, fresh batch of inter-communal vendettas steaming on the stove of Balkan politics.[25]

The Serbian war effort of 1914–1915 must be considered remarkable simply by virtue of how long it lasted; it managed to ward off Austro-Hungarian conquest for a full year. With the country's armies arrayed against the forces of a European great power, this period witnessed an unprecedented marshaling of national resources and accompanying politicization of the population. The government undertook a propaganda effort on behalf of its official war aim of unifying all Serbs, Croats, and Slovenes under the Serbian crown. The seat of government itself was moved south to Niš, as Belgrade came under repeated bombardment and was briefly occupied by the Austro-Hungarians in December

1914. The atmosphere in the temporary capital was one of intense nationalist fervor, as the town became crowded with embittered Serb refugees from Bosnia and other parts of the Habsburg-ruled South Slav lands.[26]

Bulgaria's entry into the war combined with the arrival of German troop reinforcements finally led to the defeat of the Serbian army by December 1915. This was itself the occasion for a great upsurge of national solidarity and collective pride, however: led by the Serbian government and high command, the remnants of the army fought and marched their way across the frozen mountains of Albania to the Adriatic coast. Many civilians, fearful of the conquerors, accompanied this death march. Some 143,000 people perished during this Exodus, either of cold, fatigue, and famine, or at the hands of hostile Albanian peasants. Approximately 140,000–170,000 survived to be rescued by Allied ships that transported the Serbian government to Corfu (over Greek objections), and that brought Serbia's troops to Salonika, where they participated in the opening of a new inter-Allied front against Bulgaria. The refusal of the Serbian government to surrender to the Central Powers and the fighting retreat of its armed forces reinforced the themes of heroism and martyrdom as central aspects of the Serbian nationalist self-image.

Serbian territory was divided into Austro-Hungarian and Bulgarian occupation zones (in the north and south of the country, respectively), while the Germans engaged in economic exploitation of the entire land. Bulgaria and Austria–Hungary intended to integrate Serbian territory into their respective states after the war, and they pursued cultural policies designed to further that long-term goal while simultaneously busying themselves with the more immediate task of raping the country. On the one hand, the zeal with which the occupation authorities promoted their cultural and linguistic agendas suggested that they understood what a dangerous problem popular nationalism could pose for them. On the other hand, their methods of dealing with Serbian nationalism reflected a naive optimism about how easy it would be to manipulate and reshape popular identity.

The Bulgarians were particularly heavy-handed in their imposition of a program of cultural assimilation on their occupation zone. Their propaganda claimed that not only Slavic Macedonians, but also ethnic Serbs, were in truth nothing but Bulgarians who had somehow gone astray and forgotten who they were. All they needed was a firm hand to guide them back to the refreshing waters of Bulgarian language and culture. The use of Serbian in all public functions was banned, the sale of Serbian books was declared illegal, Bulgarian theater replaced Serbian theater in occupied Niš, and Bulgarian teachers and textbooks were brought in to transform the school system into an instrument of cultural assimilation. A campaign was even launched to convert Serbian names into Bulgarian ones (in a move that foreshadowed Communist Bulgaria's cultural war against its Turkish minority in the 1980s).

For their part, the Austro-Hungarian authorities seemed less sure about what the Serbs should be transformed into. They focussed instead on trying to eliminate whatever distinctive ethno-cultural consciousness and political initiative the conquered population did have. The Austrian military governor's official instructions were "to apply the utmost energy and ruthlessness about the needs of the war and the military forces and to destroy every sign of rebellion and carry out the most far-reaching exploitation with the firmest hand and insensitivity."[27] Thousands of members of the intelligentsia and political activists of every description were deported to internment camps, the University of Belgrade was closed down, and the use of the Cyrillic alphabet – the key feature distinguishing Serbian from Croatian – was severely curtailed. The one Serbian-language newspaper published in occupied Belgrade contained nothing but censored war news, and the city's public cultural life seemed to consist of little more than endless performances by Austrian military bands.

Accompanied as they were by the conscription of Serbian men into the Bulgarian armed forces, the expropriation of vital material resources, and violent abuses of power by their armies, the cultural and linguistic policies of the occupying powers served only to confirm the popular impression that their ultimate objective was the annihilation of the Serbs as a nation. The struggle for physical survival and the fight for cultural self-determination could be seen as different aspects of the same life-and-death battle against implacable enemies. In trying to eradicate the cultural and political expressions of Serbian national identity, the Austro-Hungarians and Bulgarians merely reinforced the sense that redemption from the material ravages of war could only come in the context of renewed national independence. And as long as total liberation remained a distant prospect, the secret cultivation of Serbia's ethno-cultural heritage was a meaningful way of defying the enemy; the occupiers had themselves defined the contest in such terms.

Their unusually harsh experience under occupation contributed to the Serbs' sense of exceptionalism and to their self-image as the hardy vanguard of the South Slav peoples. This, in turn, contributed to the widespread popular assumption that Serbs would hold pride of place in the kingdom of Serbs, Croats, and Slovenes that emerged in the wake of the war – a perspective that would not be shared by the other constituent peoples of the Yugoslav state.

There were many more experiences of wartime conquest and occupation than this section could possibly survey. The further German and Ottoman advances into Russian territory under the terms of the March 1918 Treaty of Brest-Litovsk varied enormously in their impact, and do not lend themselves readily to generalization.[28] The advance of British armies into Palestine–Syria and Mesopotamia inaugurated decades of Anglo-French imperial hegemony in the Middle East, which had a formative impact on the development of the region's nation-states, as we shall see in the next chapter. But before moving from wartime occupation to postwar boundary and identity formation, we must consider the impact of exile movements on the development of wartime and postwar nationalisms.

The Politics of Exile

The experience of exile has often formed the backdrop for propagandist and conspiratorial activity on the part of revolutionaries of every description, including nationalists. Napoleon I organized a legion of Polish expatriates who fought in the ranks of the Grande Armée in the hope of helping their partitioned homeland regain independent status within a Bonapartist European order. During the mid-nineteenth century, Giuseppe Mazzini coordinated the passionate if ineffectual activities of his Young Italy organization from his refuge in London, while also – rather more successfully – cultivating the support of British high society for the cause of Italian national unification. Other examples from the nineteenth century abound.

During the First World War, this pattern became the order of the day for a wide array of nationalist activists. As the European great powers engaged in their life-and-death struggle, each of their respective territories served as a potential base of operations for malcontents from the other side. The multinational empires did not shy away from attempts at mutual subversion through support for each other's separatist movements. Ukrainian émigrés in Galicia organized a Union for the Liberation of (Russian) Ukraine (Soiuz Vyzvolennia Ukrainy – SVU) in August 1914, which enjoyed limited financial support from the Austro-Hungarian and German governments and eventually transferred its headquarters to Berlin. The SVU was authorized to gain access to POW camps, where it conducted nationalist agitation among Ukrainian prisoners. Both Germany and the Habsburg empire also hosted nationalist conferences and publication campaigns by Finnish, Muslim, and other émigrés from the Russian empire. The German government also smuggled Irish nationalist leader Sir Roger Casement (as well as arms shipments) by submarine into Ireland (where the Easter Rising broke out in 1916) and spurred the Ottomans to conduct pan-Islamic propaganda designed to loosen Britain's grip on Egypt and India (see Chapter 4).[29] For their part, the Russians sought to undermine Austria–Hungary's cohesion by appealing to the nationalist sentiments of Czechs, Slovaks, and South Slavs, while to the south, they encouraged Dashnak activists in their efforts to incite rebellion among the Armenians across the border in the Ottoman empire.[30] The Ottomans in turn sought to incite anti-Russian uprisings among the Muslim peoples of Transcaucasia as well as to cultivate contact among Georgian nationalists.[31]

The neutral countries also served as bases of activity for expatriate nationalists from throughout Eastern Europe who held conferences and established committees and information bureaus in Switzerland, Sweden, and other non-belligerent states. These organizations issued propagandist literature in Western languages,[32] organized conferences of oppressed nationalities, and lobbied the international diplomatic corps on behalf of their respective causes, even trying to play the Allied and Central Powers off against each other. The direct impact of such efforts may have been minimal, but some of these committees fulfilled an important function as channels of communication – surreptitious or otherwise – with the outside world (especially with diaspora communities in the Americas) for activists in the zones of war and occupation.[33]

Of course, the gap in perspective between diaspora and native land, émigré nationalists and activists in occupied territory, could also create discord and political tensions over a wide variety of issues. Exile in the Allied countries created the incentive and opportunity for propagating more radical or ambitious political programs than could be openly contemplated by community leaders back home, who were living under continued imperial rule or military occupation.[34] The gap between exile front and home front produced both synergies and tensions – a dialectical relationship that assumed center stage in the nationalist arena when these divergent wartime paths suddenly converged in 1918.

The expatriate leaders were few in number and their wartime experiences were completely unlike those of their countrymen. Yet because they operated out of the Allied capitals and identified themselves with the victorious Western cause, some of them were unusually well positioned to influence the course of events in their homelands in the immediate aftermath of the Central Powers' defeat. Given this disproportionately significant role in the shaping of the new nation-states of 1918, their atypical wartime trajectories – and the distinctive political perspectives that these experiences helped shape – demand particular attention.

The Czechoslovak National Council

The most striking example of how wartime exile in the Allied countries could propel a hitherto respected but relatively powerless figure into the seat of power is that of Tomáš Masaryk. By 1914, Masaryk had come to the conclusion that the Austro-Hungarian state was too retrograde and authoritarian to be susceptible to reform. Its alignment with Wilhelmine Germany in the war only reinforced his sense that full independence rather than autonomy within a German-dominated Central Europe represented the only meaningful form of self-determination for the Czech nation. By the same token, the war seemed to open up the first realistic possibility of breaking up the Habsburg empire. To this end, in December 1914, Masaryk left Austria–Hungary for Switzerland, where he began to plan a campaign from abroad on behalf of Czech independence. Prior to his departure from Prague, he had entrusted his confidant Edvard Beneš with the responsibility of organizing an underground network of activists committed to working for Czech independence. Known as the Maffie, this conspiracy brought together leaders from the younger, second-tier level of several parties' leaderships as well as a variety of intellectuals and cultural figures from outside the framework of party organizations. It functioned both as a channel for secret communication between the exiled Masaryk and his sympathizers in Bohemia, and as a framework of cooperation and coordination among those Czech politicians committed to pushing their respective party leaderships into a more confrontational stance toward the Habsburg authorities. For instance, the Maffie helped organize the pressure campaign that led to the radicalization of the Czech Union's political platform in the course of 1917–1918 (see Chapter 3).[35]

Following Beneš' own departure from Austria–Hungary in late 1915, Masaryk and he established themselves in London and Paris, respectively, where they proceeded to cultivate contacts in British and French journalistic, academic, and political circles. In 1916, joined by a handful of other exiles and by representatives of Czech immigrant communities, they launched the public phase of their independence campaign by establishing the Czechoslovak National Council. Claiming to represent the national interests of the Czech and Slovak peoples, the Council sought to convince the Allies that the breakup of the Habsburg empire and independence for its constituent peoples was the only sure means of breaking the grip of Germandom and autocracy on Central Europe. Czech political culture in particular was presented as offering a secular, democratic, Western-oriented alternative to the Catholicized, authoritarian institutions of a decrepit empire that had already effectively fallen into the clutches of militaristic Germany.[36]

Masaryk's solid credentials as a pro-Western democrat earned him a sympathetic ear in the British, and later American, intellectual and political establishments. In *The New Europe*, a London-based wartime weekly founded in 1916 by the scholar Robert Seton-Watson and the journalist Sir Henry Wickham Steed, Masaryk found a mouthpiece for his views that published his articles regularly and enthusiastically espoused the cause of political independence for all the Slavic peoples of the Habsburg empire. *The New Europe* was read by an educated British public, and its editors were extremely well connected in Whitehall. Indeed, academic contributors to the paper constituted a dominant element among the regional specialists appointed to the Foreign Office's Political Intelligence Department, charged with preparing recommendations regarding the future peace settlement. There is no question that the paper functioned as a powerful instrument in shaping British policy toward the Czechoslovak National Council in 1917–1918.[37] *La nation tcheque*, published in Paris, served a similar function in the French context. Masaryk was also able to earn considerable sympathy for his cause during his trip to the United States in 1917, not only by campaigning among the Czech and Slovak immigrant communities, but also by meeting with his fellow professor, President Woodrow Wilson.[38] The exploits of the Czechoslovak Legion in Russia (of which more below) generated admiration and support for Masaryk's cause among the broader Western public.

In most respects, Masaryk's wartime platform was constructed on the intellectual foundations he had laid before 1914. What changed most radically during the war years was the status and influence of his ideas. The polarized political culture of total war created a ready audience for his anti-Austrian views among Western elites, and the collapse of Allied–Habsburg peace feelers in Spring 1918 helped pave the way to Allied recognition that summer and fall of the Czechoslovak National Council and endorsement of national self-determination for the Czechs and Slovaks, as well as the South Slavs.[39] The Czechoslovak National Council's remarkable diplomatic success abroad, and its use of the

Maffie connection to forge what amounted to a long-distance coalition with pro-independence forces in Bohemia, propelled its formerly marginal leaders into the political cockpit in 1918. For its part, the neo-Slavic wing of Czech nationalism was obliged to accommodate itself to the achievement of the Western, liberal nationalists. A Russophile figure on the Czechoslovak National Council was dismissed from the organization after overplaying his hand in an internal power struggle,[40] while in Prague, by 1918, Karel Kramář was so impressed by Masaryk's and Beneš' apparent influence in Allied councils that he did not dispute their claim to a leadership role in the future Czechoslovak state. In any event, the Bolshevik Revolution made a pro-Russian orientation impractical in the immediate term. Thus, Masaryk and his associates were able to parlay their position as mavericks and political outsiders into the assumption of decisive roles in the creation and shaping of Czechoslovakia.

While there were strong elements of continuity between Masaryk's pre- and post-1914 positions, the process of inventing a state in the diplomatic cyberspace of wartime exile certainly helped shape his program and had a far-reaching impact on the institutions and political dynamics of interwar Czechoslovakia. Masaryk's decision openly to attack the legitimacy of the Habsburg state was itself a function of the war. More interesting is the manner in which his wartime circumstances shaped the future of relations between Czechs and Slovaks. Being unencumbered by direct involvement in the political life of his homeland, Masaryk was free to take his ideas on the Czech–Slovak connection to their logical conclusion by advocating the creation of a Czechoslovak nation-state.

Masaryk's effective wartime constituencies were Western elites and Czech and Slovak immigrant communities. Both groups proved receptive to his ideas on Czech–Slovak affinity. His Anglo-French–American audience was sympathetic to his rhetoric about the need to forge a common national identity among the two Slavic peoples on the basis of the Czechs' liberal-democratic values, with the new Czechoslovakia to become a bastion of the West in German-dominated Central Europe. For their part, the Czech and Slovak communities of the United States were much more aware of their similarities in the context of their common encounter with American urban life than were their brethren in the old country. It was in Pittsburgh, of all places, that Masaryk met with American Czech and Slovak leaders to issue a joint declaration calling for the creation of an independent Czechoslovakia. The Pittsburgh Declaration of 1917 was an effort to lend Masaryk's efforts the legitimacy of popular approval by the largest community of Czechs and Slovaks living outside the Austro-Hungarian empire. Yet while Masaryk regarded it as an affirmation of his vision of Czechoslovak unity, the document also contained assurances of Slovak autonomy within the framework of the future state – assurances that were to remain unfulfilled. As such, it was to be the subject of increasingly venomous disputes during the interwar years.[41]

The problem with Masaryk's program was that it could easily be taken as little more than a façade for Czech cultural imperialism. Masaryk clearly regarded Czech culture as the ideal medium for the dissemination of progressive values to the Slovaks. He seemed uncertain over how to deal with the fact that Slovak was linguistically distinct from Czech. In his wartime propaganda, he referred to Slovak as nothing more than a dialect of Czech, while promising that this dialect would be used in Slovak schools and administration.[42] He made no mention of employing Slovak at the level of higher education, and insisted that the linguistic issue would not constitute a stumbling block, indeed, that "there can be no language question, because every Slovak, even without an education, understands Czech and every Czech understands Slovak."[43] The latter observation was quite true, yet it also reflected a rather naive obliviousness on Masaryk's part to the "narcissism of minor difference" that can play so powerful a role in the formation of national identities and in the generation of ethnic conflicts.[44] Masaryk's pre-war contacts with Slovakia's Hlasists (see Chapter 3) and the active leadership role that the Slovak astronomer Milan Štefánik played along-side Beneš and himself in the Czechoslovak National Council doubtless encouraged Masaryk in his belief that political union would pave the way to cultural integration of the two peoples. But the fact was that the Hlasists consti-tuted a tiny Czechophile intellectual circle whose links to Slovak popular culture were extremely tenuous. Štefánik himself had been educated in Prague and had spent years abroad, becoming an officer in the French army. His personal ties to Slovakia were hardly stronger than those of Masaryk himself.[45]

The Czechoslovak National Council's success at gaining diplomatic recogni-tion from the Allies in 1918, combined with the vacuum formed by the collapse of the Austro-Hungarian empire, did create a momentum that not even the generally cautious, conservative Slovak nationalist elite could resist – especially given that this seemed to offer the most immediate chance of escape from Hungarian rule. Gathering hastily in October 1918, a self-appointed Slovak National Council voted in favor of union with the Czechs in an independent state.[46] But there was no broad-based Slovak movement underpinning this deci-sion – nothing analogous to the popular embrace of the exiled nationalists' program by a wide spectrum of Czech social classes and political parties in 1918 (as described in Chapter 4). The creation of Czechoslovakia served only to raise Slovak expectations of self-determination that were not to be fulfilled. The Slovaks' sense of having been hoodwinked into an unfair bargain led to deep bitterness on their part that was to plague the politics of the interwar republic.

The Yugoslav Committee

The South Slav political leadership also experienced a bifurcation of paths during the war. In this case, it was the exiled Yugoslav activists whose goals were ultimately frustrated by the outcome of events in their homeland. But their wartime political campaign was nonetheless significant in helping set the stage for the establishment in 1918 of the kingdom of Serbs, Croats, and Slovenes, as well as in promoting a vision of Yugoslavia whose failure to materialize would contribute to a growing sense among Croats and Slovenes of having been cheated of their birthright.

Following the occupation of Serbia in 1915, open opposition to Austro-Hungarian policies could only be undertaken from abroad. The key figures in this enterprise were Croat leaders from the Croat–Serb Coalition (HSK – see Chapter 3) who had begun organizing an anti-Habsburg campaign soon after the outbreak of hostilities. Frano Supilo had escaped Habsburg harassment by going into exile in Italy in 1910, and he was joined in 1914 by Ante Trumbić and a number of other activists – most notably, the internationally acclaimed Croat sculptor Ivan Meštrović – who either happened to be out of the country at the outbreak of the war, or managed to slip out during the early weeks of the conflict. Given the polarizing atmosphere of the Austro-Serbian war and the often brutal suppression of dissent within the Habsburg monarchy, these figures were ready to make a complete break with Vienna. The fact that they were cut off from regular contact with the complex dynamics of Croatian politics freed them of the need to negotiate and compromise, and facilitated their formulation of a clear-cut separatist program. The fact that their claim to speak on behalf of the oppressed Croat, Slovene, and Serb masses of the southern Habsburg lands was inherently unverifiable only made it easier for these leaders of the nationalist intelligentsia to issue whatever proclamations they chose in the name of the people. Following contacts between these émigrés and the Serbian government, the latter lent its moral and financial support to the émigrés' formation of the Yugoslav Committee, which committed itself to the liberation of all South Slavs from the Habsburg yoke and their unification with the kingdom of Serbia in an independent Yugoslav state. The Serbian government regarded this committee as a potentially useful propaganda organization in Britain and France, whose governments' attempts to lure Italy into the war by offering it the prospect of territorial gains along the eastern Adriatic coast conflicted with Serbia's own war aims.[47]

By 1917, London had become the *de facto* center of operations for the Yugoslav Committee. Indeed, while the leaders of the Yugoslav Committee claimed to represent the national will of their countrymen, their actual wartime constituency was limited to Croat immigrant communities in the New World, the narrow coterie of British journalists, intellectuals, and diplomats specializing in East Central European affairs, and beyond them, the educated Western public. The process of dialogue with men such as Robert Seton-Watson and Henry Wickham Steed helped shape the way in which Supilo and Trumbić articulated their own conception of a future Yugoslavia. It is very difficult to define where the propagandistic element of the Yugoslav activists' rhetoric ended and their real views began, for the crystallization of their political platform took place within the context of this ongoing engagement with the educated elites of wartime Britain. The line between propaganda and policy within the British government was itself blurry. In March 1918, Seton-Watson and Steed were given the responsibility of forming the Austro-Hungarian section of the Department of Propaganda in Enemy Countries. They used their position within the governmental apparatus to help convince Lloyd George's cabinet to abandon the thought of a compromise peace with Austria–Hungary and to move toward all but formal endorsement of full-fledged independence for its constituent peoples. Thus, propaganda could help shape diplomacy.[48]

The Yugoslav Committee and its supporters argued that a South Slav state would create the best possible framework for the cultivation of a pluralistic, culturally inclusive form of nationalism that would help transform the pattern of inter-communal rivalry and narrowly ethnic chauvinism that had dominated Balkan politics since the late nineteenth century. Serbia would provide the military brawn needed to carve out and defend the new state, while the Croats and Slovenes would contribute their liberal-democratic values to the polity and serve as its link to the culture and commerce of the West. The cultivation of fraternal ties among the constituent peoples of Yugoslavia would not come at the expense of their individual traditions and identities: while Serbs, Slovenes, and Croats would cultivate a common political culture (defined by the outlook of the Dalmatian urban elite), the individual ethno-territorial components of the state would enjoy autonomy and maintain some of their own distinctive institutions. Finally, Supilo and Trumbić were willing to compromise the purity of their liberal-democratic, national self-determination doctrine by reverting to arguments of historic state right in their effort to justify maximal territorial claims for the prospective state. (They were particularly concerned over Italy's territorial claims in Dalmatia, which were secretly recognized by the British and French governments as the price for Italian entry into the war in 1915.) The historical reference point for their state-right claims was the medieval Croatian kingdom founded in the tenth century by King Zvonimir, under whose crown Dalmatia had been united with Croatia–Slavonia.[49]

During the first months of the war, the beleaguered Serbian government, from its retreat in Niš, had encouraged and helped finance the formation of the Yugoslav Committee and had officially endorsed the ideal of Yugoslav national unification. The quest for cultural expression of the fraternal ties among the South Slavs received official sanction and support in the form of a government-sponsored scholarly commission composed of historians, linguists, and geographers who set about compiling "scientific" proof that Serbs, Croats, and Slovenes were indeed "tribes of one people." Finally, in December 1914, the Serbian Parliament had issued the Niš Declaration, which defined Serbia's central war aim as "the liberation and unification of all our unliberated brothers: Serbs, Croats and Slovenes."[50]

Yet as the war progressed, profound fissures appeared in the façade of Yugoslav solidarity. For one thing, the Yugoslav Committee's open adoption of the Serbian cause as its own did not initially seem to reflect broader sentiments among the Croat public, although this changed as the war dragged on (see Chapter 4).

Of more immediate concern to the Yugoslav Committee was the ever more unpredictable behavior of the Serbian government. The harrowing retreat of the Serbian government and army across the mountains of Albania into exile on the Greek island of Corfu in the fall and winter of 1915 did not break the spirit of the Serbian leadership. Quite to the contrary, the Serbian authorities emerged from the ordeal all the more determined to reap a fitting reward for the Serbian people's suffering once the war ended in Allied victory. Moreover, they remained active in the Allied war effort by committing their troops to the new Salonika (Greece) front that was opened in the summer of 1916. The problem was that their conception of their anticipated reward for this dedication to the war effort sounded more like a Greater Serbia than a united Yugoslavia. While the Serbians seemed increasingly amenable to the idea of compromise with Italy over prospective territorial spoils along the Adriatic, they seemed ever less interested in guaranteeing equal status to the Croat and Slovene communities in the South Slav lands that might come under their control. It became painfully apparent that they were thinking in terms of *annexing* parts or all of Bosnia, Dalmatia, Croatia–Slavonia, Vojvodina, and Slovenia rather than achieving *national unification* with the populations of these regions. The precedent of Serbia's inconsistent policies in Macedonia following its conquest in 1912–1913 preyed ever more on the minds of the Yugoslav Committee: the inhabitants of this newly "liberated" province had immediately been subjected to all the obligations of the Serbian citizenry, such as taxation and conscription, while attempts were made to postpone the extension of full constitutional rights to this population. This hardly boded well for the prospects of fraternity and equality among the ethnic communities of a Serbian-dominated Yugoslavia.

One of the first public manifestations of the tensions between members of the Serbian diplomatic corps and the Yugoslav Committee came on the occasion of a London exhibit of Ivan Meštrović's work. The Dalmatian sculptor, and member of the Yugoslav Committee, had won international attention before the war for his attempt to create an artistic genre expressive of Yugoslav fraternity. Meštrović's work celebrated themes from Serbian history, focussing on images of heroic resistance to foreign conquest and domination. He hoped to inspire Croats with the warlike traditions of their Serb brothers while showing the Serbs that their historical identity could be expressed in a modern art form developed by a Croat. The sense of being engaged in a common cultural struggle against Austro-Hungarian domination reached its high point in 1911 at an international art show in Rome. When the Habsburg authorities refused to permit a separate Croatian sub-pavilion to be set up under the auspices of the Habsburg pavilion, a number of Croatian artists – with Meštrović in the lead – staged a cultural defection, displaying their work in the Serbian pavilion instead.[51]

His international reputation as an artist lent an aura of legitimacy and respectability to the wartime Yugoslav cause in the eyes of the educated Western public. An exhibition of his work in London in June 1915 drew a large public and earned him laudatory reviews in the press.[52] Seton-Watson described the exhibition as "a presentation of the Southern Slav idea in stone ... " designed "to show that the Croats and Serbs have a culture of their own, and that its best representatives regard themselves as a single people with two names."[53] Yet in an ironic variation on the incident at the pre-war Rome art show, the Serbian ambassador to London refused to attend the 1915 exhibition because of Meštrović's refusal to call himself a Serbian artist! The more moderate Serbian ambassador to Paris crossed the Channel to appear at the exhibition in his colleague's place.[54]

This snubbing incident was a superficial manifestation of a deep-seated difference over the role of the Yugoslav Committee. The Serbian government regarded the Yugoslav Committee as a propaganda instrument pure and simple; as such, it had no business formulating an independent political agenda. Serbian efforts to reassure the Yugoslav activists only served to highlight how arrogant their fundamental premises seemed to be. When the Corfu-based authorities expressed their intention of tolerating the rights of Catholics in the future Yugoslavia, Supilo angrily insisted that toleration was not the issue: Catholics and Orthodox needed to enjoy full and unquestioned equality of rights, and this could best be guaranteed by a total separation of Church from state. The official status enjoyed by the Orthodox Church in the kingdom of Serbia was incompatible with the idea of Yugoslav unity. In a letter to Seton-Watson, Supilo complained that the Serbians simply were not mature enough to grasp such a concept.[55]

By 1916, Supilo was ready to break off relations with Serbia and to forge ahead with plans for an independent Croatian state. Yet the very multiethnic character of the Yugoslav Committee made it impossible to push such a decision through. The Slovene members of the Committee felt that their small nation would fare better as one of several ethnic groups in a South Slav state than as an isolated minority in an overwhelmingly Croat state. The ethnic Serbs on the Committee were naturally loath to sever the link to Serbia. Trumbić was also unwilling to forsake the possibility of compromise with Serbia, and Supilo eventually resigned from the Committee in protest, dying soon afterwards.[56]

The internal politics of the Serbian government in exile were extremely intricate and turbulent, and its unhappy relationship with the Yugoslav Committee served as a pivotal issue around which the confrontation between the cabinet of Prime Minister Pašić and leaders of the parliamentary opposition took place. Insofar as the Yugoslav Committee enjoyed the sympathy of certain circles within the British establishment, the leaders of the Serbian opposition may have hoped that their relative openness to dialogue with the Yugoslavists would earn them London's support in their confrontations with Pašić. Matters came to a head in the spring and summer of 1917, following the show trial and execution of the independent-minded officers at the head of the Union or Death ("Black Hand") organization, many of whom had had close ties to the parliamentary opposition.[57] Having used trumped-up charges of treason to eliminate this long-standing locus of resistance to the authority of his government, Pašić found his cabinet losing ever more support in parliament. With his coalition reduced to a minority, Pašić began making renewed overtures to the Yugoslav Committee as a way of neutralizing those segments of the Serbian opposition that had employed the Yugoslav cause as a platform for their attacks on his government. This openness to dialogue with the Yugoslavists was also designed to align Serbia more closely with the rhetoric of national self-determination espoused by Russia's new Provisional Government as well as by the United States, which had declared war on Germany in April. Finally, in May, the South Slav political parties within the Habsburg empire had responded to overtures from the new emperor, Karl, by issuing a declaration calling for their unification within the framework of a reconfigured Habsburg monarchy – a propaganda coup for the Austrians that Serbia needed to counter.[58]

The Serbian government's newly rediscovered openness to the Yugoslav idea led to the successful negotiation of the Corfu Declaration in July 1917. This document, jointly issued by the leaders of the Yugoslav Committee and the Serbian government, defined their common aim as the establishment of a democratic, constitutional kingdom of Serbs, Croats, and Slovenes under the Serbian ruling dynasty. Critical institutional details, such as the degree of local autonomy to be granted the ethnic regions, were to be left for a popularly elected, constitutional assembly to iron out once the war had ended. Only the cultural and religious rights of each constituent people were to be guaranteed.[59]

The convening in April 1918 of the Rome Congress of Oppressed Nationalities marked a high point in the Yugoslav Committee's campaign for international recognition. In its eagerness to exploit the propaganda value of hosting this two-day assembly of exiled nationalists from the Habsburg empire, the Italian government was willing to tolerate the participation of the Yugoslavs as long as they did not use the occasion to publicize their claim to territories the Italians were determined to annex. The Congress received great publicity in the Western press and support from the Allied governments. It was marked by speeches calling for the dismemberment of the Habsburg monarchy and its replacement by democratic nation-states. Potentially divisive territorial questions were side-stepped, as stress was laid on projecting an image of solidarity among the subject nationalities of East Central Europe and between those nationalities and the Italians.

While the Corfu Agreement and the Rome Congress succeeded as propaganda exercises directed at Western public opinion, they had little long-term impact on relations among the nationalist movements themselves. The Corfu Agreement had legitimized Serbia's territorial aspirations without really committing it to any specific institutional arrangements. Pašić actually used the agreement to undermine the Yugoslav Committee's attempts to gain international recognition, arguing that the Serbian ruling dynasty could now legitimately claim to speak on behalf of all South Slavs. The Italian government did its own part to block Allied recognition of the Yugoslav Committee, leaving Trumbić and his associates with little diplomatic or political leverage in their dealings with Serbia.

In the endplay of October–November 1918, the Yugoslav Committee was completely marginalized. Serbian prime minister Pašić disarmed his own internal opposition by inviting its leaders to join a broad coalition government that would preside over the reconstruction of liberated Serbia; the opposition leaders promptly abandoned their opportunistic advocacy of compromise with the Yugoslav Committee as they embraced the prospect of wielding power in a Serb-dominated Yugoslavia. Most significantly of all, the Croat social and political elites looked to the Serbian army to protect their territory against Italy and social order against the Green Cadres (see Chapter 4). The Yugoslav Committee was rendered obsolete on 1 December, as the Zagreb government's delegation granted essentially unconditional recognition to Serbian Crown Prince Alexander as King of the new kingdom of Serbs, Croats, and Slovenes.

Having fulfilled their function as propagandists for the South Slav cause, the leaders of the Yugoslav movement found themselves cast aside at the moment of truth. It seemed that they enjoyed a much more devoted following in Britain than in Serbia, or indeed in Croatia. The short-lived Zagreb government's eagerness to see order restored in the countryside overrode all other considerations, and it accepted a formula for unification with Serbia that involved the creation of a kingdom of Serbs, Croats, and Slovenes in name, which was nothing but an expanded Serbian state in practice. The Croat peasantry was duly suppressed by the Serbian army, while Serbian administrators established their bureaucratic dominion in the towns (see Chapter 7).

Yet the historical legacy of the Yugoslav Committee cannot be dismissed as insignificant. Its propaganda among the Western public and its cultivation of contact within the British establishment had paved the way for international recognition of a Yugoslav state including all of Croatia and Slovenia. At one and the same time, it was the gap between Supilo's and Trumbić's vision of a South Slav federation and the reality of a centralized, Serb-dominated Yugoslavia that was to serve as the central grievance of a resurgent Croat nationalism during the interwar period.

The Polish National Committee

In the case of Poland, the divide between those nationalists who gained diplomatic recognition in the Western capitals and those who remained in the homeland essentially reproduced the pre-existing differences between Dmowski's and Piłsudski's camps (see Chapter 3). The outbreak of war put both men's skills to the test. An armed conflict that pitted the partitioning powers against each other held forth great potential promise for the Polish national cause, but taking advantage of such a volatile situation depended on diplomatic adroitness and an acute sense of political timing. The unusual circumstances of prolonged warfare evened the playing field between Piłsudski and Dmowski, for the latter's control of a mass organization was not of immediate benefit to him amidst the upheaval of total war. In a certain sense, the most important constituencies each of them needed to cultivate at this point were not in Poland, but in the capitals of the Great Powers. But which Great Powers? There lay the rub. In both Piłsudski's and Dmowski's cases, pre-war alignments determined their initial, wartime diplomatic orientations, but as the conflict progressed, each of them modified his position in light of changing circumstances. In the end, they (unintentionally) complemented each other rather well on the diplomatic front, even as their political and personal differences grew deeper. Piłsudski's role will be examined below, in the discussion of volunteer legions. It was Dmowski who spent most of the war years in the Western capitals, lobbying on behalf of the Polish cause.

The Russian commander-in-chief's November 1914 promise of future autonomy for Poland did little to vindicate Dmowski's longstanding commitment to accommodation with Russia, especially in light of the German advance into Russian territory in the following year. In 1915, Dmowski moved his base of operations to Britain. Following the March 1917 Russian Revolution, he established a Polish National Committee that lobbied the Western allies for support, and that sought to add legitimacy to the Polish cause by recruiting a volunteer force for the Western front among Polish POWs and expatriates. Dmowski's move to the West reflected his surmise that Britain and France might end up in a stronger position than Russia to dictate peace terms to the Central Powers at the end of the war.[60] He also hoped that Paris and London would help pressure the Russian government into making substantive concessions to the Poles in the event of Russia emerging as master of Polish territory after all.

Despite his credentials as an intellectual and his familiarity with Western European societies and cultures, Dmowski was not as readily accepted by the Western establishment as were Masaryk or the Yugoslavists. His Russophile orientation and flagrantly ethnocentric conception of nationalism raised eyebrows in Britain; although he tried to tone down and rationalize his anti-Semitism, his open hostility toward Polish Jews and unwillingness to embrace the concept of tolerance toward ethno-cultural minorities in an independent Poland rubbed many of his audiences the wrong way. *The New Europe* was critical of the National Democrats' avowedly intolerant approach to ethnic relations in Poland, and Dmowski was regarded with suspicion both by the general British press and by a number of key figures within the Foreign Office.[61]

Dmowski's great advantage lay in the fact that Piłsudski was perceived as a pro-German figure, given his willingness to collaborate for a time with the German and Austrian occupying forces in Poland. Dmowski made the most of this association, and used it to undermine the influence of Piłsudski's informal representative in London, August Zaleski.[62] Dmowski also blunted the negative impact of his own chauvinistic style by recruiting a more palatable figure as spokesman for the Polish National Committee. Ignacy Paderewski, the world-famous pianist, minor composer, and editor of Chopin's works, who had been active on behalf of Polish cultural and humanitarian causes for many years, agreed to represent the Polish National Committee in its dealings with the Allied governments. Paderewski's genteel manners, charismatic presence, and compelling oratory were highly effective at winning sympathy for the Polish cause. Not the least of his converts was President Woodrow Wilson, whose distaste for Dmowski was offset by his admiration for this musical virtuoso, who so ably placed his advocacy of Polish national rights in the framework of the universal principles of democracy and national self-determination. Although Paderewski's nostalgia for the Polish–Lithuanian Commonwealth, his romantic flair, and his rather sizable ego made him an unlikely partner for Dmowski, the National Democratic leader was prepared to let him dominate the public stage during the war as the price for legitimizing the Polish National Committee in Western eyes. This stratagem was quite successful, for, by war's end, even as Piłsudski seized power in Poland, the Polish National Committee had been recognized by the Western powers as representing Polish interests and Piłsudski was ultimately obliged to acquiesce in Dmowski's and Paderewski's leadership of the Polish delegation to the Paris Peace Conference of 1919.[63] It remained to be seen whether the two competing streams of nationalism could be reconciled within the framework of an independent Polish state.

Zionism

Already established before the War as an organized movement with branches in the major Western and Central European capitals as well as in the United States and a clandestine existence in the Russian empire, the World Zionist Organization (WZO) was the ultimate exile movement, claiming as it did to represent an entire people in exile. Its actual level of support among the Jewish diaspora was difficult to assess. Although its international headquarters were in Berlin and its founder, Theodor Herzl (1860–1904), had been a Viennese Jew, Zionism held greater appeal among the Jews of Eastern Europe than among their much more assimilated Western and Central European counterparts, who were much more inclined to identify themselves as nationals of their host countries. Yet its activities in the great Jewish population centers of the Russian Pale of Settlement and Russian Poland were limited by the tsarist government's political repression. It also encountered competition in East European urban centers from rival Jewish political movements such as the Marxist Bund and met with suspicion and opposition on the part of the traditional, orthodox communities that dominated Jewish small-town (*shtetl*) life. Indeed, most orthodox rabbis regarded exile as a divinely ordained condition from which only the Messiah – not a self-appointed, predominantly secular, political organization – would redeem the Jewish people.[64]

During the years since its formal founding at the Basel Congress of 1897, the Zionist movement had undergone a significant internal upheaval over its choice of tactics and the nature of its fundamental objectives. The so-called political Zionism of Herzl and his circle had focussed on the use of personal diplomacy to win an internationally endorsed charter for the settlement of European Jewry as an autonomous society in Palestine. As repeated efforts to win clear-cut support for this project from European governments and to overcome the suspicions of the Ottoman government came to naught, leading members of the movement, Herzl among them, turned to the possibility of an alternative territorial option – possibly in British East Africa – for the future Jewish state. The uproar this provoked and the reaffirmation of the unbreakable tie between the Jewish people and the Land of Israel by the Sixth Zionist Congress of 1903 marked not only the defeat of territorialism but a decisive power shift within the movement away from political Zionism and toward the advocates of "practical Zionism." This group favored an incremental approach focussed on developing the existing Jewish agricultural settlements in Palestine by circumventing the restrictions of the hostile but bribable Ottoman authorities, and encouraging the growth of a distinctively Jewish, Hebraic national culture in the nascent *yishuv* (the Zionist community in Palestine). This strategy, it was argued, would foster the gradual development of the social, economic, and cultural infrastructure of a core national community in the ancestral homeland, creating facts on the ground rather than waiting interminably for the diplomatic version of messianic deliverance.

This approach was more than just an alternative means to a common end. Its advocates, who were mostly middle-class Jewish intellectuals from the Russian empire, shared a common opposition to what they saw as the condescension, moral vacuity, and cultural sterility of political Zionism. The political Zionists' seemingly futile diplomacy was conducted on behalf of the Jewish masses, but without their involvement. Completely focussed on the Holy Grail of a Jewish state, to be organized according to liberal, rationalist, technocratic ideals, they seemed disinterested in the question of what would make the new Jewish society distinctively and authentically Jewish. Theirs could be seen as a culturally assimilationist form of Central European Zionism; indeed, it was their assumption that German would be the lingua franca and language of high culture in the new society.

By contrast, the practical Zionists, among whom a core group known as the cultural Zionists were particularly influential, saw the cultivation of agricultural settlements in Palestine as laying the foundation for an egalitarian society connected directly to the ancestral land through the medium of labor. The quality of the Zionist project in Palestine was, to their mind, much more important than the quantity of Jews that could be transported there. Influenced by the mentality of the radical Russian intelligentsia, with its deeply ingrained hostility toward the institutions of state power, cultural Zionists such as the Russian Jewish essayist Ahad Ha'am (Asher Ginzberg, 1856–1927) stressed that a Jewish commonwealth in Palestine would never be able to accommodate the millions of destitute and persecuted East European Jews and thus could not offer the material solution to the Jewish problem that the political Zionists claimed it could. Its role should rather be that of a cultural and emotional center for world Jewry, where a modern national culture organically rooted in Jewish history and tradition and using Hebrew as its living tongue could be developed free of the overshadowing and assimilationist influence of non-Jewish forms of modernity. The influence of this core community would radiate outward into the diaspora and serve as the inspiration and model for the revitalization of Jewish life in Europe and around the world.[65]

The triumph of practical Zionism within the WZO did not bring about instantaneous success for the movement. The development of the *yishuv* seemed to grind to a halt during the last years before the war, its population leveling off at 35,000 (in addition to the 50,000 Jews from Palestine's pre-Zionist Jewish community) in the face of grievous economic problems and of a Young Turk regime even more hostile than its predecessor toward the settlement of foreign nationals on its territory.[66] Moreover, the elitist aspects of practical Zionism, with its emphasis on the role of a pioneering vanguard in creating a model society in the Land of Israel and on the revival of Hebrew to the exclusion of Yiddish – the everyday tongue of the East European Jewish masses – served to limit the mass appeal of the movement, whose leadership seemed unable to move beyond vehement theoretical debates toward creating the facts on the ground about which they held forth so eloquently.

It was amidst this atmosphere of stagnation and lack of direction in the Zionist movement that the First World War broke out. The initial response at the top levels of the organization was to adopt a cautious wait-and-see attitude and, as a movement with branches and constituencies in each of the major belligerent countries, to maintain a policy of strict neutrality toward the conflict. Berlin was to remain the location of WZO executive headquarters, with neutral Copenhagen serving as the site for an international liaison office and for periodic conferences bringing together leaders of the country branches.

Needless to say, maintaining liaison in wartime proved to be an awkward and haphazard affair. In practice, the branch offices functioned independently of one another, their perspectives and policy orientations shaped increasingly by local political constraints and opportunities. Close identification with their respective countries' causes also eroded the official stance of neutrality, particularly in Germany and Britain. Rather than compromising the prospects of the movement, this lack of coordination and breakdown of neutrality actually worked to its long-term advantage, as German and British Zionist leaders were able to win unprecedented and critical support from their respective governments in the context of wartime national and imperial rivalries. The particularly notable success of the British-based Zionists led by Chaim Weizmann (1874–1952) in creating a *de facto* alliance with the world's greatest imperial power propelled Weizmann and his supporters to the postwar leadership of the WZO and, more importantly, created a new synthesis of political and practical Zionism in the context of a suddenly revitalized *yishuv*.

The attempt by German Zionists to influence German policy toward the Jews of occupied Poland and Lithuania, as described earlier in this chapter, was largely unsuccessful, although the Zionist movement in the occupied zones benefited indirectly from the opportunities created by German occupation. German Zionist lobbying on behalf of the small *yishuv* in Ottoman-controlled Palestine, by contrast, did bear fruit. Concerned that Jemal Pasha's expulsion of the Jews of Jaffa in April 1917 was the prelude to a complete dismantling of the *yishuv*, German Zionists prevailed upon the Kaiser's government to intervene. The German government feared that the destruction of the *yishuv* by Germany's Ottoman ally would antagonize Jewish opinion in Russia (which Germany hoped shortly to knock out of the war) as well as public opinion in America and in neutral countries and serve to undermine the image and negotiating position of the Central Powers at the prospective peace conference. Intervention by German diplomats in Istanbul and by General von Falkenhayn in Palestine did in fact help restrain Jemal Pasha from massive retaliation against the *yishuv* following the arrest in October 1917 of a ring of Jewish spies that had been reporting to British intelligence. German support thus proved crucial in saving the badly battered *yishuv* as a core community around which the Zionist project could develop in the aftermath of the war.[67]

The fear – never realized – that German interest in Zionism might eventually blossom into a far-reaching expression of support for the Jewish national cause helped spur dramatic developments in British policy. Critical to this turn of events was the personal initiative of Chaim Weizmann and a small coterie of associates. A relatively obscure figure until the war presented him with a golden opportunity to enter the political stage, Weizmann was a native of the Russian Pale of Settlement who had studied chemistry in Germany and Switzerland and assumed a faculty position at the University of Manchester in 1904, all the while remaining actively involved in the Zionist movement. His wartime appointment to the Ministry of Munitions, where he made decisive contributions to the development of a new technique for the production of acetone (an important ingredient in the manufacture of cordite, an artillery-shell propellant), helped him forge useful political connections and gain personal renown in government circles. His enthusiastic Anglophilia and adeptness in the cultivation of a genteel manner, combined with his unabashed self-identification as a Russian Jew, was ideally suited to appeal to the British upper crust's fascination with the exotic foreigner.[68]

A cultural Zionist and disciple of Ahad Ha'am, Weizmann nonetheless saw in Britain's war against the Ottoman empire the perfect opportunity for forging a lasting political alliance between Zionism and a Great Power that, he was convinced, would have a decisive role to play in shaping the peace settlement and in allocating the spoils of war in the Middle East. His central objective was to gain British endorsement of the Jewish right to national self-determination in Palestine. Essentially, as David Vital has argued, this represented a reversion to the political Zionists' obsession with the idea of a charter. But whereas Herzl and his followers had failed to secure the support of any power, Weizmann was correct in perceiving a unique opportunity to do just that in wartime Britain.

A variety of concerns and interests converged to create a receptive audience in Whitehall. Linking British imperial interest in Palestine (which was seen as a potential protective buffer for British-controlled Egypt) to the Zionist campaign for a Jewish national home would give Whitehall a bargaining chip in any potential peace talks with Germany and might help preempt any similar moves by the German government. In the aftermath of the 1916 Sykes–Picot agreement in which British and French diplomats agreed on the partition of the Middle East into spheres of influence, British statesmen began to second-guess the section of the agreement providing for international control of Palestine. Once again, sponsoring the Jewish national cause could serve as a lever with which to nudge the French out and assume undivided control of Palestine. British concern, following the March 1917 Revolution, over Russia's continued commitment to the war effort also reinforced interest in Zionism. Because many prominent figures in Russian socialist parties were Jewish, British diplomats labored under the misapprehension – encouraged by Weizmann – that a dramatic pro-Zionist gesture could secure their support for the common war effort. Finally, various personal preconceptions and prejudices combined to awaken pro-Zionist sympathies among some key actors in the British establishment, such as Mark Sykes, an anti-Semite who regarded the Zionist program as an attractive alternative both to the machinations of "international Jewish finance" and to "Godless Jewish socialism" – and who also saw its sponsorship by Britain as an opportune escape route from the Palestine provisions of the Sykes–Picot agreement that bore his name.[69] The upshot, following the commencement of General Allenby's invasion of Palestine, was Foreign Secretary Lord Balfour's November 1917 declaration that:

> His Majesty's Government views with favour the establishment in Palestine of a national home for the Jewish people, and will use its best endeavours to facilitate the achievement of this object, it being clearly understood that nothing shall be done which may prejudice the civil and religious rights of existing non-Jewish communities in Palestine, or the rights and political status enjoyed by Jews in any other country.[70]

There were elements of ambiguity to the wording of this text, which did not define what a national home was, and neither specified whether the national home was to be coextensive with Palestine's borders nor defined where those borders might lie. But although the Declaration fell short of maximal Zionist political desiderata, the decision to issue it marked a watershed event that led to the postwar establishment of a British-held League of Nations mandate as an internationally recognized framework for Jewish emigration to Palestine and the development there of the institutional foundation of Jewish self-government.

Weizmann's diplomatic success helped generate the sort of mass Jewish support for his policy that he had claimed to enjoy in the first place. In other words, his claim to represent mass opinion among East European Jewry had a self-fulfilling quality. Given the inaccessibility of the Jews of German-occupied Eastern Europe and the remoteness and chaotic conditions of Russian Jewry, there was no way definitively to ascertain Jewish popular sentiments in the midst of the war. Jewish opinion abroad could be whatever a convincing, if self-appointed, spokesman in London said it was.[71] In fact, Russian Zionist leaders refused officially to abandon Zionist neutrality in favor of Weizmann's openly pro-British stance, but his failure to sway them did not significantly detract from his argument that a bold initiative by Britain would win international Jewish support. Indeed, there was a large measure of truth to this line of argument – with the notable exception that Jewish opinion did not have the kind of influence on Russian revolutionary politics that His Majesty's Government thought it did.[72]

Weizmann also had to overcome the opposition of the British Jewish establishment, whose representatives sat on the Conjoint Foreign Committee of British Jews. Convinced that claiming Palestine on the basis of Jewish national identity would compromise the Jewish claim to civil equality within their host countries, the assimilationist leaders who dominated the Conjoint Committee took the unusual step of attacking Weizmann's policy in the mainstream British press. This only redounded to Weizmann's benefit, as none other than Sir Henry Wickham Steed, editor of *The Times*, friend of oppressed nationalities, and believer in the anti-Semitic notion of an international Jewish conspiracy (and hence, perhaps, in the power of world Jewry to help Britain's cause?), weighed in on behalf of the Zionists. The open attack on Zionism also backfired within the British Jewish community, and led to a vote of censure against the Conjoint Committee by one of its constituent elements, the Board of Deputies of British Jews.[73]

Once again, then, a self-selected coterie of committed activists had success-fully employed their connections to the British academic, journalistic, and political establishments and their familiarity with, and genuine commitment to, liberal political rhetoric and values, to propel themselves into the role of repre-sentatives of their nation and to gain the qualified endorsement of a great power for their nationalist objectives. Weizmann's political triumph was the triumph of a liberal nationalism over the liberal assimilationism of the West European Jewish establishments as well as over the cautious incrementalism and neutralism of the pre-war Zionist establishment. It marked the synthesis of political Zionism with practical Zionism – a synthesis whose specifically Anglophile and ideologically moderate orientation would be called into question by the socialist Zionist leaders of the growing *yishuv* during the 1930s – but whose main outlines reappeared in the form of David Ben-Gurion's social-democratic *étatisme* and Israel's subsequent alliance with the United States in the second half of the twentieth century.

Although Zionism was but one of many ideological currents among European Jewry during and after the Great War, its claim to representative status was in some senses less problematic than that of the East European national committees described above, since it could not and did not set out to impose its vision on diaspora Jewry. Its constituency was a self-selected one, consisting of those Jews who chose to emigrate to Palestine or to support the effort. But within Palestine itself, of course, the democratic principles embraced by Zionists ran into a tougher dilemma, and one which had not been systematically examined in advance – the presence of some 600,000 Arabs whose collective identity or inter-ests could hardly be reconciled with the Jewish aspiration to national self-determination.

Synopsis

In each of the above cases, a small group of activists based in Allied capitals forged a program for national independence that gained significant public acceptance and official recognition in the West. Removed as they were from the political constraints of their native lands, they were free to promote agendas that anticipated the defeat of Germany and called for the dismantling of the

Habsburg or Ottoman empires. Their locations in London and Paris enhanced the liberal-democratic tenor of their rhetoric. This was partly a function of self-selection: those who were predisposed to favor the political values of the West (the Czechoslovak activists, the Yugoslavists) or who had strong cultural and personal connections to the West (Masaryk, Štefánik, Paderewski, Meštrović, Weizmann) were most likely to turn to Britain, France, and the United States for support. Their liberal-democratic inclinations were also reinforced by their role as propagandists addressing a Western audience during a war that was, by 1917, portrayed in the Allied and Associated countries as a struggle between democracy and autocracy. In Dmowski's case, the use of such verbiage was a calculated ploy, but, among the other figures dealt with here, ideological inclination and political necessity reinforced each other. At the same time, however, their programs were filled with the oversimplifications and facile solutions that are the hallmarks of propaganda. The notion of historic state right was conflated with liberal self-determination doctrine in an attempt to justify maximal territorial claims. Endorsement by leaders of immigrant communities was held up as a valid source of legitimacy for interethnic (especially Czechoslovak) federation schemes that did not necessarily have strong potential for broad-based support in the homelands. And yet, precisely because they enjoyed Allied support, these national committees and their political programs had a substantive impact on the postwar course of events in their countries, either by being catapulted directly into a position of power (as in the case of the Czechoslovak National Council becoming the Provisional Government of Czechoslovakia, the Polish National Committee becoming the Polish delegation to the Paris Peace Conference, or the Zionist Organization establishing the framework for Jewish emigration to, and self-rule in, Palestine) or – in the case of the Yugoslav Committee – by representing a counterfactual scenario, the non-realization of which would form a basis for challenges to the legitimacy of the postwar successor state.

Volunteer Legions

A closely related category of wartime nationalist activism was that of the volunteer legions. The legions were variously based on both Central Power- and Allied-controlled territory; their contributions to their host countries' war efforts were intended to win support for the self-determination of the nations whose aspirations they claimed to represent. As in the case of the national committees described above, with which many of them were affiliated, a number of these military formations gained a significance far out of proportion to the numbers of men enlisted in their ranks. Their impact could take a variety of forms. In some cases, their wartime exploits provided a kernel of truth around which nationalist myths were woven by the postwar successor states. In a number of instances, veterans of legions went on personally to play powerful roles as self-made nationalist elites that laid claim to political hegemony in the successor states.

Prisoners of war constituted a major recruitment pool for volunteer legions on both sides of the conflict. In the Central Powers, émigré organizations such as the Union for the Liberation of Ukraine (SVU), mentioned above, lobbied successfully for the establishment of separate camps for their co-ethnics among POWs from the Russian army. Such facilities were established in Austria–Hungary and Germany for Ukrainian, Polish, Finnish, Georgian, and Muslim POWs. Transfer to these camps was voluntary, although it had potential rewards in the form of more lenient treatment; in the case of Ukrainian prisoners, approximately 80,000 chose the option of being housed in camps set aside for them in Germany and Austria–Hungary. This act of self-differentiation and the subsequent experience of living in an ethnically homogeneous camp doubtless enhanced whatever pre-existing sense of national identity these soldiers may have had. It was from ethnic POW camps, in turn, that many men were drawn into volunteer legions such as the Finnish Jäger Battalion and Georgian Legion organized by the German army in 1915 and 1916, respectively. Ukrainian volunteers were trained and transported to the Ukrainian sector of the front, but were never actually allowed to participate in the fighting for fear that they might turn against their Central Power patrons.[74]

Habsburg POWs in Russia constituted a major recruitment pool for volunteer legions affiliated with the Allied powers. One of the less prominent examples was the Serbian Volunteer Corps, whose brief and unhappy history of dissension between Serb officers and other South Slav recruits seemed to highlight the tremendous potential for divisions among South Slavs rather than to embody the idea of Yugoslav unity.[75] By contrast, the Czechoslovak Legion stands out as an example of a volunteer force that carved out a prominent role for itself in the foundation myth of the Czechoslovak state.

The Czechoslovak Legion

From the beginning of their political activity in the West, Masaryk, Beneš, and Štefánik lobbied hard for the formation of separate contingents of Czech volunteers in the French and Italian armies. France was the first country to respond positively, and the Italians gradually followed suit. These Czech legions were recruited from among Habsburg POWs in Italy and from Czech and Slovak émigré communities in the United States and other countries overseas. The Czech contingent in the Russian Army, known as the Družina, was linked to a pan-Slavic and pro-tsarist umbrella organization formed in September 1914 by representatives of Czech communities from the major Russian urban centers, calling itself the Association of Czechoslovak Societies in Russia.[76]

In the spring of 1917, following the overthrow of the tsarist government, Masaryk was able to gain the Russian Provisional Government's recognition of his authority over the Association of Czechoslovak Societies in Russia, displacing the influence of pan-Slavs in the organization. The Družina was now integrated into an autonomous Czechoslovak Legion answerable to the authority of Masaryk's National Committee, and an active recruitment campaign was initiated among Czech and Slovak prisoners of war. Finally, it was agreed that the expanded Czechoslovak force would be free to leave Russia (by way of the Trans-Siberian railroad and the Far Eastern port of Vladivostok) for the Western Front as soon as possible.[77] Some 10 per cent of Czech prisoners volunteered for the Legion. Czechs of middle-class, educated backgrounds were disproportionately represented in the expanded force, but most of the Legion's rank-and-file were of lower-class background, and there were some Slovaks in their number as well.

By the time the Legion was prepared to set forth, the Bolsheviks were in power and had signed the Brest-Litovsk peace treaty. As all semblance of public order broke down in the country, POWs of all nationalities found themselves increasingly free of formal camp discipline, but mostly unable to find a way of returning home immediately. Many of them either joined one of the broad array of rival Russian militias that were competing for followers as they braced for civil war, or formed their own political committees and military units (often in affiliation with Russian ideological groups, ranging from monarchist to Bolshevik).

Under these conditions, it is not surprising that the initial Bolshevik commitment to upholding the previous government's understanding with the Czechoslovak Legion quickly gave way to mutual suspicion: the Bolsheviks feared that the Legion would make common cause with their enemies, while the Czech fighters were suspicious of Bolshevik attempts to disarm them. Persistent efforts by pro-Bolshevik ("Internationalist") former POWs – many of them Magyars and Germans, though also including Czechs – to win the rank-and-file of the Legion over to their cause led to violent incidents and heightened tensions.[78] In the wake of an armed clash at Chelyabinsk in May 1918, the understanding with the Bolsheviks broke down completely. The officers of the Czechoslovak Legion met in council and decided to fight their way to Vladivostok in the face of Bolshevik opposition. As they traveled in their armored rail cars, the highly motivated Czechs seized one town after another from local Bolshevik authorities. In so doing, they became *de facto* participants in the Russian Civil War, allying themselves with Socialist Revolutionaries, Mensheviks, and other, mostly left-wing, Russian elements opposed to the Bolsheviks. The activities of the Legion attracted great attention in the West, where the Czechs were seen first as the potential kernel for a reconstituted Eastern Front against Germany and later also as a core element in the Western military intervention against the Bolsheviks. In the end, these Anglo-French pipedreams came to naught, but the Czechoslovak Legion emerged with its honor and reputation intact in the eyes of the victorious powers.[79]

Ships to evacuate most of the Czech and Slovak fighters from Vladivostok did not become available until 1920, long after the guns had fallen silent on the Western Front.[80] But the epic journey across Siberia had already assumed a political and propagandist significance far out of proportion to any material contribution it could have made to the Allied war effort. The Legion's demonstration of self-sacrifice and heroism on behalf of the anti-German cause was successfully played upon by the exiled Czech leaders in their struggle to gain

Western recognition of their country's independence and of their territorial demands. Beyond that, it rapidly acquired the status of national myth within the newly founded state.

The transformation of the Legion's experiences into a national-cultural artefact began during the actual course of its trek across Siberia. Using money and equipment provided by Czech émigré associations, the legionaries recorded their progress toward Vladivostok in photos and moving pictures, produced newspapers and other publications on board one of their train cars, entertained themselves with theatrical productions, and designed monuments in honor of their martyred comrades. Much of this imagery and material was subsequently incorporated in the propagation of the Legion's story in interwar Czechoslovakia.[81] The nationalist version of history that arose from this downplayed or ignored the relative quiescence down to 1917 of the majority of the Czech populace and leadership, while portraying the exceptional experience of the legionaries as emblematic of the determination and solidarity that had animated every true son and daughter of the nation during the Great War.[82]

Piłsudski's First Brigade

A distinctive variation on this theme was developed by Piłsudski's First Brigade – the most renowned of the Polish military formations that came into being under the protection of the Central Powers.

Among the various Polish armed formations created on one part or another of that partitioned country's territory during the war, the ones that maintained the most continuous corporate identity and most steadfast commitment to a measure of autonomy were those under Piłsudski's command. Piłsudski initially enjoyed a luxury unmatched by that of his Czech or South Slav counterparts – the support and encouragement of the Austrian government. Given that the primary focus of his activity was directed at the undermining of tsarist authority in Russian-ruled Poland, the Austrian authorities had allowed him to use Galicia as a base for the organization of an underground, nationalist militia fronting as a sharpshooting club. Most of the volunteers for this force were students of an urban, middle-class background, people with a strong sense of history whose imaginations were fired by the association of their formation with the tradition of Dąbrowski's legions that had fought alongside Napoleon a century earlier.[83]

Austrian sponsorship soon proved to have its liabilities. At the outbreak of the First World War, Piłsudski's force conducted a brief, unsuccessful incursion into Russian Poland, but soon thereafter found itself obliged – under threat of dissolution by the Austrian authorities – to merge into a broader formation known as the Polish Legions, which came under the nominal oversight of a tenuous coalition of rival Galician–Polish political parties. In the eyes of Austrian military intelligence, the Legions were to serve as an instrument for promoting and legitimizing the extension of Habsburg rule over Russian Poland.[84]

Piłsudski was given the command of only one brigade (the First Brigade) in the Polish Legions, and his challenge was to maintain a distinctive role for this force that would compensate for its small size and that would counteract Austrian attempts to dilute the distinctive identity of the Legions. He met this challenge by investing his 5,000 men with an egalitarian ethos and an *esprit de corps* that enhanced their discipline and battlefield performance. Members of the force addressed each other as "citizen" as well as by military rank and there were no gradations of pay among officers. By the same token, the Brigade did not present itself as a narrowly ideological grouping; Piłsudski broke off his formal ties to the Polish Socialist Party and made it clear that acceptance into his brigade was contingent on personal commitment to the cause of national liberation rather than party affiliation. The educated background of most of its members, their high degree of political motivation, and the democratic-revolutionary atmosphere that suffused the First Brigade contributed to its outstanding performance in combat during the bloody campaigns of 1915–1916.[85]

As Russian Poland fell under an increasingly exploitative and arbitrary German and Austrian military occupation, Piłsudski's political orientation shifted away from cooperation with Vienna and Berlin and toward resistance. His alliance with Austria had always been tactical in nature, and as the Central Powers consolidated their grip on Poland, he took measures to distance himself and his men from any hint of collaboration. From 1915 on, he began directing new volunteers away from the First Brigade and into the Polish Military Organization (the "POW" according to its Polish initials) – a clandestine force that he had secretly created in skeletal form months before the outbreak of war, and which remained outside the purview of the Austrian authorities.

The German and Austrian military authorities' decision to bring all Polish legions under their direct command provoked Piłsudski into ordering the 20,000 men of the POW to undertake sabotage operations against the German and Austrian occupation forces. At the time of his resignation from the Provisional State Council two months later (July 1917), Piłsudski tried to organize the mass defection of his men to Russia, where the new Provisional Government had expressed its qualified support for an independent Poland. Although these plans were disrupted by his arrest and confinement at Magdeburg fortress, near Berlin, Piłsudski's reputation for political virtue and military prowess was such by now that his captivity only enhanced his image as a leader whose role transcended the petty squabbles of party politics. As the end of the war approached in November 1918, the Germans released Piłsudski from prison and transported him to Warsaw, where the German-appointed Regency Council handed over power to him.[86]

Sundry other militias and armies were formed in the various parts of Poland during these years. In their multiplicity of affiliations and objectives, these formations reflected the fragmented nature of Polish politics rather than embodying a sense of national unity. At the beginning of the war, Piłsudski's main political rival, Roman Dmowski, created the Puławski Legion that fought as part of the Russian army.[87] When the Russian Provisional Government recognized Poland's right to independence in 1917, it suited action to words by separating some half-million Polish soldiers from the regular armed forces and organizing them into separate formations. As the Russian army disintegrated, some of these units ended up joining the Red Army, while others fought the Bolsheviks. One formation was cut to pieces by armed Ukrainian peasants in June 1918, as it fought to protect the estates of the Polish landed gentry against social revolution.[88]

Only in February 1918, when the Germans and Austro-Hungarians signed a peace treaty with Ukraine that promised the cession of Polish territory to the new Ukrainian state, did broad segments of Polish society begin to coalesce around a position of opposition to the Central Powers' policy, vindicating Piłsudski's earlier break with the occupation authorities.[89] The Polish Regency Council issued a protest against the Ukrainian treaty, members of the Polish Circle in the Austrian Reichsrat were harshly critical, demonstrations broke out in Galician cities, and the Austrian-backed Legions attempted to escape to Russia. The one brigade that actually succeeded in crossing the lines was commanded by General Józef Haller, who subsequently left for France, where he assumed the command of an army of 100,000 Poles (former POWs and recruits from émigré communities) fighting on the Western Front.[90]

The number of men involved in Piłsudski's operations was minute compared to the hundreds of thousands of Poles who served as conscripts in the armies of the Great Powers (especially in the Russian army), and in the various other Polish party militias and volunteer corps. But it is precisely in the face of this bewildering and seemingly incoherent historical record that Piłsudski's contribution acquired its significance. Before the war was over, he was already looked to as a potential leader by units beyond his immediate control, including the Polish forces created under the auspices of the Russian Provisional Government.[91] When an independent Poland emerged, battered and dazed, from the wreckage of three empires, Piłsudski towered above the political scene as a figure whose supporters felt he had never compromised his principles, never collaborated with occupying powers beyond the clear limits of the national interest, and had led one of the most cohesive and militarily successful Polish armed formations. The experience of his brigade constituted a meaningful story line that could serve as the backbone of a unifying nationalist myth. In its official histories, school textbooks, and public rituals, the interwar Polish republic was to portray the exploits of the First Brigade as a microcosm of the national experience and as emblematic of the whole people's single-minded struggle for national liberation.[92] A quarter of a century later, de Gaulle's Free French forces were to play a loosely analogous role in the reconstruction of a positive French national self-image.

As with the Free French, this myth was a form of overcompensation for the reality of a society whose response to the war had highlighted its deep internal divisions. In fact, the ethos of the First Brigade had a double-edged quality: Piłsudski's legionnaires worshipped the idea of the nation as a supreme value for which they were eager to lay down their own lives; by the same token, they came to see themselves as a natural elite whose own conduct had embodied nationalist ideals that the nation as a whole had failed to live up to. This self-image as an unappreciated vanguard of the nation crystallized in the first weeks of the war, in the wake of the First Brigade's initial foray from Galicia into Russian Poland. This incursion had been undertaken in the hope of stimulating a general uprising against the tsarist oppressors. The legionnaires' dismay over the popular apathy that greeted them was channeled into the cultivation of a bitter pride in the loneliness of their noble mission. As the last words of the Brigade's anthem put it:

> We no longer need recognition from you,
> Neither your words, nor your tears,
> The days of seeking your compassion are ended,
> To hell with you![93]

According to Andrzej Garlicki, Piłsudski actively fostered this sense of camaraderie-in-alienation, encouraging his followers to value collective self-reliance, group discipline, and obedience to their leader as the most important principles shaping their mental outlook and governing their behavior.[94] In the postwar years, this mentality was to manifest itself in a self-serving form of political elitism that contributed to the erosion of democratic principles in the Polish republic.

The Arab Revolt

In the very difficult cultural and geopolitical circumstances of the Arab world, a striking analogy to the case of Piłsudski's legionnaires is to be found in the military and political trajectory of the leaders of the Arab Revolt.

The term Arab Revolt – as the events described below came to be known in the Arab world – is itself somewhat misleading, suggesting as it does a general uprising of the Arab masses against their Turkish overlords. This was in fact a much more limited revolt against the Ottoman state by Hussein, Sharif and Emir of Mecca and ruler of the Hejaz (the province running along the western coast of the Arabian peninsula and containing the Islamic holy cities of Mecca and Medina). The original motives of Hussein cannot be said to have been nationalist in nature. As the local potentate of a province on the periphery of the Ottoman empire, Hussein began to clash with Istanbul in the last years before the war as he attempted to preserve the functional autonomy of the Hejaz in the face of a centralizing Young Turk administration that was encroaching upon it. Hussein had been appointed Sharif of Mecca in 1908 by the Ottoman Sultan against the wishes of the CUP, creating tension between the Young Turks and the Sharif from the start. Moreover, the completion of a railway line south to Medina in the year of Hussein's appointment had facilitated the imposition of much more direct Ottoman administrative control over the city and surrounding province; the prospect of a further extension of the line to Mecca aroused Hussein's concern. An additional source of strain came with the onset of the war, as revenue from the Muslim pilgrimage (*hajj*) to Mecca was drastically reduced by the British naval blockade. By the same token, the war increased the likelihood that the British, based in Egypt, would respond favorably to Hussein's overtures, as in fact they did. The correspondence in 1915–1916 between Hussein and Sir Henry McMahon (British High Commissioner in Egypt) led to British military support for Hussein's revolt against Ottoman rule, which began in June 1916.[95]

The population of the Hejaz cannot be said to have been nationally conscious either. Most of the population was nomadic and the first local newspapers had not appeared until after 1908. Apart from some members of the ruling family itself (for which Hussein adopted the name "Hashemites" at the beginning of his revolt in 1916), the province was in many ways removed from the political and cultural pulse of the great population centers of the Arab world.[96] The rank-and-file of the Hashemites' armies was composed of Bedouin tribesmen whose personal loyalty was to their sheikhs, and whose sheikhs in turn had to be cajoled, threatened, and bribed into line by Hussein and his sons who led the military forces.

Once he had decided to risk open confrontation, Hussein's ambitions did extend beyond the confines of the Hejaz. Yet, here too, his operative mental framework was not strictly nationalist. In his Arabic-language propaganda, he attacked the Young Turk regime as at heart secular and un-Islamic, suggesting that he would restore true Islamic rule to the lands that fell under his sway.[97]

And yet, the revolt of the Hejaz did take on the political mantle of Arab nationalism by virtue of the triangular linkage that connected it with the secret nationalist societies of Syria and Iraq (Mesopotamia) and with the British. During two trips to Damascus in 1915–1916, Hussein's son Faisal had established contact and explored the possibility of cooperation with leaders of al-Fatat and al-'Ahd, and was inducted as a member of the latter society. Faisal went on to become commander of the Northern Army, the most important military arm of the Hejazi revolt, which was to enter Syria alongside the army of Britain's General Allenby in 1918. The British government itself looked upon the Sharif's rebellion as a spark that might ignite the flames of Arab nationalism in the population centers of Syria and Iraq. This view was encouraged by Arab defectors from the Ottoman forces and political exiles who belonged to al-'Ahd and al-Fatat and made wildly exaggerated claims to British officials in Cairo about the membership figures and extent of support for the societies among Arab officers serving in the Ottoman armed forces. The Hussein–McMahon correspondence was partly shaped by these considerations, and resulted in a British undertaking to support Hussein in the establishment of Arab independence across much of present-day Jordan, Syria, and Iraq.[98]

Hussein's alliance with Britain was thus framed in terms of the Arabs' right to national self-determination[99] and the revolt was directly tied to Arab nationalism through the person of Faisal. Rhetorically and symbolically, the revolt of the Hejaz took on the aura of an Arab Revolt, even though the promised uprising in Syria failed to materialize (see Chapter 4).

Not only was the symbolic significance of the Revolt to grow in the aftermath of the war, as its myth was cultivated by the Arab regimes that traced their origins to it. It also had a concrete, functional impact on postwar nationalist politics, particularly in the case of Iraq. For the Revolt served as a framework for the formation of a self-selected nationalist elite, loosely analogous in its experience and self-image to the cohort of Polish legionnaires who rose to positions of power in interwar Poland.

The central figures in this case were a small group of Arab defectors from the Ottoman army. Out of the hundreds of thousands of Arab soldiers who deserted on a variety of fronts during the course of the war, the overwhelming majority simply tried to make their way back to their homes rather than rally to a new military-political cause. But a few hundred officers from Syria and Iraq crossed over from Ottoman positions to Allied lines along a variety of fronts, eventually making their way to the Hejaz to join the military campaign led by Sharif Hussein and his sons. Other recruits were drawn into the Revolt from among the ranks of Iraqi prisoners held in British camps in India and Egypt.[100]

Numerically, these Syrian and Iraqi contingents were a drop in the bucket, given that the Hejazi forces numbered some 40,000 men (including 30,000 irregulars).[101] Their numbers were also very small in relation to those Syrians and Iraqis who remained loyal to the Sultan to the end of the war. Moreover, only around seventy were members of al-ʿAhd and al-Fatat. But they formed very distinct, tightly knit groups of experienced, Ottoman-trained officers, who assumed dominant roles in the command structure of the Hejazi forces. Those who were members of al-ʿAhd and al-Fatat had already been actively engaged in the politics of nationalism before the Sharif's uprising, and by casting their lot with the Ottomans' enemies, they had committed themselves irrevocably to the realization of a new regional order based on the idea of Arab independence. Their cohesion along lines of regional origin (there were severe strains between Iraqi officers and their less numerous Syrian colleagues),[102] their connections with nationalist societies in Syria and Mesopotamia, and their opportune affiliation with a cause that enjoyed the support of the victorious British army, all made them prime candidates for positions of power and influence in the new Arab polities that took shape in the aftermath of Ottoman defeat. As in so many of the cases reviewed above, it was precisely the exceptional nature of their wartime experience that, in the transformed circumstances of the postwar period, legitimized their claim to have acted on behalf of their captive people's desire for independence.

Their vision seemed to be on the verge of fulfillment when Faisal's Northern Army entered Damascus in October 1918 as an independent contingent allied with the advancing British forces.[103] Many of them went on to assume positions of leadership in the short-lived Syrian monarchy established by Faisal in 1918 (see Chapter 6). France's subsequent imposition of its rule on Syria and Britain's assertion of imperial oversight over Iraq was a bitter disappointment to the officers who had led the Arab Revolt. And yet, as we shall see in Chapter 7, the temptation of gaining high office within the framework of the British mandate in Iraq was to prove difficult to resist.

Conclusion

While within the multinational empires the stresses and strains of total war widened socio-political fissures along lines of ethnicity and class, outside the imperial frameworks the war opened up new spaces for experiments in mass mobilization, political organization, armed action, and the creation of heroic legends. German (and, for a much shorter period, Ottoman) armies of conquest and occupation removed extensive territories from the control of the Russian empire, and proceeded to introduce schemes of bureaucratic categorization, façades of national self-determination, and divide-and-rule policies that lent new institutional and political significance to ethnic identity and that sharpened the lines of distinction and division among nationalities. National committees based in Allied, Central Power, or neutral capitals prepared the propagandist and diplomatic groundwork for the realization of separatist programs. POW camps contained captive audiences for the propaganda of national committees and the legions' recruitment campaigns. The legions, in turn, sought to flesh out the romantic image of nations in arms.

With the fragmentation of the multinational empires into nation-states in 1917–1918, romantic images were transformed into founding myths, national committees became provisional governments or peace-conference delegations, and ethno-cultural identities that had been reified and institutionalized by occupying powers for reasons of political expediency took on new life as frameworks for national self-determination efforts. It was precisely those nationalist groups that had operated outside the boundaries of the Romanov, Ottoman, and Habsburg empires during the war that were, in many instances, best prepared to seize the day upon the collapse of those empires, assuming leading roles in the successor states or seeing their programs and political values – which tended to be of a liberal or liberal-democratic cast – incorporated into the new states' institutional and ideological structures.

Such apparent success stories contained the seeds of their own undoing. The sudden convergence in 1918 of wildly disparate perspectives and experiences – from home fronts, war fronts, occupation, and exile – within the framework of newly formed nation-states may have occasionally produced fleeting images of national triumph and unity, but in fact added to the intense discord that immediately arose over how to define the boundaries of political and national identity. Moreover, as we shall see in Chapter 7, it was to be one of the many bitter ironies of the postwar world that the very elements that had fought the hardest for a fundamental redistribution of power, themselves sometimes congealed into hardened ruling classes that jealously monopolized power in the face of mounting social changes and ideological challenges.

6 Defining the Boundaries of the Nation, 1918–1923

The end of the Great War was also the end of the three multinational empires. In their place arose a multitude of new polities with uncertain borders and ill-defined identities. Many of them were ravaged by civil conflicts and inter-state wars for several more years. Even where fighting ceased early, peace did not automatically bring about a restoration of stability and prosperity. Economic pressures that had been held under the lid by government controls during wartime were released explosively in the war's aftermath. Inflation was high everywhere, and reached astronomical proportions in many parts of Eastern Europe. Battered economies could not reabsorb the millions of soldiers and refugees who returned to their homes. The social and economic dislocation that followed the war was almost as violent in its own way as the continent-wide military conflict that had just ended. It was amidst these centrifugal forces that far-reaching decisions had to be made about the boundaries of identity in the new polities.

Although the new boundaries were justified as reflections of pre-existing identities or objective ethnographic criteria, the very process of drawing them actually played a powerful role in shaping national identities and in changing or limiting the terms of debate about nationhood. The problem was that most ethnic groups did not come in neatly wrapped territorial packages. Languages, cultures, and religions were both dispersed and intermingled in a kaleidoscopic fashion throughout the regions we have been examining. Cut-and-dried notions about the congruence of nation with state were far removed from the ethnographic realities the new states faced. Indeed, the definition of boundaries presented a multidimensional challenge. Lines of demarcation between neighboring states were the most obvious and immediate subject of contention. Another issue concerned the exercise and division of sovereignty within states. Were ethnic minorities to be awarded territorially bounded autonomous zones, extraterritorial autonomy, or no collective recognition whatsoever? Was citizenship and full juridical equality to be extended to all who resided within the territory claimed by the state, or were lines – visible or invisible – to be drawn around certain groups deemed alien to the polity? Conversely, in cases where people who saw themselves as one nation were divided from one another by "artificial" frontiers, how were those barriers to be transcended?

Political and institutional responses to these dilemmas were hastily improvised in the immediate aftermath of the war amidst the often violent clash of conflicting interests and general conditions of upheaval and chaos. Yet many of the resulting arrangements were to remain in place for years to come, with far-reaching consequences for the subsequent evolution of ethnic politics and nationalist ideologies in East Central Europe, Russia, and the Middle East.

Defining Frontiers in East Central Europe

The events of October–November 1918 in East Central Europe were a curious mix of anti-climax, high drama, and uncontrollable confusion. In the space of just a few weeks, the region's political map was transformed beyond recognition. With his troops deserting in droves, national committees seizing power in provincial capitals, and the Allied and Associated Powers responding to his desperate diplomatic overtures by tersely referring him to those national committees, Kaiser Karl accepted (on 27 October) the departure of the Czechs, Poles, and South Slavs from the imperial fold and handed over power on 11 November to a newly declared Austrian republic formed in the German rump of the former empire.[1] To the north, Germany's defeat by the Western powers spelled the end of its short-lived empire in Eastern Europe, although German Free Corps units remained active (ostensibly as an anti-Bolshevik volunteer force) in the Baltic region well into the following year.[2] To the East, the Russian polity was being consumed by civil and ethnic war.

Given the abruptness of the Central Powers' final collapse, the locus of political authority within many newly declared states was intensely contested, as was the delineation of borders among them. The establishment of administrative structures and the marking of frontiers throughout the region was a matter of makeshift arrangements and awkward improvisations – and often the subject of violent confrontations.

The political entities that engaged in these struggles for legitimacy and control ranged in nature from self-styled provisional governments formed by wartime émigrés and resistance leaders to governments of pre-existing nation-states that now sought to make good on longstanding irredentist claims against imperial territories. In Poland, Piłsudski was released from prison and placed in power by his German captors while Dmowski's Polish National Committee represented the country's interests in Paris. The leaders of Masaryk's Czechoslovak National Council returned to Prague with their status as the new country's provisional government already recognized by the major Czech parties, and with a more general statement of support for Czech–Slovak unification from a self-declared Slovak National Council, which expected regional autonomy on the basis of the Pittsburgh Declaration. Local leaders of the Ukrainian (Ruthenian) community in Subcarpathian Rus' (the province that became the eastern fringe of the interwar Czechoslovak Republic), following in the steps of their émigré community in the United States, also declared themselves in favor of secession from Hungary and adhesion to Masaryk's new state, on condition of autonomy. (The Ruthenians of this province were in fact granted a measure of local administrative control, unlike the Slovaks – as we shall see in Chapter 7.)[3] Hungary also faced the secession of Croatia and the loss of southern and eastern territories to Serbian and Romanian forces, respectively. Count Mihály Károlyi's left-of-center coalition government, in charge of the newly declared Hungarian People's Republic, deployed military forces to resist the detachment of these

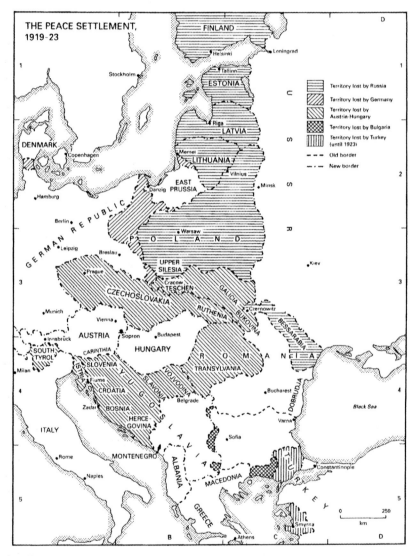

Map 3   The Peace Settlement 1919–1923

Source: Richard and Ben Crampton, *Atlas of Eastern Europe* (London: Routledge, 1996)

lands, but ultimately bowed to the Allied powers' demands for the withdrawal of Hungarian troops from wide swaths of disputed territory. The short-lived Hungarian Soviet Republic that replaced Károlyi's discredited government in March 1919 attempted to recoup some of its predecessor's losses in the name of international socialism, but was unable to mount effective resistance to a renewed Romanian offensive that ended with the fall of the Hungarian Communists and the occupation of Budapest at the beginning of August.[4]

In Lithuania, the Taryba, which had for months before the November 1918 armistice played a cat-and-mouse game with the German authorities who had created it as a façade for their own control, declared itself the Provisional Government of Lithuania in November 1918 – and promptly found itself defending the country against the Bolsheviks on the one hand and Piłsudski's Polish forces on the other. In Estonia and Latvia, German defeat on the Western Front enabled provisional governments led by anti-socialist nationalists to come to power, while the continued presence of German Free Corps formations contributed to the defeat of the invading Red Army and to the suppression of the sizable pro-Bolshevik elements within the Estonian and Latvian populations.[5] The German-assisted victory of the anti-socialist Whites in Finland's 1918 civil war left the surviving leaders of the left politically marginalized and the country deeply divided for decades, although parliamentary democracy did survive in Finland throughout the interwar years.[6]

It is not my intention here to provide a detailed narrative of the post-1918 diplomatic, political, and military struggles throughout East Central Europe. Instead, I will use selected examples – focussing in particular on the Polish case – to illuminate this chapter's overarching theme: how the very process of establishing political authority and fixing boundaries under these chaotic conditions shaped the structure of political institutions and the development of national identities.

With the Western democracies in the position of hegemons at the Paris Peace Conference, and the United States apparently playing the leading role among them, Wilsonianism served as the rhetorical framework within which the diplomatic battles of this period were fought out. The aspect of Wilsonianism most immediately relevant to the problems of East Central Europe was its affirmation of national self-determination as the logical corollary of, and foundation for, a liberal-democratic political order. As we have seen, there had been advocates of a marriage of liberalism and nationalism among the nationalist intelligentsias of the region both before the war and – most notably among the national committees in Western exile – during the war itself. But to preach was one thing, to practice another. This became apparent in the unfolding of the diplomatic effort at Paris and in the interplay between that effort and events on the ground in East Central Europe.

Woodrow Wilson's own ideas about the principle of national self-determination were highly ambiguous in their practical implications. His pre-war writings indicate that he regarded the existence of a common national identity as essential to the success of a democratic society. The example of the United States, which was foremost in his mind, suggested that national identity need not be based on ethnicity – indeed, that it could and should be based on a common historical experience and common set of values that transcended ethnicity. Of course, as an immigrant society, the United States constituted an exceptional case which marked it apart from the European experience. How then could Wilsonian doctrine be applied to postwar Europe?[7]

During the war, Wilson delivered a variety of public addresses and policy statements that appeared to elevate national self-determination to the status of an overarching principle for any future peace settlement, but without clarifying what constituted a nation or what, for that matter, was entailed by self-determination. The practical application of Wilson's doctrine evolved largely in response to immediate circumstances and to the political realities taking shape over the course of 1918–1919. As long as there appeared to be a chance of negotiating a separate peace with the Habsburg empire, for instance, it seemed more politic to call for autonomy for its constituent peoples than for their full-fledged independence. The failure of the secret diplomatic contacts with Austria–Hungary and the growing assertiveness of nationalist movements within the empire during the last months of the war led to official American and Allied endorsement of Czechoslovak and Yugoslav independence. In the case of Poland, its past history as a sovereign state earned it Wilson's early endorsement (in the January 1918 Fourteen Points speech) as a candidate for full-fledged independence. It was of crucial importance to all three of these causes, as it was to the Zionist cause, that their spokesmen in Western capitals spoke the language of liberal democracy and painted visions of their future nation-states as societies bound together by common historical and cultural experience and shared political values rather than by narrowly ethnic ties (see Chapter 5). Wilson also appears to have had a rather poor grasp of the complexity of the region's ethnography and little sense of how potentially wide was the gap separating the perspective of, say, Milan Štefánik from that of the Slovak peasantry or of the Yugoslav Committee from the Croatian man on the street.[8] He came to rue his ignorance:

> When I gave utterance to those words ("that all nations had a right to self-determination"), I said them without the knowledge that nationalities existed, which are coming to us day after day. ... You do not know and cannot appreciate the anxieties that I have experienced as the result of many millions of people having their hopes raised by what I have said.[9]

Initially, then, Wilson, did not realize how deep might run the tension between civic and ethnic categories of political identity among the soon-to-be-liberated peoples of East Central Europe. Yet the very process of determining the American position on future boundaries among the new states highlighted the criterion of ethnic identity to an unprecedented degree. The American Inquiry (a commission of experts formed to lay the groundwork for the American position on the European peace settlements) focussed its efforts on investigating the distribution of ethno-linguistic groups in disputed territories, while trying to balance the ethnic criterion with economic and strategic considerations. The approach of British Foreign Office experts – many of them drawn from the circle of academics associated with the pro-Czechoslovak and pro-Yugoslav propaganda paper, *The New Europe* – was not dissimilar.[10]

If ethnographic research seemed to be the most objective way of resolving territorial disputes, the result was to magnify the importance of ethnic identity as a source of political legitimacy far more than Wilson or Lloyd George had ever intended. As William Keylor has argued, the very nature of a boundary-marking process based on quantifiable criteria drew the Anglo-American architects of the Peace into emphasizing an ethnic basis for nationhood.[11] To be sure, senior members of the American delegation to Paris, including Secretary of State Lansing, had long harbored serious doubts about the wisdom of implementing national self-determination doctrine in such a culturally and linguistically diverse region.[12] But given the collapse of the multinational empires, and in the absence of someone capable of putting those Humpty Dumpties back together again, such critics had no principled or internally consistent method to propose in lieu of the ethnographic approach.

For their part, the interested parties in East Central Europe were quite eager to introduce additional, non-ethnographic, criteria wherever it might be to their territorial advantage to do so. Strategic and economic arguments were put forward on behalf of claims to such regions as the Sudetenland (the Austro-German-populated territorial perimeter of Bohemia, whose mountain ranges were deemed vital for the defense of Czechoslovakia) or the Polish Corridor (the stretch of formerly German territory that gave Poland access to the sea). While such arguments were best suited to convincing the Western powers, historical claims were often even more compelling from the point of view of nationalist sentiment. As we saw in the preceding chapter, already during the war, the liberal nationalists of the Yugoslav Committee and Czechoslovak National Council had articulated territorial claims based on the principle of historic state right, in a sharp departure from their earlier, principled opposition to this undemocratic notion. In Poland, as discussed in Chapter 3, the typical left-of-center and right-wing positions on historic state right had long been inversed, with Piłsudski arguing in favor of a restoration of Poland within some approximation of its 1772 boundaries, while Dmowski urged against this in favor of an ethnically more homogeneous state.

Historic claims raised a fundamental conundrum, for the boundaries referred to were those of early modern states that had not drawn their legitimacy from the principle of national self-determination or popular sovereignty. The wedding of such claims to the principle of national self-determination was incongruous by purely liberal-democratic standards, insofar as it could lead to the incorporation of territory regardless of its inhabitants' wishes.[13] And yet, it was precisely the immutability of territorial configurations based on frozen moments in history that lent them appeal as symbols of nationhood.[14]

Where historic claims overlapped with convincing strategic or economic ones (as in the case of the Sudetenland), the Western powers were likely to endorse them, especially when such demands came at the expense of the defeated powers or their rump successor states – Germany, Austria, Hungary, Bulgaria, and Turkey. Where claims were put forward on historic bases alone, the Allied and Associated Powers generally sought to restrain the nationalist enthusiasm for territorial aggrandizement. In either event, the unilateral use of military force was the surest means of making good on territorial demands, with Western recognition often coming in the wake of facts created on the ground.

Thus it was that armed action and diplomatic manipulation, rather than the gradual building of popular consensus, served as the means for assembling diverse regions and populations into East European "nation-states." We have already seen how Serbian military suppression of the Green Cadres laid the foundation for the creation of the kingdom of Serbs, Croats, and Slovenes. The Prague government's claim to Slovakia was realized, not through a mass uprising of the Slovak people against their Magyar masters, but through a combination of Czech military operations and Allied diplomatic support that forced Hungarian forces out of the region. Czech forces also clashed with their Polish rivals in a confrontation over the coal-rich Teschen district, which was partitioned between the two countries (with Czechoslovakia obtaining control of Teschen's main coalfield and railroad) by Allied arbiters in 1920.[15] Within its final frontiers, the Czechoslovak "nation-state" ended up with a population that was, according to data from the 1930 census, 51 per cent Czech, 22 per cent German, 16 per cent Slovak, 5 per cent Magyar, and 4 per cent Ruthenian.[16] Failure to create a common sense of national identity between the two main Slavic groups (Czechs and Slovaks) would obviously leave such a polity vulnerable to complete fragmentation.

In Poland, the dispute over Teschen, mentioned above, was only one item on a long menu of conflicts that included military operations against Ukrainian independence forces in Eastern Galicia, and fighting with Lithuania over Vilnius, which was captured by an ostensibly independent Polish militia in 1920 and formally annexed by the Polish parliament two years later. In 1920, Piłsudski's regime negotiated an anti-Bolshevik alliance with Symon Petliura's Kiev-based Ukrainian regime, based on the cession of Eastern Galicia to Poland. Piłsudski then undertook a full-scale war against the Soviets in which the fortunes of the opposing armies and the position of the front line see-sawed dramatically back and forth from Kiev at the height of Polish success to the outskirts of Warsaw at the climax of the Bolshevik offensive. The Polish–Soviet Treaty of Riga, which ended the conflict in March 1921, left Poland in control of a wide stretch of territory to the east of the Bug river, that is to say, well beyond the Polish ethnographic frontier (the so-called Curzon Line) as defined by a committee of the Paris Peace Conference. To the west, a combination of military actions, popular uprisings by ethnic Poles, and terms imposed by the Western powers in the Versailles peace treaty helped determine Poland's boundaries with Germany (with Germany ceding Posen [Poznań] and eastern Pomerania to Poland).[17]

In the case of Upper Silesia, a coal-rich, industrialized region of mixed Polish and German population, a plebiscite called for by the Western powers resulted in a majority vote in favor of keeping the province in Germany. When this was followed by Polish uprisings and a 1921 League of Nations decision to partition the province, many Germans were reinforced in their perception that the national self-determination principle was being applied only to their detriment and never in their favor.[18]

The Polish example merits examination in greater detail as a case that vividly illuminates the close relationship between the process of boundary-formation and the evolution of nationalist political cultures. It also encapsulates the half-hearted, self-contradictory, and inconsistent character of the Western powers' effort to promote liberal nationalism in East Central Europe.

The two most mettlesome subjects of negotiations between the Poles[19] and the Council of Four[20] concerned Poland's eastern frontiers and the future status and treatment of minority communities within the Polish state. On the first point, the conflicting Polish and Ukrainian claims to Eastern Galicia constituted a particularly maddening issue, which, like so many others, was ultimately resolved by force. In the Paris talks, Ignacy Paderewski freely acknowledged that the majority of Eastern Galicia's population spoke Ukrainian, but insisted that the mostly Polish town of Lwów (also known as Lviv in Ukrainian, Lvov in Russian, and Lemberg in German and Yiddish) could not conceivably be left stranded to the east of Poland's frontiers.[21] Coming at a time when Czech, Romanian, and Yugoslav forces were busily creating *faits accompli* at the expense of Hungary, the Polish military advance in Eastern Galicia awakened the anger and frustration of the Big Four over an Eastern Europe that seemed to be spinning out of control, defying all Western efforts at implementing a stable postwar settlement. As British Prime Minister David Lloyd George put it to Paderewski:

> We liberated the Poles, the Czechoslovaks, the Yugoslavs, and today we have all the trouble in the world preventing them from oppressing other races. I myself belong to a small nation [the Welsh]. I have the warmest and most profound sympathy for small nations which are fighting for their independence, and I am seized with despair when I see them more imperialistic than the great nations themselves.

Even more blunt was Lloyd George's outburst four days later, *à propos* the attacks on Hungary by its Czech and Romanian neighbors: "They are all little brigand peoples who only want to steal territories."[22]

In a word, the Western leaders were impatient with what they regarded as petty ethnic disputes unleashed under the cover of the national self-determination principle, and eager to get such annoying matters off their agenda as quickly as possible. In the absence of any clear-cut set of principles that could resolve such intractable disputes, and given the sense that some solution was urgently needed, *de facto* arrangements tended to form the basis for *de jure* solutions. Western fear of Bolshevism also played into the hands of nationalist regimes that portrayed themselves as vital buffers against the Red threat. In the case of Eastern Galicia, the upshot – after a stream of ineffectual threats against the Poles – was a retroactive validation of the Polish military advance. On 26 June 1919, the peace conference's Supreme Council[23] issued a ruling awarding Poland the responsibility for creating a provisional civil administration over Eastern Galicia. This, in turn, eventually led to the recognition of Polish sovereignty over the region.[24]

The Polish case vividly illustrates how both the use of military force to make good on territorial claims, and the process of diplomatic negotiation, served to blur the distinctions between liberal-civic and ethnic-chauvinist conceptions of national identity and, indeed, to favor the latter over the former. Piłsudski may have justified his military campaigns in the east as part of an effort to forge a federative framework for national self-determination that would at the same time create a strong bulwark against Russian expansionism. But in practice, he was engaged in a process of conquest that was bitterly resisted by Lithuanians and Ukrainians (except when the latter's defeat by the Bolsheviks left them with no one else to turn to but Piłsudski). In any event, Polish war weariness and lack of support from the Dmowski bloc obliged Piłsudski to compromise with the Soviets in the Peace of Riga and to abandon his program for a federation with Ukraine, Belorussia, Lithuania, Latvia, and Estonia. The upshot, by 1921, was a Poland one-third of whose population consisted of non-Poles, many of whom felt bitterly alienated from a state that had forcibly incorporated them into itself. By the same token, the Polish government felt it had little reason to negotiate terms of autonomy with minorities upon which it had already successfully imposed its rule. In practice, the vicissitudes of warfare had left Piłsudski in charge of a Polish state whose territorial configuration and whose denial of political space to non-Polish minorities conformed more closely to Dmowski's preconceptions than to his own. Moreover, the central role of the military in shaping and defending the frontiers of the state served to enhance its role as symbol of national honor and its self-image as vanguard of the nation. This was to have a significant impact on Polish political culture in subsequent years, as we shall see in Chapter 7.

Given the haphazard nature of boundary formation, the blurriness of ethnographic frontiers, and the unwillingness or inability of the Big Four to restrain some of these small-power expansionist initiatives, it was unavoidable that large minority populations would be left stranded within the new, so-called nation-states. It was with a view to regulating the treatment of such communities through a regime of international law that the drafting and negotiation of minorities treaties was initiated by the Big Four.[25]

The issue that brought the matter of minorities to the formal attention of the Paris Peace Conference concerned the fate of Jews in Poland. We have seen (in the preceding chapter) how the German occupation of Poland and Lithuania catalyzed the institutionalization of Jewish cultural and political life and stimulated debate about the possible forms that Jewish national autonomy might take in a restored Polish state. The wartime plight of East European Jews, particularly under the impact of the Russian military's abuses in 1914–1915, had also generated an outpouring of concern on the part of the Jewish public and Jewish organizations in the United States, Britain, and France. Wartime activity by such organizations had focussed on furnishing material relief to refugees and destitute communities.[26] With the war over, attention shifted to protecting Jewish individual and communal rights in the framework of the new nation-states – particularly Poland, which, with some three million Jews (roughly 10 per cent of its population) in its final territorial configuration, ended up as the European country with by far the largest number of Jewish inhabitants outside of Russia. The existence of widespread popular and political anti-Semitism in Poland, as manifested by the continued boycott (initiated in 1912) of Jewish businesses by Dmowski's National Democrats and in outbursts of violence against Jewish inhabitants upon the entry of Polish forces into Lwów and Vilnius during 1918–1919, made the future of Jewish life in that country the subject of particular concern to world Jewry.

Jewish organizations and political movements were divided over how to define the communal rights of Poland's Jews. Zionists, who dominated the joint committee of East European Jewish delegations at the Peace Conference and enjoyed the support of the American Jewish Congress, demanded that Poland and other East European states recognize their Jewish residents as members of a distinct nation, with the right to collective representation at both state and international levels. This would entail the creation of a separate Jewish parliament in Poland,[27] alongside a state parliament representing all the country's inhabitants, and it would mean the creation of a Jewish seat at the League of Nations.[28]

In demanding formal, corporate, political/diplomatic status for a territorially dispersed nation, as distinct from a state, the Zionists were challenging traditional notions about the indivisibility of state sovereignty and proposing a radical and potentially precedent-setting new formulation of the relationship between national identity and government authority. In so doing, they were underlining and responding to the deepseated contradiction between the liberal-democratic and ethno-cultural dimensions of the national self-determination principle.[29] But the response this program evoked among East European and Western governments alike was not based on the originality of its contribution to political theory. As a potential model that other ethnic minorities – and especially ethnic Germans – might seek to emulate, it was regarded as having the potential to unleash uncontrollable centrifugal forces in a region already suffering from deep instability. Neither the American, British, nor French delegations to the Paris Peace Conference were willing to promote an approach to the minorities question that would create what they saw as a nightmare scenario of states arising within states.[30]

Some non-Zionist Jewish organizations, such as France's Alliance Israélite Universelle or the delegation representing Poland's Jewish assimilationists, were utterly opposed to any policy that would formalize the status of Polish Jewry as a separate, corporate entity. Their focus was on the protection of Jews' individual rights to citizenship and equal treatment in the countries they inhabited, and on their right to practice their religion freely. Any institutionalization of Yiddish or Hebrew as officially recognized languages was opposed by these groups as an undesirable barrier to the integration of Jews into surrounding cultures.

Steering a middle course between Zionists and assimilationists was Lucien Wolf, "foreign secretary" and representative at the Paris Peace Conference of the Joint Foreign Committee of British Jews, the successor to the Conjoint Committee (see Chapter 5). Wolf forged a platform that he felt stood a reasonable chance of winning Foreign Office endorsement while granting a considerable measure of protection under international law to the Jews of Poland. He advocated a program that would involve Polish state sanction and funding for autonomous Jewish national-cultural institutions, such as a Yiddish-language school network linked to the general education system. Moreover, he lobbied hard in favor of making full Western recognition of Poland contingent on that country's submission to League of Nations oversight over its treatment of Jews and other minorities, with minority groups having the right of direct appeal to the League Council – and thence to the Permanent Court of International Justice – over alleged infringements of their rights. Fair treatment would include full civil rights for Jews as individuals as well as guarantees of freedom of religious practice and freedom to develop cultural and communal institutions without state interference. Wolf also sought to ensure that Jews would be exempted from a general ban on Sunday trading, given their own observance of Saturday as a day of rest.[31]

Intense lobbying by the American and British Jewish organizations, conducted amidst an atmosphere of public outrage over violence against Jewish communities by Polish forces operating in the fledgling country's war zones, spurred the Council of Four into placing the issue of minority rights in Poland specifically, and Eastern Europe generally, on its agenda. A hastily formed Committee on New States was charged with formulating a Polish Minorities Treaty that would serve as a model to be applied throughout the region. At the core of this initiative was an effort to make the Polish state's obligations toward its minorities – including its obligation to concede them some institutional guarantees of cultural self-expression and self-perpetuation through communal organizations and native-language school instruction – a matter of international law, under the guarantee of the League of Nations.[32]

Negotiations with the Polish delegation over the matter were a prickly affair. The very idea of making the Polish state treaty-bound to observe an externally prescribed set of guidelines regarding an aspect of its domestic affairs was deemed offensive. If, in the Poles' eyes, the international framework of such a minority-rights program infringed on Polish sovereignty, its substance threatened Polish national unity. Rather than acknowledging the need to create some system of cultural autonomy that might help accommodate the ethno-cultural pluralism of the territories claimed by the Polish National Committee, Paderewski invoked the West European ideal of civic unity to protest against what he saw as an attempt to undermine Poland's cohesion as a nation-state. Blaming Jewish disloyalty for the prevalent mood of anti-Semitism in Poland, and displaying more than a hint of such sentiment himself, Paderewski argued that:

> The Great Powers ... by distinguishing with the aid of special privileges the Jewish population from their fellow-citizens – create a new Jewish problem. ... It is to be feared that the Great Powers may be preparing for themselves unwelcome surprises, for, taking into consideration the migratory capacities of the Jewish population, which so readily transports itself from one State to another, it is certain that the Jews, basing themselves on precedent thus established, will claim elsewhere the national principles which they would enjoy in Poland.[33]

In its final form, the Polish Minorities Treaty signed on 28 June 1919 fell far short of the cultural autonomy framework proposed by Wolf, let alone the national-political autonomy called for by the Zionists. Individual rights to equality under the law and religious freedom were protected, but the collective rights of minorities remained quite limited. Minorities were to be free to create their own cultural and social institutions and private schools, but, in public schools, minority tongues could be used as the language of instruction only at the primary-school level.[34] Articles dealing specifically with the Jews likewise gave them the right to employ Yiddish as the language of instruction in some public primary schools, but not in secondary education. And while the Jews' right to observe the Sabbath was protected, no provision was made exempting Jews from the general ban on commercial activity on Sundays. This left observant Jews in the position of being obliged to observe a compulsory second day of rest that placed them at a disadvantage *vis-à-vis* their non-Jewish competitors. While the League of Nations Council (the executive committee of Great Powers) was named as the treaty's guarantor, alleged violations of its provisions could only be brought before the Council by one of the Council members; Jewish organizations were to have no direct channel of appeal to the League of Nations.[35]

The Polish Minorities Treaty served as a model that was applied throughout Eastern Europe and the Balkans. Its provisions were replicated, with minor variations, in the minority treaties signed by thirteen other European states seeking Western diplomatic recognition of their independence or of their revised boundaries, or negotiating peace treaties with the West. Yet, from the point of view of the Western powers, the fundamental objective of the treaties was to smooth the path to peaceful assimilation of minorities into state-promoted frameworks of national identity. As far as the East European and Balkan regimes were concerned, the treaties were either affronts to their countries' dignity as sovereign states or tools to be employed opportunistically in regional territorial and political rivalries. The weakness of the treaties' enforcement mechanisms meant that, in practice, the new and expanded states were free to subject their minorities to systematic patterns of abuse.[36]

In Poland, as elsewhere throughout Eastern and Central Europe, right-wing parties regularly whipped up and exploited popular hostility toward minorities – especially Jews – as a means of bolstering their own electoral support among the majority group's population, while left-wing parties expected to pick up minority votes by default, without overly exerting themselves on behalf of those ethnic groups' special interests.[37] In the 1922 elections, a Jewish-initiated minorities' electoral coalition (the Bloc of National Minorities; Blok Mniejszosci Narodowych – BMN), which included Jewish, German, Ukrainian, Belorussian, and Lithuanian parties, emerged with what appeared to be a powerful swing vote in the lower house of parliament – this despite a gerrymandered districting system designed to limit minority votes. But the hostility of the Polish Right, combined with the reluctance of the PPS and other left-wing formations to tarnish their own nationalist credentials through overt cooperation with ethnic parties, limited the influence of the BMN. Its brief moment of success in helping elect a left-of-center Piłsudskiite, Narutowicz, as President of the Republic in 1922 only played into the hands of the National Democrats' propaganda, which vilified Narutowicz as the plaything of Jews and other non-Polish nationalities. Following Narutowicz's assassination and replacement by a more conservative figure, the BMN declined as a political force, with some of its constituent parties seeing greater immediate advantage in trying to cut limited, bilateral deals with Polish governments than in continued cooperation with one another, while others retreated into bitter opposition.

Such political dynamics both reflected and contributed to the minorities' vulnerability to oppression and abuse. Poland's eastern lands (referred to as the *kresy* in Polish) were governed virtually as colonial territories. The Belorussian population, whose national consciousness was deemed least distinctive and developed, was targeted for Polonization. A mixture of forced Polonization and divide-and-rule strategies were attempted among Ukrainians, as manifest in such policies as the unsuccessful – indeed, provocative – attempt to cultivate a separate Ruthenian ethnic identity among members of the Uniate Church. Half-hearted efforts at land reform in the *kresy* repeatedly ended with the bulk of property remaining in the hands of the Polish landlords – a regional socio-economic elite whose support was courted by both Dmowski's and Piłsudski's political camps. The prime beneficiaries of whatever real redistribution did take place tended to be Polish settlers rather than indigenous Ukrainian or other non-Polish peasants. Violence ensued as terrorist tactics by right-wing Ukrainian nationalists provoked brutal responses from the state authorities.

Intermittent attempts at appeasement of, or compromise with, regional minorities proved abortive, even after Piłsudski's dramatic return from political retirement through a *coup d'état* in 1926 (see Chapter 7). Although Piłsudski did curb official anti-Semitism, his credibility as a champion of minority rights rapidly dissipated as administrative inertia and local resistance by right-wing Polish nationalists impeded the implementation of liberal policies designed to provide equal access to economic and educational opportunity and local administrative authority for minorities. It soon became apparent that limited concessions were all Piłsudski could deliver in return for parliamentary support from ethnic-minority parties. In consequence, relations between state authorities and minority populations in the *kresy* (especially Eastern Galicia) rapidly degenerated into violence once again. In September 1934, Poland unilaterally withdrew from the system of international oversight of minorities' treatment that had been enshrined in the 1919 Minorities Treaty.

While the Polish state's repressive policies succeeded in maintaining the country's territorial integrity until 1939, they were utterly counterproductive from the point of view of national unity. The more powerless and exploited minority groups felt, the stronger grew their sense that ethnicity was the most important element in determining their fate and in shaping their identity. At the same time, the fact that interwar Poland did tolerate political activity and privately funded cultural and educational endeavors by some of its minorities (notably Jews and Germans) enabled them to develop institutional expressions of their ethnonational consciousness.[38] This dynamic, in which coercive attempts at the nationalization of culture and identity by the state only stimulated the consolidation of distinct ethnonational identities among minorities, was replicated to various degrees in virtually all the other states of interwar East Central and Eastern Europe.[39]

Thus, in Romania, whose territory and population had doubled (at the expense of formerly Austro-Hungarian and Russian territory) under the terms of the peace settlement, an early experiment with regional administrative autonomy (albeit favoring local ethnic Romanians) gave way in 1922 to a rigidly centralist governmental and educational structure, justified as the best way of rapidly inculcating a sense of national unity among the hitherto fragmented Romanian people. This impatient, top-down approach to forging a cohesive nation was partly an overcompensatory response to the fact that the urban, middle-class, educated population of the new territories was overwhelmingly composed of Germans, Magyars, and Jews, while the bulk of the peasantry was ethnically Romanian.[40] Antagonism toward non-Romanians – who now constituted 30 per cent of the country's population as opposed to 12 per cent before the war – ran all the deeper because of the fact that Germans and Magyars had been members of the hegemonic nationalities in the Habsburg empire, while the Jews had tended to assimilate into Magyar and German culture, or else retained their Yiddish language, rather than adopt the peasantry's Romanian.[41]

Here again, attempts to forge interethnic political coalitions proved unsuccessful. Divide-and-rule tactics pursued by the authorities in Bucharest contributed to this, but perhaps more interesting is the fact that the general geopolitical framework of the Greater Romanian nation-state constituted an environment that reversed earlier trends toward cultural assimilation among ethnic groups. In the formerly Hungarian-ruled Banat, Germans, many of whom had begun adopting the language of the regional Magyar elite under the old regime, were now at pains to distinguish themselves from an identity that was associated with the irredentism of the rump Hungarian republic (and hence seemed to constitute a political liability). Magyarized Jews were likewise more inclined than before to stress that their love of Hungarian culture did not mean they saw themselves as part of the Hungarian nation. At the same time, there was no tradition among any of these groups of adopting as their own a Romanian language more closely associated in their experience with peasant life than with high culture. Each minority's sense of vulnerability *vis-à-vis* the national state, combined with the broadening of cultural and political gaps among the ethnic minorities, strengthened the tendency toward ethnic particularism in the new territories of Greater Romania.[42] At the same time, the Romanian government failed to fulfill its professed goal of empowering the ethnically Romanian rural masses in the country's newly acquired regions. In Transylvania, for instance, large estates were expropriated from Magyar landowners and much of the income from local industrial production was siphoned off through taxation, but the beneficiaries of these blows against the non-Romanian elites were wealthy Romanian financiers and investors based in Bucharest rather than the local Romanian peasantry.[43] Such frustrating patterns of development, combined with the Romanian government's discrimination against minorities and toleration of anti-Semitic violence, fed the growth of the fascist Iron Guard movement, which brought together Romanian students and peasants in an organized challenge to the legitimacy of parliamentary government and provoked the establishment of a royal dictatorship in 1938.[44]

Serb insistence on running the kingdom of Serbs, Croats, and Slovenes on a centralist, Serb-dominated basis had a similar impact, as did the denial of autonomy to Slovaks in Czechoslovakia (see Chapter 7). In one case after another, the attempts of the new or enlarged East European nation-states to assimilate, marginalize, or suppress their minorities only served to reinforce the sense that ethnicity was the critical element that determined one's status, social-support network, identity, and even ideological orientation. The less willing nationalist regimes were to create political space or public fora for the expression of collective identity by minorities, the more alienated the latter became and the more deeply ingrained their sense that they constituted nations unto themselves. The fact that so many wartime programs of national liberation had held forth the promise of federal structures to accommodate ethno-cultural pluralism made the denial of such rights all the more galling. In many cases, the resultant atmosphere of political polarization and fragmentation among ethnic groups led to ever more drastic turns toward right-wing, intolerant forms of nationalism and helped disable and discredit liberal-democratic institutions and values.[45]

Finally, the division of empires into nation-states also meant the fragmentation of large economic units into smaller ones. The determination to build self-reliant national economies in each of the new or enlarged states led to a raising of tariff barriers, which only served to impede the flow of goods and services and to cut off producers from their markets. This in turn made these countries – most of them economically underdeveloped in the first place and grievously afflicted by the infrastructure damage of the First World War – all the more vulnerable to the impact of the Great Depression of the 1930s, which cut short the beginnings of economic recovery in the late 1920s. The resultant hardships – persistent agrarian crises, shortage of capital and tightness of credit, decline in industrial profits and in state revenue, unemployment, low standards of living – also played into the hands of right-wing nationalists eager to scapegoat minorities or neighboring states for the material woes of their people.[46]

The Political Geography of Soviet Ethnofederalism

Of the three imperial realms examined in this volume, the only one mostly to be reconstituted as a unitary state following its wartime disintegration was the area formerly known as the Russian empire. But of course, the ideological orientation and institutional structure of the regime under whose auspices this reassembly took place represented the most radical of departures from earlier political norms. With respect to the nationality question, the Soviet Union implemented the principle of ethnofederalism on an unparalleled scale and to an unprecedented degree of systematization. In this case, therefore, it is the drawing of national frontiers *within* the new, supranational state that primarily concerns us. This system developed from an unusually complex interplay of Communist ideology, opportunism, and political experience gained in the course of the Russian Civil War.

The Ethnic Dimension of Russian Political Collapse and Civil War

In the course of the Russian Civil War (1917–1921), the non-Russian nationalities were caught between Bolshevik and White (anti-Bolshevik) armies (not to speak of German and Ottoman forces until late 1918, the Allied intervention forces from 1918 until 1920, and the invading Polish army in Ukraine and Belorussia during 1920). Many ethnic groups were themselves internally divided between conservative and revolutionary factions that were sporadically aligned with corresponding elements in the chaotic Russian political scene. Given the anarchic state of affairs prevailing across the length and breadth of the former empire, it is very difficult to make any meaningful generalizations about the development of national consciousness or nationalist institutions among the non-Russian peoples during the Civil War.[47]

In the Baltic theater, geopolitical circumstances – notably, German intervention in the Finnish civil war of January–May 1918, the persistence of German Free Corps units in Latvia and Estonia following the November 1918 armistice, eventual British naval support and arms deliveries to the Latvians and Estonians in the wake of a 1919 takeover bid by the Free Corps, and the Bolsheviks' distraction by military threats from first White Russian and then Polish forces – allowed centrist and right-wing nationalists to consolidate independence and to suppress pro-Bolshevik elements within their own populations.[48]

In Transcaucasia, the Ottoman advance and Russian military disintegration had spurred the creation of a Transcaucasian regional government that functioned as an uneasy coalition of Georgian, Armenian, and Azerbaijani leaders. Following the Bolsheviks' signing away of Transcaucasian territory to the

Ottomans (under the guise of the national self-determination principle, whose implementation in the region the Ottomans were supposedly to oversee) in the March 1918 Treaty of Brest-Litovsk, Georgian and Armenian leaders' reluctance to break away entirely from Russia gave way to a recognition that they were functionally on their own in any case, and that they might gain a better bargaining position in the framework of an independent state. The Azerbaijanis were essentially pro-Ottoman to begin with, and eager to break their ties to Russia.

It was on the basis of these highly mixed and incompatible motives that the Transcaucasian legislature (Seim) voted on 22 April 1918 in favor of creating an independent Transcaucasian Federation, which fell apart into three independent republics by the end of May. There had been no basis here for a true union, as renewed attempts at military resistance to advancing Ottoman forces failed and as the Georgian, Armenian, and Azerbaijani leaderships developed different diplomatic and military postures toward the Germans and Ottomans – allies who were each other's rivals for influence in resource-rich Transcaucasia. The Georgian declaration of independence (26 May 1918) – which precipitated the breakup of the Transcaucasian federation – freed the Georgian government to sign agreements with the Germans that gave the latter control over ports, railroads, and mining concessions in Georgia in return for German support against the encroachment of the Ottomans. The latter were accordingly limited to annexing a relatively small chunk of Georgian territory in the peace treaty of June 1918 (signed simultaneously with the Armenian–Ottoman and Azerbaijani–Ottoman peace accords). The Armenians – whose territory was of less strategic significance – were unsuccessful at engaging the interest of the Germans and hence obliged to accept more difficult terms for peace with the Ottomans, only to attempt the occupation of formerly Armenian-inhabited territory in northeastern Turkey after the Allied–Ottoman armistice of October 1918. The Azerbaijanis welcomed the Ottomans with open arms and were rewarded by Istanbul's recognition of their independence and territorial integrity, only to lose faith in Ottoman professions of pan-Turkic solidarity during the months of oppressive, if informal, military occupation that followed.[49]

Much of this region remained beyond the reach of Russian armies during the height of the Civil War, thanks in part to the effective cover of British forces that occupied Transcaucasia during 1918–1919, following the Central Powers' defeat. This enabled the three republics' governments to consolidate some measure of internal control and to gain *de facto* diplomatic recognition from the Western powers (who had, however, no serious intention of renewed military intervention on their behalf) in November 1919.[50]

In the case of Georgia, the gaining of political independence was an ostensibly incongruous development, since its Menshevik leaders were officially opposed to nationalism and had in fact been prominent participants in all-Russian Social Democratic politics until November 1917. However, having declared independence under the force of circumstances, the Georgian government soon found itself caught up in that crucible of nationalism, the fight over frontiers. It engaged in military campaigns against the Armenian republic (which was also intermittently at war with Azerbaijan) over disputed territory, while suppressing internal minorities (Abkhazians, Ossetians) seeking their own self-determination. The fact that the Russian heartland was controlled by the rival Bolshevik Party lent ideological legitimacy to the Georgian Mensheviks' new-found commitment to their country's independence. It was not until early 1921 that Bolshevik forces gained control over Georgia. They had already subjugated Armenia and Azerbaijan in 1920 through a combination of polit-ical subversion and military operations – a process of territorial consolidation that was facilitated by Moscow's alliance of convenience with Mustafa Kemal's forces in eastern Turkey (see below).[51]

In other regions, the repeated passage of rival armies, foreign and domestic, created such social and political havoc as to defy coherent descrip-tion. The Ukraine, for instance, was nominally governed during 1917–1920 by a succession of nine different regimes, none of which succeeded in estab-lishing its authority throughout the countryside. Many of the Muslim territories also experienced tremendous political upheaval, with some left-wing Jadids allying themselves with the Bolsheviks, while guerrillas (Basmachis) backed by both peasants and clerical elites offered armed resistance to Bolshevik conquest and occupation in Turkestan.[52] It is safe to say that the chaotic conditions of revolution and war were not conducive to the blos-soming of liberal-democratic or social-democratic institutions in any of these regions.[53]

One of the political tactics employed by the Bolsheviks in their life-or-death struggle in the Civil War was their promise of cultural and political autonomy to the non-Russian nationalities. The tsarist generals who commanded the various anti-Bolshevik armies, by contrast, paid little heed to the ethnic factor and openly adhered to a traditional, autocratic, Russocentric approach to the nationalities issue. As Bolshevik forces advanced into ethni-cally non-Russian territories, they set up national republics and autonomous regions. The regions were incorporated directly into the Russian state, which was constituted as a federated republic (the Russian Soviet Federative Socialist Republic (RSFSR)). The republics initially enjoyed nominal independence, but were subordinated in key policy areas to the authority of RSFSR ministries. In practice, local Bolshevik authorities were often ethnic Russians (or people who had become Russified in language and identity) who rode roughshod over the sentiments and interests of the local population. This ethnic tension was often compounded by an element of class conflict: Bolsheviks tended to be recruited from among Russian and Russified urban workers who had little in common with the predominantly non-Russian peasantry of the surrounding countryside.

The ethnic dimension of the Civil War helped shape Lenin's approach to the nationality question. It reinforced his growing conviction that transcending ethnic division in the interests of class solidarity depended on reining in the ethnic intolerance of many Russian Bolsheviks, and indulging the self-esteem of non-Russian nationalities, while keeping political power firmly in the hands of the party. It was this approach that was to shape the formal architecture of the Union of Soviet Socialist Republics (USSR).

The Soviet Ethnofederal Experiment

As we saw above, the Western powers at the Paris Peace Conference had limited control over events transpiring in Eastern Europe. They often found themselves in the position of retroactively legitimizing locally imposed solutions to boundary disputes. They were also generally befuddled by the seemingly insuperable challenge of reconciling civic-democratic ideals with ethnographic notions of nationhood. The Bolsheviks, in the aftermath of the Russian Civil War, were in a very different position. They were the undisputed masters of most of former imperial Russia's territory, and relatively free to impose whatever approach to the nationalities question that they saw fit. They too had an ideal of civic (class-based, rather than democratic) patriotism that they wished to promote, but precisely because they were pursuing their experiment within a single, multinational state, they had the luxury (or so they thought) of implementing the ethnographic principle on a systematic basis without in any way derogating from the power and authority of their supranational state. In their dialectical formula, ethnic identity was to be decoupled from state-wide political identity, and thereby reconciled with it, and, ultimately, transformed into a conduit for it.

Prior to 1917, the Bolshevik platform[54] had endorsed the principle of national self-determination, interpreting it in the radical sense of the right of nationalities to break away from the Russian empire to form independent nation-states. This stance allowed them to distance themselves completely from Russian nationalism and to form tactical alliances with separatist movements, while at the same time providing ideological cover for their rejection of the federalist approach endorsed by more moderate socialist parties. In other words, what they proposed was an either/or solution: those nationalities whose revolutionary classes wished to break away from Russia would be free in principle to do so, while those remaining within the Russian fold would make no claim to territorial or cultural autonomy. The principle of the centralized socialist state would thus not be compromised; the only question was whether in the short run, pending worldwide revolution, there would be one centralized socialist state or several such polities.

Following the November 1917 Revolution, Lenin performed an ideological about-face, convincing his comrades to endorse the principle of federalism both as a practical means of drawing the borderlands of the crumbled Russian empire into the Soviet fold and as a propagandist gesture designed to inspire revolutionary zeal among the subjects of the European colonial empires in Asia by demonstrating how equitably a socialist state treated its non-European peoples.[55]

During the Civil War, a Commissariat of Nationality Affairs headed by

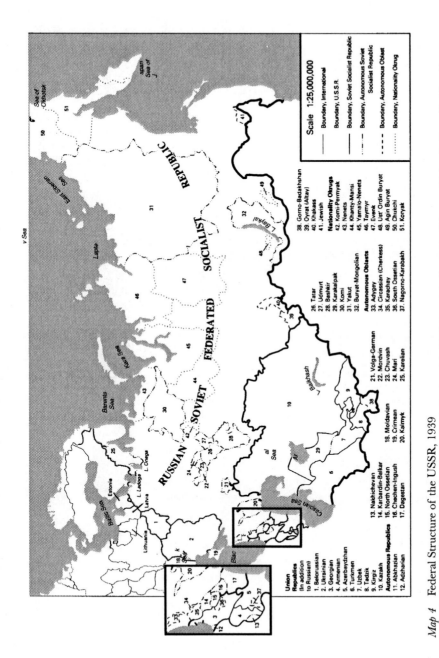

Map 4 Federal Structure of the USSR, 1939

Source: Robert S. Kaiser, *The Geography of Nationalism in Russia and the USSR*, copyright © 1994 by Princeton University Press. Reprinted by permission of Princeton University Press.

Within the map:

Scale 1:25,000,000

Boundary, International
Boundary, U.S.S.R.
Boundary, Soviet Socialist Republic
Boundary, Autonomous Soviet Socialist Republic
Boundary, Autonomous Oblast
Boundary, Nationality Okrug

Union Republics
(in addition to Russian)
1. Belorussian
2. Ukrainian
3. Georgian
4. Armenian
5. Azerbaydzhan
6. Turkmen
7. Uzbek
8. Tadzik
9. Kirgiz
10. Kazakh

Autonomous Republics
11. Abkhazian
12. Adzharian
13. Nakhichevan
14. Karbardin-Balkar
15. North Ossetian
16. Chechen-Ingush
17. Dagestan
18. Moldavian
19. Crimean
20. Kalmyk
21. Volga-German
22. Mordvin
23. Chuvash
24. Mari
25. Karelian
26. Tatar
27. Udmurt
28. Bashkir
29. Karakalpak
30. Komi
31. Yakut
32. Buryat-Mongolian

Autonomous Oblasts
33. Adygey
34. Circassian (Cherkess)
35. Karachay
36. South Ossetian
37. Nagorno-Karabakh
38. Gorno-Badakhshan
39. Oyrat (Altay)
40. Khakass
41. Jewish

Nationality Okrugs
42. Komi-Permyak
43. Nenets
44. Khanty-Mansi
45. Yamalo-Nenets
46. Taymyr
47. Evenk
48. Ust Ordin Buryat
49. Agin Buryat
50. Chukchi
51. Koryak

Joseph Stalin had been created to oversee relations with and policy toward the national minorities, but, as indicated above, improvisation and inconsistency characterized wartime nationality policy. Having ultimately fought a campaign to reconquer as much as possible of former imperial Russian territory from the embryonic nation-states that had sprung up on its soil, the Communist regime moved in the early 1920s toward the creation of a system that would pave the way for the propagation of a new, state-wide, Soviet identity based on the organizing principle of international working-class solidarity and common commitment to Communist ideals.[56]

The ethnic dimension of this social-engineering project was addressed through an extraordinarily methodical attempt to recognize, organize, modernize, and control ethnonational identities through formal institutional structures. It was Lenin's firm belief – reinforced by the successes and failures of Bolshevik nationalities policy during the Civil War – that separatist sentiments among the non-Russian masses were a product not only of manipulation by self-interested elites, but of the long history of state-sponsored Russian national chauvinism and exploitation. The bitter resentments that this had caused could be defused, he contended, by eliminating chauvinist impulses in Russian society (and within the Bolshevik party itself) and by granting the non-Russian nationalities recognition of their cultural and linguistic identities. By placing all ethnic groups – including the Russians – on an equal standing with one another, within the framework of a political system that enshrined class consciousness and ideological orientation as the criteria for membership or exclusion, the sources of interethnic tension and separatist sentiments would be removed.

Soviet nationalities policy in the 1920s rested on three pillars: the territorial-juridical, the cultural, and the socio-economic.

The character of the Soviet Union as multinational polity was enshrined as an integral aspect of the December 1922 Union Agreement (ratified as the foundation of the USSR's Constitution in 1923–1924). This established the formal political architecture of the state as a federation of sovereign national republics – the Union of Soviet Socialist Republics (USSR). Not only was every major ethnic group allocated a republic of its own, but minorities within each republic were awarded autonomous sub-units of their own. This hierarchical structure of bounded territorial units was in some cases even extended to the level of individual villages whose association with a particular nationality was formally recognized.[57]

The political sovereignty of the republics and of their sub-units was purely notional. While the USSR's constitution guaranteed each republic's right to secede from the union, any actual hint of separatism was ruthlessly repressed as a manifestation of anti-Communist subversion. Moreover, the highly centralized authority of the Communist Party of the USSR (as the Russian Communist Party was renamed in 1925) – the only legal political party in the country – belied the federative structure of the government.[58]

But Soviet federalism did have cultural content. Each territorial unit cultivated its own language as its official tongue, to be taught in schools, used in newspapers and journals, and employed in literary, theatrical, and cinematic productions. Precisely because Marxist doctrine conceived national identity to be a relatively ephemeral phenomenon on the path to a classless society, Lenin felt that multifarious languages and folkloric traditions could and should be used to convey the identical ideological message – a message that was "national in form, socialist in content."

In pursuing this approach, the Bolsheviks clearly went far beyond classical Marxism's facile dismissal of national identity as a socio-political force. Indeed, the methods of the architects of Soviet nationalities policy were partly modeled on the system developed by Nikolai I. Il'minskii (1822–1891), a nineteenth-century lay missionary who sought to draw non-Russian peoples (Tatars, Chuvash, and others) of the Middle Volga region into the ranks of the Russian Orthodox Church by legitimizing and encouraging the use of their native languages for liturgical purposes. This in turn led to the establishment of native-language schools. In the case of peoples whose languages had no written form, Il'minskii and his disciples created literary versions through transcription into the Cyrillic alphabet, standardizing grammar and phonology in the process.[59] The Soviet ethnographers of the 1920s played a similarly active role – albeit on a far more extensive scale – in defining a uniform linguistic standard for each ethnic group. (The Arabic scripts used by most Muslim peoples were replaced by the Latin alphabet in the 1920s, which gave way in turn to Cyrillic in the 1930s.) This endeavor itself was part of an all-encompassing effort to map out the entire country's ethnographic composition, using linguistic, anthropological, cultural, and socio-economic criteria to differentiate among the hundreds of nationalities. Having applied a unidimensional ethnic label to each segment of the population, the Soviet state could go on to assign it its territory, standardize its language and folklore, reify its identity, and employ its language, officially sanctioned folklore, and identity as conduits for the inculcation of socialist ideals and of loyalty to the Soviet state that had made this realization of national self-determination possible.

The showcasing of the USSR as a harmonious, voluntary community of autonomous nations was also an integral aspect of Soviet foreign propaganda: it suggested the possibility of other nations joining the union[60] and it was held up as a model of how to reconfigure relations between imperial nations and their subjects, in contrast to the continued subjugation of large segments of the globe to European colonialism. Indeed, the prospects of stimulating nationalist revolutions against European imperial hegemony in Asia seemed brighter than the chances of provoking an immediate proletarian uprising on the streets of London or Paris; hence the convening in Baku in September 1920 of the Congress of the Peoples of the East, an abortive and at times (as when the head of the Communist International called for an anti-imperial *jihad*) comical attempt by the Bolsheviks to create a framework of coordination for an unlikely assortment of nationalists and/or Communist sympathizers from across the Asian continent (including Soviet Central Asia).[61]

Finally, Soviet nationalities policy of the 1920s was intimately linked to the

Communists' modernization agenda. Cultural modernization, as described above, was part of this program: the Soviet state would take each ethnic minority by the hand and guide it through the process of acquiring the full cultural apparatus of modern nationhood – a native-language press, literature (with an indigenous writers' union in charge of defining ideological and aesthetic standards for it and facilitating its production), educational system (at least through primary or secondary school; Russian remained the language of higher education), etc. The creation of this cultural superstructure, in a reversal of the classical Marxist paradigm, would help pave the way for the development of a modern, state-funded and controlled, socio-economic base and infrastructure. The process was to be facilitated and accelerated through a policy known as *korenizatsiia* (indigenization). *Korenizatsiia* sought to root each republic's major ethnic group in the infrastructure of modernization by favoring its members for promotion up the territory's economic, administrative, and Communist Party ladders. Longstanding imperial patterns of unequal development, discrimination, and exploitation were to be reversed in this civilizing-mission-through-affirmative-action, as state-funded economic development and state-supported native-language education provided the means for peasant peoples and even nomadic groups to leap-frog into the modern, socialist, internationalist age.

At least that was the idea in principle. In practice, not only did Soviet nationalities policy present a far less pretty picture, it also contained a number of fundamental paradoxes and contradictions.

Most prominent among these was the glaring gap between the formal recognition of each republic's sovereignty and the reality of Moscow's iron grip – a depth and uniformity of centralized control that far surpassed that exercised by the Old Regime. This was true even during the 1920s, the era of the New Economic Policy (NEP), when small-scale private enterprise and private ownership of land was permitted. The brutality of the totalitarian state became even more pervasive and inescapable following Stalin's abandonment of NEP in 1928.

Moreover, no matter how much the Party sought to portray itself as internationalist in both orientation and composition, there was no getting around the fact that ethnic Russians were disproportionately represented in the Communist Party of the USSR, in the upper echelons of the Party apparatus, and in central government institutions, and that Russian continued to be promoted as the lingua franca of Soviet higher education and of the country's political and technocratic elites. The tendency toward cultural/linguistic Russification grew rather than diminished over time and was accompanied by ever more prevalent manifestations of chauvinistic attitudes toward non-Russian – and especially non-Slavic – ethnic groups. This shift was accentuated by the Communist Party's transition from a relatively small, self-selected group of committed revolutionaries to the ruling apparatus of the country, whose rapidly expanding ranks were filled by career-minded people for whom the incantation of internationalist clichés represented a prerequisite for their ascent up the bureaucratic ladder rather than an expression of deeply held convictions. Joseph Stalin's growing power within the party apparatus rested in large measure on the support of this new cohort, and – his own ethnic Georgian background notwithstanding – he employed thinly veiled language and actions to encourage Russians' sense of primacy within the Soviet Union.

It was one of the ironies of the Soviet ethnofederal system that the Russian republic was the least distinctly and cohesively constituted of the federal units. On the one hand, the administrative overlap between its governing structure and that of the central Soviet government was particularly extensive. On the other hand, it was itself formally constituted as a federated republic, to accommodate the unusually large multitude of autonomous ethnic regions that pockmarked its territory. The fact that little effort was made to cultivate a Russian ethnoterritorial consciousness distinct from Soviet identity served to reinforce Russians' tendency to identify the entire extent of the Soviet Union as their homeland – a form of national identity that often seemed to approximate a neo-imperial mentality. This perspective was further strengthened by the wide distribution of ethnic Russians across the territory of non-Russian republics.[62]

Conversely, Communist ethnofederalism did not automatically neutralize autonomist impulses among the non-Russian nationalities. On the contrary, the period leading up to the conclusion and ratification of a Union treaty in 1923–1924 was marked by strong tensions between Moscow and republican leaders objecting to the ongoing abuse of authority by RSFSR officials and concerned that the prospective constitution of the USSR lacked sufficient guarantees against the continuation of this pattern of arrogance and intrusiveness on the part of the Moscow authorities.

In the Ukrainian SSR, notably, Communist Party leader M. Skrypnik objected strenuously to systematic violations of the Ukraine's official sovereignty. A committed Bolshevik of long standing, he contended that this phenomenon was but one manifestation of a pernicious pattern of renewed Russian chauvinism that could undermine support for the revolution among the peoples of the Soviet Union. Likewise, in Georgia, whose independent Menshevik government had been overthrown by invading Bolshevik forces in 1921, the newly installed Communist authorities soon found themselves at odds with the head of the Russian Commissariat of Nationality Affairs, Joseph Stalin – himself an ethnic Georgian who promoted an unabashedly centralizing policy with strong Russian-nationalist overtones. However committed they themselves may have been to internationalist principles, the Georgian Communists found themselves playing the functional equivalent of nationalists as they strove to preserve those aspects of sovereignty guaranteed them by their 1921 treaty with the RSFSR but negated by the intrusive machinations of Stalin and his henchmen. The latter sought to force Georgia, Azerbaijan, and Armenia back into a Transcaucasian federation that would enter the USSR as one republican unit, undercutting Georgia's equality of status with other founding republics of the Soviet Union. Lenin himself strove at the last minute to intervene on behalf of the Georgian Party leaders in a vain attempt to preserve some credible division of power between the Russian-dominated Communist center and non-Russian

Communist periphery. However, he was soon incapacitated by a stroke and unable to prevent the Georgian leaders' ouster and replacement by Stalinist loyalists who embraced the creation in December 1922 of a Transcaucasian Federated Soviet Socialist Republic. By the time the federation was dissolved and Georgian republican sovereignty notionally restored in 1936, the local party organization had been systematically purged of all potential autonomist elements, and a new purge – part of the Stalinist terror unleashed throughout the Soviet Union – was under way.[63]

In the Ukrainian and Georgian cases, local Communist elites were trying to maintain equality of status for their republics by working within the formal ideological and constitutional system, attempting to make the spirit of Soviet policy conform to the letter of the law. But there was also a more systematic, ideologically distinctive challenge to the Soviet regime's centralism-in-the-name-of-internationalism. This was Sultan Galiev's National Bolshevism. A Volga Tatar from Kazan who had served as a Russian-language teacher in the Caucasus, had gone on to work for the All-Russian Muslim Congress of 1917 (see Chapter 4), and had joined the Bolshevik Party around the time of the November Revolution, Mirza Sultan Galiev was a left-wing, ideological heir to the *jadid* movement of the pre-war period (see Chapter 3). As in the case of the *jadids*, his frame of reference encompassed all the Muslims of the former Russian empire, in whose united action there would be more strength and more universal significance than in the ethnic particularism that had fragmented Russia's Muslims in 1917–1918 and that the Soviet regime was institutionalizing through its ethnofederal system.

Sultan Galiev took as his point of departure the premise (shared by Lenin) that the Russian empire's Muslims – particularly those of Central Asia – had been the victims of systematic economic exploitation on the part of Russian colonists, merchants, and manufacturers, who had enjoyed the backing and encouragement of the Russian government. His radically revisionist conclusion was that the Muslim population as a whole, therefore, constituted a proletarian nation. Internal class distinctions among the Muslims paled by comparison with the stark contrast between their historical role as the exploited and the Russians' role as the exploiters. The attainment of Muslim national self-determination (in the form of far-reaching, substantive autonomy for a unified Republic of Turan that would encompass all the Soviet Union's major Muslim populations) would thus constitute a revolutionary step forward according to Sultan Galiev. Indeed, adapting Lenin's justification for his socio-economically premature socialist revolution in Russia, Sultan Galiev argued that the national liberation of the Soviet Union's Muslim-populated regions would serve as the revolutionary spark that would set off a global revolution of oppressed, proletarian nations and the consequent collapse of imperialism, and hence capitalism. This was, in a sense, a doctrine of Soviet–Muslim chosenness or exceptionalism, a nationalist ideology couched in terms of universalistic, socialist values. This ideological heresy led to Sultan Galiev's purge from the party in 1923 and his subsequent arrest and disappearance in 1928, followed by the systematic liquidation of all Muslim Communists suspected of harboring National Communist inclinations.[64]

The suppression of Sultan Galievism marked the end of any organized or ideologically articulate form of neo-pan-Islamic nationalism in the Soviet Union. Throughout the USSR, the official cultivation of ethno-cultural particularism continued to serve as an instrument of Communist indoctrination and as a fig leaf of tolerance and pluralism that ill-concealed the brutal socio-economic and political upheavals and mass terror of the years following Stalin's abandonment of the NEP in 1928. Indeed, there was a strong element of divide-and-rule strategy and of a sort of ethnographic cultural imperialism in Soviet nationalities policy. The drawing of political, linguistic, and institutional boundaries among ethnic groups was often arbitrary and seemed designed to make the objects of this policy dependent on the Soviet state for their very identity. This appears to have been the case, for instance, in Turkestan, which was reconfigured into five Soviet republics (Turkmenistan, Uzbekistan, Kirghizistan, Kazakhstan, and Tajikistan) and numerous autonomous sub-regions over the course of 1924–1936. This novel political geography was based on ethnographic research by Soviet academicians who imposed ethnic labels on peoples whose cultural and historical heritages were so diverse, complex, overlapping, and intertwined as to defy simple categorization by any truly objective standard. (By the same token, the integration of such populations into a monolithic Turkestan would have been at least as contrived and arbitrary a nation-building project.) Each republic's educational system then set about the task of propagating a standardized and homogenized "national" language and an official historical myth that linked the recently created entity to an ancient state or ethnic group. (Thus, the Tajiks were declared to be descendants of the Sogdians.)[65]

While this approach may have served to ward off the coalescence of pan-nationalist or interethnic resistance movements, it did not automatically lead to the consolidation of a purely class- and ideology-based Soviet identity either. The political geography of ethnofederalism continued to serve as a frame of reference for collective identity, particularly because it was reinforced by the other aspects of Soviet nationalities policy. The *korenizatsiia* policy of the 1920s had given members of each republic's majority group a very concrete, material stake in the preservation of their identity, which served as a springboard for upward social mobility. That ethnic majorities and minorities were formally distinguished from one another was itself a function of another paradoxical feature of the system: territorial identity was offset by "passport nationality."[66] The latter term refers to the fact that the internal passports issued from 1932 on identified every Soviet citizen as a member of a particular ethnic group. Personal ethnic identity was determined by parentage, not by place of birth.[67] By thus combining the principles of territorial and extraterritorial or personal identity, while pursuing policies of affirmative action for the eponymous group of each republic except the RSFSR, and at the same time giving preferential treatment to ethnic Russians when it came to staffing certain key administrative and Communist Party positions throughout the Soviet Union, the regime further institutionalized barriers and resentments among intermingled nationalities. *Korenizatsiia* was abandoned as an official policy in the 1930s, but aspects of it were subsequently revived. The reification of distinctions among ethnic groups continued to be sustained by the dual-tiered, territorial and extraterritorial frameworks of identity, as well as by Stalin's intermittent use of ethnicity as a category for the classification – and collective punishment – of entire groups of people as foes of the regime.[68]

Finally, the Soviet assumption that national culture, language, and folklore could be freely manipulated to serve the goal of ideological homogenization was also questionable. Crushing blows certainly were struck at any expression of identity that did not conform to the officially designated mold. And yet, even the tightly constrained cultures of official identity were not completely neutral media for the transmission of the official line. The medium did affect the message.

The case of Jewish culture can serve as an illuminating example. Designating the Jews a nationality like any other (notwithstanding their lack of a territorial base),[69], the Soviets virtually eliminated Jewish religious education and severely limited public worship, attacked Hebrew as the language of religion and of Zionism, and promoted Yiddish as the official language of the Jewish toiling masses. The Jewish sections (generally referred to in the singular as the *Yevsektsiia*) of the Russian Communist Party, which were staffed by Jewish cadres and charged with overseeing cultural policy and propaganda among the territorially diffuse Jewish population, gained a notorious reputation in the 1920s as zealous enforcers of the regime's anti-religious and anti-Hebraic policies.[70]

Yet even in the context of this rigorously enforced cultural overhaul, in which traditional communal, religious, and educational institutions were destroyed and liturgical forms stripped of their content and transformed into vehicles for the propagation of Communist propaganda, elements of an autonomous Jewish identity continued to manifest themselves.[71] Traditional forms could not be voided of their content quite as easily as Soviet social engineers imagined. For instance, recent research by Jeff Veidlinger has shown that many plays produced by Moscow's Yiddish Theater from the 1920s through 1940s were marked by tension between their overt Marxist-Leninist message and sentimental themes that crept in between the lines. Some plays that pilloried pre-revolutionary *shtetl* (Jewish small town) society for its social inequalities and religious obscurantism nonetheless conveyed a sense of nostalgia for the lost world they were repudiating. Indeed, a number of these scripts were Marxist adaptations of classics such as the works of Sholom Aleichem (Solomon Rabinovitz, 1859–1916), the Yiddish writer whose fondly sardonic depictions of *shtetl* life were also to serve as the basis for Broadway's and Hollywood's ode to the Jewish past, *Fiddler on the Roof*. Original scripts could also contain such ambiguities, as in the case of one play that turned the story of Bar Kochba's second-century AD anti-Roman revolt into a parable about class conflict, yet in so doing also conveyed an unmistakable sense of nationalist pride (perhaps even with Zionist overtones) in the heroic deeds of Jewish freedom fighters.[72]

As in the case of the Germans' much more limited wartime experiment in the manipulation of East European ethno-cultural identities (see Chapter 5), the Soviet attempt to shape ethnicity into an instrument of imperial or supranational control was ambiguous in its results. The Soviet authorities themselves vacillated in their approach, reverting to overt Russification policies in some areas during the 1930s, officially abandoning *korenizatsiia*, integrating many small autonomous districts into the larger SSRs, deporting entire ethnic groups suspected of pro-German sympathies during the Second World War from the Caucasus to Central Asia, shutting down Yiddish theaters and executing the Soviet Union's leading Yiddish writers in 1952, then reverting to a toned-down version of *korenizatsiia* as part of the overall de-Stalinization process of the mid-to-late 1950s.

Yet through it all, the basic institutional and juridical structures of ethnofederalism – the territorial republic and the designation of personal nationality in identity documents – remained in place (and were copied or adapted, in turn, by Communist Yugoslavia and the People's Republic of China). Even as the industrialization of the USSR's economy, the collectivization of agriculture, and the uniformity of the educational curriculum created greater similarity in material conditions and socio-economic structures among various peoples, the impulse to resist complete homogenization and loss of identity may have grown stronger among some.[73] The fading of the ideological zeal of the Soviet Union's early years increased the attractiveness of national culture as a frame of reference for personal and collective identity. Amidst the final decline of Soviet Communism in the late 1980s through 1991, the legacy of Lenin's ethnofederalism stood ready to hand as the only institutional alternative to the now discredited principle of proletarian internationalism. The dialectic of Leninist nationalities policy backfired, as the very structures designed to defuse separatist impulses and transcend interethnic jealousies and resentments now formed the fault lines along which the Soviet state disintegrated into independent national republics.

Reconfiguring the Boundaries of Identity in the Middle East

The Turkish Settlement and the Kemalist State

Unlike the Romanov and Habsburg empires, the Ottoman state did not collapse in 1917 or 1918. It simply lost more and more of its territory to the advancing British-commanded armies in the Arab Middle East. The impending capitulation of its German and Austro-Hungarian allies and the steady advance of British forces in the Middle East in the fall of 1918 made the inevitability of Ottoman defeat apparent. As the discredited CUP leadership fled the country to avoid arrest by the Allied powers on war crimes charges stemming from the Armenian massacres of 1915, the Sultan's newly appointed government signed the Armistice of Mudros on 30 October 1918, opening the country to occupation by Allied forces.[74]

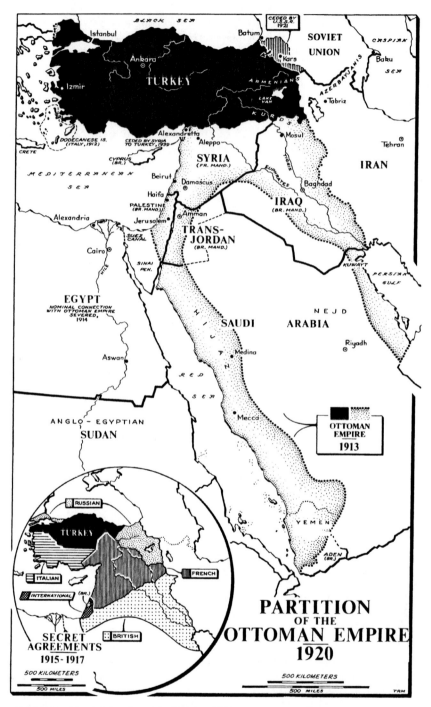

Map 5 Partition of the Ottoman Empire, 1920
Source: Sydney N. Fisher and William Ochsenwald, *The Middle East: A History*, Fourth Edition (New York: McGraw-Hill, 1990). Reproduced with permission of the McGraw-Hill companies.

The peace settlement that followed – the Treaty of Sèvres (10 August 1920) – was dictated by the victorious Allied powers. It ratified the partition of the Arab Middle East by the British and French, who were to administer their respective territories under mandates from the League of Nations. Anatolia itself was to be carved up into Greek-, Italian-, and French-administered zones, an independent Armenia, an autonomous or independent Kurdistan, and a weak and vulnerable Ottoman rump state to be left under the control of the Sultan.[75]

The Turkish nationalist societies and secret military formations that had been created by the CUP to mobilize public support for the war effort and to strike at ethnic groups perceived as enemies (see Chapter 4) were now called upon by former CUP member and army officer Mustafa Kemal to sustain a resistance effort against the occupying and invading powers and the Sultan who was collaborating with them. Based in central and eastern Anatolia, Mustafa Kemal's movement rejected the authority of the Sultan, established a parliamentary body (the Grand National Assembly) in Ankara, and, over the course of 1919–1922, succeeded – with the help of military supplies and financial aid from the Soviet Union, which saw in Kemal a useful counter to Western imperialism – in defeating a series of military adversaries. His forces triumphed over a Greek army attempting to expand Greece's occupation zone. He forced the French into a negotiated withdrawal from Cilicia (on the Syrian border). Northeastern Anatolia, scene of the Armenian massacres of 1915, had, with the Western powers' blessing, been occupied by the independent Armenian republic in early 1919. It was retaken by Kemal in September–October 1920 in a military victory that pushed the Armenian government into the over-protective arms of the Russian Communists. Moscow duly proceeded to sign away on its behalf the territories it had disputed with the Turks.[76] Having gained control of Istanbul and abolished the Sultanate by late 1922, Kemal's government capped its triumph by scrapping the humiliating Treaty of Sèvres and negotiating the Treaty of Lausanne (24 July 1923), which established Turkey's full sovereignty, territorial integrity, and international legitimacy.[77]

Thus, the one state that emerged fully independent from the debris of the former Ottoman empire was based on the Turkish core of that empire. Critical to this development was the fact that a new ruling elite had emerged in the empire during the last years of its existence. The Young Turks had been torn between their efforts to hold the multiethnic empire together on the one hand, and their increasing commitment to Turkish nationalism on the other. The defeat of the Ottoman empire resolved the tension between the conflicting interests and agendas that had informed the policies of the CUP regime. The consolidation of Bolshevik control over Central Asia put an end to the pan-Turkist dream, while the Anglo-French occupation of the Arab lands freed Turkish nationalists of the need to clothe their agenda in pan-Islamic garb. Although the CUP as such was discredited and disbanded in the aftermath of the military defeat, Musafa Kemal's nationalist movement is now widely recognized by historians[78] as in many ways a direct heir to the Young Turks. Mustafa Kemal (who was later renamed Kemal Atatürk [Great Turk]) retained or adapted many of the former regime's ideological perspectives and mobilization techniques, with none other than Ziya Gökalp (see Chapter 3) becoming chief exponent of the official line.

The defeat of the Greeks provided an occasion for consolidating the ethnically Turkish base of the new nation-state, with 1.1 million Greeks fleeing from western Asia Minor to Greece while 380,000 Turks moved in the opposite direction in a population transfer sanctioned by international treaty and endorsed by the Western powers. (Religious affiliation was used as the marker of ethnic identity in this population transfer, with thousands of Turkish-speaking adherents of Eastern Orthodoxy finding themselves deported to Greece, and vice versa.) The Armenian population had already been drastically reduced by the massacres and expulsions of 1915, with additional tens of thousands of Armenians fleeing from Cilicia into Lebanon and elsewhere following French withdrawal from that province in 1921. The Kurds, a largely peasant population with no religious, cultural, or commercial ties to the West and which did not compete economically with the rising Turkish urban elites, were deemed suitable for assimilation into Turkish culture and identity. Any attempt on their part to resist the authority of the Turkish nation-state or to assert their collective self-interest as a distinct nationality was brutally crushed.[79]

While ethnic groups that had traditionally turned to the Western powers for protection were treated as alien elements to be eliminated from the Turkish body politic, Turkish identity was itself defined in strictly secular, Western-oriented terms. Turkey was declared a republic in October 1923, the vestigial spiritual authority of the caliphate was abolished in 1924, and Mustafa Kemal's dictatorial state used its arbitrary powers to impose its notion of modern, secular national identity from above over the course of the 1920s by criminalizing the wearing of the fez (itself introduced in the early nineteenth century as part of a new look associated with the Tanzimat reform movement), encouraging the adoption of Western-style dress, fully secularizing family law (the last legal domain to have escaped complete secularization under earlier regimes), expanding the legal rights of women, adopting the Latin alphabet, and trying to "purify" the Turkish language by purging it of much of its Arabic and Persian vocabulary. This can be seen as an attempt to create an all-embracing civic consciousness (propagated more successfully among urban middle classes than among the peasantry) based on a synthesis of Western civilization and Turkish culture. But Turkish civic nationalism was built on a legacy of genocide and ethnic cleansing and propagated by a dictatorial regime with little patience for the niceties of pluralistic politics.[80]

The concerted use of state institutions to forge a Turkish national consciousness and to modernize the country's socio-cultural and economic institutions seemed relatively successful at the time, and served as a powerful model that other budding nation-states in formerly Ottoman territories sought to emulate.[81] Unlike Turkey, however, the Arab world remained overshadowed by European imperial power and divided by profound internal differences over the meaning and geopolitical parameters of Arab nationalism.

European Imperialism as Framework for the Genesis of Middle Eastern Nation-States

In the lands to the south of Turkey, the British and French gradually settled differences arising from Britain's drive to revise their 1916 spheres of influence agreement. At the 1920 San Remo Conference, they settled on British control of Mesopotamia (Iraq) and Palestine (with the territory east of the river Jordan marked off by the British in 1921–1922 to form a separate entity called Transjordan) and French control of Syria and Lebanon. League of Nations mandates (approved in 1922) were to form the international legal framework for this arrangement.[82] The rationale for the mandates rather awkwardly wedded Wilsonian principle with colonial practice. The inhabitants of the Arab lands were deemed politically immature – not yet quite capable of governing themselves. They were accordingly to be placed under the benevolent tutelage of the British and French, who were to guide them toward eventual independence. While the mandatory authorities were required to report periodically to the League on the progress of their assignments, no final due date was assigned for the handover of power to indigenous authorities. The mandates were, in fact, a convenient instrument for the imperial policies of the British and French, who had agreed on the postwar partition of the region into spheres of influence in their 1916 Sykes–Picot agreement, and who gained control of these territories through military conquest followed by the suppression of indigenous resistance in Iraq and Syria.

Yet to suggest that Anglo-French policy was shaped by imperial interests and values is not to say that the institutional form of the mandates had no impact on their approach to governance,[83] nor is it to say that this period did not mark a watershed in the development of Middle Eastern nationalisms – it did. The very arbitrariness of the borders dividing one mandatory regime from another had a significant impact on the development of states and identities in the region, as did British and French experimentation with variations on the theme of linking their imperial overlordship to local nationalism.

In the case of Palestine, Britain's claim to the territory was strongly linked to its endorsement of the Zionist movement's aspiration to establish in Palestine a "national home for the Jewish people," as the November 1917 Balfour Declaration had cautiously phrased it.[84] The League of Nations mandate for Palestine constituted the international legal framework for this nation-building project. It incorporated the language of the Balfour Declaration and obliged the British to facilitate Jewish immigration and to cooperate with a Jewish Agency in the settlement and development of the land, while protecting the rights of the territory's Arab population.[85]

To the north, the French established themselves in Lebanon in 1919, then – following the withdrawal in 1919 of British occupation forces from Syria and the San Remo agreement of April 1920 – employed military force in 1920 to make good their claim to Syria, where Faisal, son of Hussein, had been declared king in a final act of nationalist defiance. Faisal's army was defeated at the Battle of Maisalun in July and the king himself fled into exile, clearing the way for the establishment of French mandatory rule. The French exercised their authority in Lebanon and Syria in a highly intrusive manner, experimenting with the cooptation of various coalitions of local notables into puppet governments, while ultimate authority remained in the hands of the French high commissioners.[86]

By contrast, the British were inclined to move fairly rapidly toward the granting of more substantive self-government or even formal independence in the Middle Eastern lands under their control – other than Palestine, where the growing conflict between Jews and Arabs begged the question of who would exercise power in an autonomous government. In Transjordan (corresponding to today's kingdom of Jordan), Faisal's brother Abdullah was installed as Emir under the supervision of a British High Commissioner. In Iraq, following the suppression of an anti-British popular uprising led by traditional notables in 1920, Faisal was established as king in 1921 in compensation for his loss of Syria and as a way of creating a mediating system between British hegemony and the indigenous population. Iraq was awarded formal independence in 1932 within the framework of a 1930 treaty that left Britain with a preponderance of military, economic, and political power in the country. In 1936, a similar arrangement was negotiated in Egypt, which had been under British rule since 1882.

By creating a façade of Arab self-government and by wrapping their hegemony in Transjordan and Iraq in the mantle of the Hashemite dynasty, the British hoped to build on their wartime policy of using Arab nationalism as the handmaiden of their imperial ambitions. Yet, however self-interested their motives and manipulative their methods, in undertaking these policies they put in place some of the basic structures within which Arab political identity was to take shape. Their preferred method of indirect rule and their affiliation with the family that had led the Arab Revolt also brought pressure for reform to bear upon the French, whose rule in Syria and Lebanon appeared more oppressive and less legitimate by contrast. Under the left-of-center Popular Front government of 1936, France attempted to imitate the British model by negotiating what turned out to be a short-lived agreement with Arab nationalists in Syria that seemed to put that country on the road to quasi-independence under the French imperial canopy.

Unlike their East Central European counterparts, then, the Arabs did not achieve full-fledged national independence in the immediate aftermath of the war. Nonetheless, the conceptual and institutional frameworks of independent states were established under the auspices of the imperial powers. To be sure, Britain and France used these state apparatuses as instruments of economic, political, and military control over the Middle East. Yet by the same token, the newly formed states became the primary vessels within which Arab (and, in Palestine, also Jewish) nationalism took root as a hegemonic political ideology and assumed some of its distinctive typological forms. At the same time, the intrusive presence of the non-Islamic European authorities had the potential to stimulate the growth of nationalism among the general population in a way and on a scale that Ottoman rule never did. Indeed, it opened the door to propagandist experiments by embryonic populist organizations that linked familiar Islamic imagery and symbols to resentment of the foreigner in nationalist syntheses more readily intelligible to a mass audience than the essentially secular ideology of the Arab nationalist elites.[87]

All this is to suggest that the roll-back of the Ottoman empire constituted a more significant turning point in the development of the region's nation-states than did the disintegration of European control after the Second World War, and that post-First World War developments here therefore merit inclusion in this chapter despite the anomalous factor of the French and British imperial presence.

Statehood vs. Nationhood in the Arab World

The geopolitical transformation of the Middle East shaped the evolution of identities in various ways and at a number of levels. To begin with, the disappearance of the overarching Ottoman framework presided over by a sultan/caliph meant that the notion of the *umma* – the unbounded socio-religious community of Muslim faithful – no longer corresponded to any existing political structure. Arab intellectual and social elites were left casting about for alternative frames of reference.

The most attractive idea was that of Arab nationalism, whose adherents no longer had to restrict their activities to secret societies now that the Turks had departed from the scene.[88] Jemal Pasha's harsh wartime policies had succeeded in disrupting the organizational structure of the secret societies while lending credibility to their claim that the Arabs as a people were being oppressed by the Turks. The apparent triumph of the Arab forces upon their entry into Damascus in October 1918 rapidly assumed a mythical aura, rendered all the more poignant and evocative by the subsequent ouster of Faisal by the French. The assumption of the Transjordanian and Iraqi thrones by the Hashemite brothers ensured that the dream of uniting the Arabs[89] under one dynasty would continue to appear a concrete possibility, with the potential leaders of such a movement already in positions of power in self-governing political entities. By the same token, pan-Arabism held particular appeal as a modern, secular substitute for the *umma* (and also as a substitute for the discredited idea of Ottomanism, which itself had served as a secular, socially integrative alternative to the *umma* – see Chapter 3) precisely because it transcended the arbitrary lines of division the Western powers had imposed on the region.

Yet here lay the rub. The advocates of Arab political unification tended to look to the Hashemite rulers, or at least to the state apparatuses over which they presided, as the instruments for achieving their objectives. But which ruler, which government, which army was to take the lead in this enterprise? The fact was that, arbitrary though it might have been, the Anglo-French partition of the Middle East had created a paradoxical situation in which a multiplicity of political elites felt compelled at least to pay lip service to the goal of one day eliminating the frontiers that divided them, while competing with one another for pride of place in this endeavor.

Indeed, the steady stream of rhetoric about the destiny of the Arab nation was belied by the rapid crystallization of state-centered political identities among the elites of Syria, Iraq, and the Arabs of Palestine. Even during Syria's brief heyday of independence in 1918–1920, clear tensions between pan-Arab and regionalist impulses had manifested themselves. Faisal found himself playing a delicate balancing act among local notables, whose rapid rhetorical shift from Ottomanism to Arabism ill-concealed their unchanged preoccupation with securing and preserving their administrative offices, patronage networks, and political influence under whatever regime happened to be in power, and the motley crew of Sharifian officers and members of the nationalist secret societies who looked upon Faisal's regime as a springboard for the fulfillment of pan-Arab aspirations. This latter group, which won a majority of seats to the Syrian Congress in elections held in 1919, was itself divided among the mostly Syrian members of al-Fatat, the Iraqi officers of al-ʿAhd (including both former Sharifians and those who had continued to serve in the Ottoman army until the end of the war), and a small but vocal contingent of Palestinian Arabs that joined the assembly (now renamed the General Syrian Congress) in March 1920. The last group was frustrated by its inability to win Faisal's regime over to a more actively anti-Zionist position (indeed, Faisal had concluded a tentative *modus vivendi* with Chaim Weizmann in January 1919, in the hope of gaining Zionist and British support against the French),[90] while the Iraqi and Syrian Arab nationalist groupings competed with one another for political influence over the regime. Faisal's effort to reach a compromise arrangement with the French had won the support of Syrian notables, but provoked a backlash from the committed nationalists who dominated the General Syrian Congress. Backed by widespread public unrest (possibly the first clear manifestation of nationalist sentiment – itself more Syrian-centered than pan-Arab in outlook – among the general populace),[91] the Congress essentially forced Faisal to accept the title of King of an independent Syria on 8 March 1920 as a gesture of defiance toward the French. The April 1920 San Remo Conference, French military invasion and victory at the Battle of Maisalun in July, and Faisal's flight into exile followed in short order.[92]

With the crushing of Syrian independence, Damascus lost its role as a locus of common effort and internecine struggle among Arab nationalists from throughout the region. The Iraqi contingent eventually followed Faisal to Baghdad, the Syrian Arab nationalists lay low or withdrew into British mandatory territories where they continued to focus their attention on developments back home (most were sooner or later amnestied by the French as part of intermittent efforts at political accommodation), and the Palestinian Arab activists returned to Palestine. Committed as many of them remained to the dream of Arab unification, their only way of remaining politically active was to operate within the frameworks of their respective mandatory regimes.[93]

The Palestinian Arab nationalists are a case in point. Like their Syrian coun-

terparts, many of them hailed from the class of urban notables that had dominated local politics and patronage networks for the last half century or so of
Ottoman rule, but were distinguished by characteristics such as their relative
youth and their exclusion (due partly to the reforms of the Young Turks) from
offices and perquisites that historical precedent had led them to regard as theirs
by right (see Chapter 3). During 1918–1920, a number of these activists had
participated in the General Syrian Congress, while those remaining in Palestine
had looked to Damascus for inspiration and leadership. Many belonged to a
Palestine-based sister organization of al-Fatat, and these elements had dominated the first Palestinian Arab Congress of January–February 1919, which had
passed resolutions in favor of the creation of a Greater Syria encompassing
Palestine. The term Palestine, after all, had until recently referred to a vaguely
defined geographical area that had religious or socio-cultural significance, but
that did not correspond to any administrative unit under the Ottomans (any
more than Syria did). Faisal's government in Damascus seemed like the obvious
candidate to lead all the Arabs of the region to independence.

With the fall of Faisal's regime, the young nationalist elite in Palestine was left
with little choice but to operate within the confines of mandatory Palestine,
where the older generation of notables had already begun to cultivate the notion
of Palestinian patriotism as a vehicle for the assertion of their local interests *vis-
à-vis* the British authorities and in the face of the Zionist challenge. The younger
generation's shift of focus to the mandatory arena was reflected in the resolutions
of the Third Palestinian Arab Congress of December 1920, which abandoned
all talk of a Greater Syria in favor of resolutions calling for home-rule for the
Arabs of Palestine.[94]

The rapid development of the Zionist enterprise under the aegis of the
British mandate played a critical role in catalyzing the development of a distinctive Palestinian Arab national consciousness during the interwar period.
Opposition to early Zionist settlement had already been expressed vociferously in
the local press and by Arab parliamentary representatives during the last decade
of Ottoman rule, but it was in the post-Ottoman, post-Maisalun framework, that
this opposition began clearly to take the form of a distinctive Palestinian Arab
nationalism that responded to the Zionist claim to the territory as a Jewish
homeland by conceiving of the same territory as the collective birthright of its
Arab population. The Zionist program of land acquisition, which concentrated
on the purchase of individual Arab estates from absentee landlords, accelerated
the development of a nationalist consciousness among both the Palestinian Arab
elites and the peasantry, specifically the tenant farmers and sharecroppers whose
concern over the prospect of eviction from their individual plots could readily be
linked to a broader sense of nationalist territoriality. The Zionists designated the
land they purchased as inalienable property owned by the Jewish National Fund
in the name of the Jewish people; this land could be leased to Jewish agricultural
settlements, but it could never be sold. Palestinian Arab leaders responded by
emphasizing the centrality of Arab land tenure to the preservation of their
homeland's integrity. To sell an individual farm to the Zionists was construed as

handing over a piece of the motherland to the enemy. Within Palestine, it was the very absence of a defined frontier between the rival nationalist movements that fueled the struggle between them and that turned every instance of local friction (clashes between neighboring Jewish and Arab settlements, tensions over Arab claims to pasturing rights on lands purchased by the Jewish National Fund, etc.) into an incident burdened with nationalist implications.[95]

As the Palestinian case suggests, while the Battle of Maisalun put an end to the already fragile Damascene framework for pan-Arab cooperation, it led to the coalescence of more cohesive political elites within the frameworks of individual mandatory states. Mandatory borders and sectarian differences shaped distinct communities of political identity, many of which employed the rhetoric of Arab nationalism in the service of their rival interests.[96]

Sectarianism and Ethno-Regional Politics in the Framework of Arab Nationalism

Indeed, because its aspirations were so disconnected from the existing configuration of political boundaries in the post-Ottoman Middle East, and were in fact so ill-defined geographically and culturally, Arab nationalism was an extremely malleable ideology, which lent itself to multiple interpretations and applications. It was seized upon by a wide variety of regional interests and sectarian communities throughout the Middle East, be it as a source of legitimation for their own particular interests, as an ideological basis for coalition building among groups with shared interests, or, by the same token, as the encapsulation of existential danger for minority groups that feared the prospect of violence or repression committed in its name and who responded by cultivating their own sense of ethnonational distinctiveness.

The specific orientation of any given sectarian or ethno-regional[97] community toward Arab nationalism – and toward the Sunni Muslim elites that dominated nationalist regimes and organizations – was influenced by a host of factors and was subject to change over time. Indeed, many communities were internally divided over the question. Policies pursued by the mandatory authorities played an influential role in shaping such alignments. This is particularly striking in the case of the French-controlled territories.

For decades if not centuries prior to the First World War, France had sought to play the role of protector of Catholic communities in the Middle East. It had established a particularly close cultural and political bond with the Maronites of Mount Lebanon – members of a Nestorian Church that recognized the spiritual authority of the Pope. France had played a leading role in the European military and diplomatic intervention that had ended massacres of Maronites by their Druze[98] neighbors in 1860. In the wake of this crisis, the autonomy traditionally enjoyed by this region was reaffirmed and formalized in an international treaty, which created the Mutasarrifate (district) of Mount Lebanon as a territory with a 60 per cent Maronite majority, enjoying special privileges and a measure of self-rule under an Ottoman-appointed, Christian governor.[99]

Their experience of Jemal Pasha's wartime political repression and of the devastating wartime famine that killed off nearly a fifth of Mount Lebanon's population left the Maronites' communal and clerical leaders all the more loath to accept Muslim political dominion and all the more eager to turn to French support in restoring and expanding the juridical and territorial scope of their autonomy. Although some Maronite leaders sought to reach an understanding with Faisal in Damascus, the influential Church authorities remained steadfastly opposed to the integration of Mount Lebanon into an Arab state. For the majority of Maronites, Arab nationalism represented the latest incarnation of the age-old Muslim threat. What they demanded instead was the creation of an independent Maronite state with borders extending well beyond Mount Lebanon to encompass territories claimed on historic and economic grounds. The combination of local pressure from the Maronite patriarch, lobbying in France by émigrés, and the breakdown in French relations with Faisal, helped convince the French authorities to grant the Maronites their wish through the transfer of territories that had historically been part of the Ottoman province of Damascus.

The resultant state of Greater Lebanon (declared in September 1920), which remained under the authority of the French high commissioner for Syria and Lebanon but was granted a republican constitution in 1926, encapsulated all the possible dilemmas and contradictions that the creation of a nation-state could entail. The new territories added on to Mount Lebanon contained a majority Muslim population, albeit divided between Sunnis and Shi'ites. Christians comprised a bare majority of the new state's population, with the Maronites themselves constituting no more than 32 per cent – a proportion that declined progressively over time due to differential birth rates. Members of the Greek Orthodox, Greek Catholic, Armenian, and various other churches did not particularly care to play a subordinate role in a Maronite-dominated state. The fact that the Maronites' mainstream leadership defined the Maronites as non-Arabs[100] created all the stronger an incentive for their disgruntled Muslim neighbors to demand reunification with Syria in the name of Arab nationalism. As early as 1919–1920, territories in and around Mount Lebanon under French occupation had been the scene of attacks against the French as well as their Maronite allies by armed bands from Druze, Sunni, and Shi'ite communities – attacks led or incited from within those communities by advocates of Arab nationalism with close ties to Faisal's regime. To be sure, inter-communal violence was nothing new to this region, but Arab nationalism and Maronite Lebanese nationalism formed modern legitimizing frameworks for its perpetuation, as well as for its eventual transposition from the domain of traditional mountain communities to ostensibly cosmopolitan commercial centers such as Beirut.

In an effort to accommodate the interests of the various communities in the new state, the French supported the drafting of a constitution that enshrined and extended a principle that had existed in embryonic form in the Ottoman Mutasarrifate – the allocation of all seats in the legislature to members of the various sectarian communities according to a fixed formula based on census figures. While all adult residents of a given district, regardless of religious affiliation, took part in the election of its multiconfessional slate of representatives to the Chamber of Deputies, this system nonetheless reinforced the notion that the country's political leaders were answerable first and foremost to their respective religious communities. Intended as a method of reconciling the various non-Maronite groups with their incorporation into Greater Lebanon, this system may have helped ease tensions, but it also served to reinforce and institutionalize the vertical segmentation of political consciousness along sectarian lines, as did the informal understandings about the distribution of executive and ministerial positions among the major religious communities.

Lebanon's profound inter-communal differences were eventually papered over in the 1943 British-supported[101] National Pact, a binding oral agreement in which Maronite and Sunni leaders jointly signaled their break with France and assertion of full independence. The rhetorical framework for this alliance was a statement that described Lebanon as "a homeland with an Arab face seeking the beneficial good from the culture of the West."[102] Yet this formula, suggestive of a new civic identity rooted in a synthesis of Arab roots and Western values, was belied by the Pact's reinforcement of the traditional political quota system, designating which high offices were to be assigned to leaders of which communities. The brittleness of the system was underlined by the fact that 1932 was the last time (as of 2000) a census was taken in Lebanon; any renegotiation of the distribution of legislative seats and political offices in accordance with demographic changes was a scenario so likely to lead to an impasse that it threatened the continued existence of the state.

In Syria, French incompetence and inconsistency actually contributed to the forging of intercommunal coalitions based on an Arab nationalist political platform. This was most striking in the case of the Druze of southwestern Syria (a region known as Jebel Druze – the Mountain of the Druze). This largely peasant community was still organized around a clan structure, yet some of its most influential leaders had been educated in the urban centers of the Middle East and had been involved in Arab nationalist politics since before 1914. The mandatory authorities hoped to break the Druze link to Arab nationalism and to pursue a divide-and-rule strategy by granting separate administrative status and local autonomy to Jebel Druze as well as to the Alawite[103] territory in the northwest. But the inconsistency and arbitrariness of French policies helped provoke a 1925 Druze rebellion that spread like wildfire throughout much of Syria.

The leaders of the revolt were those Druze figures with the closest links to Arab nationalist organizations. They were quickly joined by Arab nationalist leaders from Damascus and other Syrian urban centers in what became a full-fledged Syrian revolt that spilled over from Jebel Druze into the very heart of Damascus (as well as into Druze communities in Lebanon) and gained unprecedented levels of mass support and involvement in many regions, both rural and urban.[104] While the French succeeded in using military force to crush the revolt in 1926–1927, some of the more astute observers among them were left with the inescapable conclusion that their divide-and-rule policies had backfired and that France would have to reach a compromise with the Syrian Arab nationalist leadership on the model of what the British had done in Iraq. This led to the empowerment of the National Bloc (led by leading veterans of the political resistance to French rule) in 1936–1939 and an unsuccessful attempt at concluding a Syrian treaty of independence (which was signed by both sides but which the French parliament failed to ratify).[105]

The political practices of Faisal's Iraqi regime highlighted both the possibilities and the limitations of using Arab nationalism as an ideological foundation for state building. While attractive to a growing number of high-school and university students as well as army officers, and increasingly acceptable as a rhetorical frame of reference for the traditional Sunni notables, it was embraced less wholeheartedly by Shi'ite leaders, whose followers represented a majority of the country's Arab Muslims but constituted an economic and political underclass. Arab nationalism was appealing to them insofar as it gave them a claim to equality of status, but threatening if used – as it was – by the Sunni elites to legitimize their own continued grip on power. As for the Kurds of northern Iraq, they shared the Sunni faith with the country's elite, but Arabic was not their native tongue. For them, constructing Iraqi political identity on a foundation of Arab nationalism could not fail to be profoundly alienating, suggesting as it did that they faced a choice between cultural assimilation or political marginalization. Their repeated uprisings against Baghdad's rule were forcefully suppressed.[106]

This handful of examples is illustrative of how extreme the divergence was among the political geography, ethnic and religious composition, and nationalist ideologies of the post-Ottoman Middle East. While Arab nationalism served as a convenient framework for building coalitions of Sunni Muslim elites within the bounds of the mandatory states, and in some cases (notably that of Druze clans in Syria) functioned as an ideological bridge between sectarian communities, it was also fatally flawed in several respects: it threatened to undermine the legitimacy of the very regimes or political elites that espoused it, insofar as the borders of their states cut across the notional Arab world. The consequent struggle by each regime to present itself as the natural leader of pan-Arabism threatened to pit one state against another in a never-ending game of rivalry and mutual subversion. The position of minority groups that were manifestly not Arab, or whose sectarian identity was threatened by the prospect of assimilation into a Sunni-dominated, Arab nationalist mainstream, was potentially even more marginal and vulnerable than it had been under the Ottoman system, where non-Arab Sunnis (such as the Kurds) had been juridically equal members of the Islamic *umma*, and where many non-Muslim sectarian groups had had the subordinate, but juridically recognized and defined, status of *millets*.[107]

The enormous gap between the promise and reality of Arab nationalist politics also engendered alienation and anger among a new generation of nationalists, reared on the language of Arab unity and frustrated by the division of the Arab world, the continued domination of the Middle East by European powers, and the lack of connection between elites and masses. Indeed, as the next chapter will argue, the political culture of the elites in both the post-1918 Middle East and East Central Europe was in many ways marked by continuities that seemed to fly in the face of their own talk of change and renewal.

Conclusion

Throughout the vast expanses of the former empires, the drawing of new boundaries in the aftermath of war was a relatively rapid and often haphazard process that left an indelible mark on the political cultures of the new polities. Where formerly a wide range of nationalist visions – ranging from narrowly ethnic to pan-nationalist, from liberal to chauvinistic – had competed for attention and popular support, there had now come into being, virtually overnight, a new, post-imperial political geography that closed off many potential paths of development. The regimes that had helped create, or were forced to operate within the constraints of, the new political geography vigorously promoted their own particular visions of national identity, obliging all communities – regional, religious, linguistic – that found themselves within the confines of the new states to align themselves with or against the official model of identity.

In East Central Europe, the blurriness of ethnographic frontiers and the non-congruence between historic and ethnographic claims to territory was a recipe for conflict. The use of armed force to determine boundaries was irreconcilable with any attempt to negotiate federative solutions or to introduce a credible, supraethnic, civic dimension to national identities. This reinforced the tendency to define the basis for state legitimacy in narrowly ethnic terms and to polarize relations between those nationalities associated with the official, state-promoted identity and those ethnic groups left stranded within polities in which they both felt and were perceived as alien.

In the former Russian empire, the Soviet regime created a highly structured, cultural, territorial, and individually ascriptive framework for the definition of ethnic identities, with a view to shaping them according to a common Soviet Communist mold. Yet, no matter how manipulative and oppressive the regime may have been in its use of ethnic identity as a medium for the propagation of what might be termed a Soviet civic patriotism, the politics of nationality could hardly fail to take on a life of its own in a system where it was so heavily institutionalized.

In the Arab countries, the connection between state legitimacy and national identity was the most tenuous – and was all the more divisive a source of contention for that. The notion of the Arab nation was so broad and ill-defined that, on the one hand, it could be used as a legitimizing principle by a wide range of communities and interests that were in fact sectarian or regional in nature; on the other hand, no existing polity corresponded geographically to anyone's conception of the Arab nation. The credibility of regimes that staked their claim to power on their commitment to the Arab nationalist cause was further undermined by the overshadowing presence of the European imperial overseers – the very elements that had determined the borders of the individual states in the first place.

In all three regions, the drawing of territorial and ethnographic boundaries was a highly transformative process. Indeed, in some cases, one could go so far as to say that it did not so much reflect pre-existing ethnonational consciousness as it shaped its development. In a system of sovereign states legitimized by the principle of national self-determination, there was little or no margin left for ambiguous or multidimensional identities. Everyone had to be fitted into an ethnonational box, by ascriptive means if necessary. Whether under the highly formalized Soviet system of state-sponsored ethnic particularism, or in the framework of the East Central European and Balkan states' dogged and counterproductive efforts to bring diverse popular identities into alignment with official nationalism (be it through forced assimilation, repression, or expulsion), or in the context of Middle Eastern leaders' propagation of a pan-Arab identity that transcended their own states' frontiers, the politics of national identity became a high-stakes game from which none could afford to exclude themselves. Opportunities for education and upward social mobility, access to administrative or political power, the securing of advantages *vis-à-vis* rival individuals or communities, sometimes even the very prospects for life or death – all were conditioned as never before by one's affiliation or lack thereof with the official national identity of one's political unit.

Yet it would be misleading to end this book on such a note of radical change. In East Central Europe and the Middle East, strong elements of continuity in political mentality and norms were clearly manifest, especially among the nationalist elites themselves. This introduced an element of inconsistency and self-contradiction that contributed to the fragility of the new nation-states, as we shall see in the next chapter.

7 Old Elites and Radical Challengers in the New Nation-States, 1918–1939

The First World War precipitated an intense escalation of expectations of change among the diverse ethnic groups of the multinational empires. The rhetoric of national liberation appeared to constitute a common currency – an ideological medium of exchange – among different social strata and political factions within each nationality. This proved to be misleading, as profound social and ideological divisions rapidly manifested themselves over precisely what sorts of changes national self-determination would in fact entail, and over how the territorial, demographic, and cultural boundaries of nationhood were to be determined. Yet the transition from empire was not marked exclusively by varying demands for change. There were also powerful elements of continuity that soon manifested themselves in the newly established states – pre-existent institutional structures and traditional forms of political culture that belied nationalist themes of integration and transformation. This was most apparent in East Central Europe and the Middle East (although it certainly was not absent from the Soviet political scene), and it is on these two regions that this schematic overview of trends during the interwar period will focus.

The late Ernest Gellner linked the growth of nationalism to the bureaucratization of state and society. Drawing on Max Weber's writings, he argued that the state cannot function effectively without the services of a disciplined body of administrators whose primary loyalty is to the state itself, rather than to any tribal or corporate structure outside the framework of the polity. Indeed, in a certain sense, the modern, Western political system seeks to transform the entire citizenry into servants of (or participants in) the state. A government-run educational system, Gellner argued, serves to standardize language and inculcate common values and identity among the entire population, so that people can function as interchangeable components of the vast bureaucratic apparatus and as standardized cogs in the integrated industrial economy.

Nationalism, in this formulation, is a by-product of the growth of the modern state and the modern, industrial economy. That part of the population whose native dialect and educational opportunities allow it easily to master the standardized official language, achieves rapid social advancement and comes to regard the state as an expression of its own national identity. Those ethnic groups that are disadvantaged because their native languages or dialects are very different from the official state language, and whose opportunities for upward social mobility are therefore compromised, can react in either of two ways: they can rush to learn the hegemonic tongue and assimilate into the rapidly advancing ethno-cultural majority; alternatively, they can respond by developing separatist movements aimed at creating independent nation-states within which their own languages and cultures will predominate.

According to Gellner, the separatist scenario is the exceptional one. It is most likely to occur during the early phases of industrialization, when the gaps between haves and have-nots are at their greatest and the social tensions accompanying modernization are most acute. He contended that, if the state manages to remain intact beyond the critical threshold of early industrialization, the ongoing process of administrative and educational modernization is normally successful at integrating and assimilating ethnic minorities (who come to realize that they have more to gain by learning the dominant language and moving up the existing socio-political ladder than by taking the risk of breaking off to form small and potentially vulnerable new states). Gellner's main model for the separatist scenario was the experience of the multinational Habsburg empire, where, he argued, administrative-modernization and cultural-assimilation efforts, combined with the early onset of industrialization, served to heighten tensions and aggravate inequalities between ethnic groups such as the Magyars and Slovaks. For him, the breakup of the Habsburg monarchy was the exception that proved the rule: most contemporary nation-states themselves contain many ethnic minorities, yet tend ultimately to be successful at integrating them politically and, to some extent at least, assimilating many of them culturally.[1]

Gellner's paradigm brilliantly illuminates many aspects of the genesis of modern nationalism and explains many features of its early development. Yet his suggestion that the nation-state is essentially a manifestation, and successful promoter, of the twin processes of modernization and socio-cultural integration needs to be balanced by a greater recognition of the pre-modern elements that continue to play powerful roles in most twentieth-century states,[2] particularly in the case of that majority of contemporary polities that arose from imperial frameworks. In their sudden transition to independence, most so-called nation-states have carried over into their administration ways of thought and styles of governance inherited from the *ancien régime*. Indeed, old elites often succeed in holding on to power by latching on to the rhetoric and imagery of nationalism.[3] In its bewildering combination of integrative aspirations and alienating practices, the nation-state's administration can contribute actively to the fragmentation of society and the disenchantment of ethnic minorities. All too often and all too quickly, coercive measures are resorted to as the only reliable means of maintaining the outward unity of the nation-state – and even the use of force has its limitations. Events in Yugoslavia, Czechoslovakia, the Soviet Union, Iraq, Somalia, Liberia, Sierra Leone, and elsewhere since 1989 suggest that Gellner's guardedly optimistic assessment of the integrative potential of the modern state may need to be revised.

The Janus-faced nature of modern state bureaucracies was highlighted by

Max Weber. Weber observed that democratization and bureaucratization go hand in hand, yet are also at odds with each other. The essence of democratization, in his broad use of the term, is the elimination of corporate privileges and juridical distinctions among the various social strata – a leveling effect that is premised on the equality of all citizens before the law (and that is an essential feature of the Gellnerian nation-state). Such a transformation can only be carried out if the personal authority of notables is replaced by the impersonal (hence impartial) authority of a professional, salaried bureaucracy. Yet a highly disciplined cohort of trained administrators functioning at all levels of government may itself crystallize into a new socio-political elite of specialized education and narrow, idiosyncratic values, an elite that stifles civic initiative and undermines the vitality of democratic institutions. A modern, impersonal bureaucracy is thus both indispensable to the functioning of mass democracy, and incompatible with its spirit. This dialectical relationship underlies much of modern political history according to Weber.[4]

Gellner fails to give adequate consideration to this paradox. More particularly, he underestimates the capacity of old elites to adapt to the political environment of freshly minted nation-states, seeking to influence or control their administrative and propagandist apparatuses even as they themselves absorb the nationalist ideologies that legitimize authority in the new polities. Many of the states that gained independence in the wake of the First World War had perforce to borrow much of their personnel from the remains of the imperial political and bureaucratic elites. Many nationalist leaders themselves seemed incapable, once in power, of shedding attitudes and mentalities that accorded better with the culture and mores of the old regimes than with the ideological frameworks of the new nation-states. The juxtaposition of elements of the old regimes' political cultures with the democratic, populist rhetoric and imagery of nationalism was jarring, and created long-term tensions within the new polities that arose between the Vistula and the Tigris after the First World War.[5]

One major line of division to which this phenomenon contributed was that between the constituent nationalities of the new states. In addressing this phenomenon, this chapter's first section essentially continues with the topic of ethnic polarization raised in Chapter 6, looking at it from the perspective of political and administrative continuities.

The persistence of old patterns of elitism in the new polities also contributed to bitter and often violent rifts within dominant nationalities. This chapter's second section compares such developments in Poland and the Middle East, where the irony of the situation was enhanced by the role of former underground nationalist activists and legionnaires in forming the new ruling circles whose attitudes and practices often seemed so reminiscent of times gone by. The glaring inconsistencies in the political praxis of the new nation-states' founding fathers contributed to the rise of an angry new generation of nationalist extremists in the course of the interwar years.

Institutional Continuities and Disaffected Ethnic Groups: the Czechoslovak and Yugoslav Cases

Czechoslovakia

The case of Czechoslovakia illustrates the problems of post-imperial transition most vividly precisely because this was the only East Central European state that retained its democratic institutions and practices throughout the interwar period. The Czechoslovak state administration approximated Weber's ideal typology of the modern, rational bureaucracy more closely than any of the other examples; moreover, its power was curtailed by democratic institutions. Nonetheless, the Prague government failed in its attempt to foster a common political identity among Czechs and Slovaks.[6]

Czechoslovakia inherited from the imperial regime a body of experienced Czech bureaucrats and administrators, who provided a considerable measure of continuity and stability to the running of affairs in the new state after the collapse of the Habsburg empire. Local civil servants in the Czech provinces were simply kept in place under the new republic, and Czechs who had worked for the central ministries in Vienna were brought back to help set up new ministries in Prague. The Czech civil service retained something of the self-image of the Habsburg administration as a semi-autonomous institution playing an integrative and constructive role in society (rather than merely a mechanism for the enforcement of existing law).

Czech political life was rich and diverse, with well-organized parties from across the ideological spectrum that had gained experience in grassroots organization, electoral politics, and parliamentary tactics within the framework of the old Austrian constitutional system. Ethnic fragmentation had been the bane of the Austrian parliament, but the ceaseless confrontations between Czechs and ethnic Germans had reinforced the need for cooperation among the Czech parties. The Czechs thus had a leadership cohort that had grown used to what might be termed "managed competition" in politics. That is to say, they stood ready to compete for power within the Czechoslovak state according to well-established liberal-democratic norms, in an atmosphere of mutual tolerance, and with an ability to form fairly effective governing coalitions once elections were over.

The situation in Slovakia was markedly different. Although Slovakia contained some of the most heavily industrialized zones of the Hungarian kingdom, its economy remained overwhelmingly agrarian. Moreover, ownership of capital had remained much more exclusively in the hands of non-Slavs (Germans, Magyars, Jews) than was the case in the Czech lands. The Hungarian constitutional system had denied the Slovaks proportional representation in parliament, with the result that the Slovak political parties that emerged in 1918 were inexperienced and unsure of themselves. Budapest had in fact pursued an active policy of assimilating the tiny Slovak elite into Magyar culture, while denying social advancement to the peasant population. There had been no opportunities for higher education in the Slovak language. Those Slovaks who wished to pursue their higher education in a Slavic language had been obliged to study in Prague (if they could circumvent Hungarian restrictions on that option).

Slovakia's administration had been run exclusively in the Magyar language and had been completely dominated by Magyars and Magyarized Slovaks. These elements remained overwhelmingly loyal to Hungary, as was demonstrated in 1919, when railway and postal officials went on strike in an attempt to disrupt Czechoslovak communications and transportation during the (unsuccessful) Hungarian invasion of Slovakia. When the bureaucracy was duly purged of Magyars, there was no more than a tiny handful of qualified Slovaks available to replace them.

Therefore, the political fissure that opened up between the Czech and Slovak communities almost as soon as the republic had been formed was not simply the result of different conceptions of national identity. In the brave new world of the nation-state, institutional continuity was superimposed on political change. This made it all the more difficult to achieve the cultural synthesis that lay at the heart of Masaryk's vision for Czechoslovakia. The deep gap between the levels of political sophistication and bureaucratic self-sufficiency of the Czech and Slovak provinces was locked into place and perpetuated by the inclusion of Slovakia in a Czechoslovak state. A wave of Czech judges, administrators, schoolteachers, clerks, and notaries filled the vacuum left by the elimination of the Hungarian administration.

In principle, the organization of Czechoslovakia's electoral system was designed to help overcome such disparities by guaranteeing proportional representation to every region and interest group. Yet, while the five political parties (known collectively as the Pětka) that dominated the parliamentary stage and that consistently participated in governing coalitions all defined themselves as Czechoslovak in orientation, they were direct successors to pre-war Czech parties, and continued to be led and dominated by Czechs. The votes garnered by the Pětka in general elections never added up to much more than 50 per cent of the total. Nonetheless, the pattern of cooperation the Pětka's leaders had established during their days in the Czech Club of the Austrian parliament, combined with the ease of access and regularized contact some of them enjoyed with the powerful presidency of the Republic – an office occupied by Tomáš Masaryk until his death in 1937 – served to facilitate their collective domination of the political system. Czechoslovak governments were formed and dissolved with dizzying frequency, but the main players from coalition to coalition remained the leaders of the Pětka.

The distribution of power at the highest levels of government had its counterpart in the state bureaucracy. Each party tended to maintain control of specific ministries even as one coalition gave way to another. This was precisely the sort of unwritten understanding that facilitated the division of power among the leading Czech-dominated parties; it also created a patronage system that reinforced their grip on power and linked them to grassroots interests. Indeed, many of the Slovaks who joined or voted for one or another of the Pětka parties did so in order to secure access to state resources for their districts or enterprises, rather than out of ideological conviction or class consciousness. Yet in most government ministries, Slovaks constituted no more than 1.6 per cent of the bureaucratic staff. Those Slovaks who were co-opted into the system tended to be Czechophiles, many of them members of Slovakia's enterprising and highly educated Protestant minority. Slovakia's rural, Catholic majority was left feeling all the more alienated from the system.[7]

In the army, a similar situation prevailed. The rank and file, to be sure, consisted of conscripts from all regions and ethnic groups. The army's only official language, though, was "Czechoslovak" – which in practice meant Czech, not Slovak.[8] Moreover, almost 80 per cent of the officer corps was Czech. This severely undermined the credibility of the army as an instrument of national integration.[9]

It should come as no surprise that the very elements of institutional continuity that served the interests of Czechs and led them to identify closely with the new state profoundly alienated many Slovaks (not to speak of the ethnic Germans of the Sudetenland and the Magyars of southern Slovakia, whose individual civil rights were fully respected, but whose collective identities were not embodied either symbolically or institutionally by the state).[10] Rather than promoting the creation of a new Czechoslovak identity, the Czech socio-political establishment's imposition of its institutions on Slovakia provoked the crystallization of a Slovak nationalism whose defining characteristic was a sense of promise betrayed. In the eyes of Father Andrej Hlinka's clerical-conservative, Slovak Populist Party – which maintained a plurality of Slovak votes in parliamentary elections from the mid 1920s on – the prospect of self-determination in an autonomous republic had given way to virtual colonization by the Czechs. Suffering from a sense of socio-economic inferiority[11] and political helplessness *vis-à-vis* the central government, Slovak nationalists cultivated what Liah Greenfeld (borrowing from Nietzsche) refers to as *ressentiment*: a sense of resentment and injured dignity on the part of an underdeveloped, traditional society, that manifests itself in a compensatory assertion of moral superiority over the materialistic and permissive culture of the (unfairly advantaged) Other.[12] In this case, the role of the Other was played by Prague, and all the ills suffered by Slovakia were blamed on the Czech-dominated political system. Slovak culture and identity were seen as besieged by an arrogant Czech intelligentsia and political leadership that was reluctant to recognize the equality of the Slovak language and way of life. Czechoslovakism was regarded as nothing more than a façade for the imposition of Godless Czech values on a Slovak society that took pride in its Catholic traditions. The growth of the Slovak educational system under the auspices of the interwar republic only served to create a more politicized and articulate intelligentsia that was acutely aware of how great the developmental gap between Slovakia and the Czech lands still was, and all the more inclined to point an accusing finger at Prague.

Thus, even in the most democratic of the successor states that emerged from the rubble of empires, the nation-integrating roles of government and bureaucracy were undermined by legacies of the old regime.[13] The polarizing impact of institutional continuities on ethnic relations was all the more dramatic in other newly established or newly expanded polities in the region – most notably Yugoslavia.

Yugoslavia

From its very establishment, the kingdom of Serbs, Croats, and Slovenes was run as an extension of the old kingdom of Serbia. The kingdom of Serbia had defined itself as a nation-state, and this case therefore diverges from this chapter's theme of imperial legacies burdening the political cultures of new nation-states. But the basic problem of regime continuity in the face of a radically reconfigured ethnographic scene manifested itself dramatically here. For the sake of simplicity, I will focus on the particularly troublesome case of Serb–Croat relations here, although the country's ethnographic map included many other nationalities.

During the parliamentary democracy of 1918–1929, the old Serbian Radical Party that had led the country into war in 1914 remained almost constantly in power at the head of shaky coalitions, despite the opposition of Stjepan Radić's Croatian Peasant Party (see Chapter 3) to its centralizing policies. The Radicals patched together parliamentary majorities by playing on the multinational makeup of the electorate to their advantage. Ethnic parties that demanded an alleviation of this or that local grievance were negotiated with, so that compromise could be avoided with those that demanded a devolution of power to their historic provinces or a substantial share of power at the center. This tactic was effective for a number of years, but in the long term it only accentuated the fragmented nature of the country's body politic. In 1929, parliamentary politics were suspended as the country fell under a monarchic dictatorship.[14]

The Serbs' political hegemony was reinforced by their disproportionate representation at the highest levels of government, as well as in the administration and army. Although they constituted no more than roughly 40 per cent of the country's population, Serbs virtually monopolized the top cabinet positions throughout the interwar period, and exploited their control of the civil service for purposes of political patronage and ethnic favoritism. Seventy-nine per cent of the officer corps was Serb, the diplomatic service was overwhelmingly Serb in composition, and the state-owned banks – cornerstones of the country's financial system – were all headed by Serbs.

This political-bureaucratic elite was deeply intermeshed with the most influential Serb commercial and financial circles, the higher clergy in the Serbian Orthodox Church, and the wealthiest stratum of Serb peasants. The government catered to these groups through its patronage networks and served their financial interests through favorable tax laws, tariff policies, and cheap loans from the state banks. The distinction between public service and private profit was blurred as members of the socio-economic elite moved in and out of public office, exploiting their political power to enrich themselves and their associates. Outright corruption was also rampant.

What made this situation particularly galling to the Croat elites was that their average level of education and economic development was higher than that of the Serbs. Whereas in Czech-dominated Slovakia there was a genuine shortage of skilled administrators, Croatia had a fairly sophisticated intelligentsia that found its path to upward mobility in the civil service blocked by what was seen as a policy of blatant discrimination. The entrenchment of the Serb ruling classes was seen as part of a deliberate policy of Greater Serbian nationalism that was not only excluding Croats from a fair share of power in Belgrade, but marginalizing them within their own provinces.

The result of Belgrade's policies was not just to alienate the Croat elites, but to exacerbate the suspicions and resentments of the Croat peasantry as well. At first glance, this may seem surprising, for one of the first acts of the kingdom of Serbs, Croats, and Slovenes was to promise agrarian-reform legislation that would abolish the last vestiges of feudalism and redistribute land more fairly among the peasantry of the new territories which had fallen under Belgrade's control.[15] This program responded to one of the most deeply felt grievances among the peasantry of the South Slav lands, whose attachment to, and claim to personal ownership of, the soil they tilled had antedated their development of national consciousness and sense of collective territoriality.

However, land reform was a complex process that, in some regions, was not entirely completed by the end of the interwar period. While the reform did result in a more equitable division of land, many of the smaller farms to which this gave rise did not prove economically viable, afflicted as they were by problems such as rural overpopulation, unfavorable price structures, heavy tax burdens, and tight credit. The state-owned banks' tendency to use their relatively cheap lines of credit in a selective and discriminatory manner certainly did not enhance the credibility of the state among the peasantry in general.[16]

Resentment of the state was particularly deep-seated among the peasants of the largely non-Serb, newly acquired territories, since this is precisely where the expectations of a rapid and radical break with past socio-economic patterns had been the highest. Moreover, *faux pas* were committed and misunderstandings arose that might have been avoided had a greater effort been made to grant autonomous political and administrative roles to native leaderships in the non-Serb regions (although the situation was complicated by the existence of sizable Serb minorities in Bosnia and Croatia). To take just one example, the Serbian army had a longstanding practice of branding superior-quality draft animals as a way of identifying them for potential requisitioning in the event of war. When introduced overnight in Croatia, where the practice was unknown, it was greeted with incomprehension and anger by farmers who felt that their finest animals were being gratuitously mutilated. The issue contributed significantly to the outbreak of the Croatian peasants' rebellion of 1920.

Thus, the imposition of the pre-existing Serbian political-administrative system throughout the newly expanded post-1918 kingdom confirmed non-Serbs' impression that the ideology of Yugoslav fraternal union and national integration was nothing but a sham. Notably, in Croatia, Belgrade's repressive tactics spurred a steady growth in support for the Croatian Peasant Party among the intelligentsia and middle classes. In other words, Croatia's inclusion in a Serb-dominated state turned out to be an important catalyst for the growth of a Croatian ethnonational identity that narrowed the gap between rural under-classes and urban elites, while distancing itself from the discredited ideal of Yugoslav unitarism. The progressive alienation of Croat peasants and elites alike culminated in their shocked reaction to the fatal shooting of Stjepan Radić and the wounding or killing of several of his colleagues on the floor of the national parliament in June 1928 by a Serb nationalist deputy. The political crisis that ensued led to the dissolution of parliament and creation of a royal dictatorship in January 1929.

During the 1930s, the political brittleness of the new regime, combined with the impact of the global Depression, accelerated the process of political polar-ization and fragmentation along ethnic lines. The Croatian Peasant Party, now under the leadership of Vladko Maček, continued to expand its base of support by turning to the right – abandoning the anti-clerical principles of its founders (who, it will be recalled, had been strongly influenced by the teachings of Tomáš Masaryk) and forging an alliance with the Catholic Church. At the same time, the seeming futility of the Peasant Party's continued openness to dialogue with the Serbs and embrace of democratic methods earned it the hostility and deri-sion of a small but active rival on the far right of Croatian politics – the Ustaša. Founded in the late 1920s by veterans of the old Frankist party, the Ustaša updated the virulently chauvinistic Croatian nationalism of the Frankists by dressing it up in fascist garb: a leadership cult was organized around the move-ment's founder, Ante Pavelić, racist themes were highlighted in the Ustaša's anti-Serb propaganda, and the militaristic structures and ethos of Italian fascism were incorporated into the movement. The Ustaša, which enjoyed Italian and Hungarian backing, compensated for its limited popular support by resorting to terrorist attacks, including the assassination of King Alexander during his visit to France in 1934, in its campaign to subvert the authority of the Belgrade regime. It was eventually catapulted into power in Croatia by the Axis forces that invaded Yugoslavia in 1941.

Just as in the Czechoslovak case then, only more so, the Yugoslav political elite's domination by members of one ethnic group who adhered to pre-war norms in the governance of an ethnographically transformed state had helped undermine the credibility of the ethos of interethnic Slav fraternity from which the state derived its legitimacy. Indeed, Belgrade's policies contributed to the consolidation of Croatian national identity among an unprecedentedly broad cross-section of the Croat population and had a similar effect on the country's other ethnic and ethno-religious communities, while at the same time under-mining and discrediting democratic institutions and inter-communal compromise or coalition-building.

Revolutionary Elites in Reactionary Roles: Poland and the Arab Middle East

Continuities between old regime and new could have a significant impact not only on interethnic relations, but also on the development of national conscious- ness and nationalist politics among the dominant nationalities of the new states. In East Central Europe, it is the Polish case and in the Middle East, Iraq – and, to some extent, Syria – that illustrate the incongruities of the postwar transition most dramatically, for in all these instances, veterans of wartime nationalist legions and clandestine organizations assumed prominent roles in the new states' political leaderships, yet, once in power, fell back on old practices in their pursuit of novel goals.

Having played the role of self-selected nationalist vanguards during the war, figures such as the officers of Piłsudski's First Brigade or of the Sharifian Army thought of themselves as a self-contained essence of the nation, whose *esprit de corps* and discipline had provided a glimmer of what their people as a whole might achieve once its full potential was unleashed. By the same token, such groups thought their wartime exploits entitled them to positions of privilege in the new nation-states. Over time, so they thought, they would use their power to shape the masses in their own image and help achieve the ideals of freedom and unity that had animated their own wartime actions. But in the name of political equality and collective liberty, socio-political hierarchies and modes of gover- nance took shape that seemed remarkably reminiscent of older political cultures.

Poland

Interwar Poland was riven not only by interethnic tensions (as described in Chapter 6), but by deep political and ideological divisions among the ethnic Poles themselves. Here, as elsewhere, the imperial legacy weighed heavily on the new state, one of whose major challenges was how to bring administrative and judicial unity to the three former imperial partitions of Poland.[17] This was a task made all the more difficult by the devastation of the First World War, the occu- pying German forces' systematic ransacking of the country's industrial infrastructure, and the ravages of the 1920 Polish–Soviet war.

What made matters worse was the ongoing rivalry between Piłsudski's and Dmowski's camps – itself a legacy of pre-war ideological divisions over how to respond to Russian imperial repression. This political blood feud drove a wedge through Polish society and politics at every level, as each side strove to infiltrate, or forge alliances with, as broad a cross-section of socio-economic interests and political parties as possible. The army's officer corps was divided between associ- ates of Piłsudski and veterans of rival wartime volunteer formations such as General Józef Haller's Polish Corps. There were also many Polish officers absorbed from the old Habsburg, Russian, and German armies, many of whom were regarded by Piłsudski's legionnaires as unpatriotic elements that had no rightful place in a Polish national army. The former imperial officers (especially the large Habsburg contingent), in turn, despised the ex-legionnaires as amateurish upstarts who had no place in a professional military force.[18]

The turbulence and polarization of parliamentary politics in the early 1920s was aggravated by violent incidents – most notably the assassination in 1922 of Gabriel Narutowicz, the man Piłsudski had backed to succeed him as President – as well as by corruption among parliamentary deputies, rising unemployment, labor unrest, and the inconsistent and half-hearted implementation of already modest land-reform legislation. It was in this context that Piłsudski carried out his 1926 *coup d'état* with the support of his loyalists within the army and of a general strike called by the Polish Socialist Party (PPS). Seizing Warsaw after a three-day battle that cost nearly 400 lives, Piłsudski did not assume personal control of the presidency or premiership, but made sure that those offices were occupied by candidates of his choice; constitutional reforms were also quickly enacted granting new powers to the presidency. Piłsudski's position in the new government as Minister of War gave him command of the army, and this allowed him to exercise ultimate control over political power while maintaining an aura of legality.

The coup held forth the promise of containing the forces of right-wing chauvinism and social conservatism and of reforming Polish political institutions and culture along broadly integrative lines. It brought to power veterans of Piłsudski's wartime military formations, who saw themselves as a nonpartisan, selflessly patriotic elite that would make a final break with outdated mentalities and corrupt values born of over a century of servitude to imperial masters.

But the legionnaires' sense of commitment to the Polish nation had always been colored by a deep distrust of the feckless masses who had failed to flock to their standards in 1914 (see Chapter 5). Their self-image as unrewarded heroes had deepened into a virtual cult of their own victimhood under the impact of the political turmoil of the early 1920s. This was a mentality that was actively cultivated by Piłsudski himself. His speeches of those years were characterized by a bitter and gloomy view of himself and his former comrades of the Legions as virtuous heroes surrounded by poisonous slanderers and evildoers who were unworthy of Poland and who must ultimately be swept out of power one way or another. In an address delivered just after his 1923 resignation as Army Chief of Staff, he described his experience as an embattled leader in the following terms:

> I was set up higher than anyone had ever been set before, so that I cast my shadow upon all, standing alone in the light. Yet, there was a shadow which encircled me, which went before me, which remained behind me. There were many such shadows. These shadows surrounded me always, intangible, following me step by step, pursuing me and mimicking me. Whether on the field of battle, whether quietly at work ... or caressing my child, this shadow pursued me inseparably. A monstrous dwarf on crooked legs, spitting out his dirty soul, spitting at me from every side, sparing nothing that should be spared, neither my family life nor my friends, following my steps, making monkey grimaces, distorting every thought. ... This dwarf was my insepa-

rable companion ... in good fortune and ill, in victory and defeat. Do not imagine, gentlemen, that this is only a metaphor. ...

After going on to speak of the murder of Narutowicz, he concluded:

> In recalling these things to your minds, in sketching the history of the past five years, I do not in the least wish to make an impression of tragedy. I only wish to state that here is filth, and that it is given honour and power in Poland. ... If Poland succeeded in reforming the republic in the first period, it began subsequently to fall back into its old habits and ... great efforts are necessary ... to restore Poland to the path of reform.[19]

The self-righteous and morbidly self-pitying tone of this call for reform did not augur well for the ex-legionnaires' prospects as the vanguard of political progress in Poland.

Piłsudski's post-coup regime was known as the Sanacja (literally, the "purification" or "sanitization"). Largely composed of non-party civil servants, it was intended to eliminate corruption and factionalism from Polish government and to promote the economic regeneration and national integration of the country. Personal ability and commitment to reform, rather than political connections, were henceforth supposed to determine appointments and promotions in the state administration. Yet this supposedly nonpartisan, national government soon degenerated into a pattern of corruption and abuse of power that discredited it in the eyes of much of the public, and that contributed to the political momentum of Poland's nascent fascist movement. It soon became apparent that former service in Piłsudski's legions was the most important measure of merit in the new system. This was most immediately manifest in the ranks of the army's officer corps, which was methodically purged of anti-Piłsudski figures, who were replaced by loyal veterans of the First Brigade and the POW (see Chapter 5). By 1939, some 65 per cent of the army's high officers were ex-legionnaires. This legionnaire-ridden army was elevated in the public eye to the status of untouchable symbol and protector of national unity. To criticize it was to be unpatriotic. The officer corps, in turn, served as a recruitment pool for high administrative and political appointees.[20]

Over the course of the late 1920s and early 1930s, Piłsudski disappointed his would-be allies in the PPS by abandoning all pretense of social reformism and seeking the support of conservative agrarian and industrial interests and the Church. His aim was to isolate the Endecja and to build a strong, "non-ideological," centrist consensus as the foundation for his power. A "Non-Party Bloc for the Support of the Government" (BBWR) was formed as the parliamentary wing of the Sanacja, consisting, as usual, of ex-legionnaires as well as a number of influential landowners. The personality cult that grew around Piłsudski and the cultivation of the legend of the First Brigade functioned as substitutes for any coherent political program.[21] The more resistance Piłsudski's authoritarian style provoked, the more arbitrary his rule became. The façade of legality became increasingly difficult to maintain in the face of mounting opposition from the political center and left, to which Piłsudski responded with increasingly repressive measures. The unavoidable consequence of the Marshal's[22] autocratic rule was a growing alienation between Polish society and the self-appointed elite that was running it. The precipitous drop in agricultural prices and rise in unemployment during the Depression of the 1930s, which the government's 1936 recovery program could only begin to redress, made matters even worse.[23]

During the 1930s, while the Sanacja monopolized power in the name of ill-defined *étatist* principles, Dmowski's Endecja gained popular support, especially among the university students and young intelligentsia whose dim employment opportunities in a period of economic crisis heightened their resentment of Jewish academic competition. Unlike the left-center opposition, Dmowski did not defend parliamentary democracy as such. Instead, from 1926 on, he launched a frontal attack on the regime's central claim to power – the notion that it somehow transcended class interests and political factions, that it embodied the true will of the nation. Dmowski portrayed the Sanacja as nothing but a cabal of Jews and freemasons determined to exploit the Polish people for their own ends. Openly rejecting the liberal-democratic façade that he had himself helped construct for the National Democrats, Dmowski fostered the development of fascism among the radical right-wing youth of the movement.

The legionnaires' self-image as the vanguard of the Polish nation had become a self-serving and corrosive myth. During 1914–1918, the men of the First Brigade and the POW had been a bold band of rebels in the nationalist cause, dedicated amateurs who despised those professional officers who remained unquestioningly loyal to the Habsburg military, and who were firm in the belief that their willpower, their *esprit de corps*, and their devotion to their commander could prevail in the face of the apathy of the masses and the tyranny of the occupying powers. While inspired by the romantic image of Poland's nineteenth-century aristocratic rebels, they undertook their own actions in a spirit of egalitarian camaraderie, valuing men for their deeds and not their birth. They saw themselves as the forerunners of a whole new generation of Poles, a generation that would be born into freedom rather than imperial servitude. At one and the same time, they saw themselves as a natural elite – an elite of courage and self-sacrifice, rather than birth or wealth, and thus the ideal leaders of a republican meritocracy.

By the time of Piłsudski's death in 1935, the legionnaires had become corrupted by power, drunk on their own myths, and unable to strike a resonant chord among either the intelligentsia or the masses. Their claim to power rested on assumptions that seemed to parody the old notion that the gentry constituted the political nation and that the masses were simply objects of their patriarchal care. In fact, having discredited parliamentary democracy, Piłsudski and his followers were unable to construct a viable alternative to it. The Endecja's fascist, violently anti-Semitic brand of nationalism moved into the breach, playing an increasingly dominant role in shaping public opinion and popular conceptions of national identity. Following the Marshal's demise, the Sanacja remained in power, but its repressive practices and its own increasing exploitation of anti-Semitism were a testimony to the bankruptcy of its values. The final, bitter hurrah of the Legions came in 1939, when the former legionnaires who now made up the bulk of the officer corps led the country's hopeless resistance to the invading German and Soviet forces that annihilated both them and the state they had created.

Syria and Iraq

In Syria and Iraq, the closed nature of the political elites and their reliance on traditional, patrimonial forms of wielding authority clashed directly with the myths and images of national unity and mass engagement that they themselves diffused. As we have seen (Chapter 3), Ottoman authority in Syria and Mesopotamia had been anchored in the support and cooperation of the class of absentee landlords and bureaucrats commonly referred to as the urban notables. These public officials belonged to a very distinct socio-economic class; their independent wealth and their personal influence in specific regions or even neighborhoods were essential to their ability to gain public office in the first place and to carry out their duties once in office. It was also taken for granted that they would exploit their position in the administration to enrich themselves. Bribery was endemic, though not officially condoned. At the same time, the reforms of the nineteenth century had created a more centralized administrative structure and better lines of communication between Istanbul and the Arab provinces than ever before. Increasingly, aspirants to high office were expected to receive formal training, most commonly at the *Mülkiye* – the administrative school in Istanbul. Thus, as in the case of the imperial Russian bureaucracy, the status, functions, education, and mentality of this stratum were such as to place it in between Max Weber's two typologies of state service: patrimonial administration and modern, rationalized, impersonal bureaucracy. The former design remained basically in place, but elements of the latter were being woven into it.[24]

This pattern carried over into the political culture of the post-First World War nationalist elites in Syria and Iraq. The young Arabists of the pre-First World War period had plunged into their political careers enthralled by the prospect of Western-style free discourse and parliamentary government that was opened up by the Young Turks' revolution of 1908. They had espoused Arab nationalism partly in response to the Young Turks' failure to fulfill that prospect. Yet by the 1930s, it had become apparent that the methods and mentalities of nationalist political parties in the Arab countries were themselves more akin to the corrupt and autocratic political culture of the Ottoman empire than to the liberal-democratic ideals over which the Arab nationalists had once seemed so enthusiastic.

Philip Khoury's study of the National Bloc that led opposition to the French in Syria has shown that its growing power was grounded not in electoral politics *per se*, but in the ability of the notables who led it to dole out favors, mediate disputes, and enforce their will in specific quarters of their native towns. They used local merchants and religious dignitaries, as well as neighborhood strongmen (*qabadayat*), as day-to-day intermediaries with the lower classes. This form of influence was then used to gain success at the polls. The Syrian nationalist leaders certainly evinced no interest in socio-economic reform: the personal financial independence so vital to their participation in politics was based on the unequal distribution of resources – particularly the glaringly disproportionate concentration of agricultural land in their hands; their ideological legitimacy was derived from their ability to bring pressure to bear upon the French authorities, on whom all social and economic ills were blamed.[25]

At the time that they began to oppose Ottomanism, the Syrian Arab nationalists had been office *seekers*, denied by the Young Turks the opportunity to hold the positions of influence and respect that they considered their rightful due. Frustrated and resentful, they sincerely felt that the time had come for radical changes in the rules of the political game. By the 1930s, when the opportunity to become office *holders* seemed at last to present itself within the framework of continued French influence in Syria, the former office seekers were reverting to mentalities and behavior patterns characteristic of their fathers and grandfathers, who had held positions of authority in the region during the second half of the nineteenth century. Much like the Italian political leadership after the Risorgimento, they continued to define themselves as a heroic nationalist vanguard while behaving more and more like an abusive and self-serving officialdom. Moreover, their ranks had grown to include many figures who had in fact held positions of authority down to the last days of the Ottoman empire, and whose conversion to Arab nationalism was more a matter of opportunism than of conviction. The political outlook of the leading Syrian nationalists was limited by a narrow-mindedness and arrogance that betrayed their origins as a landowning elite that had purchased its way into the Ottoman bureaucratic apparatus.[26]

This gap between ideological form and cultural content manifested itself in everything from the formal attire of the urban notables to their political tactics. They combined the fez with the frock-coat, in an awkward synthesis of Middle Eastern and Western garb.[27] The Bloc's leaders used their traditional, segmented power base to promote a vision of the Syrian nation as an integrated political community of which they were the sole legitimate representatives.[28] They conceived of independent Syria as a secular republic, while encouraging preachers in mosques to rally popular support by depicting the French as enemies of Islam. They attacked the mandatory government for inhibiting the development of parliamentary democracy in Syria, but ran their own party like a Mafia organization. They sought to instill the virtues of discipline and self-sacrifice among their followers, yet grasped hungrily at the perquisites of public office.

In Iraq, the post-First World War political elite was dominated by officers from the Northern Army of the Arab Revolt, who rose to power under the auspices of the Hashemite monarchy that was established with the support of the British mandatory authorities. Linked by years of common experience in the Istanbul military academy (the *Harbiye*), in secret political clubs like al-'Ahd, and in the Sharifian army, this cohort saw itself as the natural leadership of the Iraqi nation and the pan-Arab cause. Like the ex-legionnaires of Piłsudski's post-1926 regime, they saw themselves as history's chosen elite whose role it was to forge a sense of common identity among the country's fragmented population.

Yet their methods of governance did not adequately serve their professed aspirations. Iraq's new governing clique rapidly fell into habits and mindsets more commonly associated with a jaded, old ruling class than with a radical political vanguard. The co-optation of existing power structures offered the path of least resistance for a new regime seeking to establish its legitimacy and authority. In tribal areas, *shaykhs* were made responsible for tax collection, in return for all sorts of personal exemptions and the institutionalization of their customary (and not so customary) powers. In the agricultural village, the writ of the government was enforced by doling out favors to the *mukhtar* (village headman) – usually a wealthier than average peasant whose position was increasingly resented by his poorer neighbors as their livelihood was steadily undermined by the commercialization of agriculture. In the old city quarters, the local strongmen and religious dignitaries were the daily intermediaries with the masses. The new rulers sought to gain the acceptance and support of the traditional landowning bureaucrats by appointing them to high office and allowing them to consolidate their economic stranglehold on the impoverished peasantry. Indeed, members of the old and new ruling strata were increasingly interlinked through marriage ties; bonds of kinship reinforced class and political identity.[29] The Sharifians themselves quickly adopted the time-honored practice of using their political power and their control of the legal system to lay claim to huge tracts of agricultural land and to enrich themselves as rapidly as possible. The development of the oil industry by Western firms that shared their profits directly with the government served to enhance the financial autonomy of the regime as well as its leading figures' opportunities for illicit personal gain. As for the institutions of parliamentary democracy, they were treated as contrivances designed for legitimizing the decisions of the ruling class.[30]

The vocabulary of liberal democracy had been widespread in the political-reform movements of the late Ottoman empire, but like the Young Turks before them, the Iraqi Arab nationalists were a small clique that had come to power virtually overnight in an overwhelmingly illiterate, extremely heterogeneous, and profoundly hierarchical society. Imposition from above seemed to be the only possible method of effecting rapid political change. The military background of the Sharifians, their education in the German-run, Ottoman military academy, the powerful example of Mustafa Kemal's revolution-from-above in Turkey – all served to reinforce their authoritarian approach to politics. A sense of national identity and common purpose was to be transmitted to the masses from on high; there was no need to try and involve them directly in the political process.[31]

Accordingly, the Sharifian elite cultivated Iraq's military and educational institutions as instruments for the forging of a cohesive, mass-based Iraqi and pan-Arab consciousness. These programs were employed instead of, rather than in addition to, the cultivation of autonomous civic associations, the forging of broadly based bonds of material interest, and the encouragement of patterns of political cooperation and power-sharing among the diverse components of Iraqi society. The tactics of negative integration – scapegoating of minorities and propaganda against external enemies – played the most prominent role in the state's efforts to convince both itself and its popular audience that the mirage of national unity could be turned into a reality. Most notably, the attempt by the Assyrian (Nestorian) Christian community to gain official autonomy was met by a series of massacres (claiming hundreds of lives) on the part of the Iraqi army in 1933. The resultant outpouring of public enthusiasm for the army as guarantor of Iraq's unity and defender of its honor marked the highpoint (so to speak) of the Hashemite regime's national-integration enterprise.[32]

Along with the army, Iraq's educational system served as a key mechanism for the creation of a sense of national identity. The father of the Iraqi educational system was Sati' al-Husri, a pan-Arab ideologue of Syrian parentage. Interestingly, in his early incarnation as an Ottoman educator, he had been an advocate of a liberal, individualist curriculum that would breed tolerance and understanding among the diverse ethnic and religious groups of Ottoman society and had criticized Turkish nationalists for their narrow-minded chauvinism. The French occupation of Syria in 1920 had contributed to his alienation from the liberal West European conception of nationalism and reinforced his growing fascination with Germany's populist-authoritarian *völkisch* tradition. As Iraq's Director General of Education during 1921–1927, al-Husri built up the public education system at the expense of the denominational schools, seeking to use pedagogy as an instrument of mass indoctrination in secular, pan-Arab nationalism. The rigidly centralized curriculum he devised rewarded students for the rote memorization of nationalist clichés.[33]

Following al-Husri's departure from office, the chauvinistic themes of primary and secondary education were further enhanced. The Zionist enterprise in Palestine, as well as the French presence in Syria and Lebanon, were portrayed as the main obstacles to Arab unification – obstacles that would ultimately be overcome by force of arms. Ancient Arab conquests were glorified as a spur to the achievement of Arab unity in the near future – with Iraq in the role of unifier, on the model of Piedmont's role in Italian unification, or Prussia's in German unification. Al-Husri's successor, Sami Shawkat, was an outspoken pro-Nazi enthusiast who expanded the school system's paramilitary training program into a full-fledged youth movement (*al-Futuwwah* – The Youth) directly inspired by the Hitler Youth. Shawkat publicly called upon Iraqi secondary-school students to devote themselves to the "Profession of Death" – that is to killing and dying on behalf of the pan-Arab cause.[34] Meanwhile, in Syria, the National Bloc formed a paramilitary organization called the Steel Shirts, which was clearly modeled on fascist prototypes – right down to the raised-arm salute.[35] Yet while public rhetoric in the Arab world was dominated by the new talk of nationalism, the sinews of power remained attached to the old framework of patronage politics, regional interests, and tribal loyalties that had prevailed under the aegis of the Ottomans.[36]

Such incongruities between the professed ideology and the political culture of the Syrian and Iraqi nationalist leaderships bred growing discontent among a new generation of high-school and university students, intellectuals, and military officers (in the Iraqi case), who had been steeped in the propaganda of nationalism but failed to see the concrete realization of its goals and who were angered by their dim prospects of material or professional advancement in the face of the constricting influence of patronage politics and the growing economic difficulties of the interwar years. These elements, mostly middle class in origin, questioned the wisdom and integrity of the political establishment and began to form new parties that combined the open embrace of authoritarianism and a republican vision of pan-Arab union with advocacy of social reform and a professed concern for the dispossessed masses. Organizations such as the League of National Action, which brought together radical pan-Arab nationalists from Iraq, Transjordan, Palestine, Lebanon, and Syria at a conference in Qarna'il, Lebanon in 1933, sought to borrow and improve upon the fascist-style propaganda and mobilization tactics that the Iraqi regime and Syrian National Bloc themselves were experimenting with, with the intention of using them to create more modern, mass-based political parties that would bypass the patronage networks of the established elites and that would disregard and ultimately do away with the "artificial" state boundaries imposed upon the Arab world by the imperial powers.

During the 1930s, these embryonic movements failed to establish organizational bases among their countries' underclasses. Moreover, their leaders were vulnerable to the elites' mastery of the politics of co-optation and marginalization. But veterans of such early endeavors were to go on to play important roles in the officers' movements and political parties (most notably the Ba'ath Party that was to establish totalitarian-style nationalist regimes in Syria and Iraq in the 1960s) that transformed the political life of the Arab world in the second half of the twentieth century.[37]

Conclusion

The passage from imperial old regime to nation-state entailed more than a temporary adjustment crisis. It was in many respects a formative process that marked the political culture and institutions of the new states for decades to come. One of the cardinal features of this transition was the persistence of old ruling classes or old habits of mind and conceptions of power among the very bureaucratic and political elites responsible for promoting the integration of these societies around ideals of popular sovereignty and common national identity. The fact that the political experience of many of the nationalist movements had been limited to attacking state power rather than wielding it may have made them all the more prone to fall back upon the personnel and/or methods of old regimes as they struggled to consolidate their authority over their fragile new nation-states. Peasant populations, local elites, and ethnic minorities found themselves politically marginalized and treated like colonial subjects. Their alienation was all the greater for the apparently empty talk of unity, equal rights, and self-determination that dominated official rhetoric and that was actively propagated by state-run educational systems.

In the cases of Czechoslovakia and Yugoslavia, the domination of the political, military, and bureaucratic apparatuses by ethnic groups with pre-war experience in the exercise of administrative and political power, belied the official ideologies of national unity or fraternal coexistence and colored the implementation of policies designed to foster political integration. In Poland as well as in Iraq and Syria, veterans of nationalist legions and of clandestine resistance movements who considered themselves to be in the vanguard of change became obstacles to the fulfillment of the goals they espoused, as they reverted to the political style of another age. Their degeneration into self-enclosed, corrupt elites undermined the credibility of liberal-democratic institutions, as did their increasing tendency to resort to the politics of negative integration through the scapegoating of minorities. The severe material hardships of the interwar years further aggravated popular resentments over the gap between the promise and the reality of national self-determination and broadened the gulf of suspicion and distrust between rulers and masses.

All this is not to suggest that the founding fathers of the new states were insincere in their demands for national self-determination. Nationalism was more than a façade employed to delude the masses; as in the case of the Czech political leadership, the ex-legionnaires in Poland, and the Serbian ruling class, so too in the Middle East, nationalism provided a *raison d'être* for the old-new elites that was essential for their own sense of purpose and of self-importance. Whether they were born into notable families of long standing or were products of the military academy in Istanbul, they were convinced it was their role to dominate the political and social life of their countries – and their privilege to profit from this position of pre-eminence. With the collapse of imperial rule, nationalism offered a new logic for a continuation or revival of the old ways. In the Middle East, where new imperial oversight replaced Ottoman rule, the nationalists' function as mediators of their societies' relationships with the European mandatory powers reinforced their sense of being indispensable as their nations' leaders. At the same time, the British and French imperial presence seemed to free them of direct responsibility for whatever ills befell their people.[38] But as time went on, the political conduct of the nationalist elites seemed to grow ever less responsive to the public expectations that their own ideologies had spawned.

Such a broadening rift between governments and publics was a severe hindrance to political stability in the wake of the war and its aftermath, which had spurred the growth of political consciousness and expectations of power redistribution among broad segments of both urban and rural populations. The economic ravages of the Great Depression in the 1930s reinforced widespread sentiments to the effect that the nationalist regimes had failed to fulfill the promise of the nationalist movements. Throughout much of Europe, the liberal-democratic values that had appeared triumphant in 1918–1919 appeared to be succumbing to the onslaught of fascism.[39] This created opportunities for radical right-wing nationalist movements – some of which had roots in the pre-war nationalist right (Croatia's Frankists, Poland's Endecja) – to challenge the authority and question the integrity of the nation-states' founding fathers. The existing regimes' own opportunistic resort to minority-baiting or finger-pointing at foreign foes only helped legitimize and make respectable more extreme forms of nationalist xenophobia. High-school and university students concerned about their chances of employment in financially strapped government bureaucracies or shrinking professional and commercial sectors and, in some cases, concerned about competition from ethnic minorities, were readily drawn to political parties that accused their governments of corruption and elitism, derided parliamentary democracy (where its façade still existed) as a sham, and presented themselves as more genuinely concerned with the empowerment of the nation's masses and the unconditional realization of national unity at the expense of all internal and external "enemies."[40] The Italian Fascist and German Nazi movements were influential models for the youthful enthusiasts who flocked to Dmowski's reconstructed Endecja in the 1930s and for the Syrian and Iraqi students and intellectuals and Iraqi junior officers who were drawn to embryonic pan-Arabist parties that professed a commitment to the Arab masses and that were not tied to the patronage networks of the old nationalist elites. A similar phenomenon occurred in Romania, where the resentment of students over academic competition from Jews and of peasants over the prominent role of Jews and other non-Romanian nationalities as commercial middlemen, converged in the framework of Codreanu's fascist Iron Guard movement. In Estonia, the League of Veterans played a similar role.[41]

Even if these movements did not succeed in seizing the reins of power during the interwar years, they contributed to the breakdown of parliamentary institutions where such institutions had functioned at all, helped shift their countries' political fulcra to the right, and contributed to the deterioration of conditions for minorities. Meanwhile, in Czechoslovakia and Yugoslavia, it was among disempowered minorities that resentment over the ethnic double-standards and quasi-imperial mentalities of their new rulers contributed to the growth of reactionary or fascistic forms of nationalism. By the end of the interwar period, liberal nationalism no longer seemed viable as a framework for stability in post-imperial nation-states, while the alternatives threatened to be even worse.

8   Conclusion

A comparative overview of some of the nation-states formed in the wake of the First World War suggests that the attainment of national independence constituted a risk-laden transition into an unfamiliar political landscape, an exciting and treacherous new terrain that shimmered with utopian mirages while quicksand lurked underfoot. The societies that ventured forth into the Promised Land of national self-determination were divided by different expectations of where its borders would lie, how it should be cultivated, and who was entitled to partake of its fruits. The sense of disappointment in the reality of the nation-state was all the deeper for the majesty of the dreams that had first animated the liberation movements. The irony we are left with is that the First World War led directly to the enthronement of national self-determination as the sovereign principle of the international system, while at the same time sowing the seeds of failure for the new political orders founded on that principle.

By its third and fourth years, the Great War was leading to a rapid escalation of nationalist sentiments, activities, and expectations across a broad range of social classes, political organizations, and military formations in East Central Europe, the Russian empire, and the Middle East. A wide array of factors converged to cause and reinforce this trend. Among most of the belligerent states, the corrosive grind of total war and the political repression and economic exactions associated with it served to magnify the differences between haves and have-nots: those who were provided with the necessities of life and those who felt cheated of their livelihoods, those who had access to political power and those who felt subject to the arbitrary whims of the ruling elites, those who had a direct emotional or ideological stake in the triumph of their state's cause and those who felt alienated from it. In the multinational empires, such rifts were particularly wide, given the failure of those states to sustain the levels of production and resource management attained by Germany, France, and Britain. They also tended to coincide with ethno-cultural divisions, a factor that contributed to the depth of the rifts. More specifically, the war exacerbated tensions between ethnic groups that were closely identified with the imperial regimes or that commanded regional hegemony within the empires (Germans and Magyars in the Habsburg empire, Russian settlers in Central Asia, Turks in the Ottoman empire) and those that felt consigned to the role of subject nationalities or oppressed minorities. In some regions, differences of class and ethnicity coincided with and reinforced each other (Slovak peasants vs. Magyar landowning and political elites, Russian settlers and Kazakh nomads, Greek and Armenian commercial classes vs. their economically less successful but politically more powerful Turkish rivals). But ethnic groups with a high degree of internal class differentiation could also feel collectively exploited by other nationalities (Czechs by Germans). Even in cases where socio-economic differences created deep political fissures within a nationality (Croat urban classes vs. Croat peasants), ethnic difference (e.g. between Croat and Serb peasants) tended to hinder the building of truly internationalist, class-based movements.

At the same time, the framework of the war created opportunities for small, highly motivated groups of nationalist mavericks to form exile organizations and volunteer legions that played on the conflict among the Great Powers to advance their causes. The Great Powers themselves lent refuge and support to various of these movements as instruments of subversion against their rivals or as fig leaves of legitimization for their occupation of enemy territory and for their annexationist designs. The phrase "national self-determination" dominated the vocabulary of propaganda and legitimization among liberation movements and imperial powers alike.

Among the exile organizations and volunteer legions that helped shape the victorious Allied and Associated Powers' vision of a postwar settlement and/or that managed to gain power in their homelands in 1918, the predominant conceptions of nationhood were those that sought to root a state-centered political identity in a sense of ethno-cultural community by stretching the definition of the latter to its limits – or beyond. Czechoslovakism, Yugoslavism, Piłsudski's vision of a Polish-led, multinational federation – each of these nation-building projects was intended to complement *a priori* territorial aspirations based on strategic considerations or historical precedents. Arab nationalists transposed the expansive, virtually borderless spirit of the Islamic *umma* or of Ottomanism to their vision of nationhood. The cultivation of popular identities more or less congruent with such states' territorial expanses was to be achieved by building on the common denominators among the polities' major linguistic, religious, or regional communities – or, alternatively, through ethnic cleansing and forced assimilation. (The Western powers' imposition of minorities treaties was itself largely motivated by a desire to promote long-term political and cultural integration of the new or enlarged states – as was their reluctance to enforce the treaties as soon as the intractable nature of minorities problems became apparent.)[1] Conversely, the Soviet regime set out to reify ethnic identities with a view to transforming them into conduits for the propagation of a common, supranational Soviet identity. Each of these visions was more a program for the transformation of mass consciousness than a direct response to popular demand. Such programs did tap into the eagerness for political independence that gripped broad sectors of the populace. But popular notions of who constituted the nation, what the role of the state should be in land redistribution or social reform, and how independence would transform the exercise of political authority and the relations among classes, were usually quite different from those entertained by the newly empowered nationalist elites.

From the moment the new states were founded, therefore, there was a yawning gulf between the official nationalist synthesizing projects that had been catapulted into the role of authoritative ideologies and the highly compartmentalized, ethnonational consciousness that prevailed among the general populace and that had been enhanced by the war. The Croat rural population was drawn to the idea of a Croat peasant republic rather than to the grand Yugoslav design. The Slovak masses had little knowledge of, let alone interest in, the Czechoslovak ideal in which a handful of liberal Slovak intellectuals placed such great store. The basic communities of collective interest and action in many parts of the Middle East remained confessional, clan-based, or ethno-religious (Maronites, Druze) in nature, and, for many of these groups, the embrace of pan-Arab nationalism – or opposition to it – was essentially a means of protecting or enhancing their position *vis-à-vis* rival communities and of forming alliances with urban elites or mandatory authorities.

The process of establishing states, consolidating their authority, and fixing their frontiers further muddied these already murky waters. Internecine warfare among states with disputed frontiers did not create propitious conditions for the inculcation of tolerance or the cultivation of trans-ethnic cultural syntheses. The persistence of old elites or elements of their political culture in positions of power within the new regimes contributed to a conflict between democratic-populist rhetoric and authoritarian practices on the part of ruling circles in East Central Europe and the Middle East. The struggle by these regimes to maintain political control and cultivate some measure of popular support in the face of these tensions and contradictions, and in the midst of the often grueling economic hardships of the interwar years, reinforced the tendency to stigmatize and scapegoat minorities. The distinction between liberal and right-wing forms of nationalism, which had seemed quite clear-cut among a number of nationalist intelligentsias before the war, was steadily eroded, as ostensibly liberal-democratic elites resorted to policies that were functionally equivalent to the ethno-chauvinism espoused by their critics. This only served to create an atmosphere conducive to the rise of a new generation of radically right-wing, populist or quasi-fascist nationalists who pointed to the inconsistencies and self-contradictions of the first generation of nationalist elites and promised to replace their wishy-washy brand of politics with a purer, unapologetic, uncompromising form of ethnic chauvinism that would transcend the bitter class conflicts of the Depression era, empower the masses, and turn them loose against the nation's enemies, internal and external.

Several patterns emerge from this welter of information. One is that national identities were not simply prefabricated by intellectual or socio-political elites and then transmitted to "the masses" in a streamlined process of nation-state formation. Rather, diverse frameworks of collective action and identity, ranging from London-based national committees to rural rebellions and social banditry, suddenly converged in 1918 amidst the collapse of the imperial edifices. Under the new, post-imperial dispensation, the politics of nationalism were shaped by the struggle to fit divergent forms and conceptions of identity into unidimensional packages called nation-states (or Soviet socialist republics). Newly installed regimes had to find ways of either co-opting or suppressing the various social, regional, and ethnic identities prevalent in the territories over which they claimed control. Official nationalisms were unavoidably shaped by the ethnonational identities they sought to build on, while shaping them in turn. In the case of marginalized or oppressed minorities, a negative dialectic between state-promoted and popular identities prevailed. The very abruptness of the transition to independence accentuated these dilemmas and exacerbated the resultant conflicts.

It may seem that the circumstances surrounding the events of these years were so unusual, and the span of time addressed by this book so short, that this story can have no broader, theoretical implications. But it was precisely during this brief period of explosive change that long-term ideological, cultural, and institutional patterns – and the conflicts and contradictions inherent in them – crystallized. The events of 1914–1923 set much of the agenda for the politics of nationalism in these regions for the rest of the twentieth century and beyond. Moreover, this pattern of development – a relatively long phase of nationalist fermentation and intermittent political agitation and popular unrest followed by a sudden, almost unanticipated plunge into independence in the context of a general imperial collapse – is rather typical of the way nation-states have come into being, as post-1945 decolonization in Asia and Africa and events in Eastern Europe and the Soviet Union after 1989 suggest.[2] In many cases, therefore, studying the transition from nationalism as movement to nationalism as regime[3] may be critical to understanding long-term patterns of identity politics in post-imperial nation-states. Many theoretical studies of nationalism tend to overlook or underemphasize this vital point, so focussed are they on the incremental impact of social, economic, and cultural change in the modern world.

This study also seems to suggest that ethnic chauvinism was heavily overdetermined as the outcome of nationalist development in the great majority of cases. The most liberal and democratic attempts to reconcile ethnic identity with a broader, more inclusive, civic consciousness – such as Masaryk's Czechoslovakism – ended in policies that smacked of cultural imperialism and that alienated minorities. One of the most successful experiments in forging a new civic consciousness – Kemal Atatürk's Turkish nationalism – rested on ruthlessly authoritarian practices and on the stubborn equation of civic identity with assimilation into Turkish culture as defined by the state. In fact, whether this endeavor should be considered a long-term success even in terms of its own socially integrative priorities is debatable, given the resulting alienation of a large portion of the Kurdish population.

But to conclude that ethnicity is an atavistic phenomenon that must have no role in the forging of modern, liberal, national identity, or that there simply can be no such thing as liberal nationalism under any circumstances, would be premature. The problem with many of the political projects discussed in this book was that they pushed too hard for a perfect fit between ethnic and civic identities. Some of the most liberally minded nationalist thinkers and leaders discussed in this volume were convinced that national identity had to be shaped so as to conform perfectly to a preconceived notion of the centralized, modern state, characterized by the uniform distribution of its authority throughout its territory and governed in the name of an indivisible popular sovereignty.[4] *Mutatis mutandis*, Leninist nationality policy was intended to contribute to the eventual erosion of nationalist sentiments and emergence of an undifferentiated, class-based and state-centered identity.

What I am suggesting is that nationalism is fueled and shaped by the *intersection* of political and economic modernization (the emergence of the centralized state and the idea of popular sovereignty, the spread of literacy, the onset of industrialization or of the aspiration to industrialize) with the perennial human psychological and emotional need for a communal framework of identity. With the possible exception of culturally homogeneous (relatively speaking) societies such as Japan, nationalism is not fully congruent with the logic of the stream-lined modern state, and it certainly lends itself to horrific abuses, but neither can the state function entirely without it. Yael Tamir has developed an elegant argument to the effect that the liberal democratic form of the modern state is no less dependent on a sense of national identity for its functioning than its autocratic or intolerant counterparts. The self-interest alone of the individual "rational actor" is not sufficient to maintain political cohesion and a commitment to common values in a liberal society; some shared sense of identity is indispensable. By the same token, the very existence of borders between liberal-democratic states suggests that their political identities are not coextensive with all humanity, but circumscribed by the boundaries of nationhood. Conversely, Tamir argues, an individual's identity is shaped by the sense of belonging to a cultural community, and the public – perhaps even political – expression of collective identity can thus be construed as an individual right, which squares nationalism with liberalism's focus on the rights of the individual.[5]

How then to reconcile cultural diversity with political cohesion? Tamir's concluding vision of an ethno-culturally neutral, supranational framework of political sovereignty within which a menagerie of national identities could peace-fully coexist (in the spirit of the European Union (EU)) contradicts her earlier argument to the effect that a liberal state's political cohesion depends on its society's sense of shared national identity. In a sense, she falls into the same trap as the liberal nationalists of the First World War era – the belief that the structure of the modern state, the institutions of electoral democracy, and the contours of national identity can all be made to fit perfectly together, like the pieces of a puzzle.

It was Isaiah Berlin (Tamir's mentor, and himself a proponent of liberal nationalism) who pointed out that many of the values we hold most dear – such as liberty and equality, or individual freedom and collective sovereignty – are inherently in tension with one another. Having more of one inescapably means having less of the other, and no one can prove conclusively where the perfect balance may lie.[6] Liberal nationalism *is* a contradiction in terms – but that does not invalidate it. A completely and consistently liberal society devoid of any sense of national identity would lack political cohesion and would, for that matter, have no borders. States in which the cult of national identity serves as the exclusive source of political legitimacy unfortunately abound in the real world, with consequences that need not be elaborated upon here. To accommodate both liberalism and nationalism within the bounds of a polity requires a readiness to recognize that there exists tension between the two principles and a willingness to accept a certain degree of conceptual and institutional messiness and inconsistency as a consequence. Pre-existing ethnic identities cannot be stitched together overnight into new national patterns that neatly conform to the territorial configuration of the state. Nor should ethnic or regional identities that fail to conform to the integrative proclivities of the state be dismissed, let alone suppressed, as incompatible with an *a priori* conception of modern, state-centered, civic nationalism. Imaginative compromises and idiosyncratic improvisations – be they in the form of border adjustments, power-sharing agreements, regional autonomy, extraterritorial autonomy, shared sovereignty over contested territories – provide the best means of squaring the circle. Most of the regimes that came to power amidst bloodshed and destitution in the wake of the First World War lacked either the inclination or the opportunity to approach the problem in this spirit. In this sense, the EU does in fact offer an invaluable framework for experimenting with new, flexible notions of sovereignty that can more readily mediate the tension between humans' need for cooperation and their drive to define themselves by what sets them apart.[7] Whether such ideas gain acceptance, either in Europe or in the rest of the world, remains an open question.

Notes

1 Introduction

1   On the relationship between nationalism and liberalism, see in particular Liah
    Greenfeld, *Nationalism: Five Roads to Modernity* (Cambridge, MA: Harvard University
    Press, 1992) and Yael Tamir, *Liberal Nationalism* (Princeton, NJ: Princeton University
    Press, 1993). For works that explore nationalism as an aspect or function of socio-
    economic, cultural, and political modernity, see Karl Deutsch, *Nationalism and Social
    Communication. An Inquiry into the Foundations of Nationality* (Cambridge, MA: The MIT
    Press, 1966); Ernest Gellner, *Nations and Nationalism* (Ithaca, NY: Cornell University
    Press, 1983); Eric Hobsbawm, *Nations and Nationalism since 1780: Programme, Myth,
    Reality* (Cambridge: Cambridge University Press, 1990); Eric Hobsbawm and Terence
    Ranger, eds, *The Invention of Tradition* (Cambridge: Cambridge University Press, 1983);
    John Breuilly, *Nationalism and the State* (Manchester: Manchester University Press,
    1982); Benedict Anderson, *Imagined Communities* (rev. edn, London and New York:
    Verso, 1991; 1983). For a recent critique of the modernist interpretation of nation-
    alism, see Adrian Hastings, *The Construction of Nationhood: Ethnicity, Religion and
    Nationalism* (Cambridge: Cambridge University Press, 1997). Anthony Smith has
    explored the pre-modern roots of modern nationalism as well as the role of ethno-
    nationalism as a force that both reflects the conflict between, and reconciles, the
    impersonal and alienating aspects of modernization and defensive, neo-romantic
    reactions against it. Anthony Smith, *The Ethnic Origins of Nations* (Oxford: Blackwell,
    1986); *idem, Nationalism in the Twentieth Century* (New York: New York University Press,
    1979), chap. 7. On nationalism as a backlash against the bureaucratic state, see also
    Isaiah Berlin, "The Bent Twig: On the Rise of Nationalism," in *idem, The Crooked
    Timber of Humanity* (New York: Vintage, 1992), 238–261.
2   Miroslav Hroch, *Social Preconditions of National Revival in Europe: A Comparative Analysis of
    the Social Composition of Patriotic Groups among the Smaller European Nations* (New York:
    Cambridge University Press, 1985).
3   On the need to integrate the role of historical contingency and of the historical event
    into the theoretical study of nationalism, see Rogers Brubaker, *Nationalism Reframed:
    Nationhood and the National Question in the New Europe* (Cambridge: Cambridge University
    Press, 1996), chap. 1: "Nation as Form, Category, Event."
4   On the need to develop comparative perspectives on nationalism, see Peter
    Stearns, "Nationalisms: An Invitation to Comparative Analysis," *Journal of World
    History*, vol. 8, no. 1 (1997), 57–74.
5   See Seamus Dunn and T.G. Fraser, eds, *The First World War and Contemporary Ethnic
    Conflict* (London: Routledge, 1996).
6   See Greenfeld, *Nationalism*; Rogers Brubaker, *Citizenship and Nationhood in France and
    Germany* (Cambridge: Harvard University Press, 1992); George Schöpflin,
    "Nationalism, Politics and the European Experience," *Survey*, 28 (4) (Winter 1984),

67–86; *idem*, "Nationalism and Ethnicity in Europe, East and West," in Charles Kupchan, ed., *Nationalism and Nationalities in the New Europe* (Ithaca, NY: Cornell University Press, 1995). For early typological and historical distinctions between liberal and illiberal forms of nationalism, see Carlton Hayes, *The Historical Evolution of Modern Nationalism* (New York: R.R. Smith, 1931); Hans Kohn, *The Idea of Nationalism: A Study in its Origins and Background* (New York: Macmillan, 1944), chaps 6–8; *idem*, *The Age of Nationalism: The First Era of Global History* (New York: Harper & Row, 1962), part I; *Nationalism: A Report by a Study Group of Members of the Royal Institute of International Affairs* (London: Frank Cass, 1963; 1st edn, 1939), chaps 2–4.

7   See Charles Tilly, "Reflections on the History of European State-Making," in Charles Tilly, ed., *The Formation of National States in Western Europe* (Princeton, NJ: Princeton University Press, 1975).

8   A classic statement of this thesis is to be found in Ernest Renan's March 1882 Sorbonne lecture, "What is a Nation?" translated by Martin Thom and reprinted in Geoff Eley and Ronald Grigor Suny, eds, *Becoming National: A Reader* (New York: Oxford University Press, 1996). For a critical view of the French Third Republic's role in the cultural homogenization of rural France, see Eugen Weber, *Peasants into Frenchmen: The Modernization of Rural France, 1870–1914* (Stanford, CA: Stanford University Press, 1976), esp. 112–114.

9   Karen Barkey also makes this point in "Thinking about Consequences of Empire," in Karen Barkey and Mark von Hagen, eds, *After Empire – Multiethnic Societies and Nation-Building: The Soviet Union and the Russian, Ottoman, and Habsburg Empires* (Boulder, CO: Westview Press, 1997). See also Rasma Karklins, *Ethnopolitics and Transition to Democracy: The Collapse of the USSR and Latvia* (Washington, DC: Woodrow Wilson Center Press and Baltimore, MD: Johns Hopkins University Press, 1994), 44–47.

10 See Tamir, *Liberal Nationalism* (discussed in Chapter 8 of this book).

11 There are no completely standardized definitions for any of these terms. For discussions of such terminological problems, see Walker Connor, *Ethnonationalism: The Quest for Understanding* (Princeton, NJ: Princeton University Press, 1994), chap. 4; Greenfeld, *Nationalism*, 3–14; Aira Kemiläinen, "The Idea of Nationalism," *Scandinavian Journal of History*, vol. 9, no. 1 (1984), 31–64.

2 Ethnicity and Empire: An Historical Introduction

1   See Dominic Lieven's useful comparative analysis in "The Russian Empire and the Soviet Union as Imperial Polities," *Journal of Contemporary History*, vol. 30, no. 4 (October 1995), 607–636. See also the older treatment by Hugh Seton-Watson, *Nations and States: An Enquiry into the Origins of Nations and the Politics of Nationalism* (Boulder, CO: Westview, 1977), chap. 4.

2   Ernest Gellner, *Nations and Nationalism* (Ithaca, NY: Cornell University Press, 1983), 62.

3   See Steven Beller, *Francis Joseph* (London: Longman, 1996).

4   The German word for Austria is *Österreich*, meaning "eastern realm" (of the Holy Roman empire).

5   Robert A. Kann, *A History of the Habsburg Empire, 1526–1918* (Berkeley and Los Angeles, CA: University of California Press, 1974), chaps 1–3 and pp. 156–170.

6   Kann, *Habsburg*, 218–221.

7   For convenience sake, I will continue to use the terms Habsburg empire and Austria–Hungary interchangeably.

8   A unitary Reichsrat had been created under the February Patent of 1861. In the wake of its mitosis in 1867, a committee consisting of delegations from both parliaments met regularly to decide upon joint appropriations for military and foreign affairs.

9   Information on nineteenth-century developments in the Habsburg empire is drawn from: Kann, *Habsburg*, 332–342; Robert A. Kann, *The Multinational Empire: Nationalism*

and National Reform in the Habsburg Monarchy (New York: Columbia University Press, 1950), vol. 1, chap. 4; Alan Sked, *The Decline and Fall of the Habsburg Empire, 1815–1918* (London: Longman, 1989), chap. 5; Samuel R. Williamson, Jr, *Austria–Hungary and the Origins of the First World War* (New York: St. Martin's Press, 1991), chap. 2.

10 Ivo Banac, *The National Question in Yugoslavia* (Ithaca, NY: Cornell University Press, 1984), 91–93.

11 The Ukrainians of Galicia and Bukovina were called Ruthenians. I will employ the term 'Ukrainian' in reference to them, since linguistically they were virtually indistinguishable from the Ukrainians of the Russian empire, and since the younger generation of their nationalist leaders advocated the cultivation of national bonds with Russia's Ukrainians. The Galician Ukrainians were adherents of the Uniate (Eastern Rite Catholic) Church, in contrast to their predominantly Orthodox co-ethnics across the Russian border.

12 Sked, *Decline*, 213.

13 Beller, *Francis Joseph*, 140–189 and *passim*; Sked, *Decline*, 218–234; Carl E. Schorske, *Fin-de-Siècle Vienna: Politics and Culture* (New York: Vintage, 1981), 120–133. For a critique of the Habsburgs' anachronistic and paternalistic dynasticism, the hollowness of Austrian civic education, the ethno-cultural chauvinism of Hungarian civic education, and the latent intolerance and extremism of minority nationalisms in the empire, see Oscar Jaszi, *The Dissolution of the Habsburg Monarchy* (Chicago, IL: University of Chicago Press, 1961; 1929), parts IV–VII.

14 The Slovenes were also increasingly included in the designation South Slav.

15 This discussion relies upon: Banac, *The National Question*, 76–80, 85–91, 110–111, 209–214; John Lampe, *Yugoslavia as History: Twice There Was a Country* (Cambridge: Cambridge University Press, 1996), 43–46; Dimitrije Djordjevic, "The Idea of Yugoslav Unity in the Nineteenth Century," in Dimitrije Djordjevic, ed., *The Creation of Yugoslavia, 1914–1918* (Santa Barbara, CA and Oxford: Clio Press, 1980), 3; Kann, *Habsburg*, 384–405; Hugh and Christopher Seton-Watson, *The Making of a New Europe: R.W. Seton-Watson and the Last Years of Austria–Hungary* (Seattle, WA: University of Washington Press, 1981), 58–59.

16 The most dramatic example of this phenomenon actually dates from 1846, when a *szlachta*-led Polish nationalist uprising in Galicia was defeated by mostly Polish peasants who slaughtered their hated masters in the name of the Habsburg Emperor. Lewis Namier, *1848: Revolution of the Intellectuals* (Oxford: Oxford University Press, 1992; reprint of text in *Proceedings of the British Academy*, Volume 30, 1946), 12–17; Sked, *Decline*, 63–64.

17 One of the ironies of these programs of national revival was that their intellectual leaders were themselves often more comfortable speaking and writing the empire's hegemonic tongue than communicating in their own national language. Thus, the historian František Palacký, one of the architects of the nineteenth-century Czech cultural revival, did his early writing in German. Jonathan Sperber, *The European Revolutions, 1848–1851* (Cambridge: Cambridge University Press, 1994), 97.

18 Schorske, *Vienna*, 120–133.

19 Kann, *Multinational*, vol. 1, chap. 3.

20 This was the term used to distinguish peoples who were widely recognized as the heirs to historic state traditions. Kann, *Multinational*, vol. 1, chap. 2.

21 Robert B. Pynsent, *Questions of Identity: Czech and Slovak Ideas of Nationality and Personality* (Budapest, London, and New York: Central European University Press, 1994), 152–169.

22 The Uniate Church served as a focal point for Ukrainian nationalism in eastern Galicia, with the currents of Russian Ukrainian populist nationalism beginning to ripple across the border in the last decades before the First World War.

23 Gellner, *Nations and Nationalism*, 62; Miroslav Hroch, *Social Preconditions of National Revival in Europe: A Comparative Analysis of the Social Composition of Patriotic Groups among*

the Smaller European Nations (trans. from the Czech by Ben Fowkes, Cambridge: Cambridge University Press, 1985), chap. 13 and pp. 139–147.

24 John F.N. Bradley, *Czech Nationalism in the Nineteenth Century* (Boulder, CO: East European Monographs, 1984), 24, 35, 53–54; Hans Kohn, *Pan-Slavism: Its History and Ideology* (Notre Dame: University of Notre Dame Press, 1953), 184; Paul Vysny, *Neo-Slavism and the Czechs: 1898–1914* (Cambridge: Cambridge University Press, 1977), 23–26. The prototype for the Sokol movement was Turnvater Jahn's early-nineteenth-century, German-nationalist, gymnastic organizations.

25 Bohemia's large coal reserves contributed significantly to its late-nineteenth-century transformation into Austria's industrial powerhouse. David F. Good, *The Economic Rise of the Habsburg Empire, 1750–1914* (Berkeley and Los Angeles, CA: University of California Press, 1984), 129–134.

26 Bradley, *Czech Nationalism*, 33–37; Kann, *Habsburg*, 439–441; Kann, *Multinational*, vol. 1, 205.

27 This discussion of Austro-Marxism draws on: Otto Bauer, *Die Nationalitätenfrage und die Sozialdemokratie* (Vienna: I. Brand, 1907), 23–95; extracts from Bauer's and Renner's writings in Tom Bottomore and Patrick Goode, trans. and eds, *Austro-Marxism* (Oxford: Oxford University Press, 1978), 102–117; Mark E. Blum, *The Austro-Marxists, 1890–1918* (Lexington, KY: The University Press of Kentucky, 1985), chaps 3 and 5; Kann, *Multinational*, vol. 2, chap. 20.

28 Bauer, *Die Nationalitätenfrage*, 282–316; Bottomore and Good, *Austro-Marxism*, 102–107; Richard Pipes, *The Formation of the Soviet Union* (Cambridge, MA: Harvard University Press, 1964), 24–26.

29 See Chapter 3.

30 Bauer was an assimilated Jew and Renner an ethnic German.

31 Kann, *Multinational*, vol. 1, chap. 5 and vol. 2, chap. 23; Sked, *Decline*, 208–234.

32 Lieven, "The Russian Empire," 623.

33 Andreas Kappeler, *Russland als Vielvölkerreich: Entstehung, Geschichte, Zerfall* (Munich: C.H. Beck, 1993), provides the definitive treatment of this theme. This section draws extensively on his work.

34 Lieven, "The Russian Empire," 624–625. There were exceptions to this pattern, such as the autonomy of the Cossack Hetmanate according to the terms of the treaty that brought the Ukraine under the tsar's protection in the seventeenth century, the constitutional distinctiveness of the Russian partition of Poland (Congress Poland), or Finnish autonomy following its acquisition from Sweden in 1808–1809. Such exceptions were never allowed to last for long, however. Hans Rogger, *Russia in the Age of Modernisation and Revolution, 1881–1917* (London: Longman, 1983), chap. 9.

35 Richard Pipes, *Russia under the Old Regime* (2nd edn; New York: Macmillan, 1992), chaps 2–4.

36 *Ibid.*, chap. 5; Kappeler, *Russland*, chap. 4; Theodore R. Weeks, *Nation and State in Late Imperial Russia: Nationalism and Russification on the Western Frontier, 1863–1914* (DeKalb, IL: Northern Illinois University Press, 1996), 194–196.

37 Kappeler, *Russland*, 29–36. Marc Raeff argues that the co-optation of native elites into the tsarist nobility should be seen as an indirect form of Russification. See his "Uniformity, Diversity, and the Imperial Administration," and "In the Imperial Manner," in Marc Raeff, *Political Ideas and Institutions in Imperial Russia* (Boulder, CO: Westview Press, 1994).

38 For a counter-example – the persecution of the Jews – see John Doyle Klier, *Imperial Russia's Jewish Question, 1855–1881* (Cambridge: Cambridge University Press, 1995); Hans Rogger, *Jewish Policies and Right-Wing Politics in Imperial Russia* (London: Macmillan, 1986).

39 Lieven, "The Russian Empire," p. 629, no. 7.

40 Kappeler, *Russland*, chap. 7.

41 Michael Boro Petrovich, *The Emergence of Russian Panslavism, 1856–1870* (New York: Columbia University Press, 1956), 254–269; Kohn, *Pan-Slavism*, 137–175; Frank

Fadner, S.J. (The Society of Jesus – The Jesuit order), *Seventy Years of Pan-Slavism in Russia: Karazin to Danilevskii, 1800–1870* (Haarlem, The Netherlands: Georgetown University Press, 1962), 293–301 and 314–349.

42 Weeks, *Nation*, 8; Nicholas P. Vakar, *Belorussia: The Making of a Nation* (Cambridge, MA: Harvard University Press, 1956), 68–70; Kappeler, *Russland*, 189; Geoffrey Hosking, *Russia: People and Empire, 1552–1917* (Cambridge, MA: Harvard University Press, 1997), part 4, chap. 3.

43 Hosking, *Russia*, 377, 380–385.

44 Kappeler, *Russland*, chap. 7. On Russian government attitudes toward the pogroms, see Rogger, *Jewish*, chap. 4; I. Michael Aronson, "The Anti-Jewish Pogroms in Russia in 1881," in John D. Klier and Shlomo Lambroza, eds, *Pogroms: Anti-Jewish Violence in Modern Russian History* (Cambridge: Cambridge University Press, 1992).

45 This mentality is more commonly associated with the Soviet era, but Peter Holquist has found strong manifestations of it in the memoranda and reports of nineteenth-century tsarist military planners. See the introduction to Peter Holquist, " 'Conduct Merciless Mass Terror': Decossackization on the Don, 1919," *Cahiers du Monde Russe et Soviétique*, vol. 38, nos 1–2 (1997), 127–162.

46 Sir Bernard Pares, *The Fall of the Russian Monarchy* (New York: Knopf, 1939), 307–309; Allan K. Wildman, *The End of the Russian Imperial Army*, vol. 1: *The Old Army and the Soldiers' Revolt (March–April 1917)* (Princeton, NJ: Princeton University Press, 1980), 110–113; Lieven, "The Russian Empire," 613; Hubertus Jahn, *Patriotic Culture in Russia during World War I* (Ithaca, NY: Cornell University Press, 1995), 171–177. Russia's February Revolution occurred during March according to the (Western) Gregorian calendar, to which all dates in this book refer.

47 The Cossack tradition was romanticized and reified into an ideal expression of human freedom by the mid nineteenth-century poet Taras Shevchenko (1814–1861), who played a central role in elevating the language of Ukrainian peasants into a medium of literary expression and who achieved the status of national bard. John Reshetar, *The Ukrainian Revolution, 1917–1920: A Study in Nationalism* (Princeton, NJ: Princeton University Press, 1952), 5–6.

48 The Grand Duchy of Lithuania's union with Poland (dating to 1386 and confirmed as indissoluble in 1569) had led to the Polonization of its socio-political elites, whose previous medium of high-cultural expression had actually been Belorussian. Ronald Grigor Suny, *The Revenge of the Past: Nationalism, Revolution and the Collapse of the Soviet Union* (Stanford, CA: Stanford University Press, 1993), 32–33.

49 Reshetar, *Ukrainian*, 146.

50 Vakar, *Belorussia*, chap. 6.

51 Finland's autonomous status also created the foundation for a distinct political identity.

52 Kappeler, *Russland*, 183–191.

53 Henry J. Tobias, *The Jewish Bund in Russia: From Its Origins to 1905* (Stanford, CA: Stanford University Press, 1972), 251–252.

54 The Armenians had converted to Christianity in the fourth century AD. Ronald Grigor Suny, *Looking Toward Ararat: Armenia in Modern History* (Bloomington and Indianapolis, IN: Indiana University Press, 1993), 8.

55 *Ibid.*, chap. 2; Ronald Grigor Suny, *The Making of the Georgian Nation* (2nd edn, Bloomington and Indianapolis, IN: Indiana University Press, 1994), 139–143.

56 This discussion of Russia's Muslim populations draws upon: Kappeler, *Russland*, 149–168; Hélène Carrère d'Encausse, *Islam and the Russian Empire: Reform and Revolution in Central Asia* (Berkeley and Los Angeles, CA: University of California Press, 1988), chaps 2–4; Martha Brill Olcott, *The Kazakhs* (Stanford, CA: Hoover Institution Press, 1987), chaps 3–4; Steven Marks, *Road to Power: The Trans-Siberian Railroad and the Colonization of Asian Russia, 1850–1917* (Ithaca, NY: Cornell University Press, 1991), 162.

57 Z.A.B. Zeman, *The Break-up of the Habsburg Empire 1914–1918: A Study in Social and National Revolution* (London: Oxford University Press, 1961), chap. 1; James Joll, *The Origins of the First World War* (2nd edn, London: Longman, 1992), 110–111; L.C.F. Turner, *Origins of the First World War* (New York: Norton, 1970), 80–81.

58 Constantinople became known to the Islamic world as Istanbul – a mispronunciation of the Greek phrase (*eis ten polin*) meaning "to the city." The city continued to be referred to as "Konstantiniyye" on coins and in official documents.

59 This discussion of the Ottoman empire draws upon: Stanford Shaw, *History of the Ottoman Empire and Modern Turkey. Volume 1: Empire of the Gazis: The Rise and Decline of the Ottoman Empire, 1280–1808* (Cambridge: Cambridge University Press, 1976), chaps 2–5; Stanford J. Shaw and Ezel Kural Shaw, *History of the Ottoman Empire and Modern Turkey. Volume 2: Reform, Revolution, and Republic: The Rise of Modern Turkey, 1808–1975* (Cambridge: Cambridge University Press, 1977), 55–133, 157–158, 174–187, and 255–259; Bernard Lewis, *The Emergence of Modern Turkey* (London: Oxford University Press, 1961), chaps 1–2; Erik J. Zürcher, *Turkey: A Modern History* (London: I.B. Tauris, 1993), chaps 1, 5, 7–8.

60 The relationship between ethnicity and religion was highly fluid in the late Ottoman empire. In some cases, rising ethno-national consciousness divided religious communities (most notably that of Sunni Islam). In other cases, nationalists aspired to transcend religious differences. Religious identity could itself become ethnicized.

61 Lieven, "The Russian Empire," 613–614.

62 The *millet* system may have served as a loose model for the Austro-Marxists' concept of extraterritorial autonomy (discussed above).

63 Ronald Grigor Suny, *Looking Toward Ararat*, 98–106; Manoug Somakian, *Empires in Conflict: Armenia and the Great Powers 1895–1920* (London: I.B. Tauris, 1995), 15–31.

64 See, for instance, Philip Khoury, *Urban Notables and Arab Nationalism: The Politics of Damascus 1880–1920* (Cambridge: Cambridge University Press, 1983), chaps 1–2; Shaw and Shaw, *History of the Ottoman Empire*, vol. 2, 221–245.

65 *The Other Balkan Wars: A 1913 Carnegie Endowment Inquiry in Retrospect with a New Introduction and Reflections on the Present Conflict by George F. Kennan* (Washington, DC: Carnegie Foundation for International Peace, 1993), 155–157.

66 The case of the Serbo-Croatian-speaking Muslims left stranded in Bosnia after Ottoman withdrawal from the province in 1878 is particularly illuminating: many Muslims almost arbitrarily designated themselves as Serbs or Croats, for want of any distinctive national identity of their own. Banac, *The National Question*, 58–59, 66–67, 362–366.

3 On the Eve of War: The Intelligentsia as Vanguard of Nationalism

1 Britain, France, and Germany constituted the most influential prototypes. After the Russo-Japanese war of 1904–1905, Japan was also the object of attention on the part of Central Asian and Turkish nationalists, as well as of the Polish nationalist, Roman Dmowski.

2 The term "integral nationalism" refers to a chauvinistic, right-wing form of nationalism that holds up the nation's self-interest as an absolute value, to which all other ethical considerations and moral values are subordinate (or by which they are informed).

3 This discussion of pre-war Polish politics draws upon the following works: Andrzej Garlicki, *Józef Piłsudski, 1867–1935* (ed., trans., and abridged by John Coutouvidis, Aldershot: Scolar Press, 1995); R.F. Leslie, Antony Polonsky, Jan M. Ciechanowski, and Z.A. Pelczynski, *The History of Poland since 1863* (Cambridge: Cambridge University Press, 1980); Robert E. Blobaum, *Rewolucja. Russian Poland, 1904–1907* (Ithaca, NY: Cornell University Press, 1995); Piotr S. Wandycz, "Poland's Place in Europe in the Concepts of Piłsudski and Dmowski," *East European Politics and Societies,*

vol. 4, no. 3 (1990), 451–468; Adam Bromke, *Poland's Politics: Idealism vs. Realism* (Cambridge, MA: Harvard University Press, 1967); Alvin Marcus Fountain II, *Roman Dmowski: Party, Tactics, Ideology 1895–1907* (Boulder, CO: East European Monographs, 1980); Roman Dmowski, *Problems of Central and Eastern Europe* (London: privately printed, July 1917); Wiktor Sukiennicki, *East Central Europe during World War I: From Foreign Domination to National Independence* (2 vols, Boulder, CO: East European Monographs, 1984), chap. 6; Magdalena Opalski and Israel Bartal, *Poles and Jews. A Failed Brotherhood* (Hanover, NH: University Press of New England, 1992), 105.

4 Gerd Linde, *Die Deutsche Politik in Litauen im Ersten Weltkrieg* (Wiesbaden: Otto Harrassowitz, 1965), 73.

5 Piłsudski's older brother Bronisław, who was a student in St. Petersburg, was sentenced to fifteen years' hard labor for his apparently deeper involvement in the 1887 plot. Lenin's older brother, Alexander Ulianov, was executed for his leading role in the assassination attempt. Garlicki, *Piłsudski*, chap. 1.

6 Józeph Piłsudski, *Joseph Piłsudski: The Memories of a Polish Revolutionary and Soldier*, trans. and ed. D.R. Gillie (London: Faber & Faber, 1931), 16.

7 See article by Piłsudski entitled "Russia," which appeared in *Robotnik* ("The Worker," PPS party organ) in 1895, as quoted in Garlicki, *Piłsudski*, 22.

8 Letter from Piłsudski to Feliks Perl, as quoted in Garlicki, *Piłsudski*, 59.

9 The Endecja capitalized (so to speak) on workers' disillusionment with socialist strike efforts that failed to gain significant concessions from the government or the industrialists. The National Democratic trade unions were in a position to use the Endecja's industrial connections to gain improved conditions for their members by means of legal negotiation. Blobaum, *Rewolucja*, 194–195.

10 Stanley Winters, "The Young Czech Party (1874–1914): An Appraisal," *The Slavic Review*, vol. 28 (1969), 426–444.

11 Joseph Kalvoda, *The Genesis of Czechoslovakia* (Boulder, CO: East European Monographs, 1986), 13–17; Paul Vyšný, *Neo-Slavism and the Czechs: 1898–1914* (Cambridge: Cambridge University Press, 1977), chaps 3–7; J.F.N. Bradley, "Czech Pan-Slavism before the First World War," *The Slavonic and East European Review*, vol. 40 (1961–1962), 184–205 (esp. 193–197); Caspar Ferenczi, "Nationalismus und Neoslavismus in Russland vor dem Ersten Weltkrieg," *Forschungen zur osteuropäischen Geschichte*, vol. 34 (1984), 7–127.

12 H. Gordon Skilling, *T.G. Masaryk: Against the Current, 1882–1914* (University Park, PA: The Pennsylvania State University Press, 1994), 6–7, 35–37, 101–103, and chap. 3; Robert Pynsent, *Questions of Identity: Czech and Slovak Ideas of Nationality and Personality* (Budapest: Central European University Press, 1994), 180–182; Kalvoda, *Genesis of Czechoslovakia*, 17–32; Roman Szporluk, *The Political Thought of Thomas G. Masaryk* (Boulder, CO: East European Monographs, 1981), chap. 4. For a critique of Masaryk's attempt to conflate ethno-cultural and universalist themes, and for an attack on the elitist strain in his thinking, see Eva Schmidt-Hartmann, "The Fallacy of Realism: Some Problems of Masaryk's Approach to Czech National Aspirations," in Stanley B. Winters, ed., *T.G. Masaryk (1850–1937)*, vol. 1 (New York: St. Martin's Press, 1990). On Masaryk's role in the manuscripts controversy – a highly politicized debate over the authenticity of what was alleged to be newly discovered medieval Czech epic poetry, but which Masaryk denounced as nineteenth-century forgeries – see Karel Čapek, *Talks with T.G. Masaryk*, trans. Dora Round and ed. Michael Henry Heim (North Haven, CT: Catbird Press, 1995), 120 and 133, 141–144 and translator's gloss on 251; Skilling, *Masaryk*, 4–6. On his relations with Jews and his public campaign on behalf of the accused in a turn-of-the-century anti-Semitic blood libel, see Steven Beller, "The Hilsner Affair: Nationalism, Anti-Semitism and the Individual in the Habsburg Monarchy at the Turn of the Century," and Michael A. Riff, "The Ambiguity of Masaryk's Attitudes on the 'Jewish Question'," in Robert B. Pynsent, ed., *T.G. Masaryk (1850–1937), vol. 2, Thinker and Critic* (London: Macmillan, 1989); Skilling, *Masaryk*, 81–86.

13 This discussion of Slovak nationalism and its relationship to Masaryk draws upon Peter Petro, *A History of Slovak Literature* (Montreal: McGill–Queen's University Press, 1995), 94–104; Thomas D. Marzik, "The Slovakophile Relationship of T.G. Masaryk and Karel Kalal prior to 1914," in Winters, *Masaryk*; Skilling, *Masaryk*, 73–75; Szporluk, *Political Thought*, 19–24, 139; Čapek, *Talks*, 52, 57, 169, 171.

14 The Hlasists were named for their original flagship journal, *Hlas* (meaning "Voice").

15 Naturally, the notion that the Slovak peasantry was so much clay waiting to be molded in the Czechs' image was to provoke bitter resentment on the part of many Slovaks during the interwar years.

16 This discussion of South Slav nationalism relies heavily upon Ivo Banac, *The National Question in Yugoslavia: Origins, History, Politics* (Ithaca, NY: Cornell University Press, 1984), 94–99. It also draws on the following sources: Nicholas J. Miller, *Between Nation and State: Serbian Politics in Croatia before the First World War* (Pittsburgh, PA: University of Pittsburgh Press, 1997), 30–33, 46–52, and chap. 6; Hugh and Christopher Seton-Watson, *The Making of a New Europe: R.W. Seton-Watson and the Last Years of Austria–Hungary* (Seattle, WA: University of Washington Press, 1981), chap. 3; Hugh and Christopher Seton-Watson, Ljubo Boban, Mirjana Gross, Bogdan Krizman, and Dragovan Šepić, eds, *R.W. Seton-Watson and the Yugoslavs: Correspondence, 1906–1941. Vol. 1: 1906–1918* (London: British Academy, 1976), "Introduction" (pp. 12–13); Barbara Jelavich, *History of the Balkans, Vol. 1: Eighteenth and Nineteenth Centuries* (Cambridge: Cambridge University Press, 1983), 98–99; John R. Lampe, *Yugoslavia as History: Twice There Was a Country* (Cambridge: Cambridge University Press, 1996), 77–79; Ivo Banac, "Ministration and Desecration: The Place of Dubrovnik in Modern Croat National Ideology and Political Culture," in Ivo Banac, John G. Ackerman, and Roman Szporluk, eds, *Nation and Ideology: Essays in Honor of Wayne S. Vucinich* (Boulder, CO: East European Monographs, 1981).

17 The influence of Russian populism is also clearly evident in Radić's political thought.

18 Miller, *Between Nation and State*, 137–140, 154–155, 159; Milorad Ekmecic, "Serbian War Aims," in Dimitrije Djordjević, ed., *The Creation of Yugoslavia 1914–1918* (Santa Barbara, CA and Oxford, England: Clio Press, 1980), 26–27; Hugh and Christopher Seton-Watson, *Making of a New Europe*, 68–70; Banac, *The National Question*, 99–104; Robert Seton-Watson to Ivo Lupis-Vukić (17 October 1909), Smodlaka to Seton-Watson (2 May 1912), Lupis-Vukić to Seton-Watson (15 November 1912), and Seton-Watson to Lupis-Vukić (27 November 1912) in Hugh and Christopher Seton-Watson, *Seton-Watson and the Yugoslavs*, 50–54, 109, and 117–120. Various attempts by leading Serb and Croat linguists and writers to agree on a common alphabet or common subdialect as the basis for a unitary Yugoslav literary language ended in failure. Banac, *The National Question*, 209–214; Dimitrije Djordjević, "The Idea of Yugoslav Unity," in *idem*, ed., *Creation*, note 11.

19 Geoffrey Hosking, *Russia: People and Empire, 1552–1917* (Cambridge, MA: Harvard University Press, 1997), 146–147.

20 Theodore R. Weeks, *Nation and State in Late Imperial Russia: Nationalism and Russification on the Western Frontier, 1863–1914* (DeKalb, IL: Northern Illinois University Press, 1996), 30–40, chap. 9, and *passim*; Ferenczi, "Nationalismus und Neoslavismus," 39–40. On the Russian Right's anti-Semitism and its connections to the infamous "Protocols of the Elders of Zion," see Steven G. Marks, *The Russian Century* (Cambridge, MA: Harvard University Press, 2001), chap. 5.

21 This discussion of moderate and left-wing party positions on the nationalities question draws on Richard Pipes, *The Formation of the Soviet Union: Communism and Nationalism, 1917–1923* (Cambridge, MA: Harvard University Press, 1964), 29–41; Weeks, *Nation*, 21–30. On the *realpolitisch* approach of Peter Struve, one of Russia's leading liberal thinkers, to the nationalities issue, see Ferenczi, "Nationalismus und Neoslavismus," 16–26; Richard Pipes, *Struve: Liberal on the Right, 1905–1944* (Cambridge, MA: Harvard University Press, 1980), 88–94; Hosking, *Russia*, 446–448; Weeks, *Nation*, 27–29.

22 Cf. Mark Von Hagen, "Writing the History of Russia as Empire: The Perspective of Federalism," in Catherine Evtuhov, Boris Gasparov, Alexander Ospovat, and Mark Von Hagen, eds, *Kazan, Moscow, St. Petersburg: Multiple Faces of the Russian Empire* (Moscow: OGI, 1997).

23 The national poet, Taras Shevchenko, was among the founders of this society, which was broken up by the tsarist authorities soon after its establishment in 1846, but which left its mark on later Ukrainian movements.

24 John Reshetar, *The Ukrainian Revolution, 1917–1920: A Study in Nationalism* (Princeton, NJ: Princeton University Press, 1952), 6–9; Thomas M. Prymak, *Mykhailo Hrushevsky: The Politics of National Culture* (Toronto: University of Toronto Press, 1987), 7–8, 27; Ivan Rudnytsky, "The Fourth Universal and its Ideological Antecedents," in Taras Hunczak, ed., *The Ukraine, 1917–1921: A Study in Revolution* (Cambridge, MA: Harvard University Press, 1977), 188–204; Hélène Carrère d'Encausse, *The Great Challenge: Nationalities and the Bolshevik State, 1917–1930* (New York and London: Holmes & Meier, 1992), 19–22. The idea of reorganizing the tsarist empire as a democratic federation of nations had been broached by Alexander Herzen (1812–1870), the intellectual father of Russian populism. See Adam Ulam, *In the Name of the People: Prophets and Conspirators in Prerevolutionary Russia* (New York: Viking Press, 1977), chap. 2; Frank Fadner, S.J. (Society of Jesus – The Jesuit order), *Seventy Years of Pan-Slavism in Russia: Karazin to Danilevskii, 1800–1870* (Haarlem, The Netherlands: Georgetown University Press, 1962), 170–182.

25 On the anti-Habsburg, "Old Ruthenian" movement of conservative, Russophile Ukrainians in Galicia, see Zbynek Zeman, *The Break-up of the Habsburg Empire, 1914–1918* (London: Oxford University Press, 1961), chap. 1.

26 Prymak, *Hrushevsky*, 98–102.

27 The expropriations were rescinded during the 1905 Revolution. Richard G. Hovannisian, *Armenia on the Road to Independence, 1918* (Berkeley and Los Angeles, CA: University of California Press, 1969), 17–21.

28 *Ibid.*, 21–22; Ronald Grigor Suny, *Looking Toward Ararat: Armenia in Modern History* (Bloomington and Indianapolis, IN: Indiana University Press, 1993), chaps 4–5; Anahide Ter Minassian, "Nationalism and Socialism in the Armenian Revolutionary Movement (1887–1912)," in Ronald Grigor Suny, ed., *Transcaucasia, Nationalism and Social Change: Essays in the History of Armenia, Azerbaijan, and Georgia* (rev. edn, Ann Arbor, MI: University of Michigan Press, 1996; 1983). The Dashnaks' main rival was the Hnchak ("Bell" – thus named in honor of Alexander Herzen's famous journal) Party, which also espoused a blend of socialism, populism, and nationalism, but with a slightly heavier emphasis on the socialist component. Internal splits in the party during the late 1890s left the Dashnaks with a virtual monopoly over the Armenian nationalist movement.

29 Pipes, *Formation*, chap. 1 and pp. 55–56; Hovannisian, *Armenia on the Road to Independence*, 16–17.

30 The classic exposition of this argument was laid out by the Marxist Zionist Ber Borochov, who contended that anti-Semitism had prevented Jews from developing a "normal" class structure in the diaspora, and that their establishment of a new society in Palestine was the only way to rectify this anomaly. Ber Borochov, excerpt from "Our Platform," in Arthur Hertzberg, ed., *The Zionist Idea* (New York: The Jewish Publication Society of America, 1959), 360–366.

31 Henry J. Tobias, *The Jewish Bund in Russia: From Its Origins to 1905* (Stanford, CA: Stanford University Press, 1972), chap. 7, pp. 127–130, 136–138, chaps 13 and 16, pp. 248–254, and *passim*.

32 Ronald Grigor Suny, *The Making of the Georgian Nation* (2nd edn, Bloomington and Indianapolis, IN: Indiana University Press, 1994), chap. 7.

33 *Ibid.*, p. 145.

34 See Chapter 2, pp. 16–18.

35 Pipes, *Formation*, 27–28, 41–49; d'Encausse, *The Great Challenge*, 22–25.

36 Albert Hourani, *Arabic Thought in the Liberal Age, 1798–1939* (Cambridge: Cambridge University Press, 1983 edn), chaps 5–7; John L. Esposito, *Islam and Politics* (Syracuse, NY: Syracuse University Press, 1991), 46–52; Hisham Sharabi, *Arab Intellectuals and the West: The Formative Years, 1875–1914* (Baltimore, MD and London: The Johns Hopkins Press, 1970). A very similar Islamic modernist philosophy was also articulated by the Indian Muslim Ahmad Khan (1817–1898), whose smuggled-in writings were avidly read by the nascent Muslim intelligentsia of Russian-controlled Central Asia. See Esposito, *Islam and Politics*, 52–56; Gail Minault, *The Khilafat Movement: Religious Symbolism and Political Mobilization in India* (New York: Columbia University Press), 6–8, 14–24; Hélène Carrère d'Encausse, *Islam and the Russian Empire: Reform and Revolution in Central Asia* (trans. Quintin Hoare, Berkeley and Los Angeles, CA: University of California Press, 1988), 56–58.

37 This discussion of the Jadids draws upon: Pipes, *Formation*, 13–15; d'Encausse, *Islam and the Russian Empire*, chap. 5; Jacob M. Landau, *Pan-Turkism: From Irredentism to Cooperation* (Bloomington and Indianapolis, IN: Indiana University Press, 1995), 9–12; Tadeusz Swietochoswki, *Russian Azerbaijan, 1905–1920: The Shaping of National Identity in a Muslim Community* (Cambridge: Cambridge University Press, 1985), 31–33.

38 In some Turkestani cities, such as Bukhara and Samarkand, Farsi was widely employed as a spoken language. Edward Allworth, *The Modern Uzbeks: From the Fourteenth Century to the Present: A Cultural History* (Stanford, CA: Hoover Institution Press, 1990), 38.

39 Erik Zürcher, *Turkey: A Modern History* (London: I.B. Tauris, 1993), 100–104; Hasan Kayalı, *Arabs and Young Turks: Ottomanism, Arabism, and Islamism in the Ottoman Empire, 1908–1918* (Berkeley, CA: University of California Press, 1997), 72–74, 130–134.

40 See Chapter 2.

41 Atatürk had a personal falling out with the CUP leaders and presented himself as a radical alternative to them, but recent historical research has clearly demonstrated that most of his policies can be understood as selected Young Turk conceptions taken to their logical conclusions. Zürcher, *Turkey*, 180–181.

42 The name "Committee of Union and Progress" was derived from Auguste Comte's motto, "order and progress." See M. Şükrü Hanioğlu, *The Young Turks in Opposition* (New York: Oxford University Press, 1995), 74. This discussion of pre-1908 CUP politics draws heavily on Hanioğlu's pathbreaking work.

43 See Gustave Le Bon, *The Crowd: A Study of the Popular Mind* (London: T.F. Unwin, 1896).

44 As quoted in Hanioğlu, *Young Turks*, 194.

45 Zürcher, *Turkey*, 92–93.

46 For the sake of consistency, I will employ the (original) Arabic version of this term throughout. The Turkish version is *ümmet*.

47 Uriel Heyd, *Foundations of Turkish Nationalism: The Life and Teachings of Ziya Gökalp* (London: Luzac & Company and the Harvill Press, 1950), 55; Hanioğlu, *Young Turks*, chap. 9.

48 The use of the term *millet* to denote the Western concept of nation had been introduced in the mid-nineteenth century by Namik Kemal, a prominent figure among the empire's first generation of modern political dissidents, the Young Ottomans. Zürcher, *Turkey*, 71–72.

49 This discussion of Gökalp draws upon: Heyd, *Foundations of Turkish Nationalism*, part II, pp. 55–70 and chap. 5, and part III, chap. 2; Niyazi Berkes, trans. and ed., *Turkish Nationalism and Western Civilization: Selected Essays of Ziya Gökalp* (New York: Columbia University Press, 1959), 137–138, 259–262; Ahmet Emin Yalman, *Turkey in the World War* (New Haven, CT: Yale University Press, 1930), 190.

50 It is interesting in this context to note that Dmowski spoke at a convocation of nationalist organizations organized by Ahmed Riza in The Hague during the Hague Peace Conference of 1899. Fountain, *Dmowski*, 112–113; Hanioğlu, *The Young Turks*, 128–129.

51 The idea of Asian racial superiority was given impetus by the Japanese victory over Russia in the 1904–1905 war. Hanioğlu, *The Young Turks*, 210.
52 Landau, *Pan-Turkism*, 32–33.
53 From Mehmet Emin Yurdakul's poem "Wake up, Oh Turk," published in a 1918 collection but composed some years earlier, as quoted in Landau, *Pan-Turkism*, 32.
54 *Ibid.*, 38–39.
55 Masami Arai, *Turkish Nationalism in the Young Turk Era* (Leiden: Brill, 1992), chap. 4.
56 Zürcher, *Turkey*, 93–94.
57 Erik Zürcher, *The Unionist Factor: The Role of the Committee of Union and Progress in the Turkish National Movement, 1905–1926* (Leiden: Brill, 1984), 49–51; Reeva S. Simon, *Iraq between the Two World Wars: The Creation and Implementation of a Nationalist Ideology* (New York: Columbia University Press, 1986), chap. 2.
58 Zürcher, *Turkey*, 126–133; Stanford J. Shaw and Ezel Kural Shaw, *History of the Ottoman Empire and Modern Turkey*, vol. 2 (Cambridge: Cambridge University Press, 1977), 305–309. For an exploration of the tension between ethnic Turkish nationalism and liberal Ottomanism within the intellectual circles of the Young Turks between 1908 and 1914, see Arai, *Turkish Nationalism*, chaps 1, 3–4, and Conclusion.
59 Manoug J. Somakian, *Empires in Conflict: Armenia and the Great Powers 1895–1920* (London: I.B. Tauris, 1995), 40–44. In February 1914, under Great Power pressure, the Ottoman government reluctantly agreed to an internationally supervised administrative reform plan for the Armenian provinces. This agreement was never implemented. *Ibid.*, 57–63.
60 Hasan Kayalı (*Arabs and Young Turks*) argues that, taken as a whole, the public policies of the Young Turks did not reflect a preconceived Turkish nationalist agenda, but rather a centralizing form of Ottomanism. Insofar as this led the CUP regime to propagate the use of the Turkish language in the administration and educational systems of Arab regions, and to ride roughshod over certain local interests, a backlash was inevitable. But he contends that the portrayal of the CUP as a Turkish nationalist movement was a propaganda device employed by their decentralist opponents (advocates of greater regional autonomy) in the Arab world. However, research into the private correspondence of the CUP's leadership by scholars such as Zürcher and Hanioğlu suggests that there was more than a grain of truth to this propaganda line. In any event, it is hard to avoid the conclusion that centralist Ottomanism was functionally bound to lead to Turkish nationalism.
61 Hanioğlu, *The Young Turks*, 44–49; *idem*, "The Young Turks and the Arabs before the Revolution of 1908," in Rashid Khalidi, Lisa Anderson, Muhammad Muslih, and Reeva S. Simon, eds, *The Origins of Arab Nationalism* (New York: Columbia University Press, 1991); Shaw and Shaw, *History of the Ottoman Empire and Modern Turkey*, vol. 2, 309–310.
62 Kayalı, *Arabs and Young Turks*, 34, 107.
63 *Ibid.*, chap. 5 and pp. 106, 132, 140–141, 179–180, 187; Hanna Batatu, *The Old Social Classes and the Revolutionary Movements of Iraq: A Study of Iraq's Old Landed and Commercial Classes and of its Communists, Ba'thists, and Free Officers* (Princeton, NJ: Princeton University Press, 1978), 171–172.
64 Al-'Ahd had a large number of junior military officers from Mesopotamia – many of them of lower-middle-class background – among its members.
65 Eliezer Tauber, *The Arab Movements in World War I* (London: Frank Cass, 1993), 113.
66 Philip Khoury, *Urban Notables and Arab Nationalism: The Politics of Damascus 1860–1920* (Cambridge: Cambridge University Press, 1983), chap. 3; Ernest Dawn, "The Origins of Arab Nationalism," and Rashid Khalidi, "Ottomanism and Arabism in Syria before 1914: A Reassessment," in Khalidi *et al.*, *Origins of Arab Nationalism*; Sharabi, *Arab Intellectuals*, 121–128; Bassam Tibi, *Arab Nationalism: Between Islam and the Nation-State* (3rd edn, New York: St. Martin's Press, 1997), 109–114; Hourani, *Arabic Thought*, 280–285; Zeine N. Zeine, *Arab–Turkish Relations and the Emergence of Arab Nationalism*

(Beirut: Khayat's, 1958), chap. 5; Kayalı, *Arabs and Young Turks*, chap. 4 and pp. 69–70, 174–181.

67 There were also Christian writers from Lebanon and Syria who, during the last third of the nineteenth century, espoused a secular vision of Syrian and/or Arab nationalism as a framework within which religious minorities could take their place as equals alongside the Sunni Muslim majority in the Arab Middle East. George Antonius, *The Arab Awakening* (New York: Paragon Books, 1979; 1st edn, London, 1938), 45–60; Hourani, *Arabic Thought*, 273–279; Tibi, *Arab Nationalism*, 96–105. Their influence on the development of Arabism and Arab nationalism is no longer thought to have been as profound as George Antonius suggested in his influential 1938 book (cited above). For an insightful dissection of Antonius' work as an exercise in nationalist historiography, propaganda, and mythmaking, see William L. Cleveland, "The Arab Nationalism of George Antonius Reconsidered," in James Jankowski and Israel Gershoni, eds, *Rethinking Nationalism in the Arab Middle East* (New York: Columbia University Press, 1997). See also Albert Hourani, "The Arab Awakening Forty Years After," in Albert Hourani, *The Emergence of the Modern Middle East* (Berkeley, CA: University of California Press, 1981).

68 C. Ernest Dawn, *From Ottomanism to Arabism: Essays on the Origins of Arab Nationalism* (Urbana, IL: University of Illinois Press, 1973), 143–147.

69 Egypt had been under British control since 1882, and was thus beyond the reach of the Ottoman authorities.

70 Rashid Rida, "Al-'Arab wa al-Turk" (The Arabs and the Turks), *al-Manar* (Cairo), vol. 12 (1909) as reprinted in Yusuf Husayn Ibish and Yusuf Quzma Khuri, eds, *Maqalat al-Shaykh Rashid Rida al-siyasiyyah* (The political essays of Sheikh Rashid Rida), vol. 2 (Beirut: Dar Ibn Arabi, 1994), 648–649.

71 *Ibid.*, 642; Malcolm H. Kerr, *Islamic Reform: The Political and Legal Theories of Muhammad 'Abduh and Rashid Rida* (Berkeley, CA: University of California Press, 1966), 166–175; Hourani, *Arabic Thought*, 303–306.

72 Another Syrian expatriate in Cairo, 'Abd al-Rahman al-Kawakibi (1849–1903), took the nationalist implications of Rida's ideas a step further by calling openly for the transfer of the caliphate to the Arabs. See Dawn, *From Ottomanism to Arabism*, 84–85, 138–143; Hourani, *Arabic Thought*, chaps 6, 9; Sharabi, *Arab Intellectuals*, 102–104; Sylvia Haim, "Intorno alle origini della teoria del panarabismo," *Oriente Moderno*, vol. 35, no. 7 (July 1956), 409–421; Sylvia Haim, ed., *Arab Nationalism: An Anthology* (Berkeley and Los Angeles, CA: University of California Press, 1962), 16–29. Sylvia Haim has suggested that al-Kawakibi's idea of an Arab caliphate may have reflected the influence of the British Arabist Wilfrid Blunt's writings rather than being a purely original notion. This has provoked some Arab historians to condemn her as a Zionist propagandist. See, for example, Jan Dayah, *Sihafat al-Kawakibi* (The journalism of al-Kawakibi) (Beirut: Mu'assasat Fikr lil-Abhath wa-al-Nashr, 1984), 117–135.

73 Kerr, *Islamic Reform*, 153–166, 219–223.

74 Hourani, *Arabic Thought*, 309–311.

75 See Liah Greenfeld's extensive discussion of this phenomenon as it manifested itself in Russian and German nationalism. Liah Greenfeld, *Nationalism: Five Roads to Modernity* (Cambridge, MA: Harvard University Press, 1992), chaps 3–4.

76 Landau, *Pan-Turkism*, 34; Zürcher, *Turkey*, 136.

4 Straining the Imperial Molds, 1914–1918

1 For a cogent exposition of the impact of twentieth-century warfare on social culture and mass politics, see Arthur Marwick, *War and Social Change in the Twentieth Century: A Comparative Study of Britain, France, Germany, Russia and the United States* (London: Macmillan, 1974), 11–14 and *passim*.

2 In the case of the Ottoman empire, we will also examine the wartime evolution of Turkish nationalism, which was to culminate in the creation of a new Turkish nation-state in the aftermath of the conflict.

3 It has been argued that the wartime tension between Budapest and Vienna ran even deeper than that between the subject peoples and their rulers. See Robert Bideleux and Ian Jeffries, *A History of Eastern Europe: Crisis and Change* (London and New York: Routledge 1998), 399–400, drawing on Oscar Jaszi, *The Dissolution of the Habsburg Monarchy* (Chicago, IL: Chicago University Press, 1961; 1st edn, 1929), 365.

4 Günther E. Rothenberg, "The Habsburg Army in the First World War: 1914–1918," in Robert A. Kann, Bela K. Király, and Paula S. Fichtner, eds, *The Habsburg Empire in World War I* (Boulder, CO: East European Quarterly, 1977), 80–81.

5 Richard G. Plaschka, "Contradicting Ideologies: The Pressure of Ideological Conflicts in the Austro-Hungarian Army of World War I," in Kann *et al.*, *The Habsburg Empire in World War I*.

6 Victor S. Mamatey, *The United States and East Central Europe, 1914–1918: A Study in Wilsonian Diplomacy and Propaganda* (Princeton, NJ: Princeton University Press, 1957), chap. 5; Kenneth J. Calder, *Britain and the Origins of the New Europe, 1914–1918* (Cambridge: Cambridge University Press, 1976), chap. 7.

7 German was the language of command in the Habsburg army.

8 Jaszi, *Dissolution*, 141–148; István Deák, *Beyond Nationalism: A Social and Political History of the Habsburg Officer Corps, 1848–1918* (New York: Oxford University Press, 1992), *passim*.

9 Rothenberg, "The Habsburg Army in the First World War: 1914–1918," and Jay Luvaas, "A Unique Army: The Common Experience," in Kann *et al.*, *The Habsburg Empire in World War I*; Janos Decsy, "The Habsburg Army on the Threshold of Total War," in Béla Király and Nándor Dreisziger, eds, *East Central European Society in World War I* (Boulder, CO: East European Monographs, 1985), 284–285.

10 The major exceptions to this pattern were intermittent discrimination against Jews and favoritism toward Magyars, for whose services the joint army command had to compete with the Hungarian national guard. Deák, *Beyond Nationalism*, chap. 10.

11 *Ibid.* The classic novel portraying the survival of this mentality well into the age of nationalism is Joseph Roth's *Radetzky March* (trans. Joachim Neugroschel, Woodstock, NY: Overlook Press, 1995; Berlin: Gustav Kiepenheuer Verlag, 1932).

12 Leo Valiani, *The End of Austria–Hungary* (New York: Knopf, 1973), 197–198; Richard B. Spence, "Yugoslavs, the Austro-Hungarian Army, and the First World War" (Ph.D. diss., University of California at Santa Barbara, 1981), chap. 4.

13 Jaroslav Hašek, *The Good Soldier Švejk and his Fortunes in the World War* (trans. Cecil Parrott, New York: Thomas Y. Crowell Co., 1974; 1921–1923).

14 H. Louis Rees, *The Czechs during World War I* (Boulder, CO: East European Monographs, 1992), 16; Zbynek Zeman, *The Break-up of the Habsburg Empire, 1914–1918* (London: Oxford University Press, 1961), 51–52 and 54–57; Richard Georg Plaschka, "Zur Vorgeschichte des Überganges von Einheiten des Infanterieregiments Nr. 28 an der Russischen Front 1915," in Richard Georg Plaschka, *Nationalismus, Staatsgewalt, Widerstand: Aspekte nationaler und sozialer Entwicklung in Ostmittel- und Südosteuropa* (Munich: Oldenbourg, 1985).

15 John Reed reported seeing barbed wire placed *behind* the Austro-Hungarian lines on the Serbian front, presumably so as to prevent Serb soldiers in the Habsburg ranks from abandoning their positions. John Reed, *The War in Eastern Europe* (New York: Charles Scribner's Sons, 1916), 98.

16 This discussion draws on Spence, "Yugoslavs, the Austro-Hungarian Army," pp. 38–39 and chaps 5, 9, and 10; András Siklós, "The Internal Situation in the Austro-Hungarian Monarchy in the Spring and Summer of 1918," *Etudes historiques hongroises*, vol. 2 (1985), 288–300; Karel Pichlík, "Der militärische Zusammenbruch der Mittelmächte im Jahre 1918," in Richard Georg Plaschka and Karlheinz Mack,

eds, *Die Auflösung des Habsburgerreiches: Zusammenbruch und Neuorientierung im Donauraum* (Munich: Oldenbourg, 1970), 254–260.

17 On the demoralization of the Russian army, see Allan K. Wildman, *The End of the Russian Imperial Army*, vol. 1: *The Old Army and the Soldiers' Revolt (March–April 1917)* (Princeton, NJ: Princeton University Press, 1980), chaps 3–4.

18 Luvaas, "A Unique Army."

19 The Habsburg military authorities had been reporting that inappropriate fraternization was taking place between officers and rank-and-file in the 28th regiment during the period before its ignominious battlefield performance. This was seen as bad for discipline, but it certainly cannot be construed as an indication of weak group spirit. Plaschka, "Zur Vorgeschichte des Überganges."

20 Modris Eksteins, *Rites of Spring: The Great War and the Birth of the Modern Age* (New York: Anchor Books, 1990), 175; Leonard V. Smith, *Between Mutiny and Obedience: The Case of the French Fifth Infantry Division during World War I* (Princeton, NJ: Princeton University Press, 1994), *passim*; idem, "Remobilizing the Citizen-Soldier through the French Army Mutinies of 1917," in John Horne, ed., *State, Society and Mobilization in Europe during the First World War* (Cambridge: Cambridge University Press, 1997); Stéphane Audoin-Rouzeau, *Men at War 1914–1918: National Sentiment and Trench Journalism in France during the First World War* (Oxford: Berg, 1995), chaps 5–6.

21 Nándor F. Dreisziger, "The Dimensions of Total War in East Central Europe, 1914–18," in Király and Dreisziger, eds, *East Central European Society*, 16–18; Spence, "Yugoslavs, the Austro-Hungarian Army," chap. 4; Siklós, "Internal Situation," 290–294.

22 Victor S. Mamatey, "The Czech Wartime Dilemma: The Habsburgs or the Entente?" (note no. 4) in Király and Dreisziger, eds, *East Central European Society*.

23 POWs were heavily propagandized by rival Russian revolutionary parties seeking to recruit supporters and fighters for their causes.

24 Zeman, *Break-up*, 143–144; Siklós, "Internal Situation," 294–296.

25 This was in marked contrast to the armies of nation-states such as Britain, France, Germany, Bulgaria, Romania, where front-line entertainment and propaganda drawing on elements of popular culture were actively employed by the military authorities in an effort to maintain the troops' sense of connection to their homeland. Even if many soldiers in these armies became cynical about official nationalism, they generally retained a strong sense that in holding the line they were keeping the enemy away from their loved ones and native soil. As indicated above, to the extent that troops of subject nationalities in the Habsburg empire had contact with their homelands and loved ones, it tended to reinforce their inclination to desert. See J.G. Fuller, *Troop Morale and Popular Culture in the British and Dominion Armies, 1914–1918* (Oxford: Oxford University Press, 1990); Audoin-Rouzeau, *Men at War*; Vejas Gabrielius Liulevicius, "War Land: Peoples, Lands, and National Identity on the Eastern Front in World War I" (Ph.D. diss., University of Pennsylvania, 1994), 188–196; Evelina Kelbetcheva, "Between Apology and Denial: Bulgarian Culture during World War I," and Maria Bucur, "Romania: War, Occupation, Liberation," in Aviel Roshwald and Richard Stites, eds, *European Culture in the Great War: The Arts, Entertainment, and Propaganda, 1914–1918* (Cambridge: Cambridge University Press, 1999). For a romantic, fictional account of an ethnic Romanian officer's transformation from disciplined officer in the Habsburg army to fervent Romanian nationalist, see Liviu Rebreanu's interwar novel, *Forest of the Hanged* (London: Owen, 1967; 1930).

26 As quoted in Siklós, "Internal Situation," 300.

27 Siklós, "Internal Situation," 299–300; Spence, "Yugoslavs, the Austro-Hungarian Army," chaps 9–10; Richard Plaschka, "Contradicting Ideologies"; Mark Cornwall, "Morale and Patriotism in the Austro-Hungarian Army, 1914–1918," in Horne, ed., *State, Society and Mobilization*, 184–191.

28 The Czech National Socialists were advocates for workers' rights within the framework of a non-Marxist, explicitly nationalist ideology.

29 This section is heavily indebted to Rees, *The Czechs during World War I*. It also draws on the following sources: Zeman, *Break-up*; Mamatey, "The Czech Wartime Dilemma"; Victor S. Mamatey, "The Union of Czech Political Parties in the Reichsrat, 1916–1918," in Kann *et al.*, *The Habsburg Empire in World War I*; Valiani, *The End of Austria–Hungary*; Péter Hanák, "Die Volksmeinung während des letzten Kriegsjahres in Österreich-Ungarn," in Plaschka and Mack, eds, *Die Auflösung des Habsburgerreiches*; Richard Georg Plaschka, "Widerstand 1915 bis 1918 am Modell Pilsen," in Plaschka, *Nationalismus*, esp. p. 308; Claire Nolte, "Ambivalent Patriots: Czech Culture in the Great War," in Roshwald and Stites, eds, *European Culture*.

30 I use the term Austro-German to designate ethnically German subjects of the Habsburg monarchy.

31 Zeman (*Break-up*, 51–52) points out that these soldiers were largely of working-class background, from neighborhoods that were strongholds of the somewhat Russophile National Socialist Party.

32 Rees, *The Czechs during World War I*, *passim*. For its part, by 1918, the Magyar press was claiming that Hungary was subject to more ruthless requisitions than the Austrian half of the empire, with Czech troops and officials supposedly playing a disproportionate role in enforcing such measures and then siphoning the proceeds away from the military. Siklós, "Internal Situation," 287.

33 Zeman, *Break-up*, 133–139. Zeman suggests that social revolutionary sentiments gained ground among Austro-German and Magyar workers precisely because they belonged to ethnic groups that already enjoyed predominance within the Habsburg system; they had no pressing sense of national disenfranchisement that could take precedence over class interests. *Ibid.*, 145–146.

34 John Lampe, *Yugoslavia as History: Twice There Was a Country* (Cambridge: Cambridge University Press, 1996), 106–107; Ivo Banac, *The National Question in Yugoslavia* (Ithaca, NY: Cornell University Press, 1984), 366–367; Spence, "Yugoslavs, the Austro-Hungarian Army," 69–72. Of course, the Habsburg military's approach only served to reinforce Serb hostility to the Habsburg regime and identification with the Kingdom of Serbia. See Hanák, "Die Volksmeinung."

35 Nicholas J. Miller, *Between Nation and State: Serbian Politics in Croatia before the First World War* (Pittsburgh, PA: University of Pittsburgh Press, 1997), chap. 5.

36 Banac, *The National Question*, 125; Zeman, *Break-up*, 57–60; Spence, "Yugoslavs, the Austro-Hungarian Army," 62 and chap. 7. The quotation from *Hravatska* is taken from *ibid.*, 63.

37 Seton-Watson to Ivo Lupis-Vukić (17 October 1909), Seton-Watson to Herbert Fisher (9 October 1916), and Herbert Fisher to Seton-Watson (11 October 1916), in Hugh and Christopher Seton-Watson, Ljubo Boban, Mirjana Gross, Bogdan Krizman, and Dragovan Šepić, eds, *R.W. Seton-Watson and the Yugoslavs: Correspondence, 1906–1941. Vol. 1: 1906–1918* (London: British Academy, 1976), 50–54, 275–282.

38 Wayne S. Vucinich, "Mlada Bosna and the First World War," in Kann *et al.*, *The Habsburg Empire in World War I*; Zeman, *Break-up*, 59–60; Dragan Zivojinovic, "Serbia and Montenegro: The Home Front, 1914–18," in Király and Dreisziger, *East Central European Society in World War I*, 252; Banac, *The National Question*, 129–132; Spence, "Yugoslavs, the Austro-Hungarian Army," 75–80 and chap. 7. For a fictionalized account of these events, see Ivo Andrić, *Bridge on the Drina* (trans. Lovett F. Edwards, Chicago, IL: University of Chicago Press, 1977 edn), chaps 22–23. A Croat by birth, Andrić became active in the Mlada Bosna (Young Bosnia) movement before the war and was interned by the Habsburg authorities as soon as the conflict began. In later years, he moved to Belgrade and identified himself as a Serb. Lampe, *Yugoslavia as History*, 89 and 106.

39 This discussion draws upon: Andrew Wachtel, "Culture in the South Slavic Lands, 1914–1918," in Roshwald and Stites, eds, *European Culture*; Banac, *The National Question*, 125–126; Cornwall, "Morale and Patriotism," 181–182.

40 My main source of information on the Green Cadres is Ivo Banac, "'Emperor Karl has become a Comitadji': the Croatian Disturbances of Autumn 1918," *The Slavonic and East European Review*, vol. 70, no. 2 (April 1992), 284–305. See also Banac, *The National Question*, 127, 129–131; Spence, "Yugoslavs, the Austro-Hungarian Army," chap. 8.

41 In October–November 1918, many Serb villages sent petitions to the newly formed Croatian National Council calling for immediate unification with Serbia. Banac, *The National Question*, 129–131.

42 This discussion relies primarily upon: Richard Georg Plaschka, "The Army and Internal Conflict in the Austro-Hungarian Empire, 1918," in Király and Dreisziger, *East Central European Society*; Banac, *The National Question*, 127–140; Siklós, "Internal Situation," 286–287; Lampe, *Yugoslavia as History*, 108–111.

43 Stjepan Radić, leader of the Croatian Peasant Party, was one figure in the National Council who spoke up vociferously against the virtually unconditional union with Serbia, warning his colleagues that "you evidently do not care a whit that our peasant in general, and especially our Croat peasant, does not wish to hear one more thing ... about a state which you are imposing on him by force. ..." Quoted in Tim Judah, *The Serbs: History, Myth and the Destruction of Yugoslavia* (New Haven, CT: Yale University Press, 1997), 105.

44 Hanák, "Die Volksmeinung," 63–66; Zeman, *Break-up*, 139 and 219. See also E.J. Hobsbawm, *Nations and Nationalism since 1780: Programme, Myth, Reality* (Cambridge: Cambridge University Press, 1990), 126–130. Hobsbawm contends that the quest for socialism was invariably a stronger and more fundamental impulse among the working classes than the striving for national self-determination: only when the crushing of the January strike, the conclusion of the Brest-Litovsk negotiations in March 1918 on annexationist terms, and the intensification of the war on the Western fronts made it clear that a socialist peace was not within sight, did nationalism win mass support. As long as socialism and nationalism seemed to be equally viable options, he insists, it was the former that generated the most enthusiasm. But Hobsbawm's argument is difficult to reconcile with the Czech workers' failure to strike *en masse* in January 1918 (which eased the authorities' task of suppressing the strike in German Austria and Hungary) and the grassroots pressure within the Czech Social Democratic Party that led to the movement's alignment with the Czech nationalist camp as early as the summer and autumn of 1917 (see above).

45 I use the Gregorian (Western) calendar throughout this text. The Julian (Old Style) calendar still used in Russia at the time of the revolution was thirteen days behind the Western calendar.

46 Hubertus Jahn, *Patriotic Culture in Russia during World War I* (Ithaca, NY and London: Cornell University Press, 1995), Conclusion and *passim*; Orlando Figes, *A People's Tragedy: A History of the Russian Revolution* (New York: Viking, 1996), 282–288.

47 Mark von Hagen, "The Great War and the Mobilization of Ethnicity in the Russian Empire," in Barnett R. Rubin and Jack Snyder, eds, *Post-Soviet Political Order: Conflict and State Building* (London: Routledge, 1998).

48 See Aviel Roshwald, "Jewish Cultural Identity in Eastern and Central Europe during the Great War," in Roshwald and Stites, *European Culture*.

49 Mark von Hagen, "Writing the History of Russia as Empire: The Perspective of Federalism," in Catherine Evtuhov, Boris Gasparov, Alexander Ospovat, and Mark von Hagen, eds, *Kazan, Moscow, St. Petersburg: Multiple Faces of the Russian Empire* (Moscow: OGI, 1997), 400.

50 Wildman, *The End of the Russian Imperial Army*, vol. 1, 103.

51 The contact between Finnish and non-Finnish laborers engaged in construction of fortifications also aroused fears among the Finnish middle classes that their proletariat was being infected by the dangerous mentalities and barbaric habits attributed to "foreign" workers. The notion that segments of the working class had become polluted by alien values helped pave the way for the massacres of Finland's socialist

Red Guards and their supporters during the country's White Terror of 1918, which was justified as a national cleansing operation. Anthony F. Upton, *The Finnish Revolution* (Minneapolis, MN: University of Minnesota Press, 1980), 16–17.

52 Ronald Grigor Suny, *The Revenge of the Past: Nationalism, Revolution and the Collapse of the Soviet Union* (Stanford, CA: Stanford University Press, 1993), 74–75; Andrejs Plakans, *The Latvians: A Short History* (Stanford, CA: Hoover Institution Press, 1995), 113–118.

53 The Russian capital, St. Petersburg, had been renamed Petrograd after the outbreak of the war.

54 See Wildman, *The End of the Russian Imperial Army*, vol. 2: *The Road to Soviet Power and Peace* (Princeton, NJ: Princeton University Press, 1987), *passim*.

55 Andreas Kappeler, *Russland als Vielvölkerreich* (Munich: C.H. Beck, 1993), chap. 9; Figes, *A People's Tragedy*, 380.

56 Arno J. Mayer, *Wilson vs. Lenin: Political Origins of the New Diplomacy, 1917–1918* (Cleveland, OH: World Publishing Company, 1964 edn; first published as *Political Origins of the New Diplomacy, 1917–1918*, New Haven, CT: Yale University Press, 1959), 75 and 83.

57 This discussion draws upon: Richard Pipes, *The Formation of the Soviet Union: Communism and Nationalism, 1917–1923* (rev. edn, Cambridge, MA: Harvard University Press, 1964; 1954), 29–31, 50–51; Figes, *A People's Tragedy*, 371–372, 375–376; Robert Paul Browder and Alexander F. Kerensky, eds, *The Russian Provisional Government, 1917: Documents*, vol. 1 (Stanford, CA: Stanford University Press, 1961), 321–323 and 334–335; von Hagen, "Writing the History of Russia as Empire," 398; Wiktor Sukiennicki, *East Central Europe during World War I: From Foreign Domination to National Independence* (Boulder, CO: East European Monographs, 1984), vol. 1, 325–326.

58 Poland and Finland were regarded as special cases because there were nineteenth-century legal precedents for their administrative autonomy. It should also be noted that after the outbreak of the Great War, even the tsarist government had paid lip service to the idea of Polish autonomy as a propaganda weapon in its struggle with the Central Powers.

59 Nicholas P. Vakar, *Belorussia, The Making of a Nation: A Case Study* (Cambridge, MA: 1956), chap. 7; Suny, *Revenge*, 30–35. The electoral results also reflected the heavy participation of soldiers in the Belorussian sector of the Western Front, who voted in overwhelming numbers for the Bolsheviks as the party that promised to bring about an immediate peace.

60 *Ibid.*; Pipes, *Formation*, 73–75 and 151.

61 Suny, *Revenge, passim*.

62 In referring to regions such as the Ukraine (now known simply as Ukraine) and Belorussia (Belarus), I use the English terms employed at the time.

63 This discussion of Ukrainian nationalist politics draws upon: John S. Reshetar, *The Ukrainian Revolution, 1917–1920: A Study in Nationalism* (Princeton, NJ: Princeton University Press, 1952), chap. 2; Thomas M. Prymak, *Mykhailo Hrushevsky: The Politics of National Culture* (Toronto: University of Toronto Press, 1987), chap. 6; Pipes, *Formation*, 53–73; Lew Shankowsky, "Disintegration of the Imperial Russian Army in 1917," *The Ukrainian Quarterly*, XIII, 4 (December 1957), 314–315; Figes, *A People's Tragedy*, 374. The Rada's November 1917 proclamation of Ukrainian independence was still qualified by a pledge to work toward the transformation of Russia into "a federation of equal and free peoples." Unqualified independence was declared in January 1918, in the wake of Bolshevik attacks. Ivan Rudnytsky, "The Fourth Universal and its Ideological Antecedents," in Taras Hunczak, ed., *The Ukraine, 1917–1921: A Study in Revolution* (Cambridge, MA: Harvard University Press, 1977).

64 It should be noted that the better-off peasants – the so-called agrarian middle class – were better organized and hence more vocal politically than the poorest rural strata.

65 For an attempt to minimize the significance of peasant support for the USRs, see Arthur Takach, "In Search of Ukrainian National Identity: 1840–1921," *Ethnic and Racial Studies*, vol. 19, no. 3 (July 1996), 640–659.

66 Alexandre Bennigssen and Chantal Quelquejay, *Les Mouvements nationaux chez les Musulmans de Russie: Le 'Sultangalievisme' au Tatarstan* (Paris and The Hague: Mouton, 1960), 66–69; *idem, La Presse et le mouvement national chez les Musulmans de Russie avant 1920* (Paris and The Hague: Mouton, 1964), 185–188; Pipes, *Formation*, 75–79.

67 Martha Brill Olcott, *The Kazakhs* (Stanford, CA: Hoover Institution Press, 1987), chap. 4 and pp. 118–126; Edward A. Allworth, *The Modern Uzbeks: From the Fourteenth Century to the Present, A Cultural History* (Stanford, CA: Hoover Institution Press, 1990), 159–160; Hélène Carrère d'Encausse, *Islam and the Russian Empire: Reform and Revolution in Central Asia* (trans. Quintin Hoare, Berkeley and Los Angeles, CA: University of California Press, 1988), 120; Pipes, *Formation*, 81–86.

68 On the Kazakhs, see Olcott, *Kazakhs*, 101–103, 114–118, and chap. 6.

69 The Kazakhs had been nominally Muslim for centuries, but knowledge of Muslim doctrine, let alone its practice, had remained very superficial. To the south, in Turkestan, there was widespread hostility toward the Volga Tatars as agents of Russian imperialism. Allworth, *Uzbeks*, 190–191.

70 Tadeusz Swietochowski, *Russian Azerbaijan, 1905–1920: The Shaping of National Identity in a Muslim Community* (Cambridge: Cambridge University Press, 1985), 91–94, 129–135; Suny, *Revenge*, 41–43.

71 Allworth, *Uzbeks*, 161–172; d'Encausse, *Islam and the Russian Empire*, chaps 7–8.

72 The following discussion addresses the ideas developed in Ronald Grigor Suny, "Nationalism and Class in the Russian Revolution. A Comparative Discussion," in Edith Ragovin Frankel, Jonathan Frankel, and Baruch Knei-Paz, eds, *Revolution in Russia: Reassessments of 1917* (Cambridge: Cambridge University Press, 1992) and Suny, *Revenge*, chaps 1–2.

73 Suny, *Revenge*, 16–19, 33.

74 Plakans, *Latvians*, 113–118; Suny, *Revenge*, 55–58.

75 Richard Pipes, *The Russian Revolution* (New York: Knopf, 1990), 530. The ethno-linguistic distinctiveness of the Latvian riflemen and their strong *esprit de corps* made them singularly effective as Bolshevik shock troops in the Russian capital, for it set them apart from the general population and made them immune to the blandishments of rival parties. Andrew Ezergailis, *The Latvian Impact on the Bolshevik Revolution. The First Phase: September 1917 to April 1918* (Boulder, CO: East European Monographs, 1983), 281–282 and chap. 9.

76 Stanley W. Page, *The Formation of the Baltic States: A Study of the Effects of Great Power Politics upon the Emergence of Lithuania, Latvia, and Estonia* (New York: Howard Fertig, 1970), 17–21 and chap. 5; Andrew Ezergailis, *The 1917 Revolution in Latvia* (Boulder, CO: East European Monographs, 1974), 199–202.

77 Ezergailis, *Latvian Impact*, 205–213.

78 As non-Russians, the Latvian Bolsheviks could be holier than the Pope (so to speak) on the issue of nationalism – articulating a unitarist vision of the future socialist state that left even less room for national self-determination than Lenin's stated position. Ezergailis, *Latvian Impact*, 246.

79 Ahmed Emin Yalman, *Turkey in the World War* (New Haven, CT: Yale University Press, 1930), 105–106.

80 Erik Zürcher, *Turkey: A Modern History* (London: I.B. Tauris, 1993), 97–116; Bernard Lewis, *The Emergence of Modern Turkey* (London: Oxford University Press, 1961), 225–227.

81 Jacob M. Landau, *Pan-Turkism: From Irredentism to Cooperation* (Bloomington and Indianapolis, IN: Indiana University Press, 1995), 45–51, 53; Yalman, *Turkey*, 174–177; Philip Hendrick Stoddard, "The Ottoman Government and the Arabs, 1911–1918: A Preliminary Study of the Teşkilât-i Mahsusa" (Ph.D. diss., Princeton University, 1963), 68–70. The German embassy in Istanbul actually played an active

role in urging the pan-Islamic theme upon the CUP as the basis for an anti-Entente propaganda campaign. This approach was the brainchild of German Foreign Ministry official Baron Max von Oppenheim, an archaeologist, diplomat, propagandist, and spy of Jewish origin whose Middle Eastern archaeological excavations often served as cover for intelligence-gathering operations. Donald M. McKale, "Germany and the Arab Question in the First World War," *Middle Eastern Studies*, vol. 29, no. 2 (April 1993), 236–253; Fritz Fischer, *Germany's Aims in the First World War* (New York: Norton, 1967; 1961), 123–124. Oppenheim continued to dabble in Middle Eastern espionage and anti-British incitement into the 1930s, having earned the status of "honorary Aryan" under the Nazis. Aviel Roshwald, *Estranged Bedfellows: Britain and France in the Middle East during the Second World War* (New York: Oxford University Press, 1990), 49.

82 This is the prevailing view in recent scholarship (see references below). For a dissenting opinion that plays down the significance of Turkish nationalism within the CUP, see Hasan Kayalı, *Arabs and Young Turks: Ottomanism, Arabism, and Islamism in the Ottoman Empire, 1908–1918* (Berkeley and Los Angeles, CA: University of California Press, 1997).

83 This discussion draws upon: Zürcher, *Turkey*, 114, 134; Erik Zürcher, *The Unionist Factor: The Role of the Committee of Union and Progress in the Turkish National Movement, 1905–1926* (Leiden: E.J. Brill, 1984), 49–51; Lisa Anderson, "Nationalist Sentiment in Libya," in Rashid Khalidi, Lisa Anderson, Muhammad Muslih, and Reeva S. Simon, eds, *The Origins of Arab Nationalism* (New York: Columbia University Press, 1991), 229–231; Masami Arai, *Turkish Nationalism in the Young Turk Era* (Leiden: Brill, 1992), chap. 5.

84 Also, 1916 witnessed the surrender (on 29 April) of the besieged British garrison at Kut in Mesopotamia. Martin Gilbert, *The First World War: A Complete History* (New York: Henry Holt, 1994), 211–214, 228, 241, 244.

85 German intelligence officers were also involved in some of these, and related, activities. Fischer, *Germany's Aims*, 126–131.

86 Landau, *Pan-Turkism*, 49–56; Yalman, *Turkey*, chap. 16. See also Chapter 6 of this book.

87 Yalman, *Turkey*, 182–186.

88 This discussion of Turkish economic nationalism is based on Yalman, *Turkey*, chaps 9–13; Feroz Ahmad, "Vanguard of a Nascent Bourgeoisie: The Social and Economic Policy of the Young Turks 1908–1918," in Osman Okyar and Halil Inalcik, eds, *Social and Economic History of Turkey (1071–1920)* (Ankara: Meteksan, 1980); Feroz Ahmad, *The Making of Modern Turkey* (London: Routledge, 1993), 40–46; Zürcher, *The Unionist Factor*, 76–77; Zürcher, *Turkey*, 127–131, 171; Niyazi Berkes, *The Development of Secularism in Turkey* (Montreal: McGill University Press, 1964), 335–337 and 425–427. The multifaceted Russian-Jewish Marxist intellectual, German agent, and Bolshevik-German intermediary, Alexander Helphand (Parvus), who resided in Istanbul during much of the war, played an influential role in the CUP's development of a nationalist economic doctrine modeled on Friedrich List's nineteenth-century protectionist plan for German industrialization. See Ahmad, "Vanguard," 336–337; Zürcher, *Turkey*, 130; Berkes, *Development of Secularism*, 335–337 and 425; Z.A.B. Zeman and W.B. Scharlau, *The Merchant of Revolution: The Life of Alexander Israel Helphand* (London: Oxford University Press, 1965), 127–128.

89 Yalman, *Turkey*, 197–199; Zürcher, *Turkey*, 129–131, 134–135.

90 Stoddard, "The Ottoman Government and the Arabs, 1911–1918," 52–59; Zürcher, *Turkey*, 114–115, 121, 130; Zürcher, *The Unionist Factor*, 76–77, 120–121.

91 Zürcher, *Turkey*, 120–121; Ronald Grigor Suny, *Looking Toward Ararat: Armenia in Modern History* (Bloomington and Indianapolis, IN: Indiana University Press, 1993), 114. For a defensively pro-Turkish version of these events, see Justin McCarthy, *The Ottoman Turks: An Introductory History to 1923* (London: Longman, 1997), 365.

92 Zürcher, *Turkey*, 120–121; Suny, *Looking Toward Ararat*, 109–115; Manoug J. Somakian, *Empires in Conflict: Armenia and the Great Powers 1895–1920* (London and New York: Tauris, 1995), 70–96; Yalman, *Turkey*, chap. 18. For a flat denial that the Ottoman authorities planned any of the violence against the Armenians, see Stanford J. Shaw and Ezel Kural Shaw, *History of the Ottoman Empire and Modern Turkey*, vol. 2 (Cambridge: Cambridge University Press, 1977), 314–317.

93 See Selim Deringil, "The Ottoman Origins of Kemalist Nationalism: Namik Kemal to Mustafa Kemal," *European History Quarterly*, vol. 23, no. 2 (April 1993), 165–191.

94 This section draws upon the following sources: Eliezer Tauber, *The Arab Movements in World War I* (London and Portland, OR: Frank Cass, 1993), 25–37, 62–80, 113; Philip Khoury, *Urban Notables and Arab Nationalism: The Politics of Damascus 1860–1920* (Cambridge: Cambridge University Press, 1983), 74; Sulayman Musa, *Al-Harakah al-Arabiya: sirat al-marhalah al-ula lil-nahdah al-Arabiyah al-hadithah, 1908–1924* (The Arab Movement: The History of the First Stage of the Modern Arab Awakening, 1908–1924) (Beirut: Dar al-Nahar lil-Nashr, 1977), 261–262; Stoddard, "The Ottoman Government and the Arabs, 1911–1918," 147; C. Ernest Dawn, "The Rise of Arabism in Syria," *The Middle East Journal*, vol. 16, no. 2 (1962), 145–168; Bassam Tibi, *Arab Nationalism: A Critical Enquiry* (2nd edn, New York: St. Martin's Press, 1990), 118–122; William L. Cleveland, *The Making of an Arab Nationalist: Ottomanism and Arabism in the Life and Thought of Sati' al-Husri* (Princeton, NJ: Princeton University Press, 1971), x–xi and 32–41.

95 Dawn, "The Rise of Arabism in Syria," 151; Muhammad Kurd 'Ali, *Memoirs of Muhammad Kurd 'Ali: A Selection* (trans. Khalil Totah, Washington, DC: American Council of Learned Societies, 1954), 56–58. Kurd 'Ali also argued that his pre-war advocacy of Arab autonomy had not constituted disloyalty to the Ottoman empire as such. *Ibid.*, 34–37.

96 The Government of India (Raj) authorities in charge of Britain's Mesopotamia campaign were opposed to the efforts of their counterparts in Cairo to incite Arab nationalism. See Briton Cooper Busch, *Britain, India, and the Arabs, 1914–1921* (Berkeley and Los Angeles, CA: University of California Press, 1971), chaps 2–3 and pp. 202–214; Bruce Westrate, *The Arab Bureau: British Policy in the Middle East, 1916–1920* (University Park, PA: The Pennsylvania State University Press, 1992), chap. 4; Tauber, *The Arab Movements*, 31.

5 New Arenas of Action: Nationalisms of Occupation and Exile, 1914–1918

1 This discussion draws upon: Heinz Lemke, *Allianz und Rivalität: Die Mittelmächte und Polen im Ersten Weltkrieg* (East Berlin: Akademie-Verlag, 1977), pp. 18–19, 54–73, chaps 3, 6, and *passim*; David Stevenson, *The First World War and International Politics* (Oxford: Oxford University Press, 1988), 91–95, 102–103; Fritz Fischer, *Germany's Aims in the First World War* (New York: Norton, 1967; 1961), 189–197, 244–246; Wiktor Sukiennicki, *East Central Europe during World War I: From Foreign Domination to National Independence* (2 vols, Boulder, CO: East European Monographs, 1984), vol. 1, chap. 14; Jan Molenda, "Social Changes in Poland during World War I," in Béla Király and Nándor Dreisziger, eds, *East Central European Society in World War I* (Boulder, CO: Social Science Monographs, 1985).

2 It is also worth noting that German ethnographic research in occupied Eastern Europe served as an important source of information for The Inquiry, the semi-official American commission charged with preparing recommendations – particularly regarding national boundaries – for the future peace settlement. Lawrence E. Gelfand, *The Inquiry: American Preparations for Peace, 1917–1919* (New Haven, CT: Yale University Press, 1963), 107–108.

3 Lemke, *Allianz*, 18–19. For a contemporaneous argument in favor of Germany's marrying idealism to realism by assuming the role of liberator of East European

nationalities, see Wilhelm Feldman, *Die Zukunft Polens und der deutsch-polnische Ausgleich* (Berlin: Verlag Karl Curtius, September 1915).

4 This discussion of Ober Ost draws heavily on the pathbreaking work of Vejas Gabrielius Liulevicius, "War Land: Peoples, Lands, and National Identity on the Eastern Front in World War I" (Ph.D. diss., University of Pennsylvania, 1994).

5 *Ibid., passim.*

6 It should be noted that the use of ethnography to categorize and control or co-opt indigenous peoples was a common feature of nineteenth- and twentieth-century imperial administrative culture. See the discussion in Daniel Brower, "Islam and Ethnicity: Russian Colonial Policy in Turkestan," in Daniel R. Brower and Edward J. Lazzerini, eds, *Russia's Orient: Imperial Borderlands and Peoples, 1700–1917* (Bloomington and Indianapolis, IN: Indiana University Press, 1997).

7 Liulevicius, "War Land," chap. 3. See also the Yiddish novel by Oyzer Varshavski, *Shmuglars* (Smugglers) (Warsaw and New York: Weissenberg Ferlag, 1921; 1920).

8 This section draws upon: Liulevicius, "War Land," 224–234, 260–280; Gerd Linde, *Die Deutsche Politik in Litauen im Ersten Weltkrieg* (Wiesbaden: Otto Harrassowitz, 1965), 89–170; Alfred Erich Senn, *The Emergence of Modern Lithuania* (New York: Columbia University Press, 1959), 25–46.

9 For a fuller discussion of this topic, see Aviel Roshwald, "Jewish Cultural Identity in Eastern and Central Europe during the Great War," in Aviel Roshwald and Richard Stites, eds, *European Culture during the Great War: The Arts, Entertainment, and Propaganda, 1914–1918* (Cambridge: Cambridge University Press, 1999).

10 Steven J. Zipperstein, "The Politics of Relief: The Transformation of Russian Jewish Communal Life during the First World War," in Jonathan Frankel, ed., *Jews and the Eastern European Crisis, 1914–21* (Oxford: Oxford University Press, 1988); David G. Roskies, *Against the Apocalypse: Responses to Catastrophe in Modern Jewish Culture* (Cambridge, MA: Harvard University Press, 1984), 92; S. An-sky (Shlomo-Zanvill Rappoport), *Der yidisher khurbn fun Poilen, Galitsye un Bukovina fun tag-buch 1914–1917* (The Jewish Catastrophe in Poland, Galicia, and Bukovina from the 1914–17 Diary), in *Gezamelte Shriftn* (Collected Writings), vols. 4–6 (Warsaw, Vilnius, New York: An-sky Publishing Company, 1927–1928), vol. 4, p. 11; Hans Rogger, *Jewish Policies and Right-Wing Politics in Imperial Russia* (London: Macmillan, 1986), 100–101. Peter Holquist argues that Russian wartime policy toward Jews and ethnic Germans was a manifestation of longstanding ideas prevalent in the Russian military about the potential uses of ethnic categorization and social engineering in the creation of a more cohesive body politic. Peter Holquist, "Total Mobilization and Population Politics: Russia's Deluge (1914–1921) and its European Context," paper presented at "Conference on Russia and the Great War," St. Petersburg, Russia, May 1998.

11 See Sammy Gronemann, *Hawdoloh und Zapfenstreich* (Berlin: Jüdischer Verlag, 1925), insert after p. 24. See also Zosa Szajkowski, "The German Appeal to the Jews of Poland, August 1914," *The Jewish Quarterly Review*, New Series, vol. 59 (1969), 311–320.

12 Hirsh Abramovich, *Farshvundene geshtalten (zikhroynes und silueten)* (Disappeared Figures (Memories and Silhouettes)) (Buenos Aires: Tsentral Ferband fun Poylishe Yiden in Argentine, 1958), 297–299. My thanks to the late Dina Abramowicz of the YIVO Institute for Jewish Research in New York for bringing this useful source to my attention.

13 Ezra Mendelsohn, *Zionism in Poland: The Formative Years, 1915–1926* (New Haven, CT: Yale University Press, 1981), 77; Zosa Szajkowski, "The Struggle for Yiddish during World War I: The Attitude of German Jewry," *Leo Baeck Institute Year Book IX* (London, 1964), 131–158, 140; Abramovich, "Di Vilner Gezelshaft 'Hilf durch Arbet" and "A yidishe landwirtshaft-shule in Poilen," in *Farshvundene geshtalten*, 327–339 and 340–356; see also *ibid.*, footnote on p. 292; Gronemann, *Hawdoloh*, 84–85; "Aus dem Arbeitsleben des Rabbiner Dr. Sali Levi" (pamphlet published in memory of Rabbi

Sali Levi by the board of directors of the Jewish community of Mainz, 21 April 1951), 4–6, YIVO Institute for Jewish Research, New York.

14 Egmont Zechlin, *Die deutsche Politik und die Juden im Ersten Weltkrieg* (Göttingen: Vandenhoeck & Ruprecht, 1969), chap. 12.

15 This was accompanied by a fund-raising drive on behalf of the beleaguered Jewish settlement (*yishuv*) in Palestine, whose economic and even physical survival was under threat by the hostile policies of Jemal Pasha. Mendelsohn, *Zionism*, chap. 1; Zechlin, *Die deutsche Politik und die Juden*, 176–178; *Der Moment* (Warsaw-based Yiddish-language daily), 13 July 1917 and various other articles on Palestine relief, summer 1917. German diplomatic intervention – motivated in part by concern over American public opinion prior to US entry into the war in April 1917 – had played a critical role in saving the *yishuv* from mass deportation. Isaiah Friedman, *Germany, Turkey, and Zionism, 1897–1918* (Oxford: Oxford University Press, 1977), part III.

16 Szajkowski, "The Struggle for Yiddish," 147; Steven E. Aschheim, *Brothers and Strangers: The East European Jew in German and German Jewish Consciousness, 1800–1923* (Madison, WI: University of Wisconsin Press, 1982), 165–168; Zechlin, *Die deutsche Politik und die Juden*, chaps 9–11; Gershon C. Bacon, "The Poznanski Affair of 1921: Kehillah Politics and the Internal Political Realignment of Polish Jewry," in Frankel, ed., *The Jews and the European Crisis*; idem, "Agudat Israel in Interwar Poland," in Yisrael Gutman, Ezra Mendelsohn, Jehuda Reinharz, and Chone Shmeruk, eds, *The Jews of Poland between Two World Wars* (Hanover, NH: University Press of New England, 1989); Robert Moses Shapiro, "Aspects of Jewish Self-Government in Lódz, 1914–1939," in Antony Polonsky, ed., *From Shtetl to Socialism: Studies from Polin* (London and Washington, DC: Littman Library, 1993); Mark Levene, *War, Jews, and the New Europe: The Diplomacy of Lucien Wolf, 1914–1919* (Oxford: Oxford University Press, 1992), 175–176.

17 Linde, *Die Deutsche Politik in Litauen*, 71–79; Lemke, *Allianz und Rivalität*, 288–290.

18 Aschheim, *Brothers and Strangers*, 157–160, 163; Szajkowski, "The Struggle for Yiddish"; idem, "The Komitee fuer den Osten und Zionism," in Raphael Patai, ed., *Herzl Year Book*, vol. 7 (New York, 1971), 199–240.

19 Vilna is the transliteration of the Yiddish pronunciation of this town's name.

20 Nahma Sandrow, *Vagabond Stars: A World History of Yiddish Theater* (New York: Harper & Row, 1977), chap. 8; Gronemann, *Hawdoloh*, 195–198; Luba Kadison and Joseph Buloff, with Irving Genn, *On Stage, Off Stage: Memories of a Lifetime in the Yiddish Theatre* (Cambridge, MA: Harvard University Press, 1992), 6–10; Liulevicius, "War Land," 185–186.

21 Even such a qualified reference to the rule of law in German-occupied Eastern Europe demands yet further qualification. It has meaning only within the limited framework of comparison with the former Russian administration of these lands. The very wide gap that separated the German military's rigid and authoritarian juridical practice from any true sense of justice is bitterly conveyed in Arnold Zweig's novel, *The Case of Sergeant Grisha* (published in German in 1927), discussed by Liulevicius in "War Land," 93–94. Arnold Zweig served as an officer attached to the press section of the Ober Ost administration.

22 Gronemann, *Hawdoloh*, 169–173.

23 Liulevicius, "War Land," 233; Linde, *Die Deutsche Politik in Litauen*, 37–39.

24 For a discussion of Serbian martyrdom myths, see Tim Judah, *The Serbs: History, Myth and the Destruction of Yugoslavia* (New Haven, CT: Yale University Press, 1997), chaps 3–4.

25 *The Other Balkan Wars: A 1913 Carnegie Endowment Inquiry in Retrospect with a New Introduction and Reflections on the Present Conflict by George F. Kennan* (Washington, DC: Carnegie Foundation for International Peace, 1993), passim; Barbara Jelavich, *History of the Balkans*, vol. 2: *Twentieth Century* (Cambridge: Cambridge University Press, 1983), 95–100.

26 For this discussion, I have drawn upon: C.E.J. Fryer, *The Destruction of Serbia in 1915* (New York: East European Monographs, 1997), chaps 2–6, 12, 14; Dragan Zivojinović, "Serbia and Montenegro: The Home Front, 1914–18" and Dimitrije Djordjević, "Vojvoda Putnik, The Serbian High Command, and Strategy in 1914," in Király and Dreisziger, eds, *East Central European Society*, 239–245; Jelavich, *History of the Balkans*, vol. 2, 115; John Reed, *The War in Eastern Europe* (New York: Charles Scribner's Sons, 1916), 42–49, 57–74; John Clinton Adams, *Flight in Winter* (Princeton, NJ: Princeton University Press, 1942), *passim*; Stilyan Noykov, "The Bulgarian Army in World War I, 1915–18," in Király and Dreisziger, *East Central European Society*; John Lampe, *Yugoslavia as History: Twice There Was a Country* (Cambridge: Cambridge University Press, 1996), 102, 107–108; Evelina Kelbetcheva, "Between Apology and Denial: Bulgarian Culture during World War I," in Roshwald and Stites, eds, *European Culture*; Andrew Wachtel, "Culture in the South Slavic Lands, 1914–1918," in *ibid.*, 209; Zbynek Zeman, *The Break-up of the Habsburg Empire, 1914–1918* (London: Oxford University Press, 1961), 60; Dragolioub Yovanovitch, *Les Effets économiques et sociaux de la guerre en Serbie* (Paris: Les Presses Universitaires de France, 1930), chap. 7.

27 As quoted in Zivojinović, "Serbia and Montenegro," 252.

28 See Geoff Eley, "Remapping the Nation: War, Revolutionary Upheaval, and State Formation in Eastern Europe, 1914–1923," in Peter J. Potichnyj and Howard Aster, eds, *Ukrainian–Jewish Relations in Historical Perspective* (Edmonton: Canadian Institute of Ukrainian Studies, University of Alberta, 1988, 2nd edn 1990).

29 Fischer, *Germany's Aims*, 120–138.

30 Mark von Hagen, "The Great War and the Mobilization of Ethnicity in the Russian Empire," in Barnett R. Rubin and Jack Snyder, eds, *Post-Soviet Political Order: Conflict and State Building* (London: Routledge, 1998); Oleh Fedyshyn, "The Germans and the Union for the Liberation of the Ukraine, 1914–1917," in Taras Hunczak, ed., *The Ukraine, 1917–1921: A Study in Revolution* (Cambridge, MA: Harvard Ukrainian Research Institute, 1977); Oleh Fedyshyn, *Germany's Drive to the East and the Ukrainian Revolution, 1917–1918* (New Brunswick, NJ: Rutgers University Press, 1971), 26, 30–41.

31 Tadeusz Swietochowski, *Russian Azerbaijan, 1905–1920: The Shaping of National Identity in a Muslim Community* (Cambridge: Cambridge University Press, 1985), 77–81.

32 See, for instance, Juozas Gabrys, *Ober-Ost: le plan annexionniste allemand en Lithuanie* (Lausanne: Bureau d'information de Lithuanie, 1917); Auguste Henri Forel, *Für ein freies Lettland im freien Russland!* (Basel: Latvija-verlag, 1917); Mykhailo Lozymskyi, *Les "droits" de la Pologne sur la Galicie: exposé …* (Lausanne: Bureau ukrainien, 1917).

33 Sukiennicki, *East Central Europe*, vol. 1, 217–239; Fedyshyn, "The Germans and the Union for the Liberation of the Ukraine," 314; C.A. Macartney, *National States and National Minorities* (London: Oxford University Press, 1934), 183.

34 For example, some Lithuanian émigré organizations accused the Taryba of collaborating with the Germans. See Liulevicius, "War Land," 266; Senn, *Emergence of Modern Lithuania*, 26–27, 38–39.

35 Zbynek Zeman with Antonín Klimek, *The Life of Edvard Beneš: 1884–1948* (Oxford: Clarendon Press, 1997), chap. 2.

36 *Ibid.* This argument was presented to the British Foreign Office via Robert Seton-Watson as early as May 1915. See Kenneth J. Calder, *Britain and the Origins of the New Europe, 1914–1918* (Cambridge: Cambridge University Press, 1976), 81.

37 Erik Goldstein, *Winning the Peace: British Diplomatic Strategy, Peace Planning, and the Paris Peace Conference, 1916–1920* (Oxford: Clarendon Press, 1991), 3–4, 117–119, 123–140, 257–259.

38 Although Wilson did not endorse the complete breakup of the Habsburg Empire until September 1918, he had expressed sympathy for the Czech cause as early as 1889. Victor Mamatey, *The United States and East Central Europe, 1914–1918: A Study in*

Wilsonian Diplomacy and Propaganda (Princeton, NJ: Princeton University Press, 1957), 13–14.

39 Calder, *Britain*, chap. 7 and *passim*.

40 Josef Kalvoda, *The Genesis of Czechoslovakia* (Boulder, CO: East European Monographs, 1986), chap. 5.

41 Roman Szporluk, *The Political Thought of Thomas G. Masaryk* (Boulder, CO: East European Monographs, 1981), 141; Jaroslav Krejčí and Pavel Machonin, *Czechoslovakia, 1918–92: A Laboratory for Social Change* (London: Macmillan, 1996), 9–10. Masaryk also met in Pittsburgh a year later with leaders of the émigré Hungarian Ruthenian community, who agreed to support the incorporation of their home province (Subcarpathian Rus') as an autonomous region of the prospective Czechoslovak state. Paul Robert Magocsi, *The Rusyns of Slovakia: An Historical Survey* (New York: East European Monographs, 1993), 59; D. Perman, *The Shaping of the Czechoslovak State: Diplomatic History of the Boundaries of Czechoslovakia, 1914–1920* (Leiden: Brill, 1962), 26–27. For Masaryk's defensive account of the Pittsburgh Declaration, in which he concedes that the Declaration spoke of Slovak autonomy but denies that he was bound to this provision by signing on to the document, see Thomas Garrigue Masaryk, *The Making of a State: Memories and Observations, 1914–1918* (New York: Frederick A. Stokes, 1927), 220–221.

42 Thomas G. Masaryk, *The New Europe (The Slav Standpoint)* (Lewisburg: Bucknell University Press, 1972; first edn, 1918), 138.

43 *Ibid.* See also Szporluk, *Political Thought*, 139.

44 See Michael Ignatieff, *Blood and Belonging: Journeys into the New Nationalism* (New York: Farrar, Straus and Giroux, 1993), 21–22. Edvard Beneš seems to have been even less sensitive to the distinctiveness of Slovak identity. William V. Wallace, "Masaryk and Beneš and the Creation of Czechoslovakia: a Study in Mentalities," in Harry Hanak, ed., *T.G. Masaryk (1850–1937)*, vol. 3 (New York: St. Martin's Press, 1990), 77–78.

45 Derek Sayer, *The Coasts of Bohemia: A Czech History* (Princeton, NJ: Princeton University Press, 1998), 171; Zeman, *Life of Beneš*, 24–25.

46 Stanislav J. Kirschbaum, *A History of Slovakia: The Struggle for Survival* (New York: St. Martin's Press, 1995), 150–152.

47 Gale Stokes, "The Role of the Yugoslav Committee in the Formation of Yugoslavia," and Milorad Ekmecić, "Serbian War Aims," in Dimitrije Djordjević, ed., *The Creation of Yugoslavia 1914–1918* (Santa Barbara, CA and Oxford: Clio Press, 1980).

48 *Ibid.*, "Introduction"; Calder, *Britain*, 78 and chap. 5; Ivo J. Lederer, "Nationalism and the Yugoslavs," in Peter F. Sugar and Ivo John Lederer, eds, *Nationalism in Eastern Europe* (Seattle, WA: University of Washington Press, 1994; 1969), 429–430.

49 Seton-Watson to Foreign Office (1 October 1914), in Hugh and Christopher Seton-Watson , Ljubo Boban, Mirjana Gross, Bogdan Krizman, and Dragovan Šepić, eds, *R.W. Seton-Watson and the Yugoslavs: Correspondence, 1906–1941. Vol. 1: 1906–1918* (London: British Academy, 1976), 180–186. Once he had taken a clear stance in favor of Czechoslovak independence, Masaryk similarly resorted to the argument of Bohemian historic state right in justifying his claim to strategically vital, but German-populated, regions.

50 This discussion draws upon: Ekmecić, "Serbian War Aims," 20–23; Dragan Zivojinović, "Serbia and Montenegro: The Home Front, 1914–18," in Király and Dreisziger, eds, *East Central European Society*, 242; Lampe, *Yugoslavia as History*, 100–101; Stokes, "Role of the Yugoslav Committee"; Ivo Banac, *The National Question in Yugoslavia: Origins, History, Politics* (Ithaca, NY and London: Cornell University Press, 1984), 202–209.

51 Smodlaka to Seton-Watson (29 April 1911) in H. and C. Seton-Watson, *Seton-Watson and the Yugoslavs*, 82–83.

52 *The Times* (London), 24 and 26 June 1915. Not everyone who saw the sculptures liked them. *The Times* of 30 June 1915 published a letter from the poet Selwyn Image

attacking Meštrović's work as "wilful, inchoate, amorphous, even monstrous …" and objecting to the official sponsorship of the exhibition.

53 Seton-Watson to Mabel Grukić (15 March 1915), in H. and C. Seton-Watson, *Seton-Watson and the Yugoslavs*, 199–205.

54 H. and C. Seton-Watson, "Introduction," in *Seton-Watson and the Yugoslavs*, 25.

55 Supilo to Seton-Watson (31 December 1916) in *ibid.*, 286–287.

56 Supilo to Seton-Watson (26 May 1917) in H. and C. Seton-Watson, *Seton-Watson and the Yugoslavs*, 294–295; Stokes, "Role of the Yugoslav Committee," 57–58.

57 See David MacKenzie, *APIS: The Congenial Conspirator: The Life of Colonel Dragutin T. Dimitrijević* (Boulder, CO: East European Monographs, 1989), chaps 16–25.

58 Stokes, "Role of the Yugoslav Committee," 58–59; Seton-Watson to Intelligence Bureau (1 June 1917), Milorad Drašković (Serbian opposition deputy) to Seton-Watson (21 September 1918), and Seton-Watson to Foreign Office (4 October 1918), in H. and C. Seton-Watson, *Seton-Watson and the Yugoslavs*, 296–298, 336–339, and 350–355.

59 This discussion relies upon: Stokes, "Role of the Yugoslav Committee," 58; Lampe, *Yugoslavia as History*, 60–64, 102–104, 108–111; Mamatey, *The United States and East Central Europe*, chap. 4; Judah, *The Serbs*, 104–106.

60 One of Dmowski's most consistent objectives was the inclusion of extensive German-ruled territories in a future Polish state. Those lands included Upper Silesia, Poznań, West Prussia, East Prussia (whose exclusively German-inhabited northern zone was to be granted some form of self-rule), and part of Pomerania. Roman Dmowski, *Problems of Central and Eastern Europe* (London: privately printed, 1917), 66–75.

61 Paul Latawski, "The Discrepancy between State and Ethnographic Frontiers: Dmowski and Masaryk on Self-determination," in Hanak, ed., *Masaryk*; *idem*, "Roman Dmowski and Western Opinion," in Latawski, ed., *The Reconstruction of Poland, 1914–23* (New York: St. Martin's Press, 1992); Alvin Marcus Fountain III, *Roman Dmowski: Party, Tactics, Ideology 1895–1907* (Boulder, CO: East European Monographs, 1980), 110. A broad array of Jewish organizations and personalities lobbied hard against Western recognition of Dmowski's Polish National Committee and in favor of creating a political framework in postwar Poland that would protect minority rights. Eugene Black, "Lucien Wolf and the Making of Poland: Paris, 1919," in Antony Polonsky, ed., *From Shtetl to Socialism: Studies from Polin* (London and Washington, DC: The Littman Library of Jewish Civilization, 1993), 274–275 and 291, nos. 24 and 25; Eugene Black, "Squaring a Minorities Triangle: Lucien Wolf, Jewish Nationalists and Polish Nationalists," in Latawski, ed., *The Reconstruction of Poland, 1914–23*, 22–23. The Polish National Committee did enjoy some sympathy among a number of highly placed conservative Catholic officials in the British Foreign Office. Levene, *War, Jews*, 190.

62 Levene, *War, Jews*, 188–190.

63 Adam Zamoyski, *Paderewski* (New York: Atheneum, 1982), chaps 10–12; Andrzej Garlicki, *Józef Piłsudski, 1867–1935*, ed., abridged, and trans. from the Polish by John Coutrouvidis (Aldershot: Scolar Press, 1995), 89–90; Zeman, *Break-up of the Habsburg Empire*, 195–196.

64 This section is heavily indebted to the last two volumes of David Vital's magisterial, three-volume history of Zionism: *Zionism: The Formative Years* (Oxford: Clarendon Press, 1982) and *Zionism: The Crucial Phase* (Oxford: Clarendon Press, 1987).

65 Steven J. Zipperstein, *Elusive Prophet: Ahad Ha'am and the Origins of Zionism* (Berkeley, CA: University of California Press, 1993), chaps 3–4. Zipperstein points out that in many respects, such as his questioning of parliamentary democracy, Ahad Ha'am's brand of cultural elitism was idiosyncratic and at odds with the intellectual mainstream of cultural Zionism. *Ibid.*, 150–153.

66 Neville Mandel, *The Arabs and Zionism before World War I* (Berkeley, CA: University of California Press, 1976), xxiv. In the course of the First World War, Palestine's total Jewish population would decline to around 60,000; the Arab population of what was

to become mandatory Palestine stood around 600,000 in 1914. Muhammad Muslih, *The Origins of Palestinian Nationalism* (New York: Columbia University Press, 1988), 13–14.

67 Isaiah Friedman, *Germany, Turkey and Zionism, 1897–1918* (Oxford: Clarendon Press, 1977), chaps 11–16, esp. chap. 16.

68 Jehudah Reinharz, *Chaim Weizmann: The Making of a Zionist Leader* (New York and Oxford: Oxford University Press, 1985), chaps 3–4 and 10–11; *idem, Chaim Weizmann: The Making of a Statesman* (New York and Oxford: Oxford University Press, 1993), chaps 1–6; Vital, *Zionism: The Crucial Phase,* 156–166.

69 Isaiah Friedman, *The Question of Palestine, 1914–1918. British–Jewish–Arab Relations* (New York: Schocken Books, 1973), *passim;* Leonard Stein, *The Balfour Declaration* (New York: Simon & Schuster, 1961), chap. 17.

70 As quoted in Friedman, *Question of Palestine,* 279.

71 But note the success of the Zionist petition in Poland in 1917, as described earlier in this chapter.

72 Vital, *Zionism: The Crucial Phase,* 251–252.

73 *Ibid.,* 271–280; Levene, *War, Jews,* 2–7, chaps 5–7; David Stevenson, *The First World War and International Politics* (Oxford: Oxford University Press, 1988), 178. The Conjoint Committee was dissolved, only to be reconstituted in December 1917 as the Joint Foreign Committee.

74 Von Hagen, "The Great War and the Mobilization of Ethnicity," 14; Fedyshyn, "The Germans and the Union for the Liberation of the Ukraine," 315–319; Anthony A. Upton, *The Finnish Revolution, 1917–1918* (Minneapolis, MN: University of Minnesota Press, 1980), 20–25.

75 The Serbian Volunteer Corps was answerable to the authority of Serbia's government-in-exile. Following its deployment against Bulgarian forces on Romania's Dobrudja front in 1916, where it suffered extremely heavy casualties, most of the corps' surviving Croat and Slovene officers and soldiers abandoned it in disgust over the ethnic chauvinism and anti-Yugoslavism of their Serb commanders. See Ivo Banac, "South Slav Prisoners of War in Revolutionary Russia," in Samuel R. Williamson and Peter Pastor, eds, *Essays on World War I: Origin and Prisoners of War* (New York: East European Monographs, 1983); Richard B. Spence, "Yugoslavs, the Austro-Hungarian Army, and the First World War" (Ph.D. diss., University of California at Santa Barbara, 1981), chap. 6.

76 John F.N. Bradley, *The Czechoslovak Legion in Russia, 1914–1920* (Boulder, CO: East European Monographs, 1991), 14. For a succinct account of the Czechoslovak Legion in Russia, see Rowan A. Williams, "The Czech Legion Revisited," *East Central Europe,* vol. 6, pt. 1 (1979), 20–39.

77 Josef Kalvoda, "The Origins of the Czechoslovak Army, 1914–18," in Király and Dreisziger, eds, *East Central European Society,* 423; Josef Kalvoda, "Czech and Slovak Prisoners of War in Russia during the War and Revolution," in Samuel R. Williamson, Jr. and Peter Pastor, eds, *Essays on World War I: Origins and Prisoners of War* (New York: East European Monographs, 1983).

78 Kalvoda, "Czech and Slovak Prisoners of War," 229–234. As Kalvoda points out, the clashes between the Czechoslovak Legion and Bolshevized Magyars and Austro-Germans evoke an image of a Habsburg civil war being played out on Russian soil. The threat posed by German and Magyar POWs was exaggerated by French and White Russian propaganda aimed at securing American participation in an anti-Bolshevik intervention in the Russian civil war. George F. Kennan, *Soviet–American Relations, 1917–1920,* vol. 2: *The Decision to Intervene* (Princeton, NJ: Princeton University Press, 1958), 400–403; Betty Miller Unterberger, *The United States, Revolutionary Russia, and the Rise of Czechoslovakia* (Chapel Hill, NC: The University of North Carolina Press, 1989), chaps 12–15.

79 Zeman, *Break-up of the Habsburg Empire,* chap. 7; Kennan, *Soviet–American Relations,* chaps 12–13 and 17.

80 Rowan A. Williams, "The Odyssey of the Czechs," *East European Quarterly*, vol. 9, no. 1 (Spring 1975), 15–38.

81 Claire Nolte, "Ambivalent Patriots: Czech Culture in the Great War," in Roshwald and Stites, eds, *European Culture*, 168.

82 Arne Novak, *Czech Literature*, trans. Peter Kussi (Ann Arbor, MI: Michigan Slavic Publications, 1976), 288–291. It should be pointed out that the experiences of the Legion in Siberia also gave rise to anti-war fiction. *Ibid.*

83 Leonard Ratajczyk, "The Evolution of the Polish Army, 1914–22," Leonard Ratajczyk, "Development of the Polish Officer Corps in World War I," and Leslaw Dudek, "Polish Military Formations in World War I," in Király and Dreisziger, eds, *East Central European Society*; Harold Segel, "Culture in Poland during World War I," in Roshwald and Stites, eds, *European Culture*.

84 Ratajczyk, "The Evolution of the Polish Army," 440–441; M. Kamil Dziewanowski, "Polish Society in World War I: Armed Forces and Military Operations," in Király and Dreisziger, eds, *East Central European Society*, 488; Garlicki, *Piłsudski*, chap. 4.

85 Dziewanowski, "Polish Society," 489; Norman Davies, *God's Playground: A History of Poland*, vol. 2 (New York: Columbia University Press, 1982), 381–385.

86 Dziewanowski, "Polish Society," 489–493; Garlicki, *Piłsudski*, chap. 4 and p. 88; R.F. Leslie, Antony Polonsky, Jan M. Ciechanowski, and Z.A. Pelczynski, eds, *The History of Poland since 1863* (Cambridge: Cambridge University Press, 1980), 116–127; M. Kamil Dziewanowski, *Joseph Piłsudski: A European Federalist, 1918–1922* (Stanford, CA: Hoover Institution Press, 1969), 56–57; Sukiennicki, *East Central Europe*, vol. 1, chaps 14, 18, and 29 and pp. 333–342; Davies, *God's Playground*, 385–392.

87 Dziewanowski, "Polish Society," 488; Ratajczyk, "The Evolution of the Polish Army," 444.

88 *Ibid.*, 445.

89 Zeman, *Break-up of the Habsburg Empire*, 154–157; Sukiennicki, *East Central Europe*, vol. 1, 540–565.

90 Ratajczyk, "The Evolution of the Polish Army," 444–447; Dziewanowski, "Polish Society," 494–496; Sukiennicki, *East Central Europe*, vol. 2, chap. 27.

91 Lew Shankowsky, "Disintegration of the Imperial Russian Army in 1917," *The Ukrainian Quarterly*, XIII, 4 (December 1957), 308.

92 See Chapter 7.

93 As quoted in Garlicki, *Piłsudski*, 73.

94 *Ibid.*, 74.

95 William Ochsenwald, "Ironic Origins: Arab Nationalism in the Hejaz, 1882–1914," in Rashid Khalidi, Lisa Anderson, Muhammad Muslih, and Reeva S. Simon, eds, *The Origins of Arab Nationalism* (New York: Columbia University Press, 1991); Ernest Dawn, *From Ottomanism to Arabism: Essays on the Origins of Arab Nationalism* (Urbana, IL: University of Illinois Press, 1973), chaps 1–4.

96 *Ibid.*

97 Ochsenwald, "Ironic Origins"; Dawn, *Ottomanism to Arabism*, chap. 3; Zeine N. Zeine, *The Struggle for Arab Independence* (2nd edn, Delmar, NY: Caravan Books, 1977; 1960), chap. 1. One of Hussein's attractions from the point of view of the British authorities in Egypt was as a counter to Ottoman pan-Islamic propaganda. On the other hand, the British government of India (the Raj), which was caught up in a rivalry with Cairo over influence and authority in Arabia and Mesopotamia (where the Raj was in charge of the military campaign against the Ottomans), feared that British support for a revolt against the Ottoman caliph would provoke unrest among India's Muslims. Briton Cooper Busch, *Britain, India, and the Arabs, 1914–1921* (Berkeley, CA: University of California Press, 1971), chaps 2, 4, 5; Bruce Westrate, *The Arab Bureau: British Policy in the Middle East, 1916–1920* (University Park, PA: The Pennsylvania State University Press, 1992), chap. 4.

98 Eliezer Tauber, *The Arab Movements in World War I* (London: Frank Cass, 1993), chap. 3; Zeine, *Struggle for Arab Independence*, 22. The British also recognized

Hussein as King of the Hejaz. Whether or not Palestine was to be included in the prospective sphere of Arab independence remains the subject of controversy, given the ambiguous wording of the documents. Britain's 1916 Sykes–Picot agreement with the French on partition of the region into spheres of influence and its commitment to the Zionists regarding Palestine under the terms of the 1917 Balfour Declaration further contributed to an overly complex diplomatic framework that could not fail to exacerbate tensions among rival claimants to territory and power in the Middle East. See Friedman, *Question of Palestine*, chap. 6; *idem*, "The McMahon–Hussein Correspondence and the Question of Palestine," *Journal of Contemporary History*, vol. 5, no. 2 (1970), 83–122; Arnold Toynbee and Isaiah Friedman, "The McMahon–Hussein Correspondence: Comments and a Reply," *Journal of Contemporary History*, vol. 5, no. 4 (1970), 185–201; Elizabeth Monroe, *Britain's Moment in the Middle East, 1914–1971* (2nd edn, London: Chatto & Windus, 1981; 1963), 26–37.

99 See Mary Wilson, "The Hashemites, the Arab Revolt, and Arab Nationalism," in Khalidi *et al.*, eds, *Origins of Arab Nationalism*.

100 Tauber, *The Arab Movements*, chap. 5. Many of the POWs sent from prison camps in India to the Hejaz proved unwilling to join the Sharifian forces or the Arab Legion that British authorities were trying to organize, leading the Cairo authorities to suspect the Raj, which opposed Cairo's sponsorship of the Revolt, of deliberately sabotaging the recruitment effort. Westrate, *The Arab Bureau*, 90–91.

101 Tauber, *The Arab Movements*, chap. 5.

102 *Ibid.*, 134–144.

103 Elie Kedourie, "The Capture of Damascus, 1 October 1918," in *idem*, *The Chatham House Version and Other Middle Eastern Studies* (Hanover, NH: University Press of New England, 1984 edn).

6 Defining the Boundaries of the Nation, 1918–1923

1 Robert Bideleux and Ian Jeffries, *A History of Eastern Europe: Crisis and Change* (London: Routledge, 1998), 404.

2 Robert G.L. Waite, *Vanguard of Nazism: The Free Corps Movement in Postwar Germany, 1918–1923* (Cambridge, MA: Harvard University Press, 1952), chap. 5. The Allied and Associated Powers initially allowed the Free Corps to operate in the Baltic in order to hold the Bolsheviks at bay.

3 Paul Robert Magocsi, *The Rusyns of Slovakia: An Historical Survey* (New York: East European Monographs, 1993), chap. 7 and p. 71; Piotr S. Wandycz, *France and Her Eastern Allies, 1919–1925* (Minneapolis, MN: University of Minnesota Press, 1962), 64–65, 68–69.

4 Peter F. Sugar, Péter Hanák, and Tibor Frank, eds, *A History of Hungary* (Bloomington, IN: Indiana University Press, 1990), 303–309.

5 The Bolsheviks had won 40 per cent of the Estonian vote and 72 per cent of the vote in the parts of Latvia not yet occupied by the Germans in the November 1917 elections to the Russian Constituent Assembly (which was dissolved by Lenin's regime in January 1918 after meeting for one day). Toivo Raun, *Estonia and the Estonians* (Stanford, CA: Hoover Institution Press, 1987), 103; Ronald Grigor Suny, *The Revenge of the Past: Nationalism, Revolution, and the Collapse of the Soviet Union* (Stanford, CA: Stanford University Press, 1993), 54, 57.

6 John W. Wheeler-Bennett, *Brest-Litovsk: The Forgotten Peace, March 1918* (New York: Norton, 1971; 1938), chap. 4 and pp. 243–247, 262–275; Alfred Erich Senn, *The Emergence of Modern Lithuania* (New York: Columbia University Press, 1959), chap. 3; Vejas Gabrielius Liulevicius, "War Land: Peoples, Lands, and National Identity on the Eastern Front in World War I" (Ph.D. diss., University of Pennsylvania, 1994), 271–272; Suny, *The Revenge of the Past*, 55–58, 64–72; Andrejs Plakans, *The Latvians: A Short History* (Stanford, CA: Hoover Institution Press, 1995), chap. 7; Raun, *Estonia*,

chap. 8; Anthony F. Upton, *The Finnish Revolution, 1917–1918* (Minneapolis, MN: University of Minnesota Press, 1980), chaps 12–17.

7 Lloyd Ambrosius, "Dilemmas of National Self-Determination: Woodrow Wilson's Legacy," in Christian Baechler and Carole Fink, eds, *The Establishment of European Frontiers after the Two World Wars* (Berlin: Peter Lang, 1996).

8 Victor Mamatey, *The United States and East Central Europe, 1914–1918: A Study in Wilsonian Diplomacy and Propaganda* (Princeton, NJ: Princeton University Press, 1957), chaps 2, 4, and 5; Harold I. Nelson, *Land and Power: British and Allied Policy on Germany's Frontiers, 1916–19* (London: Routledge & Kegan Paul, 1963), 30–31, 38–39; Alan Sharp, *The Versailles Settlement: Peacemaking in Paris, 1919* (New York: St. Martin's Press, 1991), 130–132, 155–157.

9 As quoted in Sharp, *Versailles*, 156.

10 William R. Keylor, "The Principle of National Self-Determination as a Factor in the Creation of Postwar Frontiers in Europe, 1919 and 1945," in Baechler and Fink, eds, *The Establishment of European Frontiers*; Lawrence E. Gelfand, *The Inquiry: American Preparations for Peace, 1917–1919* (New Haven, CT: Yale University Press, 1963), chaps 3 and 7; Erik Goldstein, *Winning the Peace: British Diplomatic Strategy, Peace Planning, and the Paris Peace Conference, 1916–1920* (Oxford: Clarendon Press, 1991), chap. 2 and pp. 123–140; Nelson, *Land and Power*, 367–370; Mamatey, *The United States and East Central Europe*, 174.

11 Keylor, "The Principle of National Self-Determination." Wilson and Lloyd George did not necessarily follow the recommendations of their experts, and the final boundaries were not shaped exclusively by ethnic criteria but also by strategic considerations, feelings of antipathy toward the former Central Powers, and events on the ground in East Central Europe. My point is that the process of investigating rival territorial claims highlighted the role of ethnicity as the foundation of national identity.

12 Robert Lansing, *The Peace Negotiations: A Personal Narrative* (Boston, MA and New York: Houghton Mifflin, 1921), chap. 7.

13 I am expanding here on a point made by Antoni Czubinski in "Les frontières de l'état polonais, 1914–1990," in Baechler and Fink, eds, *The Establishment of European Frontiers*.

14 On the state map as logo of nationhood, see Benedict Anderson, *Imagined Communities* (rev. edn, London and New York: Verso, 1991; 1983), 170–178.

15 Wandycz, *France and Her Eastern Allies*, chap. 3 and pp. 148–160. The most detailed, English-language work on the Czechoslovak territorial settlement is D. Perman, *The Shaping of the Czechoslovak State: Diplomatic History of the Boundaries of Czechoslovakia, 1914–1920* (Leiden: Brill, 1962).

16 Jaroslav Krejčí and Pavel Machonin, *Czechoslovakia, 1918–92: A Laboratory for Social Change* (London: Macmillan, 1996), 12.

17 Wandycz, *France and Her Eastern Allies*, chaps 4–6; M. Kamil Dziewanowski, *Joseph Piłsudski: A European Federalist, 1918–1922* (Stanford, CA: Hoover Institution Press, 1969), 315–319 and chap. 17.

18 Wandycz, *France and Her Eastern Allies*, 43–48, 225–237.

19 On the very eve of the Paris Peace Conference's opening in January 1919, Dmowski and Piłsudski were able temporarily to patch up their differences in the interest of presenting a common front: Dmowski's political partner, Paderewski, was appointed Prime Minister and Foreign Minister; the Polish National Committee was enlarged to include left-wing allies of Piłsudski in return for Piłsudski's recognition of the Committee as representative of Poland's interests at the Peace Conference; Dmowski and Paderewski were to serve as official delegates to the Conference; Piłsudski was confirmed in his role as Polish Chief of State. Robert Machray, *The Poland of Piłsudski* (London: George Allen & Unwin, 1936), chap. 3.

20 Often referred to as the Big Four, this was composed of the leaders of the United States, Britain, France, and Italy, whose deliberations largely shaped the outcome of the Paris Peace Conference.

21 He claimed that because the Ukrainians of Galicia had been so long under Habsburg rule, they had nothing in common with the Ukrainian Republic to the East, in former Russian territory. Interview of Paderewski by the Big Four, 5 June, 11:00am, in Arthur Link, ed., *The Deliberations of the Council of Four (March 24–June 28, 1919): Notes of the Official Interpreter, Paul Mantoux* (Princeton, NJ: Princeton University Press, 1992), 309.

22 First Lloyd George quotation from *ibid.*, 311–312; second from *ibid.*, meeting of 9 June, 11:00am, 352. It should be noted in this context that Britain was itself at that time busily integrating territories seized from the Ottoman empire and Germany into its already bloated overseas empire.

23 This was the body composed of the Big Ten heads of government and foreign ministers of the US, Britain, France, Italy, and Japan who constituted the official executive committee of the Peace Conference.

24 The Supreme Council attempted to save face by recommending that Eastern Galicia be granted autonomy and that its ultimate disposition be determined by plebiscite. In 1923, Britain and France finally recognized Poland's eastern frontiers, including its control of Eastern Galicia, after the Polish parliament had formally conferred autonomy on the region; this autonomy remained purely notional. See Michael Zurowski, "The British Foreign Office and Poland's Eastern Minorities, 1918–1941," part I, *The Ukrainian Quarterly*, vol. 46, no. 3 (Fall 1990), 262–281; Laurence J. Orzell, "A 'Hotly Disputed' Issue: Eastern Galicia at the Paris Peace Conference, 1919," *Polish Review*, vol. 25, no. 1 (1980), 49–68; Antony Polonsky, *Politics in Independent Poland, 1921–1939: The Crisis of Constitutional Government* (Oxford: Oxford University Press, 1972), 51–52; Kay Lundgreen-Nielsen, "The Mayer Thesis Reconsidered: The Poles and the Paris Peace Conference, 1919," *The International History Review*, vol. 7, no. 1 (February 1985), 68–102; Wandycz, *France and Her Eastern Allies*, chaps 5–6; H.J. Elcock, "Britain and the Russo-Polish Frontier, 1919–1921," *Historical Journal*, vol. 12, no. 1 (1969), 137–154.

25 The League of Nations Covenant, drawn up in February 1919, failed to incorporate any general guarantee of minority rights in member states, due to an impasse arising from American unwillingness to extend such rights to racial as well as religious minorities. See Mark Levene, "Britain, a British Jew, and Jewish Relations with the New Poland: The Making of the Polish Minorities Treaty of 1919," *Polin*, vol. 8, Antony Polonsky, Ezra Mendelsohn, and Jerzy Tomaszewski, eds, *Jews in Independent Poland, 1918–1939* (London and Washington, DC: Littman Library of Jewish Civilization, 1994), 14–41 (esp. 33); Carole Fink, "The League of Nations and the Minorities Question," *World Affairs*, vol. 157, no. 4 (Spring 1995), 197–205.

26 American Jewish relief organizations continued to have access to German-occupied Poland as long as the US remained neutral.

27 This could be seen as an attempt to create an updated version of the Council of the Four Lands that represented Jewish interests in the early modern Polish–Lithuanian Commonwealth.

28 The notion of one form or another of extraterritorial, national-cultural autonomy for Jews enjoyed support among other Jewish political movements in Poland, such as the Folkists (advocates of Yiddish culture) and the Bundists. Mark Levene, *War, Jews, and the New Europe: The Diplomacy of Lucien Wolf, 1914–1919* (Oxford: Oxford University Press, 1992), 215–216. On the unfulfilled precedent of Jewish autonomy in the short-lived Ukrainian republic, see Paul Robert Magocsi, *A History of Ukraine* (Seattle, WA: University of Washington Press, 1996), 503–507.

29 For a recent revival and expansion upon this approach by a scholar of international law, see Gidon Gottlieb, *Nation against State* (New York: Council on Foreign Relations Press, 1993).

30 This discussion draws on the publications of Mark Levene cited throughout this section.

31 Levene, "Nationalism and its Alternatives in the International Arena: The Jewish Question at Paris 1919," *The Journal of Contemporary History*, vol. 28, no. 3 (July 1993), 511–531; Fink, "The League of Nations." Wolf's program represented a step back from his earlier advocacy of more far-reaching cultural autonomy for Poland's Jews. These ideas had been shaped by his reading of some of Karl Renner's writings on the national problem in the Habsburg empire. Levene, *War, Jews*, 179–180; *idem*, "Britain, a British Jew," 17. For background information on Renner and the Austro-Marxists, see Chapter 2 of the present book.

32 Among the precedents for this approach was Article 44 of the international treaty settling the Eastern Crisis, drawn up at the Congress of Berlin in 1878. This attempted to protect Romania's much abused Jewish population by providing for their naturalization and guaranteeing their civil rights. The Romanian parliament circumvented these provisions in the following year by drawing up a constitutional amendment that paid lip service to its treaty obligations while setting up virtually insurmountable roadblocks to the actual naturalization of the country's Jews, most of whom were immigrants or children of immigrants from the Russian empire and Galicia. See Fink, "The League of Nations"; Fritz Stern, *Gold and Iron: Bismarck, Bleichröder, and the Building of the German Empire* (New York: Alfred Knopf, 1977), chap. 14; Keith Hitchins, *Rumania, 1866–1947* (Oxford: Oxford University Press, 1994), 52–53. The Polish Minorities Treaty sought to plug this loophole by emphasizing the civil rights of all "inhabitants" of Polish territory.

33 Memorandum from Paderewski to the Big Four, discussed at meeting of 17 June 1919, 4:00pm, in Link, ed., *The Deliberations of the Big Four*, 492.

34 On the broader cultural rights guaranteed the German minority in Poland's portion of Upper Silesia following its partition, see Janusz Zarnowski, "Le Système de protection des minorités et la Pologne," *Acta Poloniae Historica*, vol. 52 (1985), 105–124, esp. 113–114.

35 Fink, "The League of Nations"; C.A. Macartney, *National States and National Minorities* (London: Oxford University Press, 1934), 220–240.

36 Patrick B. Finney, "'An Evil for All Concerned': Great Britain and Minority Protection after 1919," *Journal of Contemporary History*, vol. 30, no. 3 (July 1995), 533–551; Fink, "The League of Nations," note 2; Macartney, *National States*, chap. 7; D.R. Gadgil, "The Protection of Minorities," in William F. Mackey and Albert Verdoort, eds, *The Multinational Society: Papers of the Ljubljana Seminar* (Rowley, MA: Newbury House Publishers, 1975), 71–72.

37 The following discussion draws on these works: Gabriele Simoncini, "The Polyethnic State: National Minorities in Interbellum Poland," *Nationalities Papers*, vol. 22, supplement no. 1 (1994), 5–28; Pawel Korzec, "Der Block der Nationalen Minderheiten in Parlamentarismus Polens des Jahres 1922," *Zeitschrift für Ostforschung*, vol. 24, no. 2 (June 1975), 193–220; Yisrael Gutman, "Polish Antisemitism between the Wars: An Overview," in Yisrael Gutman, Ezra Mendelsohn, Jehuda Reinharz, and Chone Shmeruk, eds, *The Jews of Poland between Two World Wars* (Hanover, NH: University Press of New England, 1989); Polonsky, *Politics in Independent Poland*, pp. 65, 87, 92, chaps 3–4, pp. 213–218, 371–378; Ilya Prizel, *National Identity and Foreign Policy: Nationalism and Leadership in Poland, Russia and Ukraine* (Cambridge: Cambridge University Press, 1998), 62–67; Andrzej Korbonski, "Poland: 1918–1990," in Joseph Held, ed., *The Columbia History of Eastern Europe in the Twentieth Century* (New York: Columbia University Press, 1992), 232–234; Zarnowski, "Le Système," 122–123; Norman Davies, *God's Playground: A History of Poland*, vol. 2 (New York: Columbia University Press, 1982), 404–410. On the main Polish peasant party's inclination to target minorities and form coalitions with Dmowski's National Democrats, see Olga A. Narkiewicz, *The Green Flag: Polish Populist Politics, 1867–1970* (London: Croom Helm, 1976), 185, 190, and 197–198; Dziewanowski, *Piłsudski*, 336.

38 The percentage of Poland's Jews identifying Yiddish or Hebrew, rather than Polish, as their native tongue, increased from 74.2 to 87 per cent between 1921 and 1931,

according to official census figures. This was probably not simply a reflection of the
success of private Jewish schools, but also an expression of the increased alienation of
Polish Jewry from the state's official nationalism. Prizel, *National Identity*, 65.
39 On the dynamic relationship between the "nationalizing state" and minorities, see
Rogers Brubaker, *Nationalism Reframed: Nationhood and the National Question in the New
Europe* (Cambridge: Cambridge University Press, 1996), 63–66 and chap. 4.
40 In Bukovina, no one ethnic group constituted a simple majority, and much of the
peasantry was Ukrainian.
41 Irina Livezeanu, *Cultural Politics in Greater Romania. Regionalism, Nation Building, and
Ethnic Struggle, 1918–1930* (Ithaca, NY: Cornell University Press, 1995); Hildrun
Glass, *Zerbrochene Nachbarschaft: Das deutsch-jüdische Verhältnis in Rumänien (1918–1938)*
(Munich: Oldenbourg, 1996); Hitchins, *Rumania*, 290.
42 Glass, *Zerbrochene Nachbarschaft, passim.*
43 Sam Beck and Marilyn McArthur, "Romania: Ethnicity, Nationalism and
Development," in Sam Beck and John W. Cole, eds, *Ethnicity and Nationalism in
Southeastern Europe* (Amsterdam: Antropologisch-Sociologisch Centrum, University of
Amsterdam, 1981), 44–48.
44 On Romanian fascism, see Livezeanu, *Cultural Politics in Greater Romania*, and Eugen
Weber, "The Men of the Archangel," in George Mosse, ed., *International Fascism: New
Thoughts and New Approaches* (London: Sage Publications, 1979), 317–343. For similar
developments in Latvia, see Andrejs Plakans, *The Latvians: A Short History* (Stanford,
CA: Hoover Institution Press, 1995), 118–123.
45 Geoff Eley, "Remapping the Nation: War, Revolutionary Upheaval, and State
Formation in Eastern Europe, 1914–1923," in Peter J. Potichnyj and Howard Aster,
eds, *Ukrainian–Jewish Relations in Historical Perspective* (Edmonton, 1988); Karl J.
Newman, *European Democracy between the Wars* (trans. Kenneth Morgan, London:
George Allen & Unwin, 1970), 147–173; Zarnowski, "Le Système de protection,"
109. Of course, fear of Communism also played into the hands of right-wing nationalists across Europe during the interwar years. See Eley, "Remapping." On the
synthesis of anti-Semitism with anti-Communism in interwar Polish political
discourse, see Simoncini, "The Polyethnic State," 7–8.
46 Newman, *European Democracy*, 174–179; Iván T. Bérend and György Ránki, "Die
wirtschaftlichen Probleme des Donaubeckens nach dem Zerfall der Österreichisch-
Ungarischen Monarchie", in Richard Georg Plaschka and Karlheinz Mack, eds, *Die
Auflösung des Habsburgerreiches: Zusammenbruch und Neuorientierung im Donauraum* (Munich:
Oldenbourg, 1970); Norman Davies, *God's Playground*, 410–417; Hitchins, *Rumania*,
chap. 8 and p. 416.
47 This section is heavily indebted to Richard Pipes, *The Formation of the Soviet Union:
Communism and Nationalism, 1917–1923* (rev. edn, Cambridge, MA: Harvard University
Press, 1964; 1954), chaps 3–5.
48 Waite, *Vanguard of Nazism*, chap. 5; Anthony F. Upton, *The Finnish Revolution,
1917–1918* (Minneapolis, MN: University of Minnesota Press, 1980), chaps 12–17;
Plakans, *The Latvians*, 113–115.
49 This section draws upon: Tadeusz Swietochowski, *Russian Azerbaijan, 1905–1920: The
Shaping of National Identity in a Muslim Community* (Cambridge: Cambridge University
Press, 1985), chaps 5–6; idem, "National Consciousness and Political Orientations in
Azerbaijan, 1905–1920," in Ronald Grigor Suny, ed., *Transcaucasia, Nationalism and
Social Change: Essays in the History of Armenia, Azerbaijan, and Georgia* (rev. edn, Ann Arbor,
MI: University of Michigan Press, 1996; 1983), 224–225; John W. Wheeler-Bennett,
Brest-Litovsk: The Forgotten Peace, March 1918 (New York: Norton, 1971; 1938), 272;
Firuz Kazemzadeh, *The Struggle for Transcaucasia, 1917–1921* (New York: Philosophical
Library, 1951), chaps 5–7 and pp. 272–275.
50 The Allied countries recognized Georgia's independence *de jure* on the very eve of its
conquest by the Soviet Union in early 1921.

51 Pipes, *Formation*, 98–107 and chap. 5; Ronald Grigor Suny, *The Making of the Georgian Nation* (2nd edn, Bloomington, IN: Indiana University Press, 1994; 1988), chap. 9.

52 Enver Pasha, who had briefly flirted with the Bolsheviks in the hope of gaining their support for his return to power in Turkey, defected to the Basmachis in November 1921 with the intention of transforming their revolt into a pan-Turkist military campaign. In the event, he never gained direct command of more than 3,000 fighters, and was killed in a firefight with Red Army troops in 1922.

53 Pipes, *Formation*, chaps 3 and 4; Taras Hunczak, "The Ukraine under Hetman Pavlo Skoropadskyi," and Martha Bohachevsky-Chomiak, "The Directory of the Ukrainian National Republic," in Taras Hunczak, ed., *The Ukraine, 1917–1921: A Study in Revolution* (Cambridge, MA: Harvard Ukrainian Research Institute, 1977); Magocsi, *Ukraine*, 503–507; Arthur E. Adams, "The Great Ukrainian Jacquerie," and Frank Sysyn, "Nestor Makhno and the Ukrainian Revolution," in Hunczak, ed., *The Ukraine*; Hélène Carrère d'Encausse, *Islam and the Russian Empire: Reform and Revolution in Central Asia* (Berkeley and Los Angeles, CA: University of California Press, 1988; orig. French edn, 1966), chap. 9; Eley, "Remapping the Nation."

54 In 1918, the Bolsheviks changed their name to Russian Communist Party (Bolsheviks). The terms Bolshevik and Communist will be used interchangeably here. See Pipes, *Formation*, 110.

55 *Ibid.*, 107–113.

56 This section is drawn primarily from the following sources: Walker Connor, *The National Question in Marxist-Leninist Theory and Strategy* (Princeton, NJ: Princeton University Press, 1984), chaps 2–3; Yuri Slezkine, "The USSR as a Communal Apartment, or How a Socialist State Promoted Ethnic Particularism," *Slavic Review*, vol. 53, no. 2 (Summer 1994), 414–452; Robert Kaiser, *The Geography of Nationalism in Russia and the USSR* (Princeton, NJ: Princeton University Press, 1994), chap. 3 and *passim*; Brubaker, *Nationalism Reframed*, chap. 2; Pipes, *Formation*; Suny, *Revenge*, chap. 3; Hélène Carrère d'Encausse, *The Great Challenge: Nationalities and the Bolshevik State, 1917–1930* (New York: Holmes & Meier, 1992); Andreas Kappeler, *Russland als Vielvölkerreich* (Munich: C.H. Beck, 1993), Epilogue.

57 See Kaiser, *Geography*, 109–110.

58 d'Encausse, *The Great Challenge*, chap. 8.

59 Isabelle Kreindler, "A Neglected Source of Lenin's Nationality Policy," *Slavic Review*, vol. 36, no. 1 (March 1977), 86–100; Robert Geraci, "The Il'minskii System and the Controversy over Non-Russian Teachers and Priests in the Middle Volga," in Catherine Evtuhov, Boris Gasparov, Alexander Ospovat, and Mark von Hagen, eds, *Kazan, Moscow, St. Petersburg: Multiple Faces of the Russian Empire* (Moscow: OGI, 1997).

60 There was also an irredentist twist to this theme in propaganda directed at Belorussians and Ukrainians living in Poland's *kresy*, just across the border from the ostensibly sovereign Ukrainian and Belorussian Soviet Socialist Republics.

61 Adam B. Ulam, *Expansion and Coexistence: Soviet Foreign Policy, 1917–1973* (2nd edn, New York: Praeger, 1974; 1968), 121–125; Richard Pipes, *Russia under the Bolshevik Regime* (New York: Vintage, 1994), 198–201.

62 The close overlap between the concepts of Soviet and Russian identity reached its climax in the aftermath of the Second World War. See Prizel, *National Identity*, chap. 6. For figures on the increasing dispersal of Russians across the non-Russian republics of the USSR during the interwar years, see Kaiser, *Geography*, 118.

63 Pipes, *Formation*, 263–293; Prizel, *National Identity*, 329–330; Suny, *Making of the Georgian Nation*, chap. 10 and pp. 272–273.

64 Alexandre A. Bennigsen and S. Enders Wimbush, *Muslim National Communism in the Soviet Union: A Revolutionary Strategy for the Colonial World* (Chicago, IL: The University of Chicago Press, 1979), chaps 3–4; Pipes, *Formation*, 168–170, 260–262; Hans Bräker, "Soviet Policy toward Islam," in Andreas Kappeler, Gerhard Simon, Georg Brunner, and Edward Allworth, eds, *Muslim Communities Reemerge: Historical Perspectives on*

Nationality, Politics, and Opposition in the Former Soviet Union and Yugoslavia (Durham, NC: Duke University Press, 1994), 162–163.

65 Kaiser, *Geography*, 110–112; d'Encausse, *The Great Challenge*, 177–179; Bert G. Fragner, "The Nationalization of the Uzbeks and Tajiks," in Kappeler *et al.*, *Muslim Communities.*

66 Brubaker, *Nationalism Reframed*, 30–32.

67 Initially, people were free to choose their nationality regardless of parentage, but this policy did not last long (*ibid.*).

68 See Amir Weiner, "Nature, Nurture, and Memory in a Socialist Utopia: Delineating the Soviet Socio-Ethnic Body in the Age of Socialism," *The American Historical Review*, vol. 104, no. 4 (October 1999), 1114–1155.

69 A Jewish autonomous district (*oblast*) was created in the remote Siberian region of Birobidzhan in 1934. The Jewish population of this bizarre showcase – complete with public signs in Yiddish, Yiddish schools, a local Yiddish newspaper, and a Yiddish theater – never much exceeded 30,000 out of a total population of 100,000. Birobidzhan retains its status as a Jewish autonomous *oblast* in post-Soviet Russia. Nora Levin, *The Jews in the Soviet Union since 1917: Paradox of Survival* (vol. 1, New York: New York University Press, 1988), chap. 13, pp. 488–492; Kaiser, *Geography*, 103, 353.

70 Levin, *Jews in the Soviet Union*, vol. 1, chaps 4–5, pp. 54–57; Zvi Y. Gitelman, *Jewish Nationality and Soviet Politics: The Jewish Sections of the CPSU, 1917–1930* (Princeton, NJ: Princeton University Press, 1972).

71 Having destroyed traditional Jewish cultural institutions, the *Yevsekstiia* itself became internally divided between those who wanted to build a new, Communist form of Yiddish culture and those who advocated complete Jewish assimilation. Gitelman, *Jewish Nationality*, chap. 6 and pp. 405–440, 497–498.

72 Jeff Veidlinger, "Moscow's Yiddish Stage" (Ph.D. diss., Georgetown University, 1998).

73 See Anthony Smith, *Nationalism in the Twentieth Century* (New York: New York University Press, 1979), 180–182, for a more global elaboration of this theme.

74 Bernard Lewis, *The Emergence of Modern Turkey* (2nd edn, London: Oxford University Press, 1968; 1961), chap. 8.

75 Additionally, the Straits were to be internationalized. The provision for an Italian zone was not technically part of the Treaty of Sèvres. David Stevenson, *The First World War and International Politics* (Oxford: Oxford University Press, 1988), 301–305; Sharp, *Versailles*, 171.

76 Pipes, *Formation*, 231–234; Manoug Joseph Somakian, *Empires in Conflict: Armenia and the Great Powers, 1895–1920* (London and New York: I.B. Tauris, 1995), 204–242; Bülent Gökay, *A Clash of Empires: Turkey between Russian Bolshevism and British Imperialism, 1918–1923* (London: Tauris, 1997), 83–87, 101–112.

77 Lewis, *Emergence*, chap. 8; Erik Zürcher, *Turkey: A Modern History* (London: I. B. Tauris, 1993), chap. 9.

78 See Zürcher, *Turkey*, 180–181; Selim Deringil, "The Ottoman Origins of Kemalist Nationalism: Namik Kemal to Mustafa Kemal," *European History Quarterly*, vol. 23, no. 2 (April 1993), 165–191.

79 Finney, "An Evil," 542–543; Brubaker, *Nationalism Reframed*, 152–156; Michael R. Marrus, *The Unwanted: European Refugees in the Twentieth Century* (New York: Oxford University Press, 1985), 97–106; Zürcher, *Turkey*, 176–180; Stanford Shaw and Ezel Kural Shaw, *History of the Ottoman Empire and Modern Turkey*, vol. 2: *Reform, Revolution and Republic: The Rise of Modern Turkey, 1808–1975* (Cambridge: Cambridge University Press, 1977), 381.

80 Niyazi Berkes, *The Development of Secularism in Turkey* (Montreal: McGill University Press, 1964), chap. 16; Lewis, *Emergence*, 101–102, 264–279; Shaw and Shaw, *History of the Ottoman Empire*, vol. 2, 375–380, 384–395; Zürcher, *Turkey*, 180–181. For an entertaining if unconvincing apologia for the political legacy of Kemalism, see Ernest Gellner, *Encounters with Nationalism* (Oxford: Blackwell, 1994), chap. 7.

81 On the relatively unsuccessful programs of economic modernization in the Arab states – a predicament aggravated by the policies of the mandatory powers – and on the problems (particularly in the agricultural sector) with Turkey's *étatisme*, see Zvi Yehuda Hershlag, *Introduction to the Modern Economic History of the Middle East* (2nd edn, Leiden: Brill, 1980; 1964), 167–170, 236–243, and part 7; Gellner, *Encounters with Nationalism*, 83.

82 The award of a mandate over Syria to France flew in the face of the recommendations of the King–Crane Commission, sent by Woodrow Wilson in the framework of the 1919 Paris Peace Conference to assess the state of public opinion in Syria and Palestine. Stevenson, *The First World War*, 293–299; Howard M. Sachar, *The Emergence of the Middle East, 1914–1924* (New York: Knopf, 1969), chap. 9.

83 See L. Carl Brown, *International Politics and the Middle East: Old Rules, Dangerous Game* (Princeton, NJ: Princeton University Press, 1984), 89.

84 As quoted in Isaiah Friedman, *The Question of Palestine, 1914–1918: British–Jewish–Arab Relations* (New York: Schocken Books, 1973), 279.

85 See Sachar, *Emergence*, 406.

86 For general overviews of the French mandatory regimes in Lebanon and Syria, see Stephen H. Longrigg, *Syria and Lebanon under French Mandate* (London: Oxford University Press, 1958); Albert Hourani, *Syria and Lebanon: A Political Essay* (Oxford: Oxford University Press, 1946); Philip Khoury, *Syria and the French Mandate: The Politics of Arab Nationalism 1920–1945* (Princeton, NJ: Princeton University Press, 1987).

87 See James Gelvin, "Popular Mobilization and the Foundations of Mass Politics in Syria, 1918–1920" (Ph.D. diss., Harvard University, 1992).

88 Al-Fatat remained a clandestine organization, but its leaders now established a front organization – the Arab Independence Party – to function as their public face. Philip S. Khoury, *Urban Notables and Arab Nationalism: The Politics of Damascus, 1880–1920* (Cambridge: Cambridge University Press, 1983), chap. 4; Muhammad Muslih, *The Origins of Palestinian Nationalism* (New York: Columbia University Press, 1988), chap. 6.

89 The Hashemites' pan-Arab ambitions generally encompassed only the so-called Fertile Crescent (Iraq, Syria, Transjordan, Palestine, and parts or all of Lebanon). But pan-Arabist tendencies were also developing in Egypt during the interwar years. Yehoshua Porath, *Be-mivchan ha-ma'aseh ha-politi: Erets-yisrael, achdut arvit, u-mediniyut britaniyah* (In the Trial of Political Action: The Land of Israel, Arab Unity, and British Policy) (Jerusalem: Yad Yitschaq Ben Tsvi, 1985), chap. 1 and pp. 163–174.

90 Sachar, *Emergence*, 384–388; Bernard Wasserstein, *The British in Palestine: The Mandatory Government and the Arab–Jewish Conflict, 1917–1929* (London: Royal Historical Society, 1978), chap. 2.

91 James L. Gelvin, "The Other Arab Nationalism: Syrian/Arab Populism in its Historical and International Contexts," in James Jankowski and Israel Gershoni, eds, *Rethinking Nationalism in the Arab Middle East* (New York: Columbia University Press, 1997); *idem*, "Popular Mobilization."

92 Sachar, *Emergence*, chap. 9.

93 In Transjordan, Emir Abdullah was obliged in 1924 by the British (as well as by jealous Transjordanian tribal leaders) to get rid of the pan-Arab nationalists from Syria and elsewhere whom he had appointed to his cabinet. Kamal Salibi, *The Modern History of Jordan* (London: Tauris, 1993), chap. 5; Mary C. Wilson, *King Abdullah, Britain and the Making of Jordan* (Cambridge: Cambridge University Press, 1987), chap. 5.

94 Muslih, *Palestinian Nationalism*, chaps 8–9; Yehoshua Porath, *The Emergence of the Palestinian–Arab National Movement, 1918–1929* (London: Frank Cass, 1974), Introduction and chap. 2; Rashid Khalidi, *Palestinian Identity: The Construction of Modern National Consciousness* (New York: Columbia University Press, 1997), 162–175.

95 Neville J. Mandel, *The Arabs and Zionism before World War I* (Berkeley, CA: University of California Press, 1976); Baruch Kimmerling, *Zionism and Territory: The Socio-Territorial Dimensions of Zionist Politics* (Berkeley, CA: University of California Press, 1983), chaps 1–2; Kenneth W. Stein, *The Land Question in Palestine, 1917–1939* (Chapel Hill, NC: The University of North Carolina Press, 1984).

96 Khoury, *Syria and the French Mandate*, chap. 4; Gelvin, "Popular Mobilization," 259–260; Muhammad Muslih, "The Rise of Local Nationalism in the Arab East," in Rashid Khalidi, Lisa Anderson, Muhammad Muslih, and Reeva S. Simon, eds, *The Origins of Arab Nationalism* (New York: Columbia University Press, 1991). On the development of political consciousness among the broader urban populace, see Gelvin, "The Other Arab Nationalism"; *idem*, "Popular Mobilization," parts II–III.

97 The distinction between religious and ethnic forms of identity is often virtually meaningless – or became so in the course of the developments described here – among non-Muslims in the Middle East. The Ottomans' *millet* system had institutionalized the vertical segregation of Middle Eastern society along religious and ethno-religious lines, and the ethnicization of confessional identity was reinforced in the late Ottoman and post-Ottoman periods as the nationality principle became the all-encompassing frame of reference for the assertion of collective political rights. See Kemal Karpat, "The Ottoman Ethnic and Confessional Legacy in the Middle East," in Milton J. Esman and Itamar Rabinovich, eds, *Ethnicity, Pluralism, and the State in the Middle East* (Ithaca, NY: Cornell University Press, 1988).

98 The Druze are members of a heterodox Muslim sect.

99 This account is particularly indebted to Meir Zamir, *The Formation of Modern Lebanon* (Ithaca, NY and London: Cornell University Press, 1985), chap. 2, pp. 199–215, and *passim*. See also Kemal Salibi, *A House of Many Mansions: The History of Lebanon Reconsidered* (Berkeley and Los Angeles, CA: University of California Press, 1988), chaps 1–2, pp. 171–178; Edmond Rabbath, *La Formation Historique du Liban Politique et Constitutionel* (Beirut: Publications de l'Université Libanaise, 1973), 359–379, 420–422; Walid Khalidi, *Conflict and Violence in Lebanon* (Cambridge, MA: Harvard University Press, 1979), note 27 to chap. 1; Elie Kedourie, *Islam in the Modern World* (New York, 1981), 90–91; Bishara al-Khoury, *Haqa'iq lubnaniyyah* (Lebanese Realities), vol. 1 (Beirut, 1960), 264.

100 Although Arabic was their spoken tongue, the Maronites used a form of Aramaic as their liturgical language, and cultivated a myth of descent from an ancient people.

101 British forces occupied Syria and Lebanon during the Second World War, transferring administrative control of the territories from the Vichy French to the Free French, but using their own military hegemony and political influence to undermine French authority. See Aviel Roshwald, *Estranged Bedfellows: Britain and France in the Middle East during the Second World War* (New York: Oxford University Press, 1990); A.B. Gaunson, *The Anglo-French Clash in Lebanon and Syria, 1940–1945* (London: Macmillan, 1987); Major-General Sir Edward Spears, *Fulfilment of a Mission: Syria and Lebanon, 1941–1944* (London: Seeley, Service and Cooper/Hamden, CT: Archon Books, 1977).

102 Cited in Walid Khalidi, *Conflict and Violence in Lebanon: Confrontation in the Middle East* (Cambridge, MA: Center for International Affairs, Harvard University, 1979), 162, no. 27

103 The Alawites are another Muslim sectarian group, concentrated in the northwestern Syrian district of Latakia.

104 At the same time, it must be emphasized that patterns of support for, and opposition to, the Syrian Arab nationalists among the Druze were closely linked to internal clan rivalries, suggesting that here too, Arab nationalism served as an ideological umbrella for coalition-building among distinct communal interests rather than constituting a truly cohesive, trans-communal identity. Khoury, *Syria and the French Mandate*, chap. 20. On the dynamics of minority politics in mandatory Syria, see also Itamar Rabinovich, "The Compact Minorities and the Syrian State, 1918–1945," *Journal of Contemporary History*, vol. 14, no. 4 (October 1979), 693–712.

105 Khoury, *Syria and the French Mandate*, chaps 2, 6–7, 10, 17–22. For critical analyses of French policy by contemporaneous observers, see Robert Montagne, "French Policy

in North Africa and in Syria," *International Affairs*, vol. 16, no. 2 (March–April 1937), 263–279; Pierre Rondot, "L'expérience du mandat français en Syrie et au Liban (1918–45)," *Revue des Droits Internationaux Publiques* (1948), 387–409.

106 Reeva Simon, "The Imposition of Nationalism: Iraq, 1921–1941," in Jankowski and Gershoni, eds, *Rethinking Nationalism*.

107 See Gabriel Ben-Dor, "Ethnopolitics and the Middle Eastern State," in Esman and Rabinovich, eds, *Ethnicity, Pluralism and the State*.

7 Old Elites and Radical Challengers in the New Nation-States, 1918–1939

1 Ernest Gellner, *Nations and Nationalism* (Ithaca, NY: Cornell University Press, 1983), 48.

2 Gellner's own writings on the Middle East point in this direction. See for example Ernest Gellner, "Tribalism and the State in the Middle East," in Philip S. Khoury and Joseph Kostiner, eds, *Tribes and State Formation in the Middle East* (Berkeley and Los Angeles, CA: University of California Press, 1990).

3 Arno Mayer uses the concept of the persistence of the old regime to explain the political dynamic leading up to the outbreak of the First World War in Europe. Arno Mayer, *The Persistence of the Old Regime* (New York: Random House, 1981). I am not convinced by Mayer's attempt to identify anachronistic socio-economic interests as the key determinants of the short-term diplomacy and decision-making of the July 1914 crisis. However, I do find value in the notion that long-term patterns of political and institutional development can be shaped by the struggle of old elites to maintain their hegemony through the manipulation of modernization processes. See Joseph Schumpeter, *Imperialism and Social Classes* (New York: Meridian, 1955).

4 Max Weber, *Economy and Society*, vol. 3 (New York: Bedminster Press, 1968), chap. 11.

5 For an insightful, comparative exploration of the role of imperial legacies in shaping nationalist politics, see also Karen Barkey and Mark von Hagen, eds, *After Empire – Multiethnic Societies and Nation-Building: The Soviet Union and the Russian, Ottoman, and Habsburg Empires* (Boulder, CO: Westview Press, 1997).

6 This section is particularly indebted to the incisive analysis in Carol Skalnik Leff, *National Conflict in Czechoslovakia: The Making and Remaking of a State, 1918–1987* (Princeton, NJ: Princeton University Press, 1988). It also draws upon the following sources: Helmut Slapnicka, "Die neue Staat und die bürokratische Kontinuität. Die Entwicklung der Verwaltung 1918–1938," in Karl Bosl, ed., *Die demokratisch-parlamen-tarische Struktur der ersten Tschechoslowakischen Republik* (Munich and Vienna: Oldenbourg, 1975); R.W. Seton-Watson, *The New Slovakia* (Prague: Fr. Borovy, 1924); Owen V. Johnson, *Slovakia 1918–1938: Education and the Making of a Nation* (Boulder, CO: East European Monographs, 1985); Derek Sayer, *The Coasts of Bohemia: A Czech History* (Princeton, NJ: Princeton University Press, 1998), 170–176; Peter Burian, "Demokratie und Parlamentarismus in der Ersten Tschechoslowakischen Republik," in Hans-Erich Volkmann, ed., *Die Krise des Parlamentarismus in Ostmitteleuropa zwischen den beiden Weltkriegen* (Marburg: J.G. Herder-Institut, 1967).

7 See Leff, *Czechoslovakia*, 192–193. The Czech leadership was convinced that over time, the process of economic development and political integration would lead the Slovak masses to embrace the cultural and administrative centralism of their Czechophile vanguard. See Victor Mamatey, "The Development of Czechoslovak Democracy, 1920–1938," in Victor Mamatey and Radomir Luza, eds, *A History of the Czechoslovak Republic, 1918–1948* (Princeton, NJ: Princeton University Press, 1973), 120–126.

8 István Deák, *Beyond Nationalism: A Social and Political History of the Habsburg Officer Corps, 1848–1918* (New York: Oxford University Press, 1990), 208–209.

9 Jonathan Zorach, "The Nationality Problem in the Czechoslovak Army between the Two World Wars," *East Central Europe*, 5, Pt. 2 (1978), 169–185.

10 See Fred Hahn, "Masaryk and the Germans," in Harry Hanak, ed., *T.G. Masaryk (1850–1937), Vol. 3: Statesman and Cultural Force* (New York: St. Martin's Press, 1989).

11 In his keen assessment of Czech–Slovak relations, published in 1924, R.W. Seton-Watson was critical of Czech unwillingness to compromise the principles of economic efficiency for the sake of sustaining the development of a native Slovak industrial base. By the same token, though, he emphasized that:

> the suggestion that "Prague" regards Slovakia as a colony to be exploited, and deliberately aims at destroying its economic and financial independence ... is a grotesque calumny, which none the less finds credulous believers among the inexperienced Slovak masses and even a section of the intelligentsia.
> (Seton-Watson, *The New Slovakia*, p. 96)

12 Liah Greenfeld, *Nationalism: Five Roads to Modernity* (Cambridge, MA: Harvard University Press, 1992), 15–16.

13 For a debate about interwar Czechoslovakia's significance as a touchstone for the general problems of the East European nation-state, see F. Gregory Campbell, Gale Stokes, and Roman Szporluk, "Discussion," *Slavic Review*, vol. 44, no. 1 (1985), 1–29.

14 This section draws on the following sources: Ivo Banac, *The National Question in Yugoslavia: Origins, History, Politics* (Ithaca, NY and London: Cornell University Press, 1984), 375–378; Lenard Cohen, "The Social Background and Recruitment of Yugoslav Political Elites, 1918–48," in Allen H. Barton, Bogdan Denitch, and Charles Kadushin, eds, *Opinion-Making Elites in Yugoslavia* (New York: Praeger, 1973), 59–62; Jozo Tomasevich, *Peasants, Politics, and Economic Change in Yugoslavia* (Stanford, CA: Stanford University Press, 1955), 241–260; Deák, *Beyond Nationalism*, 209; John Lampe, *Yugoslavia as History: Twice There Was a Country* (Cambridge: Cambridge University Press, 1996), 156–159, 171–173, 189–194, and chap. 7. For an attempt to place the decisions and policies of the Serbian leadership in the best light possible, see Alex N. Dragnich, *The First Yugoslavia: Search for a Viable Political System* (Stanford, CA: Hoover Institution Press, 1983) and *idem*, "The Anatomy of a Myth: Serbian Hegemony," *Slavic Review*, vol. 50, no. 3 (Fall 1991), 659–662.

15 Peasants within the pre-First World War boundaries of Serbia and Montenegro already had full title to their land, and therefore were not led to expect any dramatic change in property law.

16 Tomasevich, *Peasants, Politics*, chap. 18. Although the formation of cooperative societies combined with the general rise in grain prices to strengthen the Croatian and Slovenian rural economies in the late 1920s, the Great Depression wiped out these gains in the following decade. Lampe, *Yugoslavia*, 146–148 and 168–170.

17 Norman Davies, *God's Playground: A History of Poland*, vol. 2 (New York: Columbia University Press, 1982), 410–411; Andrzej Korbonski, "Poland: 1918–1990," in Joseph Held, ed., *The Columbia History of Eastern Europe in the Twentieth Century* (New York: Columbia University Press, 1992), 235–237. Thanks to its history of *de facto* autonomy under the Habsburgs, Galicia was able to contribute disproportionately to the personnel and juridical and institutional framework of the Polish republic. See Józef Buszko, "Das soziale und politische Erbe der österreichisch-ungarischen Monarchie im unabhängigen Polen," *Österreichische Osthefte*, vol. 36 (1994), no. 4, 741–751.

18 This section draws upon: Antony Polonsky, *Politics in Independent Poland, 1921–1939: The Crisis of Constitutional Government* (Oxford: Clarendon Press, 1972), chaps 2–4, 6, and pp. 128–136, 358–371; Joseph Rothschild, *Piłsudski's Coup D'Etat* (New York and London: Columbia University Press, 1966), chaps 3, 10, 13, 15, 18, and *passim*; Andrzej Garlicki, *Józef Piłsudski, 1867–1935* (ed., abridged, and trans. from the Polish by John Coutrouvidis, Aldershot: Scolar Press, 1995), chaps 7–9; Davies, *God's Playground*, 421–426.

19 Józef Piłsudski, *Joseph Piłsudski: The Memories of a Polish Revolutionary and Soldier* (trans. and ed. D.R. Gillie, London: Faber & Faber, 1931), 369–371.

20 The legionnaires' typical background as volunteers who had never studied in a military academy did not equip them well for long-term planning and military modernization. Polonsky, *Politics*, 202.

21 The cult of the Legion was even institutionalized: an Institute of Legionary Studies was established in 1934. Polonsky, *Politics*, 354.

22 Piłsudski was named first marshal of Poland in 1920.

23 The first years of the Sanacja had witnessed an improvement in economic conditions, but the onset of the Depression had wiped out these gains. Rothschild, *Piłsudski's Coup D'Etat*, chap. 15.

24 Philip Khoury, *Urban Notables and Arab Nationalism: The Politics of Damascus 1880–1920* (Cambridge: Cambridge University Press, 1983), chaps 1–2; Hanna Batatu, *The Old Social Classes and the Revolutionary Movements of Iraq* (Princeton, NJ: Princeton University Press, 1978), chap. 8; Weber, *Economy and Society*, chap. 11.

25 Philip Khoury, *Syria and the French Mandate: The Politics of Arab Nationalism 1920–1945* (Princeton, NJ: Princeton University Press, 1987), chap. 11.

26 *Ibid.*, chap. 10; C. Ernest Dawn, *From Ottomanism to Arabism: Essays on the Origins of Arab Nationalism* (Urbana, IL: University of Illinois Press, 1973), 160–174; Hisham Sharabi, *Arab Intellectuals and the West: The Formative Years, 1875–1914* (Baltimore, MD and London: The Johns Hopkins Press, 1970), 127.

27 Khoury, *Syria*, 564 and 603.

28 See Dhuqan Qarqut, *Tatawwur al-harakah al-wataniyyah fi Suriya, 1920–1939* (The development of the nationalist movement in Syria, 1920–1939) (Beirut: Dar al-Tali'ah lil-Tiba'ah wa-al-Nashr, 1975), 104–105.

29 In their land-tenure and tax-collection policies, the Sharifians were following in the wake of precedents set by the British imperial authorities during their wartime and immediate postwar period of direct rule over Iraq. The British, in turn, had regarded their attempts to co-opt traditional elites as a systematization of Ottoman practices. Peter Sluglett, *Britain in Iraq, 1914–1932* (London: Ithaca Press, 1976), chap. 6; Charles Issawi, *The Middle East Economy: Decline and Recovery* (Princeton, NJ: Marcus Wiener Publishers, 1995), 154.

30 Batatu, *Social Classes*, chaps 8 and 10.

31 *Ibid.*, chap. 10; Phebe Marr, *The Modern History of Iraq* (Boulder, CO: Westview/London: Longman, 1985), 69–70.

32 Reeva S. Simon, *Iraq between the Two World Wars: The Creation and Implementation of a Nationalist Ideology* (New York: Columbia University Press, 1986), 119–123; Daniel Silverfarb, *Britain's Informal Empire in the Middle East: A Case Study of Iraq, 1929–1941* (New York: Oxford University Press, 1986), chap. 4. The Assyrians, uprooted from what became Turkish territory in the wake of their unsuccessful pro-Allied revolt against the Ottomans during the First World War, had been resettled in Iraq by the British.

33 Simon, *Iraq between the Wars*, chap. 4; William Cleveland, *The Making of an Arab Nationalist: Ottomanism and Arabism in the Life and Thought of Sati' al-Husri* (Princeton, NJ: Princeton University Press, 1971), 38–41, 62–63; Bassam Tibi, *Arab Nationalism: Between Islam and the Nation-State* (3rd edn, New York: St. Martin's Press, 1997), 119, 142–154. Al-Husri emphasized that compulsory military service had a vital role to play in complementing and completing the educational task of the school system by inculcating youth from all regions with a commitment to the nation as the object of supreme loyalty. See Sati' al-Husri, "Al-khidmah al-'askariyyah wa al-tarbiyah al-'amah" (Military service and general education), in *Al-a'mal al-qawmiyyah li-Sati' al-Husri* (The Nationalist Works of Sati' al-Husri), vol. 2: *Ahadith fi-al-tarbiyah wa-al-ijtima'* (Discussions in Education and Society) (Beirut: Markaz Dirasat al-Wahdah al-Arabiyyah, 1985).

34 Simon, *Iraq between the Wars*, chap. 4. See excerpt from Sami Shawkat's "Profession of Death" (a speech delivered in 1933) in Sylvia Haim, *Arab Nationalism*, 97–99.

35 Khoury, *Syria*, 471–476.

36 For a discussion of the possibility of reconciling modernization with traditional Middle Eastern social structures and traditions, see Samir Khalaf, "On Loyalties and Social Change," in Georges Sabagh, ed., *The Modern Economic and Social History of the Middle East in its World Context* (Cambridge: Cambridge University Press, 1989).

37 Philip Khoury, "The Paradoxical in Arab Nationalism: Interwar Syria Revisited," and Reeva S. Simon, "The Imposition of Nationalism on a Non-Nation State: The Case of Iraq during the Interwar Period, 1921–1941," in James Jankowski and Israel Gershoni, eds, *Rethinking Nationalism in the Arab Middle East* (New York: Columbia University Press, 1997).

38 Albert Hourani, "A Note on Revolutions in the Arab World," in Albert Hourani, *The Emergence of the Modern Middle East* (Berkeley and Los Angeles, CA: University of California Press, 1981), 71.

39 See Mark Mazower, *Dark Continent: Europe's Twentieth Century* (New York: Knopf, 1999), chap. 1.

40 My thanks to Jerry Muller for drawing my attention to this point.

41 On Romania, see p. 170 of this book. On Estonia, see Toivo U. Raun, *Estonia and the Estonians* (Stanford, CA: Hoover Institution Press, 1987), chap. 8. On Latvia's transition to ethno-chauvinistic authoritarianism in the 1930s, see Andrejs Plakans, *The Latvians: A Short History* (Stanford, CA: Hoover Institution Press, 1995), 132–138.

8 Conclusion

1 See Patrick B. Finney, "'An Evil for All Concerned': Great Britain and Minority Protection after 1919," *Journal of Contemporary History*, vol. 30, no. 3 (July 1995), 533–551.

2 See Richard L. Rudolph and David F. Good, eds, *Nationalism and Empire: The Habsburg Monarchy and the Soviet Union* (New York: St. Martin's Press, 1992).

3 Renzo de Felice's analytical distinction between fascist movement and fascist regime offers an interesting point of comparison here. Renzo de Felice and Michael A. Ledeen, *Fascism: An Informal Introduction to its Theory and Practice* (English version of *Intervista sul fascismo*) (New Brunswick, NJ: Transaction, 1976), chap. 3.

4 This idea also manifests itself in the work of contemporary theorists of nationalism such as Ernest Gellner.

5 Yael Tamir, *Liberal Nationalism* (Princeton, NJ: Princeton University Press, 1993).

6 Isaiah Berlin, "Two Concepts of Liberty," in *idem*, *The Proper Study of Mankind* (London: Chatto & Windus, 1997). See also Michael Ignatieff, *Isaiah Berlin: A Life* (New York: Henry Holt, 1998), 225–228.

7 For some imaginative approaches to the conflict between state authority and national identity, see Gidon Gottlieb, *Nation against State* (New York: Council on Foreign Relations Press, 1993).

Index

Slovenes, Croats and Serbs 87–8;
Yugoslav Committee 88, 132–8, 146,
160, 161

Zagreb 13, 84, 86, 88
Zaleski, August 139
Zionism 25, 54, 123, 140–5, 160, 165–7,
182, 187, 190, 214; cultural 141;

General 123; in Germany 142–3;
Labor 54; political 140, 143, 145;
practical 140–2, 145; in Russia 144;
World Zionist Organization (WZO)
140–2, 146
Zürcher, Erik 63
Zvonimir, King 134
Zweig, Arnold 245 no. 21

Printed in the United States
38571LVS00005B/37-66